Management planning and control systems

Advanced concepts and cases

THE WILLARD J. GRAHAM SERIES IN ACCOUNTING
Consulting Editor   **Robert N. Anthony**   *Harvard University*

Management planning and control systems
Advanced concepts and cases

Jerry Dermer
Faculty of Management Studies
University of Toronto

1977
RICHARD D. IRWIN, INC.   Homewood, Illinois   60430
Irwin-Dorsey Limited   Georgetown, Ontario   L7G 4B3

2 3 4 5 6 7 8 9 0 MP 5 4 3 2 1 0

ISBN 0-256-01874-X
Library of Congress Catalog Card No. 76–17353

Printed in the United States of America

Preface

The purpose of this book is to familiarize the reader with the role of management planning and control systems as well as problems inherent in their design and use. The text and cases are intended to provide the core materials for a graduate, advanced undergraduate, or executive development course in systems design and evaluation. The book is unique in several respects, especially in its emphasis on planning and its message that every planning and control system must be custom made to fit the situation at hand. It should be of interest to those trained in accounting and other areas of management who wish to integrate and advance their knowledge of managerial accounting and general management, and their ability to apply this knowledge to real life problems.

Planning is a topic that is addressed from many perspectives in a management program—globally in courses on business policy and strategy, and functionally in courses on marketing, finance, personnel, and production. Courses in accounting and computer-based information systems focus on methods and techniques useful in carrying out planning activities. And these courses are supported by an abundance of pertinent literature. Yet, despite this apparently extensive coverage, the subject of planning, its relationship to control, and the role of the various methods and techniques used to carry it out usually remain fragmented issues in the mind of the student. Little time and effort are devoted to comparing and integrating within an overall framework the differing perspectives and methods and techniques available. Up to now it has usually been left to the individual student to provide the framework that is needed to conceptualize planning, to relate it to the material he or she has already covered on control, and then to integrate the various components that make up a managerial planning and control system. This book attempts to help students do this.

The text (and especially the cases) repeatedly stress the fact that the appropriateness of any planning and control system is contingent on the particular situation in which it must be used. There is considerable evidence to show that for many administrative choices, such as organizational structure or leadership style, the most appropriate solution to a given problem depends on the unique requirements of that problem. And the same is true for the design of planning and control systems. There is no one best system that applies in all situations. Organizations differ in their objectives, external environments, resources, organizational structure, and internal capabilities, and in many other ways. Therefore any recommendation concerning the benefit to be derived from using a particular approach or technique cannot be accepted as universally applicable, but must be evaluated in light of the situation in which the approach or technique is to be implemented.

This does not mean that all planning and control systems design must begin from scratch, reinventing the wheel for each occasion. Fortunately, the considerable work already done in the field can, if properly integrated, evaluated, and systematized, provide valuable input to the situational system design process. This text describes a systematic procedure for designing and implementing planning and control systems, so that the system that will best match the characteristics of the situation can be identified and specified. The approach is based on the following premises: (1) although there may not be one best system that fits all situations, there is a systematic process of systems design that is appropriate to all situations; and (2) if we understand the procedure by which a system was specified, we can then evaluate the effectiveness of its design and so continually improve the systems design process. If these two assumptions are valid, then mastery of this text will contribute significantly to the understanding of planning and control systems design and use.

The objectives of the book can be summarized as follows:

1. To present a conceptual framework that both demonstrates the generic nature of planning and control processes, and also conveys the distinguishing environmental and organizational factors that make each design situation unique.

2. To define procedures to identify and analyze the factors that determine the planning and control system most appropriate for a given situation.

3. To make the system designer and/or user aware of the alternative components that make up a system, the function that each component satisfies, and the strengths, weaknesses, and interrelationships of these components.

4. And, finally, to interrelate the discussion of methods and tech-

niques into a systematic approach to planning and control system design and implementation that can be applied to all management planning and control processes.

The book provides an orientation, a number of conceptual models, and a set of procedures which can help guide the design and evaluation process. It also surveys a number of tools and techniques, provides a systematic means of evaluating them, and gives the opportunity to apply them and test their utility in a variety of case study situations. This book is thus the next step beyond textbooks and case study courses which either simply describe a technique that the system designer could use, or only give him situations to analyze in order to help him gain experience and to develop his own theory. It is not claimed that this material constitutes a definitive theory of planning and control systems design, of course; but it is a contribution toward theory.

December 1976 JERRY DERMER

Acknowledgments

As is usually the case with undertakings of this size, grateful acknowledgments of inspiration, guidance, and assistance are due to many people. My interest in the field of management planning and control systems was spurred by the writings of the control group at the Harvard Business School and although I've never had the pleasure of being either a student or a colleague of that group, their thoughts certainly have influenced me. While at MIT I had the opportunity to be exposed to others working in the field and also to teach and develop materials for courses in planning and in control system design. Several classes at the Faculty of Management Studies at the University of Toronto pretested the material and offered innumerable, invaluable suggestions.

Of the many who have helped me in this work, I can name only a few. Many of the ideas, for example, the types of risk and reasons for control outlined in Chapter 1, originated with my colleague Jamie Poapst. Bob Anthony and Bob Malcolm thoroughly reviewed the complete manuscript and their suggestions resulted in a marked improvement in it. Maria Latimer endured the pain and suffering of typing much of this material. My sincere thanks goes to Margaret Wente, my guardian angel editor, who entered the preparation of this manuscript when I was fed up to the teeth with it and successfully translated it from Dermerese into English. And to my wife Anita, who has continually asked, "Aren't you finished with it yet?" I can finally reply, thankfully, "Yes"!

All the cases in this book are original. They have been prepared for the purpose of stimulating class discussions and not to illustrate the effective or ineffective handling of any administrative situations. The views expressed in no way represent the views of the authors or the institutions described.

Of the 21 cases included only the University of Calgary, Ford Motor Company, Raytheon Company, Pfizer International, Volvo, and United Air Lines represent real organizations. The other cases are all fictionalized composites of situations encountered in other organizations. The University of Calgary case was prepared by Douglas J. Tigert of the University of Toronto, on behalf of the University of Calgary, and R. S. Chapman assisted in its preparation. A. D. Bevacqua assisted in the preparation of North Eastern Gas. United Air Lines and Pfizer International in Africa are based on masters theses prepared under my supervision at MIT, the former by Michael Louis Henegen, June 1973, and the latter by Odunayo Bukola Olagundoye and Philip Owusu, June 1974. The material on Raytheon's planning and control system was kindly provided by the Vice President–Corporate Planning, Robert L. Seaman. The Volvo case includes articles which appeared originally in *Time, The Weekly News Magazine,* and the *Financial Post,* and are reprinted with permission.

December 1976   J. D. D.

Contents

New program generation: *Planning gaps. The generation of
new programs. Some approaches to innovation and new program generation.* Project evaluation and resource allocation: *Program life cycles. Evaluation and choice.* Specification of the long-range plan: *Key variables of the long-range
plan.* Responsibility unit planning and control. System
evaluation and adaptation.

part two   Framework and approach

A framework for design: *Differentiation and decentralization.*
Differentiation: *Vertical differentiation by hierarchical level.
Horizontal differentiation. Matrix organizations. Line versus
staff.* Decentralization: *Purpose and definition. Benefits and
weaknesses.* Behavioral differences between responsibility
units. The relationship of differentiation and decentralization
to planning and control systems design.

Responsibility unit system requirements: *Improving performance.* A systematic approach to system design: *Description of the approach. Relationship to the multicycle model.
Example. The advantages of a normative approach.* The need
for formalization.

part three   Methods and techniques of planning and control

Structured and unstructured tasks. Some techniques for
planning and controlling structured processes: *The use of
formal models in planning. Managed and engineered costs.*

Feedback and feedforward control. Motivational techniques: *The motivational role of financial objectives. Job enrichment. Human resource accounting.* Appendix: Interpreting and responding to deviations from expectation.

7   The planning and control of

Some problems of unstructured processes: *Allocating resources effectively. Increasing motivation. Establishing appropriate feedback.* Zero-base budgeting: *How zero-base budgeting works. Benefits of zero-base budgeting. Implementation of the procedure.* Management by objectives: *The goals of management by objectives. How management by objectives works. Two conceptions of MBO.*

8

The role of monetary measurements in planning and control: *Limitations of formal measurements. Choosing financial performance measurements.* The profit measure: *Strengths of the profit measure. Weaknesses of the profit measure. The role of profit in planning and evaluation.* Profit centers: *Situational requirements for successful implementation. The benefits of profit centers. Types of profit centers.* Transfer pricing: *Determining transfer prices. The significance of transfer pricing.* Two styles of profit center management: *Profit as a specific performance objective. Profit as a guiding objective.*

9

Return on investment (ROI): *Calculation of the investment base. Advantages of ROI. Disadvantages of ROI.* Residual income (RI): *Advantages of RI. Disadvantages of RI.* Effective use of investment-based performance measures. An alternative approach to planning and controlling investment centers.

part four   Organizational considerations

Three staff groups that influence system design: *The planner. The controller. The manager of management information systems (MIS).* Interrelationships among the three groups. Alternative organizational relationships: *Alternative roles for the planner. Alternative roles for the controller.* Other determinants of staff roles.

Case study 10–1. Universal Tool and Appliances, 337

Perspective and orientation: *Process models. Assumptions.* Sytematic procedure for systems design / adaptation. Selection of appropriate tools and techniques. Guidelines for successful implementation.

Case study 11–1. United Air Lines, 358
Case study 11–2. Meat Inspection Services (B), 368
Case study 11–3. North Eastern Gas, 371

part one

Perspective and orientation

Chapter outline

1

Introduction and orientation

When you have completed this chapter you will:

1. Be able to define and explain the processes of planning and control.
2. Understand some of the reasons why planning and control are required.
3. Appreciate the similarities, differences, and interrelationships between planning and control processes.
4. Be able to define and describe a planning and control system.

AN OVERVIEW OF PLANNING

What is planning?

Every organization must relate to its environment in order to survive. Determining the nature of this relationship involves choices. For example an organization can be *active* in that it shapes its environment, or *passive* in that it adapts to environmental change. Planning is the process by which an organization solves the problem of determining its relationship with its environment. It is the process of collecting information and making decisions by which management formulates objectives, and chooses the pattern of action to achieve those objectives. Planning reconciles objectives, opportunities, and capabilities. It involves selecting ends and means—deciding where you want to be in the future and the best way of getting there.

In order to understand planning, it is essential to recognize that it is a process—that is, sequence of activities, steps, or behaviors. The activities of collecting information and making decisions, for example,

3

are one way to describe planning. However, as shall be seen, there are many different ways to describe a planning process. Planning is a continual process because change is continual: both the organization and the environment being planned for change during the planning process. By collecting information and making decisions management continually establishes the purposes, guidelines, constraints, and programs of action used in guiding the organization into the future. Through planning, management achieves the communication, coordination, and motivation needed to bring about the outcomes it desires. Through planning management ensures that its organization will survive.

Planning itself is a component of the management process described by Fayol, the circular sequence of planning, organizing, communicating, coordinating, and controlling. But if the function of management is to maintain the course of the organizational unit entrusted to it, as long as a venture is under way, management has no natural conclusion or end point. So planning, one fundamental role of management, also has no apparent conclusion and is a continual process.

The process of planning has been viewed in many different perspectives. For example, planning has been defined as:

> A method of guiding managers so that their decisions and actions are set to the future of the organization in a consistent and rational manner, and in a way desired by top management (Ewing, 1968).

Alternatively, it has been defined in the following way:

> A process which begins with objectives; defines strategies, policies, and detailed plans to achieve them; which establishes an organization to implement decisions; and feedback to introduce a new planning cycle (Steiner, 1969).

It has also been regarded as a rational decision-making process:

> A process that involves making and evaluating each of a set of inter-related decisions before an action is required, in a situation in which it is believed that unless action is taken, the desired future state is not likely to occur, and that, if appropriate action is taken, the likelihood of a favourable outcome can be increased (Ackoff, 1970).

From these definitions it appears that the essence of planning is collecting information and making decisions in light of what is desired in the future. For example, planning may be concerned with deciding what must be done to make current or future activities more effective and efficient; what must be done to capitalize on unused organizational capabilities or to exploit existing opportunities; or what must be done to develop or transform the environment of the organization so that ultimate survival is more likely.

Planning versus plans. In order to fully understand what planning is, it is essential to recognize the relationship between the planning process and the plans it produces. A plan is simply the output of the planning process; for example, a decision by the operators of beef feed-lots to withhold supply until price controls are removed; by an automobile company to replace an existing car line with a new one; or by a graduate business student to take a job with one organization instead of another. A plan is a summary of the decisions made at one particular point of time in the planning process. It specifies outcomes and specific courses of action but leaves undefined the process by which these actions were decided upon. It prescribes the activities to be done and what is expected as a result of these actions. For instance, a plan may describe the scope and character of future activities sequenced over time, and the resources necessary to achieve them. Planning itself, however, is the process by which such plans are prepared.

To further crystallize the concept of planning, it is useful to differentiate it from forecasting, policy formation, and strategy development. Forecasting is the prediction of events that will take place in the future. Forecasts are one type of input information used in planning, and forecasting may be one of the activities that make up a planning process; but forecasting itself is not planning. Policies are preplanned decisions waiting to be activated by the occurrence of the situation for which they were intended. For example, an organization may have a policy to employ minority groups whenever possible, or to give to reputable charities whenever asked. Policies are thus static guidelines for repeated decisions. A strategy is a particular pattern of actions intended to attain certain desired ends. An organization may choose either to adapt to its environment or to shape it. Reaction and pro-action, therefore, are examples of broad (and possibly alternative) strategies. A strategy is generally less fixed and (perhaps) more specific than a policy. But regardless of how one chooses to define these terms, it is clear that both strategies and policies are the outputs of a process of information collection and decision making. And so strategy formulation, policy development, and similar terms are simply labels to describe certain planning processes.

Why is planning needed?

If planning is the process of deciding what has to be done today to be ready for tomorrow, why or when is planning needed? Why can't an organization forego anticipation and just respond to events as they present themselves? Some economists have long been averse to planning. They prefer to rely on an invisible hand (as conceptualized by Adam Smith) to guide the economy, with individual freedom of choice determining what is best. Similarly, within organizations, freedom to innovate and to act and react have long been proposed as an appropriate style of management. But the oil crisis, energy shortages, and the inflation of the 1970s have converted even the free market-oriented chairman of the President's Council of Economic Advisers, Herbert Stein, who now acknowledges that the United States may need a planned economy like the Japanese or the French (*Business Week*, January 5, 1974). And as evidenced by the volume of literature devoted to planning, a similar opinion exists in the business community. It is now apparent to government and to business that environmental and organizational complexity can only be managed by appropriate managerial methods.

The need for planning depends on the nature of the opportunities and threats an organization is required to deal with, and on the complexity involved in contending with these issues. The survival of any organization requires that it determine a basis for existence, obtain the resources to exploit this basis, allocate them, complete resource conversion and marketing, and secure payment for the product produced or service rendered. To meet its objectives it must anticipate the future, coordinate individual efforts, and bridge the lags inherent in matching opportunities with capabilities. Hence, an organization's need for planning is a function of its need for what planning can do for it in meeting these requirements.

To be successful in competitive industry, an organization must capitalize on opportunity. Opportunity may lie either in the external environment or in the organization's ability to differentiate itself and so capitalize on unique capabilities. But both of these areas are ever-changing and so must be continually monitored. Furthermore, responding to opportunity—by creating a problem, by developing a differential advantage, or by recognizing a particular market niche—is not instantaneous. A variety of problems and time lags are inherent in most responses. Hence in situations where environmental opportunity and external capability must be monitored, and where lags may delay an organization's response to opportunity, anticipation in the form of planning is required.

Planning is also needed because of the time required in and complexity of developing and coordinating human resources. Organizational success requires the efforts of many individuals. But management personnel are becoming increasingly mobile, capable of practising their professional skills in a variety of industries and situations. Because they are costly and demand satisfaction from the task they perform, stockpiling management is an undesirable procedure. Also, the special skills or familiarity required for a particular aspect of an operation must be accumulated over a long period of time. Therefore the efficient management of human resources requires planning.

Organizational success in a technological age is also inexorably linked to planning. Business relies increasingly on productive machinery, computers, and communications devices. The sophistication of this technology is advancing at a rapid pace so forecasting its future development is a specialized task. In addition, acquiring the technological capability and facilities to satisfy the demands of today's economies of scale requires the outlay of large capital expenditures and involves long lead times. Rapid product obsolescence, the high failure rate of new products, and ever-changing consumer orientations (e.g., from consumption to consumerism and recycling) make the risk inherent in these decisions almost debilitating. The sheer size of the capital investments and the sophistication of the analytical methodology necessary to reflect the risks in successfully acquiring and integrating technology stipulate that such decisions be deliberative processes.

Even if the development of managerial and technological capability is effectively planned, this in itself is no assurance of success: success also requires their coordination. Achieving the coordination of human and technological resources within a single organizational unit has never been an easy task; and the current spread of corporations through international networks makes these problems even more complex. There is an ever-greater need to increase the stability of organizations so that subunits can predict the behavior of, and hence coordinate with, each other—a need that planning can satisfy.

Planning is also an important influence on an organization's style of management. The pace of modern business gives rise to what is politely called an action orientation, and impolitely referred to as "fire fighting." Fire fighting is a reactive style of management that responds only when a fire (crisis) has appeared. Furthermore, the phenomenon of selective perception or "tunnel vision"—narrowing one's focus to that which is of immediate concern and for which one is directly responsible—continually distorts decision-making criteria. Planning is one way to counter fire fighting and tunnel vision. It forces management to step back, to anticipate the future, and to consider the system of interrelationships in which it operates. By planning, management can develop a consistent orientation to the unforeseen environment of the future and to the large structures in which it operates. Planning is thus a means of having management think through what is desired and how it should be accomplished. Strictly as a mental exercise, planning encourages innovation, mind-stretching, and a search for more and better alternatives.

In brief, then, planning is needed to the extent that (1) an organization must anticipate environmental change and reduce the time lags inherent in its adaptation process; (2) the management of an organization requires a common frame of reference to integrate its decisions and goals; (3) an organization requires a medium by which assumptions and premises can be made explicit; and (4) communication must be facilitated, conflicts resolved, and coordination and cooperation achieved. In short, planning is needed to the degree that an organization requires the various benefits that planning can provide.

The benefits of planning

The preceding reasons for planning ought to make it evident that there are two types of benefits planning can provide: (1) better results eminating from the plans produced, i.e., from the decisions or recommendations as to what should be done; and (2) better management eminating from the process of planning itself, i.e., from engaging in the activity that leads to the formulation of plans.

Better results. An organization can benefit from better plans to the extent that a plan can tell it what to do when continuing with its existing activity is no longer appropriate; that is, when it needs new direction or more effective or efficient operations. This may occur when:

a. It is unable to recognize environmental opportunity.
b. It is unable to capitalize on environmental opportunity by reaction.
c. It is unable to influence or shape the environment it faces.
d. It lacks awareness of either the scope of its capabilities or the constraints it faces.
e. It lacks information about the expectations it must satisfy.
f. It is having trouble translating recommendations into a basis for action.
g. It is not allocating its resources appropriately.
h. It is not accomplishing the objectives it sets out.

Therefore planning can be of use in:

1. Choosing the right things to do (direction).
2. Accomplishing them (effectiveness).
3. Achieving these results with minimum input (efficiency).

Better management. A popular management cliché goes as follows: "When you have completed a planning activity, you could lock the plans produced in a desk drawer and still derive 90 percent of the benefits of the activity." The cliché implies that irrespective of the quality of the plans produced, an organization benefits from engaging in a planning process. Some of the process benefits are the following:

a. Planning provides a *common frame of reference* for all managers who participate in the process. The conceptual structure of the planning process permits managers to view their present and future operations from a common perspective and so better understood what is expected of them (for example, in anticipating future changes or accepting more risk). Such a common frame of reference also improves the communication and coordination that every organization requires.

b. Planning improves *managerial activity and involvement.* Engaging in a planning activity forces managers to make explicit their expectations and the premises on which they are based, and hence resolves conflicts that might not otherwise surface. And to the extent that participation and self-direction are motivational, involvement in planning is also a means of increasing motivation.

c. Planning is also a *management development method.* Formal planning can make managers explicitly conscious of what they are now doing and of what they could be doing in order to perform their jobs better (for example, by forcing them to consider new opportunities they had previously ignored). Thus it can bring about a more systematic and disciplined way of managing.

The nature of and the interrelationship between these two types of benefits that planning can provide must be recognized and understood if the right type of planning for an organization is to be correctly chosen. Anyone specifying how planning is to be carried out must be aware that irrespective of the quality of the plans produced, engaging in a planning activity can yield individual and organizational process benefits such as a more disciplined way of managing, greater perspective and understanding, increased communication, learning, greater consideration of alternatives, and increased motivation. Of course such process benefits are not, in themselves, a sufficient justification for planning. Planning must also produce better results. But in many situations better management is a prerequisite to achieving better results and thus using planning to provide process benefits so as to develop a stronger organization is one way of eventually achieving better results.

The problem-solving basis of planning

Planning is defined or described in many ways, depending on the point of view of the describer. This diversity is understandable, for if planning is deciding what to do in advance, then all premeditated human activity requires planning. Clearly, since planning is a multidimensional process many dimensions can be used to describe it. The following are five of the most common dimensions that distinguish different types of planning:

1. *Time horizon.* Short-range (1 year or less), medium-range (1–5 years), long-term (5–20 years), and infinite.
2. *Organizational perspective.* Multinational, corporate, divisional, functional (e.g., marketing, finance), departmental, mission-oriented, project, product line.
3. *Hierarchical scope or organizational level.* Strategic, policy, top management, program, budget, procedural, operational.

4. *Focus.* Product or service, money, work force, market, technology, information.
5. *Purpose.* Specifying desired outcomes and results, communication, coordination, conflict resolution, consistent managerial orientation, innovation, management development.

From these five dimensions alone one sees that organizational planning processes can be differentiated by the scope they cover, the time horizon they encompass, the quantification and aggregation of the data they deal with, the uncertainty they attempt to reconcile, or the purpose they hope to achieve. It appears that the types of planning are almost infinite in number. But in spite of this apparent diversity, the similarity among them far outweighs the apparent differences. This similarity is the problem-solving nature of planning.

All planning involves formulating and solving problems. Plans can be conceived and implemented in terms of two sets of variables and the set of relationships between them. One set of variables contains the input, determining, or independent variables and the other the outcome, resultant, or dependent variables. Variables ignored are assumed to be irrelevant or insignificant to the process under consideration. Variables such as advertising expenditures may be measured exactly, while others, such as consumer demand, may be approximated in any number of ways extending from pure judgment to sophisticated quantitative market research. The relationships among the independent and dependent variables may be known exactly, estimated, or simply assumed. Any number of variables, such as profit, market share, or return on investment can be used as solution criteria or measures of success of a plan. And so, although the specification, quantification, and ultimate reliability of a plan depend on the scope and characteristics of the phenomenon it focuses on, the planning process itself can always be conceptualized in the same way regardless of the time horizon, organizational level, and so on, of the activity being planned.

Planning is just the process of abstracting and manipulating various actions and evaluating the results of these actions. It selects the variables to be considered, estimates their values, specifies the relationships among these variables, and then manipulates this configuration until an acceptable plan is achieved. Manipulating the model yields a solution; and the solution itself is the plan. Planning selects from the infinite set of possible variables and relationships those that best characterize the underlying activity, specifies the results to be achieved by a particular point in time, and then determines the actions required to produce these results.

Hence, in spite of the apparent variety in the types of planning, the traditional problem-solving sequence is the common process underlying various planning activities. Policy formulation, financial planning, strategy determination, and production planning are all, in essence, problem-solving activities. All planning activities involve the same basic steps. The differences are primarily in focus and in manner of implementation—choice of methods, techniques, and emphasis—and are differences in degree, not in kind.

Planning in organizations

The problem-solving model describes the essence of all planning processes, whether they are the elaborate procedures of a multinational corporation or the informal methods of a recent business school graduate planning an interview with a prospective employer. As well as being a useful abstraction or conceptualization that facilitates thinking about planning, it is also a normative model which describes how planning ought to be carried out. This general process model is a useful starting point to show how planning should be carried out in each unique situation.

Single-cycle planning process model. The planning needed to solve a single problem can be described by the seven-step problem-solving cycle most students of management are familiar with:

Analysis
  1. Recognize that a problem exists.
  2. Formulate the problem and specify the additional data needed.
  3. Collect and analyze the required data.

Decision
  4. Generate alternatives and express them in terms of the input and outcome variables and relationships required.
  5. Use appropriate criteria, select the best alternative.

Implementation
  6. Implement the selected alternative by translating it into a form suitable for execution; i.e., into a plan.
  7. Ensure that the plan is accomplished through appropriate control techniques.

It is recognized that this model of the analysis-decision-implementation sequence only provides a framework for a process which does not always follow a neat pattern. The process is not usually sequential. Recycling between steps is almost always required; for example, the collection of data (step 3) may result in a need to restate the problem (step 2). Most situations will require a repeated recycling of steps and only in the simplest of situations will planning follow a straight path from problem recognition to provision for control. Nevertheless, a sequential process model does give an understanding of the various steps involved in planning the ends desired and the best means of accomplishing these.

Multicycle planning. The complexity of operations for all but the smallest organizations cannot be handled as a monolithic whole guided by a single-cycle planning process. The organization's "problem" is actually a whole series of interrelated subproblems, and before it can be solved it must be subdivided into more manageable proportions. When the solution of one problem in an organization's planning activity constrains other problem-solving cycles, these form a multicycle planning process.

One way to subdivide the problem of achieving the global objectives of an organization into more manageable (single cycle) proportions is through means-end analysis. As illustrated below establishing a means-end chain of objectives and activities implies that accomplishing subgoal C contributes in turn to the accomplishment of subgoal B which, in turn, contributes toward accomplishing global goal A (C is the means to B; B is the means to A). Through means-end analysis the ultimate task of the organization can be decomposed into units, each capable of solution. The plan of one hierarchical level becomes the constraints on the level below, and so on.

```
                  Organizational level

A   Corporate office—Objectives
↑                   —Strategies
B   Marketing dept. —Objectives
↑                   —Strategies
C   Product line    —Objectives
                    —Strategies
```

In the above illustration each organizational level is involved in choosing its own objectives and strategies (ends and means) and hence is involved in a single-cycle problem-solving process. However, the planning done by the marketing department is constrained by the choices made at the corporate level and product line planning is, in turn, constrained by the marketing plans. Thus a chain of means-ends relationships decomposes an organization's problem-solving requirements into manageable units, while at the same time still linking all planning to the organization's overall mission.

Each means-end unit in the hierarchical chain can be considered as a single-cycle planning process. The actual number of cycles carried out depends, in any organization, on the complexity of the problem to be solved and on the structure of the organization solving it. In general, the more complex a problem is, the greater the number of subproblems it will be broken into and the greater the number of cycles carried out to reach a solution. Consider, for example, how many cycles might be required to solve the problem of world peace. Another point is that if responsibility for planning is distributed uniformly throughout an organization, each level in the hierarchy will carry out one cycle, and the total number of cycles will correspond to the number of hierarchical levels. Thus the number of planning cycles carried out will be contingent on the complexity of the problem to be solved and on the hierarchical structure of the organization.

Conceptualized in this way, organizational planning is a hierarchically decomposed multicycle process carried out by various organizational subunits. Each cycle is different in scope, level of aggregation, and time horizon. Proceeding downward through the hierarchy, there are an increasing number of constraints on each planning process in the form of more detailed goals and more specific planning activities and timing. Organizational planning is thus a nested hierarchical activity which depends on the organization's structure. But even though such organizational planning processes are exceedingly complex, it is important to keep sight of the fact that they are made up of single-cycle processes linked together in a hierarchical network, and that within each cycle the basic problem-solving sequence is carried out.

AN OVERVIEW OF CONTROL

What is control?

If planning is a process of continually establishing ends and courses of action, control is the process of ensuring that these courses of action are maintained and that the desired ends are achieved. It is the process of continually ensuring conformance to expectation. Control concludes the managerial cycle that begins with planning.

Control is concerned with ". . . the successful implementation of a course of action as predetermined by a decision model . . . and . . . with feedback that might (a) change the future plans given the model, and (b) possibly change the decision model itself . . ." (Horngren, 1972). Control also means ". . . observation of results to see whether plans are being carried out. . . . It implies corrective action as a result of the evaluation, or possibly replanning" (Amey and Egginton, 1973).

In other words, "management control can be defined as a systematic effort by business management to compare performance to predetermined standards, plans, or objectives in order to determine whether performance is in line with these standards and presumably in order to take any remedial action required to see that human and other resources are being used in the most effective and efficient way possible in achieving corporate objectives" (Mockler, 1972, p. 14).

Control, like planning, is a problem-solving process, but now the problems relate to the implementation rather than the formulation of plans. Control is the process of deciding if what is going on is as it should be—if it is "under control" and includes the actions necessary to rectify deviations from expectation and to make the activity under way more efficient and effective. An integral part of this process, then, is collecting information and making decisions.

One way to describe a control process is in the following five steps:

1. Determining if a problem exists, by collecting information about expectations and actual performance, and then comparing them.
2. Generating alternative courses that will close or minimize the deviation between actual and expected.
3. Evaluating the alternative courses of remedial action available and selecting the most appropriate one.
4. Implementing the chosen action.
5. Ensuring that the appropriate action did actually close the deviation between actual and expected.

The range of control and controls

Just as planning is a continuous process, so is control. Just as plans can be distinguished from planning, controls can also be distinguished from control. Control is the continual process of ensuring conformance to expectation. Controls are the means by which control is effected—they are the behaviors, conditioning influences, historical measurements, or analytical techniques used to bring about this conformance. Controls are thus the content of the control process employed at any one point in time.

Financial controls. Control has traditionally been considered the province of financial executives or controllers because they are the generators of "controls." The controls they use are formal, quantified, and money-based, and the control process they use stresses the minimization of deviations from expectation and compliance to specific financial plans.

Since control of any activity requires an understanding of its underlying cause and effect relationships, financial control requires an understanding of how financial variables behave with activity. The control process selects a particular product or organizational unit, focuses on input-output relationships, develops standards to measure efficiency, and keeps track of deviations from these expectations. Responsibility accounting is the term used to describe the identification of financial data with the persons responsible for their control.

Four types of financial control systems and related responsibility centers are commonly used for the control of organizational units. If a system measures only the costs incurred by a unit, that unit is termed a cost center. A cost center is the smallest organizational segment for which costs are traced and accumulated and over which an individual has responsibility. Although every unit classified as a cost center produces some useful output, it is usually neither feasible nor desirable to measure these outputs in monetary terms. Therefore, for cost centers, expectations are expressed and control is effected primarily in terms of inputs (i.e., costs).

When only the output of a unit is measured in monetary terms, that unit lends itself to operation as a revenue center. For this type of unit, a system may establish a budget for sales revenue, record the actual sales made, and then account for differences in terms of variances. When the performance of a unit can be measured in terms of both the revenue it earns and also the expense it incurs in generating that revenue, it can be controlled as a profit center.

The most comprehensive form of financial control system applicable to an organizational unit is an investment center. In an investment center, measures are taken not only of profit but also of the capital employed to generate this profit. The productivity of capital is used as the basis of performance expectation and evaluation. For these organizational units, return on investment is the figure most commonly employed to express expectations and to assess performance.

Financial data have been the primary means of organizational control for several reasons. The foremost of these reasons is that they allow a number of diverse organizational aspects to be measured by one uniform common denominator—money. A budget, as a simulation of activities in terms of their financial flows, is a convenient means of describing a host of diverse activities. Also, objectives and efficiencies are easily expressed in financial terms. And because of the importance of financing and cash to an organization, the focus on financial controls is natural. But in spite of the traditional association of controls with an organization's controller, it must be recognized that the spectrum of organizational control is far broader than money-based measures alone.

In fact, the number of control processes engaged in is even greater than the number of planning processes. If for every planning process in an organization there is an accompanying control process, then there are at least as many control processes as there are planning processes. But control, as the process of ensuring conformance to expectation, can also be considered from a number of differing perspectives and effected simultaneously from many sources.

Other sources of control. Perhaps the most important source of control lies within an individual himself—i.e., his internal control or self-instigated behavior change. Organizational theorists investigating self-control have shown that his degree of commitment and the feedback information he[1] receives influence an individual's ability to modify his behavior. Agreement with the objectives established, overall level of aspiration, and individual motivation and ability also affect self-directed behavior changes. But although these studies have shed considerable light on self-directed behavior change, this cornerstone of organizational control is still only vaguely understood. Yet it is a significant aspect of any consideration of control and cannot be ignored.

From the standpoint of organizational theory, control relates to influence, authority, and power; it refers to any system that determines what another person, group, or organization will do. Influence, in turn, may come from many sources—peer groups, individuals, or family. Any source of information is a potential source of influence, and so the potential range of organizational control is almost limitless.

One important source of control external to an individual is his or her supervisor. The leadership style of a supervisor may affect the control he or she is able to achieve. Control requires the perception of actual events, a comparison of those events with original expectations, and then the taking of appropriate action. The control process can be exercised by many alternative styles of leadership. One type of leader may allow a subordinate to correct a situation himself, while another may prefer to take punitive action. Taking an active versus a passive role, or using coercion and pressure to effect control as opposed to being supportive and stimulating individual learning are alternative means of achieving conformance. Accordingly, the appropriateness of a leader's style to the situation in which he or she operates is another factor in the degree of control he or she will be able to achieve.

Personnel managers as well as line supervisors are concerned with control. Perhaps the easiest way to achieve control is to match a task situation with an individual who has the predisposition and ability to behave in accordance with task expectations. Hence, personnel staffs have long used psychological and vocational aptitude tests in an attempt to fit the best employee to the job and so minimize the need for external controls. An alternative and more modern approach fits the job to the worker by designing tasks to provide both fulfillment and satisfaction, thereby taking advantage of the capabilities of each unique individual. But regardless of which way this coordination is conducted, fitting the task to the worker or matching the worker to the task, an appropriate match of task expectations with an individual's normal behavioral pattern and ability minimizes the need for external control.

Training can also facilitate control by improving workers' vocational, decision making, and communication skills so that they can carry out

---

[1] The common pronoun "he" refers to persons of either sex and is not intended to be masculine or feminine but simply "human."

their jobs more effectively. Training may also improve interpersonal skills so that they are better able to function with co-workers and subordinates and conform more readily to their expectations. The personnel staff can also use monetary rewards as a means of control. Performance contingent payment schemes, supplemental benefits, and stock option plans are now often available to assembly-line workers as well as to top executives.

The management science, operations research, and management information systems groups within an organization also contribute to organizational control. These groups analyze, optimize, and predefine and systematize what should be accomplished. Their objective is to reduce unstructured tasks requiring judgment and intuition to programmed step-by-step operations. They effect control by understanding and anticipating all possible alternatives that decision makers may face, and by providing them with alternative courses of action. And the increasingly favorable economics of computer-based information capture and processing are making possible the manipulation of large volumes of information for a great number of uses. The potential of programmed decision making, then, is another important determinant of current and future organizational control.

Although this enumeration of sources of control is by no means exhaustive, it does indicate the wide range of controls that have to be considered by a systems designer attempting to ensure conformance to expectation. These controls make up a set of complementary and supplementary choices to be selected or relied upon as required. However, the job of matching a particular portfolio of controls to an activity is a demanding design task that is situationally specific.

When is control needed?

In order to specify the portfolio of controls needed to bring about desired behavior, it is first necessary to understand why expected behavior may not be forthcoming. The need for and type of control most appropriate for any organizational activity is a direct function of those aspects of organizational life that tend to cause deviations from expectation. These can be grouped into three broad classes of reasons. Each describes a type of risk that control reduces.

1. *Conceptual risk.* Conceptual risk may be characterized as an imperfect formulation of a problem. An individual or organization may choose a behavior, or select a method of analysis, which is improperly conceived in the first place. Using an incorrect model, making the wrong assumptions, or choosing incorrect decision criteria are examples of conceptual risk. Indeed, unless an activity or operation is completely understood, any manipulation of it involves conceptual risk. Conceptual risk

is encountered whenever cause and effect relationships are not perfectly known. For example, it may not be known whether changing an advertising slogan will affect a company's image. In these situations, feedback on actual events is the primary way to accommodate conceptual risk. In fact, learning through feedback data may be the only means of testing the validity of the particular conception used to formulate a plan.

2. *Administrative risk.* Administrative risk is the risk that even a perfectly conceptualized solution may not be implemented properly. Even when one has properly conceptualized a problem and proposed a plan, implementation depends on the administrative capabilities of the organization. For example, one purpose of control is to ensure better planning. But even though an organization has properly conceptualized the task at hand and employs the most appropriate planning methods, its planners must still have their creativity and ambition tempered by the awareness that their plans will be used as a basis for action. Providing feedback on performance and holding each planner accountable for his plans are ways to reduce deviations caused by overoptimistic predictions. Thus, from the standpoint of overcoming administrative risk, control improves the probability that what is expected will actually take place.

3. *Environmental risk.* A third risk in planning is that unanticipated environmental changes may take place after plans have been put into effect. Even if planning has been appropriately conceived and administered, subsequent external changes can alter results. Control identifies these changes and provides the feedback information necessary to recognize and react constructively to change. Control thus provides data so that appropriate actions may be taken to minimize future deviations.

In sum, the amount and type of control required by any organizational unit depend predominantly on the conceptual, administrative, and environmental risks it faces.

THE RELATIONSHIP OF PLANNING AND CONTROL

Definitional confusion

The term "control" is sometimes assumed to include activities related to deciding what should be accomplished. A common example is the term "management control." Another example is the phrase "budgetary control." But budgetary control includes establishment of budget expectations, a process which begins with receiving and transforming the outputs of higher level planning. It includes the collection and processing of the additional information needed to establish budget expectations. And so the first step of a budgetary control process is actually planning—establishing the expectations that are to be accomplished. Budgetary control is then carried out by collecting and processing information about the actual activities that took place, the normal scope of control.

Budgetary control is therefore not just control: it is really planning and control. Recall that planning was defined as the process of determining what should be done—by establishing expectations—and control was defined as the process of ensuring conformance to expectations—by comparing actual results against expectations. Of course plans are expressed and control is effected in terms of the same variables, e.g., standard costs and deviations from standard; but as the terms planning and control are defined here, budgeting involves both planning and control.

Process interactions

It is important to recognize the interrelationship between planning and control as carried out in most organizational contexts. Effective control requires continuous problem solving to correct deviations and to overcome obstacles. To be effective, a control system must be modeled closely after the system used to devise the original plans. Control itself, however, is essentially based on feedback. It is management by exception, the practice of channeling management's attention to those activities or outcomes that have deviated from expectation. Corrective action is thus stimulated by deviations from original plans and is taken ex post, after the fact. Because this is so, the original planning process and the subsequent control process may appear to be discrete, since only the output of the planning process (i.e., the plan) interfaces with the control process. But only in rare instances can control be considered independently of planning.

In reality, planning and control are usually inextricably intertwined. When a deviation does occur, how does one determine to what source of risk it should be attributed? In fact, control information does not, and in most cases simply cannot, distinguish among the three types of risk previously discussed. Only when a deviation is caused by improper implementation alone (administrative risk) can planning and control be treated independently of one another. In such a case control will be able to pinpoint the cause of the ineffective implementation and correct it. But this is the exception, not the rule.

Planning identifies and measures relevant controllable and uncontrollable variables, specifies the relationships among these variables, selects criteria by which to evaluate solutions, and then manipulates this configuration until an acceptable solution is reached. This solution then becomes the plan to be implemented. Taking into account all these antecedents of implementation, it should be clear that deviations may be caused not only by ineffective implementation but by any of a number of other factors. Deviations may be due to environmental changes that have occurred since the plan was put forward (environmental risk), or to an improperly specified or improperly calibrated model (conceptual risk). Whenever a modeling or calibration error is made preceeding the formulation and implementation of a plan, the source of deviation is improper planning, not ineffective implementation.

Feedback control reveals errors in specification, calibration, and implementation. It provides information useful in countering conceptual, administrative, and environmental risk. However, in all but the most unique cases planning and control must be considered to be completely intermeshed, and not as separate and distinct processes.

PLANNING AND CONTROL SYSTEMS

This chapter has described planning and control processes in order to show the fundamental similarities and differences in the ways they are carried out. It has emphasized that the need for and appropriateness of planning and control processes depend on the situation to which they applied, and that differences in organizational style, strategy, types of management, and so on can all influence the methods of planning and control selected. An underlying premise of this book is that planning and control are situationally determined, and that different situations require different types of planning and control.

The discussion so far has been entirely in terms of processes—but this is a book on planning and control systems. In very general terms, a system is simply a set of elements and relationships viewed from a common perspective, such as a particular goal or purpose. Conceptualizing a set of elements as a system is a means of delineating and understanding the interrelationships among a complex set of elements. A planning and control system, therefore, is the set of elements (tools, people, measurements, schedules, and guidelines) used in planning and control.

A planning and control system is made up of four components:

1. A model of the planning and control processes which specifies the steps to be carried out.
2. Specification of methods—tools, techniques, and reports to be used in each step of the process.
3. Specification of who is to be responsible for each step of the process.
4. A schedule of the required activities.

At its most fundamental level, a planning system answers the questions:

What should be done?	Activities.
How should it be carried out?	Methods and techniques.
Who should do each activity?	Involvement.
When should it be done?	Timing.

A system serves as an organization's framework for the conduct of its planning and control. It channels the organization's collective creativity, innovativeness, judgment, and intuition into a focused, productive thrust. The intent of the system is to stimulate, facilitate, constrain, guide, and assist planning and control.

A planning and control system may, for instance, include a planning and control procedures manual and an implementation and follow-up program. The manual may contain chapters on the assignment of tasks, sequences of activities, required time schedule, techniques to be used, and reports to be prepared; and it may cover many details such as the particular manner in which reports are to be prepared. These many decisions about appropriate procedures and implementation must be made by the system designer.

The design of an organization's planning and control system is determined by the needs to be satisfied in each situation. For example, if it is desired that managers evaluate financial decisions in a certain way (e.g., by using the net present value method of analysis), specification of the technique in the capital expenditure section of the planning manual is one way to bring about the desired behavior. Some types of behavior may be motivated instead of prescribed by making compensation contingent on their accomplishment. Efficiency can be highlighted by reporting input and output conversion ratios. Or managerial skills can be improved by making junior managers go through an elaborate planning procedure and complete reports requiring them to explore and analyze areas believed beneficial to their development. In other words, appropriate design of a planning and control system can help elicit certain kinds of desired behavior—the behavior that will result in successful accomplishment of the organization's objectives.

THE INTENT OF THIS BOOK

Although it has already been emphasized that the design of any planning and control system is situationally specific, this fact is of sufficient importance (and potential misunderstanding) to be reemphasized here. The intent of this text is not to tell a system designer what should be done; rather, it is to convey the fact that there are a number of possibilities that might be done in any particular situation. The message carried in these pages is that systematic analysis must be applied in choosing what is best and no prescriptions should be made without knowledge of the situation.

As will be discussed in later chapters, organizations differ significantly from each other in many ways. Some are organized by product while others are arranged by the functions performed. Decentralized organizations rely more on the decision making of lower echelon personnel while in centralized firms decisions are made at the top and simply communicated to those concerned. Clearly, different organization designs have different planning and control requirements. Hence the appropriateness of any component element of a planning and control system—whether it is the activity to be carried out, the tools and techniques to be used in carrying it out, the personnel to be involved, or the schedule to be followed—depends on the situation in which it is to be used.

Many books uncritically emphasize the applicability of certain methods and techniques without qualification. This seductive promise of widespread applicability may tend to produce what can be termed a "tools in search of a problem" syndrome. That is, armed with a tool that solves a certain problem, the system designer may tend to see that problem where it may not exist. Too often, however, the exact problem for which the method is recommended rarely arises as originally described, and attempts to implement the tool run into difficulty.

In contrast to this approach, this text squarely faces the uncertain and contingent application of most of the activities and techniques which make up the planning and control system. Therefore recommendations of specific methods for solving specific problem situations will not be found in this book. What will be found, rather, is repeated emphasis that any method must be individually evaluated in light of the situation in which it is going to be used.

Because the text avoids specific recommendations and answers many questions with "it depends," it may disturb some readers who prefer a less ambiguous educational experience. Undoubtedly it will weaken the readers' confidence in each and every technique they know. However, it compensates for this by providing a conceptual framework and a systematic design procedure which encourages the system designer to look beyond problem symptoms and readily available solutions. It will increase their awareness of the conditions needed for the successful selection and implementation of all system elements, and the dysfunctional consequences that may result from blind implementation of any method. There are few simple solutions to system design problems. Caution and critical evaluation are always called for.

SUMMARY

Planning is the continual process of collecting the information and making the decisions by which an organizational unit adapts to, shapes, and exploits its environment. By planning, management establishes the purposes, guidelines, constraints, and programs of action used in shepherding its organization through the future. Although there appear to be many forms and types of planning, any single-cycle planning process can be regarded simply as a form of problem solving, which specifies desired ends and the means of achieving them. An organizational unit derives two types of benefits from planning. Good plans provide appropriate direction and contribute to the efficient and effective use of resources. An organization needs good plans to the extent that its current activities are unsuitable to future conditions. Second, irrespective of the quality of the plans produced, engaging in a planning process is an excellent way to improve communication, coordination, mind stretching, and managerial development. The amount and types of planning required by an organization depend solely on the situation in which that organization finds itself and on its particular needs.

An organization's total planning needs can be decomposed and allocated to the subunits in its hierarchy through means-end analysis. Each subunit carries out a single-cycle planning process establishing its ends and the means by which it will achieve these. Organizational planning is an interconnected network of single-cycle planning processes forming a nested hierarchy. The manner in which planning is carried out is therefore largely determined by the way an organization is structured.

Control is the continuous process of ensuring conformance to expectation. It is a problem-solving process oriented toward overcoming obstacles and taking advantage of opportunities so that deviations are minimized and expectations are realized. Control can be effected in any number of ways, from the detailed quantitative financial-based reporting schemes of the controller to the subtle interpersonal influences of a supervisor. Like planning, control is entirely situationally determined, and therefore control system design is also situationally specific. The appropriate amount and type of control depend entirely on the administrative, conceptual, and environmental risks to be contended with.

Although most of this chapter has treated planning and control as separate and distinct processes, in most organizational contexts they are closely interconnected. Control can be considered independently of planning only if the deviations identified by feedback are known to stem from administrative risk; i.e., ineffective implementation. In all other situations planning and control cannot be separated.

A planning and control system is the structure within which planning and control are carried out. It consists of a process model, a designation of the tools and techniques needed to carry out each step of the process, a specification of the people to be involved and the schedule to be followed. The specification of a particular planning and control system is determined entirely by the behavior the system is intended to affect, which in turn is determined by what an organization has to do to be successful.

QUESTIONS

1. If planning is a process of collecting information and making decisions, is all decision making planning?

2. If planning is a continuous process, why do organizations have annual planning cycles with rigid deadlines?

3. Is planning possible in a totally random environment, or needed in a completely static one?

4. In what ways does planning for the development and introduction of a new product differ from (a) planning future work force requirements, and (b) production planning?

5. Planning is a prime means of procrastination. Agree or disagree?

6. Can there be planning without control?

7. If planning involves deciding on desired ends and the means to achieve them, what do controls control—ends, or means, or both?

8. In a typical classroom situation, how are expectations established, and conformance to them assured?

9. Will managers who understand and apply the process models described in this chapter achieve better results than managers who do not?

10. Distinguish between internal and external control.

REFERENCES AND BIBLIOGRAPHY

Ackoff, R. L. *A concept of corporate planning.* New York: Wiley, 1970.

Amey, L. R., and Eggington, D. A. *Management accounting.* London: Longman Group Limited, 1973.

Cammann, C., and Nadler, David A. Fit control systems to your managerial style. *Harvard Business Review,* January–February 1976, pp. 65–72.

Corporate planning: Piercing the future fog in the executive suite, Business Week Special Report, *Business Week,* April 28, 1975.

Dalton, G. W., and Lawrence, P. R. *Motivation and Control in Organizations.* Homewood, Ill.: Irwin, 1971.

Ewing, David W. *The Practice of Planning,* New York: Harper & Row, 1968.

Gerstner, L. B. Can strategic planning pay off? *Business Horizons,* 1972, pp. 5–16.

Giglioni, Giovanni B., and Bedeian, Arthur G. A conspectus of management control theory: 1900–1972. *Academy of Management Journal,* June 1974, pp. 292–305.

Grinyer, Peter H. Some dangerous axioms of corporate planning. *Journal of Business Policy,* Autumn 1972, pp. 3–7.

Herold, David M. Long-range planning and organizational performance: A cross-valuation study, *Academy of Management Journal,* March 1972, pp. 91–104.

Hofer, Charles W. Toward a contingency theory of business strategy, *Academy of Management Journal,* December 1975, pp. 784–810.

Horngren, C. T. *Cost Accounting: A Managerial Emphasis.* Englewood Cliffs, N.J.: Prentice-Hall, Inc., 1972.

Malik, Zafar A., and Karger, Delmar W. Does long-range planning improve company performance? *Management Review*, September 1975, pp. 27–31.

McMahon, J. Timothy, and Perritt, G. W. Toward a contingency theory of organizational control. *Academy of Management Journal*, December 1973, pp. 624–35.

Mockler, R. J. *The Management Control Process*. New York: Appleton-Century Crofts, 1972.

Nanus, Burt. The future-oriented corporation, *Business Horizons*, February 1975, p. 5–10.

Patz, Alan L. Notes: Business policy and the scientific method, *California Management Review*, Spring 1975, pp. 87–91.

Pennington, Malcolm W. Why has planning failed? *Long-Range Planning*, March 1972, pp. 2–9.

Ringbaak, K. A. Why planning fails. *European Business*, Spring 1971, pp. 15–27.

Ringbaak, K. A. The corporate planning life cycle—An international point of view, *Long-Range Planning*, September 1972, pp. 28–31.

Schoeffler, Sidney; Buzzell, Robert D.; and Hoany, Donald F. Impact of strategic planning on profit performance, *Harvard Business Review*, March–April 1974, pp. 137–44.

Steiner, G. A. *Top Management Planning*. New York: Macmillan, 1969.

Stern, Ludwig. Contingency planning: Why? How and How Much? *Datamation*, September 1974, pp. 83–98.

Thume, Stanley S., and House, Robert J. Where long-range planning pays off, *Business Horizons*, August 1970, pp. 81–87.

Case study 1–1
Imperial Footwear Limited

Imperial Footwear manufactures and distributes shoes for boys aged three to ten. Sales have grown from $7 million in 1958 to $25 million in 1976. The intent now is to expand Imperial's product line to manufacture and distribute girls' shoes and to double sales volume over the next five years. Next year the first girls' shoes will be introduced.

The following exchange was part of a conversation which took place over lunch between the president of the company and the vice-presidents of finance, manufacturing, and marketing.

V.P. Manufacturing: I think we need a new approach to our long-range corporate planning! A corporate plan is a written statement of strategy, sequenced over time, delineating the scope and character of proposed future activities, and the resources needed to achieve them. It should be backed up by documented analysis of how competitors are likely to act, opportunities in the environment, industry dynamics, points of vulner-ability, and overall organizational capabilities. If that's what a long-range plan is, we sure don't have one now. All we have is a five-year financial forecast showing sources and dispositions of funds, and a one-year budget-ing procedure where we first describe next year's actions and then control against it. Other companies are now doing more formal planning and we should also.

President: The only reason companies are setting up planning departments is that it is now fashionable to do so. Strategic planning is the new "com-puter in the front window." It's just a bandwagon effect, a fad. We al-ready have very sound long-range plans and know exactly where we're going. We don't need a planning department.

V.P. Manufacturing: Well I don't agree. I don't think we're systematically thinking about the long-term future. What little strategic planning we do is usually strictly blue sky. I think the problem is serious and we should do something about it.

V.P. Finance: Formal corporate planning doesn't work. Look at our current situation. We invest a considerable amount of time and generate a lot of paper to carry out the individual work planning system the personnel de-partment started but, to be truthful, I don't see the payoffs traceable to these efforts. Are we really better off through this sort of planning? I think it causes more problems than it solves and costs more than its worth. Work planning leads to procrastination. You know, the "don't do it, plan" syndrome. Or it runs in parallel with operations and does not lead it. Our financial forecasting and budgeting system is all that we really need.

V.P. Manufacturing: In part you're 100 percent correct. A good portion of our planning focuses on procedures and documentation and timing, and not on strategic issues. We worry about numbers but we do little hard think-ing about the future. And in what little we do, we emphasize the distant future so that there is always an out if we are wrong. Our long-range plans consist of optimistic objectives agreed on at a meeting but backed by little fact. We never really explain or come to grips with our existing situation.

V.P. Marketing: Are you implying that we haven't sat down and thoroughly analyzed the nature of our business, what are our leading indicators, and are our problems? Are you saying that there is no conscious matching of organizational strengths and staffing to the requirements of the future? Are you saying that we have no commitment to the plans we generate? Well I certainly do all these things before I make decisions and I am committed to my plans.

President: Planning is the responsibility of all top managers and we do it as a normal part of our jobs. A good manager puts out fires regularly, improves his ongoing operations, and also plans for the long-term future. And you are all good managers. Otherwise you wouldn't be where you are today.

Large companies faced with diverse problems may need elaborate formal systems and planning groups to carry out their planning. We simply don't. I don't like staff groups cluttering things up; I don't like formalized procedures; and I don't believe we need either. We've been successful in the past. We will continue to be successful in the future.

V.P. Manufacturing: I agree with you completely. I believe our managerial efforts are competent. But they are far too diffused, too inconsistent, and too incomplete. For example, you have to recognize that we are not providing for all possible contingencies. What happens if public acceptance of our new lines is not as good as we expect? In addition, we are not communicating enough with the general public. People are growing very skeptical about business and we have to continually convince them that we are contributing to society. And we have to relate more closely to the government.

V.P. Marketing: Look!! The world now is far too uncertain to plan far into the future. Issues like inflation, government policies, and the general rapidity of change makes long-range planning a futile effort. A better strategy is simply to stay loose and flexible and to be ready to react to customer demands. I only plan as far ahead as I have to. Furthermore detailed planning puts you into a rigid straightjacket, limits creativity and forces conformity. Those are not the kind of characteristics we want in today's world.

V.P. Manufacturing: Good planning is not rigid! And corporate planning is more than just marketing planning and financial budgets.

What I am trying to say simply is that we should get back to basics. What we need is a systematic way of getting everyone involved in formulating strategy and managing this company. We require some sort of a common umbrella or frame of reference to guide our functional planning. I want to know more about what you're doing. We need a procedure to get us communicating and then a way of getting all our managers communicating, so that everybody can see where the organization is going. If we don't, I think we are going to have problems in the future.

Questions

Assume that you are a consultant called in by the vice president of manufacturing to help this organization think through the problems of long-range planning and to try to reach some consensus.

1. Would you take the job?
2. Who would you attempt to talk to?
3. What questions would you ask them? For each question state explicitly the reasons you would ask it, and how you think your questions fit together to solve the problem.
4. What answers would you possibly expect to these questions?
5. How would you present your conclusions to your client?

Case study 1–2

Ajax-McLeod Consultants Limited

Ajax-McLeod is a 15-person consulting firm located in San Diego. Sections I and III, following, are excerpts from *Planning Systems: A Report to Management* prepared by Ajax-McLeod and distributed free of charge to the top management of a number of major companies in the hope of developing new clients.

SECTION I: MEASURING YOUR PLANNING EFFORT

Planning is but one element of the total system of management performed by an evolving organization in a changing environment. The interactive effects of planning with organizational and environmental considerations suggests strongly that we must look at a "total system." No one element of this system can be examined independently to yield valid information. And the fact that the "appropriateness" of planning can only be identified in terms of its relationship to other elements is of critical importance. It suggests what the criteria for an effective planning effort should be. Defining criteria for effective planning involves identifying two critical factors: (1) the purpose of planning and (2) the conditions for success. This section discusses these two factors.

PURPOSE OF PLANNING

The essence of planning is concerned with the creation of a desired future state. Specifying objectives is defining the future states which the organization desires to realize. Identifying a planning gap consists of measuring the difference between the desired future state, the objective, and the state most likely to occur if no new decisions or actions are taken. Planning then focuses on identifying those decisions and actions which must be taken today, tomorrow, or next month, in order to increase the likelihood of achieving organizational objectives.

In light of this, one can identify three purposes of planning: (1) anticipatory decision making, (2) organizational learning, and (3) functional integration.

Anticipatory decision making

As planning is an activity undertaken before action is taken, planning anticipates those decisions and actions needed to achieve organizational objectives. If these could be taken immediately without loss of efficiency, planning would not be required. However, because achieving this desired future state often involves a complex set of interdependent decisions and actions, a planning system must provide a well-designed process for identifying and specifying them.

Organizational learning

In this regard, planning is a management process by which the organization learns, and thus can adapt its behavior to the changing requirements for success imposed on it by a changing environment.

Functional integration

Because decisions and actions within an organization are interrelated, horizontally as well as vertically, planning efforts must serve to integrate and coordinate activities across functional lines within the organization.

CONDITIONS FOR SUCCESS

Against this background one can proceed to identify criteria for assessing the viability of planning systems. There are five essential criteria for effective planning from a total systems viewpoint: (1) participative, (2) continuous, (3) coordinative, (4) integrated, and (5) experimental.

Participative

The first criterion is that planning should be participative. The benefits of planning are not derived from consuming its output, but from engaging in their production. Process is planning's most important product. Effective planning cannot be done to or for an organization. It must be done by an organization. Therefore, the role of the professional planner is not to plan, but to provide everyone who can be affected by planning with an opportunity to participate in it, and to provide those engaged in it with information, instructions, questions and answers that enable them to plan better than professional planners can alone. Planning must be a humanized activity in which the professional planner is basically a catalyst.

Continuous

The second essential criterion is that planning should be continuous. Since systems and their environment are changing continuously, no plan retains its quality over time. Plans must be continuously updated, extended and corrected. Planning should not be a one time thing.

Coordinative

All functions of a system should be planned for interdependently. No one function can be planned for effectively if planned for independently of other functions. The question of priorities is misleading. All issues should be dealt with simultaneously and interactively.

Integrated

In multilevel organizations, such as governments or corporations, planning is required at all levels and planning at each level should be integrated with planning at all levels.

Experimental

Because of the accelerating rate of technological change and of the accelerating rate of social change produced by it, experience is no longer the best teacher. In fact, it's not even a good teacher. It is too slow, too ambiguous, and too imprecise. Therefore, it should be replaced by experimentation—designed and controlled experiments. All implementations of planning output should take the form of controlled experiments so as to provide rapid, unambiguous, precise, and relevant feedback.

Section II of the Report, which describes problems that the firm had helped two of its clients to solve, is omitted.)

SECTION III: FINDING SOLUTIONS TO YOUR PLANNING PROBLEMS

Many organizations have experienced painful problems with their planning efforts. Some derive from the planning process itself, some from the implementation procedure. This section attempts to help in separating failures in the plan from failures in implementation. We suggest that you ask yourself the following questions to identify causes:

Failures in implementation

1. Did top management assume that it could delegate the planning function?
2. Did you forget the political nature of planning? Were there dysfunctional political forces which prevented it from working?
3. Did you ignore the fact that planning is and should be a learning process, and/or that the learning curve is quite steep initially?
4. Did you underestimate the effort involved in planning?
5. Did you fail to separate planning from your traditional budgeting

process? Did you fail to encourage managers to do more than just number-crunching?

6. If you tried to implement the plan in parts, did you destroy the co-herency of the whole plan?
7. Did you fail to integrate planning into each manager's everyday decision-making process?
8. Did you regard the plan as a static blueprint, rather than a helpful starting point in coping with a dynamic experiment?
9. Did you fail to see that the plan only turns uncertainty into quanti-fied terms; it does not reduce uncertainty? Were you able to adapt when the odds didn't pay off?
10. Did you use the planning process primarily as a learning process, without taking the output seriously? Just as in psychoanalysis, un-derstanding the problem doesn't make it go away; a decision to take action and solve the problem is necessary.
11. Were you so eager to use your plan for the short run, that you missed the long-run indications?

If you have answered "yes" to even one of these, try to remedy the problem before throwing out the plan. Despite the presence of such problems, your plan may be good. If such problems have appeared, man-agers may not have given the plan a fair trial. Consequently, a good plan may have proven infeasible. The next segment indicates some failures in the plan itself. We encourage you to consider these also. Frequently, *both* the plan and the implementation may be deficient.

Failures in the plan itself

Identifying failures in the plan itself is a much more complex process. To identify the sources of dissatisfaction with a plan, try asking the follow-ing questions:

1. Did you extrapolate rather than think through future alternatives?
2. Did you take the numbers too seriously, rather than acquire a good feel for what was going on?
3. Did you waste time on developing ridiculously precise numbers for the distant horizon?
4. Did you get embroiled in using sophisticated techniques, rather than using the most meaningful ones?
5. Did you repeat your planning procedure at fixed scheduled time intervals, regardless of the challenges of the environment and the organization?
6. Was your planning system too rigid? Did you allow flexibility for idea generation and creativity? Did you keep the plan simple enough to be meaningful?

7. Did you weigh all environmental and organizational variables similarly? Did you avoid identifying which variables are most critical to *your* company?
8. Did you have multiple objectives which were not assigned different priorities (e.g., conflict between profits and growth)?

These are some of the sources of a plan's failure. They all show up in the symptom of a plan that doesn't "fit" the situation. All parameters (constraints) are variable in the long run. Are you assuming too much as fixed and so missing opportunities?

Finding solutions to your planning problems

What mechanisms can correct deficiencies in the implementation or in the plan? Some of the following methods have worked effectively for a number of our clients:

1. Setting up a Planning Review Board with a mandate to correct inconsistencies; e.g., between the reward system and the plan, as well as change the planning process.
2. Reducing the length of time to complete a planning and control cycle dividing the process into smaller stages and planning in a modular fashion.
3. Building in more adaptability to the plan. The key is to get the plan itself to suggest necessary modifications; e.g., building in early warming criteria to signal a mismatch between product and market.
4. Building flexibility into the implementation. Over time the organizational and environmental factors affecting the implementation procedure will change. Problems can be overcome when planners and managers see it as their function to adapt their planning procedures accordingly.
5. Searching for new or better approaches. It may be that you need entirely new plan or implementation procedure. No one else may have designed an appropriate one. It is therefore necessary to institute a search process. We have found that the process of looking for "a better way to do things" is a great stimulus to inventiveness and creativity in managers (or planners!).

Questions

1. Two groups of questions regarding the purposes of planning and the conditions necessary for success are implicitly posed in Section I: (*a*) Does your way of planning facilitate anticipatory decision making, organizational learning and functional integration? and (*b*) Is your approach

to planning participative, continuous, coordinative, integrative, and experimental?

What evidence (actions or results) should an executive look for in order to answer these questions? Would all executives agree on the relative importance of these considerations? Why?

2. Can you think of an example situation that describes each of the reasons for failure listed in Section III? What reasons can you suggest for the fact that such errors are made by many organizations? Which component of the planning system—activities, methods, involvement or timing—is the most likely cause?

3. What problems does each of the solutions listed in Section III really solve?

4. Why do you think the subject of control was completely excluded from consideration in this report? Should it have been?

5. Do think this report will be successful in attracting new clients to the firm?

Chapter outline

Multicycle, hierarchical planning and control
   Steps in strategy formulation
Intelligence acquisition
   Environmental information
     Environmental subsectors
     Amount and type of scanning needed
     Techniques of environmental scanning
     The formalization of scanning
   Resources and capability evaluation
     Components of capability
     Analysis of capability
   Past performance analysis
   Stakeholder expectations
   Intelligence acquisition and organizational style
Statement of strategic mission
   Formulation
   General and specific objectives
   Key variables as a framework for planning

2

An overview of planning and control: Strategic planning

When you have completed this chapter you will understand:

1. How an organization's overall planning and control process works.
2. The role of strategic planning within this process.
3. The four types of information used in strategic planning and some of the techniques used to gather it.
4. What an organization's statement of strategic mission is.
5. How strategic plans can by synopsized and communicated by key variables.

MULTICYCLE, HIERARCHICAL PLANNING AND CONTROL

Organizational planning is a process of collecting information and making decisions in order to narrow the range of alternative behaviors until the most desirable set of actions can be specified. The multicycle approach to planning decomposes the complex problem of environmental influence and adaptation into a nested set of manageable subproblems capable of solution. Each cycle then involves solving one problem or making one decision. Thus, the global problem of deciding how best to interact with the environment is broken into a series of successively smaller problems, each of which contributes to the solution of the larger problem and which, in turn, generates other, more specific problems that have to be solved before action can be taken.

In a multicycle planning process, how to implement the solution decided on in one cycle becomes the problem to be solved by subsequent cycles. That is, the implementation phase of one cycle is, in itself, a cycle. Hence, in terms of the single-cycle problem-solving model described in Chapter 1, multicycle planning can be thought of as a hierarchy of single-cycle problem-solving processes linked to each other as illustrated below.

Analysis
Decision
Implementation { Analysis
                  Decision
                  Implementation { Analysis
                                    Decision
                                    Implementation

Implementation is thus simply a metaphor for subsequent planning. It is only in the last cycle of this process that decisions are made about the short-term activities to be carried out.

Of course, an organization may make decisions about short-term activities through a one-cycle process, without reference to any prior (longer term) planning. But the absence of a longer term perspective often means that these short-term decisions are not necessarily the best ones. Certain options may be overlooked and others inappropriately emphasized. If an organization wants to be confident that todays decisions are best for tomorrow it needs a more systematic way of making decisions.

For example, consider the following two investment opportunities

FIGURE 2–1

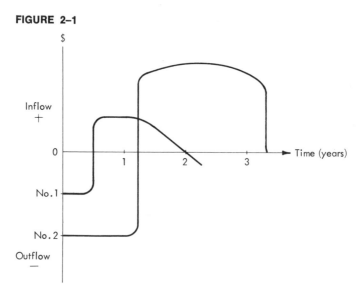

with cash outflow and inflow patterns as indicated in Figure 2–1. It is obvious from this figure that looking at year 1 activities only would lead to an inappropriate decision.

Selecting alternative no. 1 because it provides a positive return in the short run may not prove to be the best decision when a longer period is considered.

Or consider an organization faced with a choice between two mutually exclusive but equally profitable proposals. Which should it choose? Clearly the one that best fits its longer term interests. But how can it choose between these if it doesn't have some prior basis for choice?

An appropriate planning process facilitates these types of decisions. It helps steer the organization by systematically excluding possible options until the short-term activities that are best for the long-term interests of the organization can be chosen. This process can be depicted as shown in Figure 2–2. Each cycle in the planning process successively

FIGURE 2–2

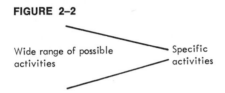

focuses on more specific actions. The cycles should address the following kinds of questions:

1. *At the broadest levels.* What should be the particular focus, mission, or purpose of our organization? What should be the product/market scope of our operations and why do we believe we can be successful in our endeavor? On what basis do we undertake some businesses and exclude others? On what basis do we say yes to some proposals and no to others?
2. *More specific.* What multiyear programs, projects, or groups of related activities should we consider? Which programs best contribute to the accomplishment of our organizational purpose? Which projects best reflect our competitive advantages? How shall we allocate our resources among projects?
3. *Most specific.* What short-term activities should we undertake? How shall we assign responsibility, motivate and control behavior?

The first of the above areas may be termed *strategic planning,* the second *program planning and resource allocation,* and the third *responsibility unit planning and control.*

Each of these three classes of questions requires a single-cycle planning process. The set of three cycles constitutes a *multicycle planning* process and describes one way in which an organization can break down the complex problem of how to interact with its environment into manageable proportions. The three cycles can be illustrated as a top-down hierarchical process (see Figure 2–3).

FIGURE 2–3

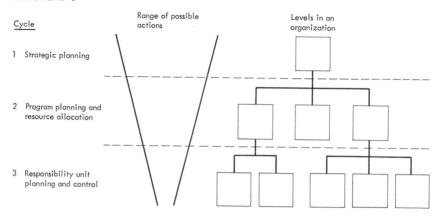

In terms of the funnel-shaped conceptualization of planning, the multi-cycle process can be depicted as shown in Figure 2–4.

FIGURE 2–4

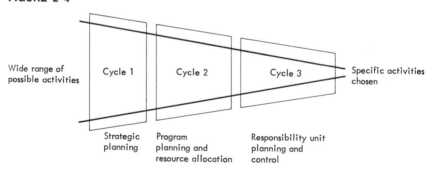

The abbreviated process model below describes in more detail the three-cycle planning and control activity.

As illustrated in Table 2–1, steps 2 to 8 make up the three distinct planning and control cycles, operating within an overall cycle of system specification and adaptation. Steps 2 and 3 describe strategic planning, the planning which prescribes, summarizes, and communicates the mission of the overall organization. Steps 4, 5, and 6 are the means by which programs are generated, resources are allocated, and the organization's scope, character, and expected performance are prescribed and expressed in terms of a long-range plan. Steps 7 and 8 make up responsibility unit planning and control, in which a calendar time portion of a multiyear program is assigned to a responsible individual for execution. Steps 1 and 9 ensure continuous overall system adaptation, as well as

TABLE 2–1
Process model of multicycle planning and control

Cycle	Step
	1. Designing the planning and control system
1. Strategic planning	2. Intelligence acquisition
	a. Environmental scanning
	b. Capability evaluation
	c. Determination of stakeholder expectations
	d. Analysis of past performance
	3. Formulation of statement of strategic mission
2. Program planning and resource allocation	4. New program generation and intelligence acquisition
	5. Program evaluation and resource allocation
	6. Specification of long-range plans
3. Responsibility unit planning and control	7. Responsibility unit planning
	8. Responsibility unit performance control
	9. System evaluation and adaptation and revision

continuous adaptation within each of the three cycles. Steps 1 through 9 inclusive describe the full planning and control process.

It should be noted that within each of the three cycles information concerning expectations, environmental changes, internal capability, and past performance is converted into a prescription for action. Expectations for the second and third cycles are influenced significantly by the output of the previous cycle. For the strategic planning cycle, however, expectations are derived both from external and internal sources.

The three cycles can be considered to be related as illustrated in Figure 2–5. The three cycles make up a means-ends hierarchical chain

FIGURE 2–5

	Planning	*Performance*
Cycle 1:	Organizational mission ←	Organizational mission
	influences and constrains	↑ which contributes to
	the choice of	the achievement of
Cycle 2:	Programs ⟸	⟹ Programs
	influences and constrains	↑ make up
	the choice of	
Cycle 3:	Activities ⟸	⟹ Activities

which describes a multicycle hierarchical process. Activity objectives are ends in themselves and are also the means to accomplish program objectives. Program objectives are ends in themselves as well as the means to accomplish the mission.

Figure 2–6 further depicts the hierarchical relationship of the three cycles. The output of one becomes the input into the next, and the results of each lower cycle provide feedback to each of the other cycles. The figure also shows that the same type of information is used in all three

FIGURE 2-6
A three-cycle planning and control process

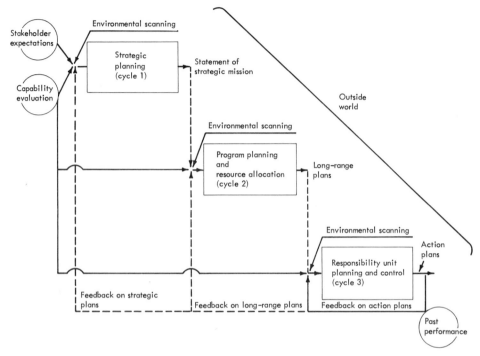

cycles, and that each cycle narrows in perspective as it moves toward specific, short-term considerations.

The connection between the three cycles is variable, and so is represented by dotted lines. The extent to which the output of one cycle prescribes or constrains the behavior of successive cycles, and the extent to which performance feedback is provided to upstream cycles, determine the degree to which they are linked together.

The remainder of this chapter describes several aspects of an organization's strategic planning cycle and develops a process model based on the information needed for strategy formulation.The subsequent cycles, program planning and resources allocation, and responsibility unit planning and control, are discussed in Chapter 3. Together, these two chapters elaborate the multicycle model diagrammed in Figure 2-6.

Steps in strategy formulation

Strategy formulation, cycle 1, is the most far-reaching, unstructured, uncertain, and least understood of all organizational planning processes.

FIGURE 2–7
Cycle 1: Strategic planning

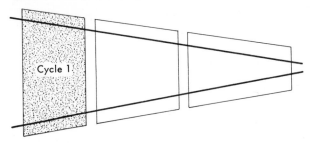

See Figure 2–7. Through a strategic planning cycle an organization determines or reaffirms its ultimate mission and the broad means of accomplishing it. It is the process by which an organization solves the problem of deciding how it will interact with, shape, or exploit its environment. The discussion below focuses on two of the most important steps of effective strategic planning: intelligence acquisition and formulation of the statement of strategic mission. Although a process model containing these two steps does not completely describe this planning cycle, it does give some insight into the essence of the process and serves to differentiate alternative modes of strategic planning.

INTELLIGENCE ACQUISITION

As in all planning processes, one of the first steps in cycle 1, strategic planning, is intelligence acquisition (step 2 outlined in Table 2–1). Four types of information are required in strategic planning, and to gather this information the organization must assess the following areas: its external environment; its own resources and capability; past performance; and stakeholder expectations. These four types of information provide the data base from which alternative objectives and strategies are generated and evaluated. Let us consider how information is acquired in each of these areas.

Environmental information

Environmental scanning is the activity by which an organization collects information about the opportunities and threats it faces. It is a continuous process because the requirements for such information are endless. Scanning involves collecting information about the state of the current environment as well as about future trends. It involves making decisions about the parts of the environment to be examined, the frequency of examination, and the communication channels within the organization through which this information should be transmitted. As illustrated in Figure 2–6, environmental scanning is an essential activity in all three planning cycles because environmental information is required in each.

An organization's external environment influences its formulation of strategic mission in two ways. First, the environment has an indirect effect on the organization through the expectations of its stakeholders (all individuals, groups, or institutions who have a vested interest in the organization's actions). The environment influences the attitudes of stakeholders, who may be optimistic, pessimistic, or concerned with maintaining the status quo; and these attitudes, in turn, influence their expectations of the firm.

Second, the environment affects the mission of the firm directly by offering specific opportunities, by presenting specific threats, or by putting definite constraints on what can be accomplished. Obviously, when trying to formulate strategic plans management must be aware of such factors as the present and projected state of the world and national economies, the nature of the competition, the possibility of governmental intervention, and the availability of trained managers.

The organization needs environmental information in order to assess its ability to shape the environment to its own advantage. Using advertising to create or change attitudes is one such method of influence. Another strategy is to take concerted action through industry associations. For example, in the spring of 1974, a Gallup poll indicated that 85 percent of Americans were in favor of gun control laws. Yet the National Rifle Association, other gun-related organizations, and the manufacturers themselves have effectively acted to prevent legislation banning hand guns. This is one instance in which environmental information and strategy formulation have gone hand in hand.

Environmental subsectors.   In order for a firm to examine its external environment, it must first delineate and then subdivide that environment into manageable subsectors which can be described by some set of relevant characteristics. The environmental subsectors most commonly selected for attention are those which reflect the main areas of action and reaction for the company. These may include the following domains:

a. Technological environment.
b. Markets and competition.
c. Economic environment.
d. Government policies.
e. Demographic shifts.
f. Social and cultural changes.

Technological environment. The production and managerial technology available to a company determines both what the firm can accomplish and how efficiently it can do so. The technology that supports management (e.g., information systems, computers, and telecommunications capabilities) is particularly important in shaping the direction of a company. Also, product and production technology differentiate companies. Contrast, for instance, the effects of technology on the semiconductor industry, which moved rapidly from transistors to large-scale integrated chips, with the electricity generation industry, whose switch from coal and oil to nuclear power has been ever so slow. The rapidity and predictability of technological change are important determinants of the amount and type of environmental scanning an organization should carry out.

Markets and competition. A company, as a seller of goods and also as a buyer of resources, is influenced by its market environment. Market structure (e.g., the number of buyers and sellers), the intensity and methods of competition (price, product differentiation, promotion, or distribution), the degree of stability and predictability, and the availability of feedback all influence the amount and type of scanning needed.

Economic environment. The economic environment of a company is the aggregation of all those who operate in the same market. Some economic considerations are the general availability of factors of production (capital and labor), and any conditions which influence the willingness and ability of buyers to buy (disposable income, rates of inflation and so on). The relationship of a firm's operating character to the general economy determines what areas it should scan for economic information. The closer a firm follows the general economy the more predictable its operating environment, and the more it can benefit from the general economic forecasting carried out by governments and financial institutions.

Government policies. Keeping abreast of governmental activity is important for three reasons. First, the government defines the legal system in which a firm must operate. It establishes antitrust policies, health and safety regulations, air and water pollution rules, and employment practices. Second, the government imposes costs on the company in the form of taxes and tariffs. And third, the government itself is often in the firm's marketplace, both as a buyer, and also as a supplier of goods and services directly, as health insurance, or indirectly, through subsidies such as those provided the troubled aircraft industries.

Demographic shifts and social and cultural changes. The last two environmental domains tend to be more diffuse than the factors already considered, and their effects are likely to be more influential in the long than in the short run. Their impact is usually subtler, and may be felt only through changes in one of the other areas. Nevertheless, they are important considerations in predicting changes in markets, the economy, and governmental services.

Amount and type of scanning needed. In the preceeding discussion several distinguishing characteristics were used to differentiate among environments, including:

1. Relative stability versus rapid rate of change.
2. Certainty versus unpredictability.
3. Complexity verus simplicity.
4. Homogeneity versus heterogeneity.

Different mixes of environmental characteristics require different amounts and types of scanning. Usually the more certain or predictable an environment, the less the need for planning. For example, stable environments require less scanning than unstable ones. In a stable environment planning assumptions do not require frequent updating. Longer time horizons can be accommodated, and routine tasks permit more fixed responsibilities. Organizations in stable environments, then, can rely on established policies and procedures over longer periods of time. Uncertain environments, on the other hand, usually require greater attention, particularly when uncertainty is coupled with instability. In these situations more resources must be devoted to scanning the environment, evaluating trends, determining and searching out alternatives, and adapting to change in general. It can be concluded, therefore, that the amount and type of scanning appropriate for a given organizational unit cannot be universally specified, but must be determined according to the nature of its operating environment.

Techniques of environmental scanning. Once the environmental subsectors most relevant to the firm have been identified and the amount of required scanning has been specified, the next task is to decide on the techniques by which the needed information is to be acquired (i.e., the methods by which the activity specified in the process model is to be carried out). Three ways to gather this information are forecasting, performance differential analysis, and the use of question-type checklists.

Forecasting. A forecast is a prediction of a future event. A major portion of an organization's scanning resources is usually devoted to providing the forecasts needed for the formulation of strategy.

Before forecasting can be carried out in any environmental subsector, a basis for the prediction must be selected, as well as a technique or procedure. Broadly speaking, forecasts may be either people-based or data-based. The following are some examples of procedures which may be used in both cases:

A. People-based. People-based techniques use the experience and intuition which people carry in their heads as the basis of the prediction and attempt to extract that information in a systematic way. They include:

1. Guesses.
2. Forecasts made by an expert.
3. Forecasts made by a group. Group methods include delphi techniques (a procedure by which a group of experts isolated from one another each makes a prediction about a future event, receives feedback about the predictions of others, makes a new prediction, and continues this procedure until a final solution is reached), consumer panels (a group of consumers of a product are questioned about its attributes), intention to buy surveys, or futuristic techniques such as scenario writing.

B. Data-based. Methods which use formally codified data, including:
  1. Data analysis only:
     a. Seasonal adjustment techniques.
     b. Trend extrapolation.
     c. Stock charting.
     d. Leading and lagging indicators.
     e. Surveys.
     f. Life-style analysis.
  2. Models:
     a. Regression.
     b. Input–output analysis.
     c. Econometric analysis.
     d. Simulation models.
     e. Systems dynamics models.

The particular forecasting techniques a company chooses will depend on the events it has to forecast, the time horizon involved, the creativity and innovation required, and its past success in using the method. The criteria for selection of one forecasting method over another are the accuracy or benefits derived from the method, the time the organization has available to do it, the cost of the method, and any other administrative or organizational constraints the method may impose.

Performance differential analysis. Although forecasting is perhaps the most widely used scanning method, it is enlightening to consider other techniques for gathering information. Performance differential analysis is a technique which compares an organization's products and performance against those of other companies so as to provide insights into opportunities or problems currently being overlooked.

Many companies compare themselves annually to their competition. By examining the annual reports of their competitors and selected information collected through distributors, trade papers, news releases, catalogs, and filings with the Securities and Exchange Commission, they

seek first to establish differentials between themselves and their competition and then to explain why these differentials exist and what can be
done to remedy them.

Table 2–2 illustrates one marketing-oriented breakdown employed by

TABLE 2–2
Performance differential analysis

Element	Characteristics	Aspect examined
Products	Components of each line Market share Phase in life cycle Recent modifications	Rate of change Current size Trends Strengths and weaknesses
End use of products	Benefits provided New applications	Key factors which determine success
Customer groups	Multidimensional classification	Problems to be faced in future
Channels of distribution	Types	
Competitive tactics	Emphasis Methods	Needs not now satisfied

companies in such a comparison. By systematically examining their
products, uses of products, customer groups, channels of distribution, and
competitive tactics; selected characteristics of each of these elements;
and how these elements have changed over time, the company is better
able to determine what information it needs to prepare its strategic
plans.

Question-type checklists. Checklists provide a simple yet systematic
guide to acquire relevant environmental information useful in even the
smallest organizations. For example, Guido Martino, a custom tailor in
Boston with a sales volume of $350,000 per year, relies on this technique.
His way of structuring the acquisition of environmental information is
by posing three simple questions:

1. Why do my customers come to me and why not go to someone else?
2. What deficiencies are there in the services I now provide?
3. What customers am I missing and what can I do to get them?

Over time, forcing himself to answer these questions led him to subscribe
to newspapers from New York, San Francisco, and several European
centers in order to see what others were doing and to get new styling
ideas. He also purchased several Italian fashion magazines regularly. The
information he collected led him to remodel his store to reflect a more
European atmosphere. To him, scanning means collecting the information
he needs in order to maintain his competitive position.

The formalization of scanning. In the past, many organizations gave no more than lip service to formal environmental scanning because the environment had little impact on them. They could function reasonably well with minimal environmental sensitivity. The situation is changing, however. It is now recognized that relevant environmental information may come from a wide range of sources, including:

1. Personal experience of executives.
2. Professional journals.
3. Reports.
4. Books.
5. Professional meetings.
6. Industrial conferences and association publications.
7. Colleagues.
8. Board members.
9. Friends.
10. Employees.
11. Suppliers and customers.
12. Governmental statistical publications.

Clearly, if the wealth of data potentially available from these sources is to be systematically acquired, screened, and communicated, a formal approach is needed.

At the Scott Paper Company, responsibility for part of its environmental scanning is assigned to the marketing research and development department. Data gathered are evaluated by the product management group concerned, and this group reports to the senior executives. This arrangement establishes accountability within the group which has the largest stake in the area being scanned. In the opinion of these executives, it is possible to obey all legal and ethical requirements and still collect all the information they require (*Nation's Business,* March 1972).

Environmental scanning is now becoming more and more formalized. One organization with an aggressive program that pays off is Health-Chem's Herculite subsidiary. Their environmental scanning efforts are as carefully structured as their financial plans. One particularly effective tool is a comprehensive "Guide to Gathering Market Intelligence" distributed to all key personnel of this company. This guide clearly spells out the scope of the environmental scanning program. It defines the kind of information the company needs, explains the role of each functional group in this process, and then pinpoints sources to probe and strategies to follow (*Nation's Business,* March 1972).

Resources and capability evaluation

A second type of information an organization needs for strategic planning is an assessment of its own available resources and distinguishing capabilities. This information is needed so that the company can define and exploit its competitive advantages, an important part of any strategic plan.

An organization that builds on its unique strengths significantly increases the likelihood of its success. An accurate internal analysis is therefore required in order to match environmental opportunities to internal capabilities, and to set realistic limits on what the firm can actually accomplish so that its planning can in fact be carried out.

Components of capability. Just as in the discussion of external environmental scanning, it is useful to break down internal capability into several areas:

a. Market positions: Proprietary product lines or brands, franchises, superior services or facilities, marketing research, public acceptance through successful past performance.

b. Technological superiority: Performance characteristics of products, price-quality-value differentials, product design, product innovation, quality, patents, technological monopolies.

c. Physical facilities: Manufacturing facilities, research and testing facilities, warehouses, branch offices, logistics, trucks, tankers, convenient locations.

d. Preferential supply position: Ownership of low-cost or scarce natural resources, vertical integration, location of resources in relation to markets.

e. Financial strengths: Money available or obtainable in the capital markets, skills in financial negotiation, working capital or inventory management, credit management.

f. Human resources: Managerial skills such as experience, ambition, desired personal advancement, effective decision making, ability to plan, interpersonal skills; nonmanagerial skills such as labor, salesmen, engineers, technologists or other workers with specialized abilities, creativity, and merchandising skills.

g. Specialized experience: Unique or uncommon knowledge of manufacturing, distribution, innovation or managerial techniques, capitalization on learning curve effects.

Analysis of capability. Once the various components of capability have been defined, each one must be systematically analyzed in order to determine if acceptable strategies can be founded on them, or if additional capabilities or resources are needed. Two common methods are an analysis of momentum and flexibility, and again, the use of a question-type checklist.

Momentum and flexibility. Capability can be analyzed from two viewpoints, momentum and flexibility. *Momentum* is the capability provided by the firm's current operations and projects. By examining the firm's momentum in each of the above areas both quantitatively (i.e., in terms of size, rates of change, and trend) and qualitatively, a company is able to assess what new projects it can easily absorb into current operations. *Flexibility*, on the other hand, concerns the adaptability of a company's resources to new uses. A flexibility examination probes the firm's ability and willingness to change. It evaluates the extent to which existing skills, physical facilities, and marketing channels can be adapted to other uses, as well as the extent to which managerial skills, knowledge, judgment, and attitudes can be reoriented to new domains. A flexibility evaluation assesses the ease with which a firm can adapt its capabilities and resources to new applications.

Question-type checklists. Having categorized its capabilities, a company can begin to question the significance of its strengths and weaknesses in each area. What loyalties can it build on? What competitive advantages does it have over competition? What areas should it be capitalizing on that it is not now involved in? Question-directed analysis of this type led a major airline which had previously restricted itself only to air travel to expand the scope of its services to include hotel and rental car reservations, ground transportation to and from the airport, and overall vacation planning.

One aggressive conglomerate with a growth objective frequently performs an internal resource audit as presented in Table 2–3. It wants to

TABLE 2–3
Internal resource audit

Organiza-tional unit	Facilities and resources	Special skills	Management ability	Capability as an organiza-tional unit
Division A	Money Technology Productive capability	Innovation Risk preferences Stamina Interpersonal skills	Adaptability Flexibility Orientation	Handle complexity pressure risk

capitalize on all available resources and so continually evaluates them by asking, for example: What complexity of problem can its managers handle? What tasks is it especially good at handling? How far can it be moved from its existing courses to face new activity? By correctly identifying the most productive resources it has available at any one time, this conglomerate has been able to combine its ability to raise money, innovate internally, and provide good managerial skills to build a successful organization.

Past performance analysis

Past performance analysis may be considered to be one part of the evaluation of resources and capability. However, the two are being kept separate to point out that resources and capabilities analysis should attempt to determine what an organization can potentially undertake which is not necessarily what it has done in the past.

For many organizations, knowledge of where they now stand—their present position and accomplishments—is an essential input to planning. So concurrent with capability evaluation, they identify, describe, and evaluate their past strategies, past performance, and the resources devoted to those accomplishments. They may use either the programs currently under way or product/market segments as their units of analysis; and data on sales by customer, product, or market to identify the scope of these segments of operations. By interrelating customer-product-market concentrations, the strategies used, and the resources deployed, a company can determine what programs management has emphasized and how they have fared. Accounting analysis may reveal the distribution of capital assets, working capital, and cash among these programs, as well as recurring and one-time expenses required to support these activities. If this is followed by a thorough evaluation of past performance, it can yield a third source of information on which to formulate a statement of strategic mission.

Past performance analysis may include an evaluation of the size and rates of growth of each program the organization has undertaken. It may evaluate market share, changes in penetration, or the impact on a particular segment of the economy. Financial and qualitative analysis may allow the organization to categorize each program in terms of its stage of life-cycle evolution, to distinguish between programs which are cash generators and those which are cash consumers; and to identify those which still offer the potential for high growth versus those that are now mature and in their declining stages. In this way a clearer definition of the risk/reward profile of each component unit of the whole business can be formed.

To stimulate further analysis and to focus attention on sensitive areas, comparative analyses may be carried out. Comparison of past performance with original expectations, historical trends, or competitors may provide the perspective against which to evaluate existing programs. Comparative analysis is especially important to incremental planning from the basis of current businesses because it reveals the extent to which these operations are not performing as desired, and therefore the extent to which planning may be needed.

Stakeholder expectations

The fourth component of any organization's intelligence acquisition is the determination of what stakeholders expect. The stakeholders of a firm are all those who have a vested interest in its behavior. They include the owners of a firm, its creditors, customers, suppliers, management, labor, competition, the government and society as a whole. Each of these stakeholders has its own set of expectations. The satisfaction of these expectations is the reason that the firm exists; and is really the driving force behind the firm.

One suggestive list of some stakeholders and their expectations is presented in Table 2–4. This list reveals that even within any one group

TABLE 2–4
Stakeholders and their expectations

Owners	Security of investment Growth—fair return Dividends
Creditors	Solvency Security
Customers	Safe reliable product Service before and after sale Continuous availability Fair price
Suppliers	Stability of sourcing Fair return Growth in usage
Management	Survival Financial rewards Recognition Enjoyable working environment
Labor	Equitable and fair treatment Just rewards Influence over organization
Competitors	Legal and ethical behavior
Society	Social conscience Responsibility Environmental, ecological, and social concern
Government	Source of tax revenues Fair competition Adherence to law

the expectations of individual stakeholders may diverge. The expectations of any one stakeholder have to do with those characteristics of the company that affect his or her own interests. It is apparent that both within a group and between groups of stakeholders, expectations may be reinforcing, or independent of each other, or possibly in conflict. For example, a substantial increase in profits will probably be welcomed by a company's stockholders and management. Yet this may evoke tremendous cries from consumers claiming price gouging, and the government may threaten antitrust action. Companies attempting to become better corporate citizens or more socially conscious are, in effect, just widening the scope of stakeholder expectations to be considered in their formulation of strategy.

Each stakeholder expectation may carry a different priority depending on its legal, moral, or ethical weight, its effect on the business, its potential impact in the long or short run, or its relationship to the particular values held by management. Clearly, evaluating stakeholder expectations necessitates establishing priorities for each expectation, determining if the interrelationships among them are reinforcing, conflicting, or independent, and then devising a means of reconciliation. The diversity of expectations can easily interject confusion into the planning process. Therefore, one solution to this dilemma is to configure these expectations into a hierarchy in which the most dominant expectations are given the highest priority and the least important given the lowest (Granger, 1964).

Intelligence acquisition and organizational style

Strategic planning (and, in fact, all planning) requires matching resources and capabilities to environmental opportunities in order to satisfy stakeholder expectations. This reconciliation process, which requires the four types of information discussed above, is depicted graphically in Figure 2–8. The resources devoted to acquiring these four types of in-

FIGURE 2–8

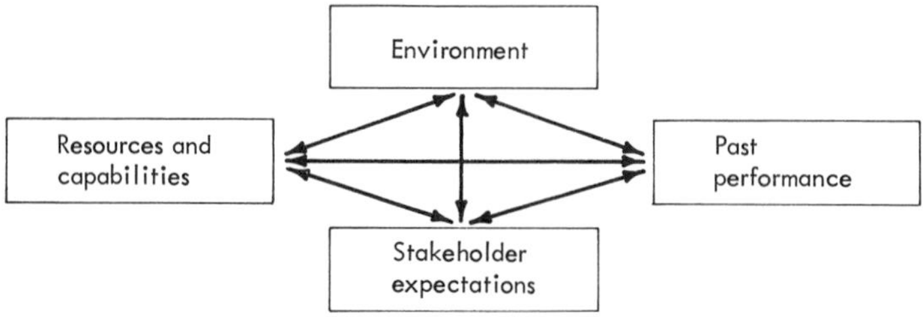

formation, and the way they are incorporated into strategic planning, are to a great extent determined by the particular style of the organization. Three distinctive and recognizable styles of operation are the entrepreneurial, the extrapolative, and the reactive.

An entrepreneurial organization is one that is externally oriented, constantly looking for opportunities to grow either by expansion of existing businesses or by diversification. Hence environmental scanning and capability evaluation play major roles in its planning process. The entrepreneurial organization is both future and externally oriented; it is anticipative, it is pro-active. It is always trying to discover new opportunities or to predict what products or services potential customers will need next.

The reactive organization, on the other hand, is internally oriented. It is satisfied with its existing scope of operations and prefers to maintain the status quo as long as possible. The reactive organization employs short-term operational planning and control through budgets, rather than considering the external environment and its own unused capabilities. Evaluation of past performance dominates its planning, since it is a deviation from desired performance that signals the need to change. A reactive organization does not employ future-oriented planning unless a significant deviation from expectation has been noted.

One difference between an anticipative and a reactive organization is described in Figure 2–9. The sales trend depicted in this figure ought

FIGURE 2–9

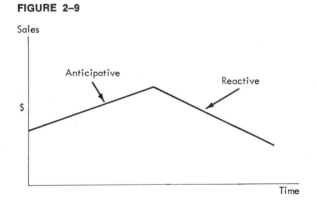

to be diagnosed and corrected through planning by both an anticipative and a reactive organization. However, an anticipative, externally oriented organization will plan to correct this situation before undesired events actively occur, while a reactive organization requires a negative deviation from expected performance to signal the need to plan.

Somewhere between these two operating modes is the extrapolative organization. This organization plans, but does so from the base of its current operations. Unlike the reactive organization it looks into the future but only to assess the appropriateness of its existing operations to these new conditions. If extrapolating past activities into the future will satisfy stakeholder expectations, this organization will then limit its planning to continue its past activities. If change is necessary, it is made incrementally from current operations. The strategic planning of an extrapolative company thus starts from the basis of its existing operations and attempts to adjust these to fit the future. Given the value of existing momentum and the investment in basic operating assets, it is not surprising that a majority of today's businesses plan in an extrapolative manner.

At one time or another, entrepreneurial, extrapolative, and reactive organizations all use the four types of intelligence discussed above in their strategic planning. What differentiates them is whether planning is triggered by a self-initiated desire to satisfy future stakeholder expectations, or by a deviation in past performance.

At some point the entrepreneurial organization must consider its past performance and the reactive organization must look to the future. But their priorities, natural inclinations, and normal modes of intelligence acquisition differ substantially from one another. Hence, an organization's style of operation helps determine how its acquires and uses planning intelligence.

STATEMENT OF STRATEGIC MISSION

Formulation

The formulation of an organization's statement of strategic mission is synonymous with many phrases, such as producing a statement of corporate purpose, establishing objectives, or setting corporate aims. Regardless of what it is called, it is the initial definition of the problems to be solved in matching capabilities and resources to opportunities so as to accomplish the expectations of the stakeholders. It provides an idea of what the organization wishes to accomplish and how it intends to do so. The purpose of the statement of strategic mission is to give an organization direction and cohesive purpose so that it can accomplish the expectations of its stakeholders.

The statement of strategic mission is a broad definition of the thrust of the organization. It identifies the organization's competitive advantages and the manner in which it will differentiate itself from its competition. The statement provides broad objectives for the organization, the strategies to accomplish these objectives, the reasoning behind these strategies, and the criteria for evaluating alternative courses of action. Its intent is to make environmental and organizational assumptions explicit so that further planning can progress in a well-focused and systematic manner based on a commonly understood rationale.

Mission definition may be simply a statement of broad purposes; e.g., making a profit, providing a service, survival, or creating and holding a customer. Or it may reflect specific decisions, such as changing management's orientation toward risk, delineating new markets, modifying organizational structure, or obtaining new sources of financing. It may specify where the organization wants to be in the future and then provide the means for evaluating how far the organization has moved in this direction. It may express the future course of the organization in terms of a statement such as, "Because we have the opportunity to do X and we have specific capabilities Y to do so, in the future this organization should. . . ." Or it may be even more specific, and define the exact scope of the organization in terms of its sales objectives by product, customer, channel of distribution, price, quality, and category, as well as the resources to be devoted to achieving these.

Remember the interrelated nature of multicycle planning and that the purpose of cycle 1, strategic planning, is to focus the subsequent planning of cycles 2 and 3. (Refer back to Table 2–1.) To be effective, cycle 1 must eliminate certain options from further consideration. It must provide some guide for when to say yes and when to say no to proposed objectives and courses of action. If the alternative to any objective, aim, or purpose stated in an organization's statement of strategic mission is not really viable, then that objective does not effectively narrow the range of alternatives for subsequent planning. Such over-general objectives are just motherhood statements which everyone agrees with whole heartedly. Making a profit, providing a service, survival, or creating and holding a customer are, without further qualification, all motherhood statements. However they are a poor guide to lower level decision makers because they provide little help in choosing among alternative behaviors. And after all, that is really what planning is all about.

The character of an organization's statement of strategic mission depends greatly on its management. Top management may possess a strong faith in research, like Watson of IBM. It may be dominated by a technical genius, such as Land of Polaroid; by the aggressiveness of a Geneen of IT&T, or even by the independence of a Howard Hughes. Because of the uncertain impact of executive intention, values, and management style on the evolution of a corporation's statement of strategic mission, the process is still a mystery to organizational researchers. The formulation of strategic mission is the most uncertain, ill-defined, and ambiguous of an organization's three planning cycles. It can best be described as a process of information reconciliation and conflict resolution, a process of balancing science against creativity, and intuitive judgment against logical reasoning.

General and specific objectives

There is considerable confusion and dispute about the meaning of the terms "objectives" and "goals" in the planning literature. Some authors use them interchangeably, some define objectives as broader than goals, and others define them the opposite way. Rather than enter this irrec-oncilable semantic debate, this book will confine itself to the term "objectives." For those readers who prefer the term "goals," conversion is straightforward.

In many companies, the formulation of strategic mission is called the determination of corporate objectives. General objectives are desired future states or outcomes without reference to a definite time dimension. They are an ideal representation of what the organization wants to accomplish. The intent underlying the specification of objectives is directional only—to provide guidance. General objectives are expressed in broad terms, such as providing the most efficient transportation services to those who require them, or maximizing the use of skills in manufacturing and marketing branded advertised goods.

Specific objectives, on the other hand, are quantified targets whose attainment is desired by a specific time. They are usually measurable and can serve as a basis for evaluating performance. Specific objectives may be expressed as a desired rate of growth, a desired profitability per year, an increase in share value, or the maintenance of specific levels of solvency and liquidity.

The specification of objectives and formulation of the strategy to accomplish them are intertwined. It is not known if objectives are stated only after strategy has been determined, or if they are stated initially and then continually redefined as strategy is formulated. To say that objectives should be set first implies that they are independent of an organization's capability to accomplish them. Alternatively, to maintain that objectives can only follow strategy implies that organizations do only what they are capable of doing, instead perhaps, of what they should be doing. It implies a tendency to extrapolate the past, even when it is no longer desirable to do so. Clearly, neither of these sequences should be followed rigidly. Any attempt to specify the particular sequence by which strategy and objectives are developed is futile. It is important only to recognize that accomplishing these two steps is a circular and intertwined process.

Key variables as a framework for planning

In any multicycle planning process, expectations in the form of purposes and objectives must be transmitted between cycles. Hence an important characteristic of multicycle planning and control is the manner in which this communication is handled. The manner of transmitting expectations and guidelines determines the extent to which each downstream cycle will be directed by the outputs of the earlier cycles. The strategic plan for any relatively dynamic organization presents such a problem in communications. Since it covers a multiyear period it must reflect and accommodate the inevitable changes that will take place. Therefore if a strategic plan is to serve as a meaningful guideline for subsequent planning, it cannot rapidly become obsolete. Thus it must be both broad and flexible enough not to become obsolete too quickly, and yet also specific enough to focus subsequent planning.

One method used to extract the essence from a statement of strategic mission and express it in a highly communicable form is the identification of key variables (KVs). A KV is simply an activity or result which is critical to the success of any plan. The KVs of any plan describe either objectives or the preconditions for their accomplishment. Of the total set of variables contained in a plan, the KVs are the most important.

The key variables of a plan consist of key result areas and the key success factors that guarantee good performance in each of these areas; i.e., the ends desired and the means of attaining them. Key result areas (KRAs) are those areas or aspects of the organization that most significantly reflect the results of its activities. What areas should be considered to be key result areas? Here is one recommendation: "Objectives are needed in every area where performance and results directly and initially affect the survival and prosperity of the business" (Drucker, 1964, p. 52). If success can be described in terms of acceptable performance in certain crucial areas of operations, then each of these areas is a key result area. Market share, profit, or public image may each be considered to be a key result area.

Key success factors (KSFs) are the controllable and uncontrollable activities and events necessary for successful performance in the key result areas. For example, if market share is a key result area, then advertising expenditures or sales effort may be a key success factor. Performance in a key result area therefore is hypothesized to be a function of one or more key success factors. The key result areas and key success factors of any plan or planning process are its key variables.

To General Electric, probably the first company to use key variables for planning and control, key variables define those areas of activity that require continuous management control. General Electric identifies key variables by asking the following question: "Will continued failure in this area prevent the attainment of management's responsibilities for advancing General Electric as a leader in a strong, competitive economy, even though results in all other key areas are good?" (General Electric, 1954). G.E.'s key result areas include: (1) profitability; (2) market position; (3) productivity; (4) product leadership; (5) personnel development; (6) employee attitude; (7) public responsibility; and (8) balance between short- and long-run goals.

Key variables are thus one way of expressing the output of any planning cycle. They describe what is to be emphasized and what should be considered only secondarily. Extracting and communicating the KVs of a strategic plan can synopsize and clarify any complexity or fuzziness that might make the plan subject to alternative interpretations. Qualitative KVs can also compensate for the limitations inherent in most quantitative plans, which by their very nature cannot fully encompass the scope and richness of an administrative situation. In sum, KVs are intended to distil a plan down to its essence, thereby providing priorities and guidance for subordinate decision making and action. Every strategic planning cycle should therefore be able to produce a meaningful set of key variables that can motivate and guide all of an organization's subsequent planning.

SUMMARY

Planning is the process of narrowing the range of alternative behaviors through a series of problem-solving cycles until a single set of actions can be specified. Strategic planning, the process of specifying or reaffirming corporate objectives and the means of accomplishing them, is the first and most complex of these cycles. It requires four types of intelligence on which to base its formulation of strategic mission.

Environmental information can be acquired by techniques such as forecasting, performance differential analysis, and question-type checklists. Internal capabilities can be assessed by being first defined and then probed in terms of momentum and flexibility or by self-questioning. Determination of stakeholder expectations and evaluation of past performance complete the intelligence acquisition phase. An organization's style—entrepreneurial, extrapolative, or reactive—is a significant factor in how it will acquire and use intelligence.

The statement of strategic mission specifies what a firm wishes to be or to accomplish, and the means it has chosen of doing so. Management style will determine how this statement is formulated and used. General objectives are desired future outcomes that do not include quantification or time dimensions, while specific objectives are quantified targets whose attainment is desired within a specific time.

Key variables are results critical to organizational success and the activities that will accomplish them. They describe either the objectives or the preconditions to the achievement of the strategic mission. As a synopsis of the ends and means chosen, key variables express the most significant key result areas and key success factors of any plan.

QUESTIONS

1. How do you distinguish between a planning cycle and a step within a cycle? When does one cycle end and another begin? Is there overlap between cycles? Is strategic planning really a one-cycle process?

2. Consider a local supermarket chain, a municipal government, a hospital,

an automobile dealership, and a university. From the standpoint of the top management of each of these organizations list several strategic decisions they could be required to make. Which are the most strategic?

3. Prepare a sample statement of strategic mission for each of the organizations listed in question 2. Be sure your statement helps differentiate and focus the direction of the organization and is not just a motherhood statement.

4. Which of the four types of intelligence required in strategic planning is most important in formulating each of the missions of question 3?

5. Do today's organizations really look at all stakeholder expectations? How is knowledge about stakeholder expectations acquired? How do you think the conflicting expectations of stakeholders are resolved in practice?

6. How could an organization justify an expenditure on formalized environmental scanning?

7. In what ways would knowledge of the key variables of last year's strategic plan be useful in this year's planning?

8. (a) How does the educational institution you are attending know when it is being successful or unsuccessful? (b) What are some of its key strategic variables (key result areas and key success factors)?

9. (a) Can key strategic variables be measured? (b) How does an organization ensure that its strategic plans are implemented properly? What kind of feedback is received?

10. Who should be involved in strategic planning?
    a. Top, middle, and/or lower management?
    b. Staff departments?
    c. Outside consultants and specialists?
    What are the advantages and disadvantages of an organization purchasing a strategic plan from an outside consultant?

11. Under what conditions is reaction an appropriate strategy? Does a strategy of reaction imply that no anticipative planning need be done?

12. How does the material covered in Chapter 2 relate to the content of courses called business strategy or policy formation?

13. What determines the time horizon (how far into the future) of an organization's strategic planning cycle?

REFERENCES AND BIBLIOGRAPHY

Anguilar, Francis J. *Scanning the Business Environment.* New York: The Macmillan Company, 1967.

Ansoff, H. I. *Corporate Strategy: An Analytic Approach to Business Policy for Growth and Expansion.* New York: McGraw-Hill Book Co., 1965.

Bauer, R. A., and Gergen, K. J. *The Study of Policy Formation.* New York: Free Press, 1968.

Bright, James R. Evaluating signals of technological change. *Harvard Business Review,* January–February 1970, pp. 62–70.

Cleland, David, and King, William R. Competitive business intelligence systems. *Business Horizons,* December 1975, pp. 19–28.

Cooper, A. C.; DeMuzzio, E.; Hatten, K.; Hicks, G. J.; and Tock, D. *Strategic Responses to Technological Threats.* Professional Papers of the Academy of Management, Division of Business Policy and Planning, Boston, 1973.

Cooper-Jones, D. *Business Planning and Forecasting.* New York: Halsted Press, 1974.

Cummings, Larry L.; Hinton, Bernard, L.; and Gobdel, Bruce C. Creative behavior as a function of task environment: Impact of objectives, procedures, and controls. *Academy of Management Journal,* September 1975, pp. 489–99.

Dalrymple, Douglas J. Sales forecasting methods and accuracy. *Business Horizons,* December 1975, p. 69.

Drucker, Peter. *Managing for Results.* New York: Harper & Row, 1964.

General Electric Company, *Professional Management in General Electric.* New York: The General Electric Company, 1954.

Granger, C. H. The hierarchy of objectives, *Harvard Business Review,* 1964, pp. 63–74.

Gross, B. What are your organization's objectives? A general systems approach to planning. *Human Relations,* August 1965, pp. 195–216.

Hatten, K. J., and Piccoli, M. L. An evaluation of a technological forecasting method by computer-based simulation. *Academy of Management Proceedings.* Boston, 1973.

Henderson, Bruce D. *Construction of a Business Strategy.* Boston: The Boston Consulting Group, 1970.

Katz, R. L. *Cases and Concepts in Corporate Strategy.* Englewood Cliffs, N.J.: Prentice-Hall, Inc., 1970.

McConnell, J. Douglas. Strategic planning: One workable approach. *Long-Range Planning,* December 1971, pp. 2–6.

Maier, N. R. F. Maximizing personal creativity through better problem-solving. *Personnel Administration,* 1964, pp. 14–18.

Mason, R. Hal. Corporate strategy: A point of view. *California Management Review,* 1971, pp. 5–12.

Meadows, A.; Parnes, S. J.; and Reese, H. "Influence of brainstorming instructions and problem sequence on a creative problem-solving test. *Journal of Applied Psychology,* 1959, pp. 413–16.

Nation's Business, March 1972.

Newman, William H. Shaping the master strategy of your firm. *California Management Review,* Spring 1967, pp. 77–88.

Thomas, Philip S. Environmental analysis for corporate planning. *Business Horizons,* October 1974, pp. 27–38.

Thompson, James D., and McEwen, William J. Organizational goals and environment: Goal setting as an interaction process. *American Sociological Review,* February 1958, pp. 23–30.

Vancil, Richard F. Accuracy of long-range planning. *Harvard Business Review,* September–October 1970, pp. 98–101.

Warren, E. Kirby.   The capability inventory: Its role in long-range planning. *Management of Personnel Quarterly*, Winter 1965, pp. 50–56.

Case study 2–1

Human Resources Incorporated

In February 1972, Robert Rosenberg, president of Human Resources Incorporated was reviewing the firm's past growth and profitability and the objectives and strategies being used. His review led him to believe that considerable improvement was required. This case study describes the ways his attempts at improvement were conceptualized and implemented.

HISTORICAL BACKGROUND

HRI was founded in 1950 by Robert's father, William Rosenberg, and a partner with an initial capital outlay of $15,000. In 1957 with some inheritance from his deceased father, William Rosenberg purchased his partner's interest. Consequently HRI went through a period of rapid expansion and, in the following ten years, reached a leadership position in the temporary help field in the United States.

Initially HRI focused on supplying temporary office help only but later expanded into supplying industrial and professional services to clients requiring sales/marketing, technical, light industrial, medical-dental, and data processing assistance. Beginning in 1968, it diversified into various service industries, most notably travel, permanent employment, equipment rentals, and business training schools. In 1970, it began franchising temporary help and service industry outlets. By 1972, HRI was operating 350 owned and franchised offices in major metropolitan areas across Canada and the United States, with franchises making up 25 percent of these.

Since 1968, however, HRI has gradually relinquished its dominant position in the temporary help field to new competitors, characterized by strong professional management and ample capital. For the last two years, while the temporary help industry was growing at a record rate of 20 percent each year. HRI's revenues stayed constant at $75 million, with a profit margin of only 3 percent of sales. And even this profitability rate was only maintained because some of the owned service businesses such as travel, were extremely profitable.

ORGANIZATION

The head office of HRI is in Chicago. Operating and franchising activities are decentralized into four geographic areas: West, East and

Central, South, and Canada. Residing in each area is a regional vice president responsible for both functions. Reporting to him are an assistant vice president—operations, and an assistant vice president—franchises.

In addition to the four regional vice presidents and the vice president—franchising, there are three staff persons reporting to the president: the director of marketing, the director of personnel, and the controller.

CURRENT SITUATION

Robert only became president in July 1971. However, his involvement in projects during college breaks and his brief period as president provided him with considerable insight into the nature of the business and its significant aspects.

Although HRI employed many well-trained managers and had successfully diversified into other businesses and franchising since 1968, Robert felt that there was a lack of professionalism in the way the firm was being managed and an overall lack of corporate direction. He was sure that these deficiencies were felt by personnel at all levels. Several times he had overheard complaints that company policies and strategies were vague and, in some cases, even conflicting.

He feared that the firm's managers were not attuned to the changes that were permeating the temporary help and service industry markets and the diverse environments in which HRI's clients operate. Furthermore, he felt that rapid changes were occurring in the labor market, the supply side of HRI's business, and that management was not sufficiently aware of these. Robert attributed much of this lack of external focus to his father's autocratic style of making all key strategic decisions himself and of running the business as his personal fiefdom.

Keeping up with change is a difficult task for HRI. For one thing there is the complexity of operating in a number of different markets. The problem is increased by HRI's growth strategy of developing a variety of new businesses, rather than competing in existing markets and acquiring ongoing enterprises. Furthermore, there is the increasing strength of their competition. Robert, therefore, felt that his managers required a more defined corporate purpose before they could begin to devise strategies to compete more effectively. And he also believed that his competent management staff must now become more involved in the firm's strategic decision processes if they were to develop the skills the firm needs to continue to grow.

For these reasons, he called a meeting of the top executives in February 1972 to discuss how they should go about setting corporate aims and modifying the way the company is being managed.

ORGANIZATION OF THE PLANNING COMMITTEE

All principal executives were present at this meeting. Robert Rosenberg acted as chairman.

Robert began the meeting by welcoming the executives and emphasizing that the purpose was to organize a planning committee, to discuss what the planning committee could accomplish, and to determine the specific roles the members of this committee should play.

Mr. Turner, regional vice-president—West, brought up the question of establishing a permanent planning committee versus an ad hoc task force. Although the group felt that it was advantageous to make planning a formal part of the way the business was operated, they recognized that a temporary planning committee was a way of working out the best operating procedure for a permanent effort and of assessing the reactions of other personnel. Furthermore, changes in objectives and strategies could necessitate organizational changes. They therefore agreed that formation of a permanent planning unit should be deferred.

Discussion then centered around some of the critical issues the firm would be facing in the future, the uncertainty surrounding their entire sphere of operations, and how these problems should be tackled. After considerable discussion members of the group agreed to do some individual thinking before they met again.

The meeting did not adjourn, however, until a planning committee was established. The committee consisted of the four regional vice presidents, the director of marketing, and the controller.

It was generally agreed that the following should take place:

1. Mr. Turner, vice president of the West region, should act as chairman of the committee.
2. Sufficient secretarial and clerical help should be provided the committee to ensure a smooth flow of work.
3. The task of setting corporate purpose should not exceed six months.
4. To accomplish this, the committee should plan to meet 10–12 times.
5. Members are to be given sufficient advance notice of each meeting to come properly prepared.
6. The committee should try to utilize all existing talents within the firm.
7. The committee should report back to the president at some convenient future time.

ACTIVITIES OF THE PLANNING COMMITTEE

The following progress report was submitted to the president by Mr. Turner, the chairman of the planning committee, on April 26, 1972.

MEMO

TO: Mr. Robert Rosenberg, President
FROM: D. Turner, Chairman, Planning Committee
RE: Progress Report on Planning Committee's Activities

April 26, 1972

Further to our conversation today, here is a summary of the progress of our Planning Committee to date and a schedule of events for the next few weeks.

We have held six sessions. During and between these sessions the Committee members conducted thorough and critical examinations of the firm's existing policies and adaptability to its environment. Involvement of lower echelon personnel was encouraged throughout by requesting information and recommendations from them. For your reference, highlights of the minutes from these meetings are enclosed (see Exhibit 1).

We are now at the stage of drafting strategic alternatives. At least three more sessions are planned since each member requires time to consolidate his own thinking before meaningful discussion can take place. We will not begin drafting proposals for alternative strategies until all information has been collected so that action programs can be compared, weighted in terms of relative importance, and manpower needs and budgets optimally allocated.

Our schedule of future activities is as follows:

1. One session will be devoted to ensuring that the committee has covered all significant aspects of corporate operations and that the decisions we have reached are thoroughly cross-checked for internal consistency.
2. To ensure communication, feedback, understanding, and agreement among all members of management we propose that an oral presentation be made to you and to other senior executives before detailed action plans are developed.
3. Our plans for the formal documentation of strategic alternatives are as follows:
    a. All write-ups will follow the same format with Purpose, and Means well spelled out, and the rationale and commitment for each action plan fully articulated.
    b. All top executives will receive the entire strategic plan containing the evaluation and choices among strategic alternatives.
    c. Specific audiences will only receive specific sections of the documentation. This will ensure efficiency and eliminate the time-consuming task of reviewing irrelevant inputs.
    d. The Committee will be responsible for appointing staff to draft these documents.
    e. Methods for controlling sensitive documents will be designed and communicated to affected parties.

In summary, I can report that the entire committee has gained a significant understanding of the structure and functioning of our organization and a significant appreciation of its individual competences. We are confident that our systematic and rational approach to the setting of corporate aims and the preparation of corporate strategy is an efficient procedure, and that a similar procedure can be used to prepare subunit goals and strategies throughout the organization.

EXHIBIT 1
Highlights of minutes

Meeting 1: Friday, February 16, 1972. 9:00 A.M.

The meeting began with each executive giving his opinion about the operation of his region, economic trends, a general business outlook, the state of competition, and/or other issues that have an impact on the company.

The discussions then focussed on three aspects in particular: (1) critical decision areas, (2) the scope and type of information needed to make decisions in these areas, and (3) sources of the relevant information.

The Committee agreed that the following decision areas are vital to HRI's functioning:

1. Profits.   How can profits be maximized?
2. Growth.   How should growth be channeled? Should growth be through internal expansion or should franchising be continued?
3. Efficiency.   Are we presently operating at maximum efficiency? If not, what must be done and what improvements should be made?
4. Diversification.   Should HRI continue its diversification program or should it attempt to capitalize on its strength in existing markets? What other marketing strategies could be adopted?
5. Management development.   Do present policies achieve the management development needed by the organization?

Discussion then turned to the scope and type of information needed to make decisions in each of these areas. The discussion was quite time consuming since a considerable effort was made to resolve misunderstandings that arose from semantic differences.

To facilitate compilation of the data needed, it was agreed to develop and use a common checklist to systematically identify critical information. Macro (big picture) and micro (day-to-day) information was to be collected separately, and then coordinated. We chose to categorize information into environmental (internal and external) factors, resources, administrative processes, and nature of outputs produced. Each of these categories is to be applied to each organizational unit and, from this, a set of information needs compiled and presented to the Committee.

Since the Committee is also responsible for interpreting and utilizing these data, each Committee member agreed to be responsible for gathering the information needed from the functional units under his jurisdiction.

EXHIBIT 1 *(continued)*

The following tasks were assigned for the next meeting: (1) The Chairman is to be responsible for developing the format and making the preliminary information checklist available to all members; (2) each member is to be responsible for gathering information from the functional units within his jurisdiction; (3) each member is to use the checklist to gather, analyze, and interpret his input data and to identify additional information needed; and (4) at the next meeting the Committee will critique the information collected by each member before deciding on the additional information needed and who is best suited to collect it.

Meeting 2: Friday, March 1, 1972. 9:00 A.M.

While some of the needed information was now available, the Committee preferred to deal with all input data at one time. It was felt that while piecemeal treatment of information would smooth the decision-making work load, it would also make assessment of relative priorities difficult. Furthermore, looking at the information in an ad hoc fashion might be misleading as interrelationships among decisions might be overlooked.

The meeting was used to allow members to gain insight into each other's attitudes toward and opinions about the existing policies of the organization, how these policies are incorporated into operations, and how they are communicated to the various units within the organization. Discussion also focused on potential improvements. It was agreed that policies should be regarded as broad statements used to assure that consistent management is applied throughout the organization.

Specific discussions then centered around four policy areas that the Committee felt were sensitive to executive discretion and where the most important improvements could be made. The following represent the conclusions of the Commitee in these four areas:

a. *Stakeholders.* The Committee felt that the previous implicit definition of stakeholders is too narrow and should be expanded to include not only owners and customers but also labor and management.
b. *Resource utilization.* The Committee agreed that corporate economic resources are not being fully utilized. Our traditional methods of economic analyses based on standard accounting methods are inadequate and have not kept up with the rapid changes in business methods. The Committee agreed that there is a need for more advanced techniques of financial analysis and more use of computers.
c. *Market analyses.* The Committee agreed that the existing market definitions had been too vague. Although HRI had undertaken diversification programs, because these were undertaken without a clear conception of where the firm was going and what kind of businesses we would like to be in, we may have suffered losses by

EXHIBIT 1 (continued)

foregoing or being unaware of other profitable investment opportunities.

d. *Management development and use.* The Committee agreed that no concerted team efforts had been attempted in the past and hence the synergistic potential of our management resources has never been fully realized. Our executives have no real appreciation of each others values, motivation, and dedication. Management development is an entirely neglected area in the company. The Committee feels that management development should be made a significant aspect of our corporate objectives and that an organizational unit should be structured to accommodate the development of competent executives. The experience of this Committee's functioning could serve as a first step toward more cooperation among members of top management.

Meetings 3, 4 and 5: Friday, March 15, 22, and 29, 1972

The purpose of these meetings was to familiarize the team with the available data and to identify additional information needed.

During these meetings presentations were made on each member's activities. To facilitate common thinking and subsequent documentation, these presentations were made under the same headings and framework, and clearly sketched on flip charts and wall displays. Some of the questions that were addressed in these presentations are given in Exhibit 2. To keep the ball rolling and to encourage members to debate and argue over opposing viewpoints, the chairmanship of these meetings was rotated.

The meetings served to stimulate participative reasoning toward corporate purpose by following a systematic procedure. Each member's presentation first identified the relevant areas he was most concerned with, examined their current status, evaluated their past performance, discussed future changes in the environment, and then synthesized and summarized the findings.

These meetings resulted in the compilation of a well-reasoned inventory of needs. These fell into three categories: need for additional information; improvement needs; and needs for achievement (goals).

To handle our needs for additional information the Committee adopted a procedure which we termed an internal request for information. An internal request for information is simply a form documenting an issue or a question which is directed to a specific individual in the organization. The individual is expected to respond to this request in a reasonable amount of time. The Committee felt that this directed search for information would serve to involve line and staff specialists in the corporate planning process and to generate innovative suggestions and alternative methods of fulfilling needs for improvement. To facilitate review of these requests, all respondents were required to use a uni-

EXHIBIT 1 (concluded)

form method of reporting that we prepared. All proposals were to be submitted within six weeks. Some of the tentative goals that were established are listed below in Exhibit 3.

Meeting 6: Friday, April 15, 1972

This was a short meeting. While waiting for the last internal requests for information to be submitted, the Committee decided to recapitulate what it has achieved so far.

Some of the last information submissions were then summarized on flip charts and individual members began to work either separately or in pairs on assessing the implications of this information on proposed strategies.

A suggestion was made that the Committee go off to a resort for two days to work on the formation of strategies. The Chairman was to look into possible accommodation and times for this meeting and to report back.

EXHIBIT 2

Questions addressed at Meetings 3, 4, and 5

Markets

What kind of technological, economic, and competitive environment do you operate in?

What are the important factors that need to be manipulated and monitored?

What is your market posture and ability to adapt to the changing environment, as compared to your competitors?

Industry

What important changes in clients' businesses need to be monitored?

What is the image of HRI among client companies?

Labor market

What important changes in demographics need to be monitored?

Are we marketing the right skills?

What kind of recruitment is necessary?

How should we deal with the growing power of unions?

Corporate resources

What are your available resources and expertise?

What important factors in the environment have direct bearings on your resources?

Are these resources being maximally utilized?

Organization

Are you satisfied with efficiency of operating methods?

What trends in operating methods are significant?

EXHIBIT 2 (continued)

What improvements should be done?

Stakeholders

What are the investments of our stakeholders?

What are their expectations?

Are we performing up to potential?

EXHIBIT 3

Guiding goal

To be leaders in the supply of human resources to business and industry; to be strong, profitable, diversified, and unified.

1. *Profits:*
    a. To obtain minimum annual earnings after income tax of 7 percent on sales and 18 percent on shareholders' equity.
    b. To retain 75 percent of net earning in the business.
    c. To earn a profit from each office and each line of service.
    d. To strive to increase profits after tax by at least 15 percent annually.
2. *Markets:*
    a. To regain the leadership position of HRI in the U.S. temporary help market.
    b. To increase our share of the Canadian market and maintain a growth rate of 20 percent.
    c. To attain a leadership position in the industrial market.
3. *Management development:*
    a. To pay competitive wage rates and benefits to all employees.
    b. To maintain an employee turnover of 6 percent.
    c. To install management development programs to ensure rational career progression and attraction of talents.
    d. To install performance evaluation procedures that will enhance motivation and dedication.
4. *Growth and innovation:*
    a. To attain our growth objectives (profits and markets) through internal expansion.
    b. To concentrate on further diversification provided all other objectives are fulfilled.

Questions

1. If you were Robert Rosenberg, what would your evaluation be of the progress the committee had made thus far and the approach they have taken? What suggestions (and/or orders) would you now make to them?

2. As an objective outsider, what is your evaluation of what has taken place since February 1972?

3. If you were the vice president chairing the committee, what would you have done differently?

Case study 2–2

The University of Calgary

In the late summer and early fall of 1975, W. A. Cochrane, the new president of the University of Calgary initiated a series of discussions with the deans of the various faculties aimed at launching a management seminar for the administrative staff of the University of Calgary.

A few weeks later, at a meeting of department heads on September 25, Cochrane opened the meeting (which had a long agenda) with a discussion about the forthcoming management seminar for department heads to be held at Banff on December 8–10, 1975.

In opening the discussion, President Cochrane commented:

> . . . the administrative officers of this university, particularly at the departmental level, play a critical role. There is not only need for greater involvement but there are perceived, in several instances, problems related to administrative skills. Departments are encouraged to attend the seminar on a voluntary basis. The workshops will deal with management strategies and management skills. Resource people will be called in from outside but we will attempt to use talent from our own campus in this area. It is hoped that the seminar will deal with precise problems of University management with respect to department heads (implementation of change, importance of strategies, resolution of conflict, etc.). The seminar is not intended to provide a great deal of management *theory*, but it is expected to emphasize the skill side of management with examples of problems and a discussion of how one might have proceeded to solve certain types of problems. . . .

HISTORICAL BACKGROUND

The University of Calgary had been an independent institution only since 1966. Prior to that period, the campus had operated as a branch of the University of Edmonton, primarily in makeshift, temporary buildings. The first two permanent buildings had been erected in 1962 and 1963. After 1966, the University of Calgary grew rapidly as enrollment shot up. After a brief pause in growth during the 1972–74 period, the university was once again in a growth pattern in 1975.

Like any new young university, the University of Calgary suffered growing pains as it struggled to cope with the ever-increasing tide of new students each fall. Through necessity, the campus operated through a highly centralized organizational structure. Day-to-day "crisis" management was the rule rather than the exception with little long-term planning taking place, especially at the faculty level.

On two occasions in the past, attempts had been made to come to grips with the appointment, role, authority and responsibility profile of the department heads. The *Schonfield Report* in 1970 and the *Flanagan Report* in 1972–73 both represented commitment of enormous man-hours of time and talent in an attempt to clarify and define the role of the department head. Both reports had been submitted to the General Faculties Council. Both had failed to pass. Consequently, in 1975, no real progress had been made in defining the role of the department head and no effort had been made to define the type of skills/administrative capabilities that were desirable for this position.

ORGANIZING AND PLANNING THE SEMINAR

After the meeting with the department heads on September 25, 1975, President Cochrane turned over the responsibility for planning and organizing the seminar to two individuals: (*a*) Dr. Donovan, the academic assistant to the president and (*b*) Dr. R. S. Chapman, associate dean of the Division of Continuing Education (DCE). Dr. Cochrane emphasized that the timing of the seminar was critical since the Faculty of Arts and Science was less than a year away from splitting into four new Faculties of Arts, Science, Social Sciences and University College. In fact, the University was at the time, searching for approximately seven new deans and a number of department heads.

A few days later, Dr. Chapman was approached by several professors from the Faculty of Commerce who offered their services and suggested they assume primary responsibility for the development and implementation of the administrative seminar. Several preliminary meetings were held with both Dr. Chapman, and eventually with President Cochrane, to discuss the seminar objectives, seminar content, and pedagogical approach.

In early October, Professor Douglas Tigert, a *Marketing Professor* at the University of Toronto's Faculty of Management Studies, received a call from a Dr. Chapman of the University of Calgary. . . .

Chapman: Professor Tigert, I'm glad I reached you at last. Let me tell you why I'm calling. We're planning on running an administrative seminar for the University of Calgary's administrative staff, at Banff on December 8–10. You come highly recommended for this type of thing and I am hoping you will agree to be one of the seminar leaders.

Tigert: Is this a marketing seminar?

Chapman: No, no . . . this is a seminar to improve the administrative and management skills of our department heads and deans. But we'd like you to provide the marketing input . . . you know . . . planning, strategy . . . that sort of thing.

The two men chatted for a while about the forthcoming seminar. Finally, Professor Tigert asked Dr. Chapman for an outline of the seminar topics.

Chapman: Let's see, I have it right here in front of me. Right, here's the list:

- *a.* Administrative perspectives.
- *b.* Planning and goal setting.
- *c.* University planning.
- *d.* Evaluating organizational effectiveness.
- *e.* Diagnosis.
- *f.* Organizational change.
- *g.* Influence.
- *h.* Interpersonal competence and group effectiveness.

Tigert: What are the basic objectives . . . to improve skills at strategic planning, budgeting, etc., or to improve interpersonal skills and leadership styles, or what?

Chapman: I think both. We really want them to become more effective administrators in all facets of their job.

After discussing objectives and seminar content for an additional four or five minutes, Professor Tigert broke in.

Tigert: Look I'm going to be passing through Calgary on November 20 and 21. Why don't you go ahead and assume that I will be one of the seminar leaders. I'll plan on spending one full day on the campus, meeting with you and the other seminar leaders to finalize the seminar outline. It might be a good idea if I met with a number of deans and department heads while I'm there, just so that I understand what they think is to be accomplished at the seminar. . . . What they want the participants to take away with them. It might even be a good idea if I met the President, since he initiated the idea.

Chapman: Fine, I'll send you the preliminary seminar outline and set up a complete schedule for your visit on the 21st.

Three days later, just as he was departing for the airport to attend a two-week seminar in Europe, Professor Tigert received the preliminary seminar outline from Dr. Chapman, (see Appendix). He tucked it into his briefcase as he was walking out the door to the airport limousine. The next day, Canada was hit with a nationwide mail strike.

On Wednesday, November 19, Professor Tigert telephoned Dr. Chapman at the University of Calgary to finalize the details of his visit:

Tigert: Hello, . . . how's everything going with the seminar?

Chapman: Fine, everything's fine. I have your schedule all ready. You're going to start off the morning with President Cochrane and then meet with several deans before having lunch with Cunningham, Lee and Robinson, the other seminar leaders from the Faculty of Commerce.

Tigert: Good. Are we all set with the reservation at the Calgary Inn? I'm sure glad we handled that early. I didn't know this was Grey Cup Week.

Chapman: What?

Tigert: Didn't you get my letter about your making the reservations? Of course you couldn't, could you. There's a mail strike on. Look, I'm just leaving for Vancouver but I'll be in Calgary on Thursday night. Why don't you just find me a bed in the residence and we'll take it from there when I arrive?

Chapman: O.K., give me a call when you arrive and I'll have it set up.

After spending two days in Vancouver, Professor Tigert arrived in Calgary where arrangements had been made for him to stay in one of the student residences. On Friday morning he met with Dr. Chapman for a brief meeting before starting on a day of interviewing with various administrative officials. They again reviewed the seminar objectives and discussed several changes in the day's schedule.

Since Dr. Cochrane was unexpectedly away in Toronto, Dr. Tigert met instead with Dr. Donovan, President Cochrane's administrative assistant and the man responsible for some of the details of the seminar's organization, including the selection of the participants. Dr. Donovan expressed the philosophy of the seminar as he saw it:

. . . many of the problems we have occur because our deans and department heads have poor management skills . . . it isn't like a company . . . if people don't get along or they don't perform, you can't fire them . . . it's not necessary, but highly desirable that they get along . . . so the most important thing is interpersonal relations. . . .

About 11 o'clock, Chapman and Tigert met with Professors Cunningham, Lee and Robinson to nail down the final details of the seminar. There seemed to be a bit of uncertainty about the seminar objectives; what to emphasize, what sequence, and so on, but there was a lot of good stuff in the total package. Each professor appeared clear on how his materials would interrelate with the other material. The four professors and Dr. Chapman discussed the two meetings that had been held with President Cochrane to make sure they all understood the seminar's purpose as Cochrane saw it.

After a quick lunch with the other seminar leaders, Professor Tigert and Dr. Chapman moved on to the next appointment with one of the faculty deans. In discussing the seminar objectives with this dean, some of the same problems were reiterated. Dean X indicated that people coming into administrative positions just don't know much about administration:

. . . they need to know more about budgeting, organizational structure and interpersonal relations . . . how to communicate downwards, up-

wards and horizontally . . . how to resolve conflict . . . the department heads want more authority . . . we also should be doing more on
evaluation . . . evaluating a unit for effectiveness. . . .

Professor Tigert casually asked about university resources that might
be the best for teaching or running a seminar on interpersonal relations
and communication. The dean mentioned that there were, over in the
Education Department, a number of people who specialized in this area.
He remarked that "Bill Goding has done a lot on communication and
Paul Adams specializes in interpersonal relations. . . ."

Tigert and Chapman then met with one of the vice presidents to get
further information on the seminar objectives. He was pretty specific:

> . . . let's train them to be more effective in managing their function
> . . . don't imprint management on them!!! . . . teach them how to
> handle situations without stress . . . let's find a way to let academic
> leaders function effectively in their discipline and yet improve planning
> and management . . . what should a particular department be doing
> in 1975 . . . or 1980 and what will it take to accomplish those objec-
> tives . . . the department head is the link between the students, the
> curriculum, the faculty and the administration . . . he is a key
> player. . . .

On his last stop for the day, Professor Tigert met with one of the
senior administrators in the Arts and Science Faculty. He had a long,
in-depth discussion with Professor Y:

> . . . you know, the department heads are suspiscious about the whole
> seminar concept . . . they face real problems, day-to-day down in the
> trenches . . . they feel hassled . . . in the fall they have to assess all
> the staff members for promotions and advances . . . they have to do all
> the course and programme changes for next year . . . they have to do
> a programme review as the first stage in the budgeting process . . .
> how would you cope with no increase in the budget . . . the budget
> adjusted for inflation is declining and quality is deteriorating . . .
>
> . . . a department headship is definitely declining in attractiveness. . . .
>
> . . . this seminar should focus on skill deficiencies and skill needs and
> they vary enormously across departments . . . one man needs to be a
> people manager, another maybe someone who needs to understand re-
> search and resource allocation. . . .
>
> . . . a third needs to be a "tough guy" . . . and a fourth needs a gen-
> uine humanistic touch. . . .
>
> . . . you know, a lot of these annual procedures are unnecessary . . .
> like the annual review of all professors. . . .
>
> . . . a lot of procedures are a waste of time . . . the Office of Institu-
> tional Research produces a book full of data and that feeds into budget
> allocation decisions . . . it's not accurate . . . a lot of factors are not

built into that data and no one understands it anyway . . . AREG [Allocation Resource Evaluation Guide] is no good but three-quarters of the budget is allocated on this formula . . . the academic vice-president should go to the department and get a real estimate of a department's needs . . .

. . . all procedures have been changed to a semi-legalistic framework . . . the old gentleman's agreement is gone . . . now we spell everything out . . .

Shortly after the last meeting, Dr. Tigert hurried off to catch his plane for Toronto.

Questions

1. Does the University of Calgary have a problem?
   Should this seminar have been initiated?
   How do you think it turned out?
2. What other alternatives could have accomplished the same objectives as envisioned for this seminar?
3. Design an appropriate planning system for this seminar.

APPENDIX

PRELIMINARY OUTLINE: UNIVERSITY OF CALGARY

SEMINAR ON ADMINISTRATION

Purpose

To expand the knowledge and management skills of those individuals who have administrative responsibilities.

To clarify the roles and responsibilities of administrators.

Tentative dates and times

9:00 A.M., Monday, December 8 to
4:30 P.M., Wednesday, December 10, 1975

Location

Banff Centre

Resource personnel

Dr. P. H. Cunningham, Faculty of Business, the University of Calgary
Dr. M. B. Lee, Faculty of Business, the University of Calgary

Dr. J. M. A. Robinson, Faculty of Business, the University of Calgary

Dr. P. Savage, Faculty of Business, the University of Calgary

Dr. D. J. Tigert, Faculty of Management Studies, the University of Toronto and small group discussion leaders from the University of Calgary

Participants

Approximately 40 individuals drawn from the vice presidents, deans and academic department heads of the University of Calgary

SCHEDULE

Sunday, December 7, 1975
  Evening   Drive to Banff and register for
                                  accommodation at Banff Centre

Monday, December 8, 1975
  7:30– 8:30 A.M.   Breakfast
  9:00– 9:15 A.M.   General Session—Overview of the
                                  Seminar and the Educational Plan
  9:15–10:30 A.M.   General Session—An Administrative
                                  Perspective—The Role of the
                                  Administrator   Dr. M. B. Lee
  10:30–10:45 A.M.   Coffee break
  10:45–12:00 noon   General Session—Planning and Goal
                                  Setting   Dr. J. M. A. Robinson
  12:00– 1:15 P.M.   Lunch
  1:15– 3:00 P.M.   Group meetings (discussion and
                                  application of concepts from the
                                  morning general sessions)
  3:00 P.M.   Coffee available
  3:00– 5:00 P.M.   Recreation break
  5:00– 5:45 P.M.   Reception
  6:00– 7:00 P.M.   Dinner
  7:00– 9:00 P.M.   General Session—Future Shock and
                                  Adaptive Competitive Strategy—
                                  Environmental Assessment: Input to
                                  the Planning Process   Dr. D. J. Tigert
  9:00–   Group meetings

Tuesday, December 9, 1975
  7:30– 8:30 A.M.   Breakfast
  9:00–10:30 A.M.   Group presentations
  10:30–10:45 A.M.   Coffee break
  10:45–12:00 noon   Process Models of Planning (including
                                  group work on a University of Calgary
                                  case)   Dr. D. J. Tigert

SCHEDULE (*continued*)

12:00– 1:15 P.M.	Lunch
1:15– 3:00 P.M.	General session—Managing Conflict *Dr. P. H. Cunningham*
3:00 P.M.	Coffee available
3:00– 5:00 P.M.	Recreation break
5:00– 5:45 P.M.	Reception
6:00– 7:00 P.M.	Dinner
7:00– 8:45 P.M.	General session—Management of Change *Dr. M. B. Lee*

Wednesday, December 10, 1975

7:30– 8:30 A.M.	Breakfast
9:00–10:30 A.M.	General session—The Influence of the Administrator (power, leadership, motivation) *Dr. M. B. Lee*
10:30–10:45 A.M.	Coffee break
10:45–12:00 noon	General session—Interpersonal Competence and Group Effectiveness *Dr. P. H. Cunningham*
12:00– 1:15 P.M.	Lunch
1:15– 3:00 P.M.	Group meetings
3:00– 3:15 P.M.	Coffee break
3:15– 4:30 P.M.	General session—Evaluation of Seminar and Follow-up Plans
4:30 P.M.	Adjourn
5:00 P.M.	Dinner available

Chapter outline

New program generation
  Planning gaps
  The generation of new programs
  Some approaches to innovation and new program
    generation
Project evaluation and resource allocation
  Program life cycles
  Evaluation and choice
    Procedure and documentation
    Evaluation criteria
Specification of the long-range plan
  Key variables of the long-range plan
Responsibility unit planning and control
System evaluation and adaptation

3

Overview continued: Program planning, resource allocation, and responsibility unit planning and control

When you have completed this chapter, which describes cycles 2 and 3 of the multicycle hierarchical planning process, you will understand the following:

1. What a planning gap is.
2. What are programs and projects and their role in organizational planning and control.
3. How programs and projects are initiated and how resources are allocated to them.
4. Some of the procedures, documentation, and decision criteria that make up a project evaluation system.
5. The role and content of a long-range plan and its key variables.
6. What a responsibility unit planning and control system is.
7. How the evaluation and adaptation of the overall planning and control system are carried out.

NEW PROGRAM GENERATION

Planning gaps

Before considering cycle 2 of the multicycle model outlined in Table 2–1, it is essential to understand the general relationship of the output of cycle 1, strategic planning, to the performance of cycle 2, and the means by which the expectations are communicated. These are best described in terms of key variables (KVs) and planning gaps.

An organization's strategic planning produces the statement of strategic mission for that organization. The objectives and strategies defined by this statement then becomes a framework for subsequent planning. When this statement is synopsized and communicated as key variables, these KVs guide cycles 2 and 3 of the nine-step planning process model described in Chapter 2.

Key variables can be used to stimulate and guide planning in two different ways. They may be used as stylistic guidelines to instill a unity of purpose or to ensure goal congruence throughout the organization. Alternatively they may be used as specific performance targets for subordinate activity. KVs, therefore, may express either general or specific objectives.

If cycle 2 is intended primarily to narrow a planning gap, then KVs will express specific objectives. A planning gap is an estimate of the difference between (*a*) what is likely to be achieved if there is no planning and the organization continues what it is doing now, and (*b*) what the organization could potentially accomplish at some future point in time. The difference between the extrapolated results of current operations and the results that planning indicates could be accomplished defines a gap to be closed by subsequent program planning.

FIGURE 3–1
Specification of planning gap

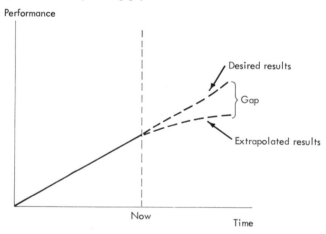

If, however, KVs are stated as general objectives then they merely provide direction, rather than defining any specific planning gap. In this mode of operation, the outputs of the strategic planning process are intended solely to help managers conceptualize the desired future of the organization and motivate them to make this future an actuality. In this situation cycle 2 determines how, when, and to what extent these unquantified objectives can be accomplished. Program planning and resource allocation are the means by which these general objectives are quantified and achieved.

A prime determinant of an organization's success in closing the planning gap either specified or implied in its statement of strategic mission is its ability to plan and fund novel and profitable programs. As outlined in Table 2–1, new program generation is step 4 in the nine-step model and the first step of cycle 2, the program planning and resource allocation phase of the multicycle process.

A program is a group of coordinated activities designed to accomplish a specific objective. Launching a new product or modernizing a plant are examples of programs. Clustering all of the activities that are intended to achieve some overall objective into programs is a means of directing attention squarely to what is to be accomplished. A project is simply the quantification and expression of a program or part of a program in terms of its financial inflows and outflows and the relative timing of these flows, so that the relative desirability of undertaking the program can be evaluated. An organization attempts to achieve its strategic mission by planning, evaluating, and implementing a set of projects. Project evaluation and resource allocation make up the second step of cycle 2, and step 5 in the model outlined in Table 2–1. The third and last step in this cycle involves translating the decisions made in these two prior steps into a long-range plan.

Several aspects of new program generation are discussed next in this section. The second and third sections consider project evaluation and resource allocation, and the specification of long-range plans, respectively.

FIGURE 3–2
Cycle 2: Program planning and resource allocation

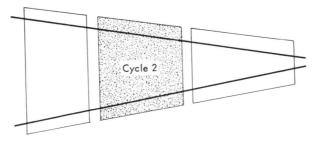

The generation of new programs

Some organizations initiate new programs spontaneously in their normal course of business. For them, innovation is not a problem. But for other organizations, the problem of stimulating new ideas and programs is among the most difficult they will face.

Program generation is a process of gathering information, generating ideas, expressing them in terms of projects, and developing them to the point where they can be evaluated. Program generation may begin with a list of problems that have to be solved so that the organization can accomplish its mission. It may also necessitate identifying the skills required to solve these problems and, if necessary, acquiring or developing these skills. Acquiring skills may, in fact, turn out to be a project in itself. Eventually, programs are translated into projects which must then be submitted for evaluation, the next step in the planning process.

Although project evaluation may be a periodic activity (e.g., part of an annual capital budget), new program planning itself is a continuous process, since good ideas can arise at any time. Therefore it is important to distinguish the continuous process of generating new projects from the periodic task of evaluating them.

Some approaches to innovation and new program generation

Organizations use a variety of techniques and methods in managing their new program generation. The members of one top-management team define the problems they feel have to be solved in order to accomplish their strategic mission. They then select the individual best qualified to handle each problem and assign him the task of formulating a specific solution. They do this by a procedure called a *request for proposal*, in which a formal request is sent to the individual, who is required to respond to it in one or two months in a form he or she thinks most suitable.

Some organizations concerned with encouraging proposals go considerably further in their approach; they attempt to create the proper climate for innovation. All managers are made aware of top management's receptivity and commitment to new ideas, and that a strong marketing staff is accessible to provide the preliminary information and evaluation necessary to screen new proposals. Management encourages support from a strong technical staff and emphasizes good communications between line and staff. They ensure the freedom to fail, so that the proposer of a project bears no stigma if it fails to be accepted. But they also identify and reward successful champions of proposals, hence fostering a spirit of entrepreneurship within their organization.

To help their search for new products or new businesses, many corporations resort to formal idea-generating techniques such as brainstorming. In this method a problem situation is given to a group of managers to solve; the managers are free to propose any solution to the problem, no matter how farfetched it may be. The purpose of brainstorming is to elicit as many new ideas as possible. The technique is founded on two basic principles: (1) in order to avoid the constraining effects of premature evaluation, the evaluation of any idea is postponed until all ideas are generated, and (2) a supportive climate must be maintained so that no individual feels threatened by or in competition with other committee members. To encourage the free exchange of ideas in many companies the ideas generated in a brainstorming session are evaluated by another group independent of the generating group.

Another stimulus to innovation is the use of temporary study groups to research specific questions. The John Hancock Insurance Company, for example, uses issue analysis: a means of identifying and resolving major issues which the company faces or will face in the near future. Top management selects the issues to be analyzed either from those nominated by company departments at the beginning of the annual planning cycle or from those that arise during the preparation and review of departmental projections for the year. They convene a task force, usually a combination of junior and senior officers, to thoroughly study an identified issue. The task force follows a specified procedure and then presents a formal report to top management. Issue analysis forces a consideration of the major problems the company faces, how these problems interrelate with corporate objectives, and what solutions appear to be viable. It also produces a record which can be used for either review or reference if the same issue comes up again (Lamphere, 1973).

A large commercial bank in Boston follows a similar practice. It holds each of its divisions responsible for one new idea each year; e.g., a new service or a new business that could be undertaken. Each division forms a team of six to eight junior and senior executives who work for two months under the direction of a vice president. Each group first meets together in a closed meeting to review its ideas, and then presents top management with proposals for future expansion.

One way to complement (and, in some cases, even replace) staff groups in new program generation is by use of the venture team. Based on the principle that the composition of a group should fit the task it has to handle, the venture team concept assembles a group best able to carry out a new program (producing and marketing a new product, for example). Team formation overcomes the problem of long-range planning departments which are too busy with other functions, and of marketing development departments which are too closely linked to the existing practices and politics of the organization. Venture teams can link research and development to production and marketing without going through normal organizational channels, and hence are a means of stimulating new ideas without normal organizational constraints. Successful venture teams are usually small (five to seven people) and multidisciplinary. They operate in a climate of entrepreneurship, receive strong support from top management, and have a flexible and indeterminate life-span. They are usually disbanded when the product has been launched successfully and turned over to regular operating groups.

These examples of systematic ways of carrying out the new program generation step in a planning process are neither exhaustive nor necessarily individually recommended. Requests for proposal, concern with climate, brainstorming, issue analysis, and venture teams are merely some of the many solutions to the problem of how best to generate new programs. And, as in the selection of methods for any planning process, the best choice is situationally specific. All of these methods have strengths and weaknesses, and only an evaluation of the specific situation to which the method is to be applied can determine which, if any, is most appropriate.

PROJECT EVALUATION AND RESOURCE ALLOCATION

All organizations have a finite amount of resources (money, facilities, people, and so on) that they must allocate among competing projects in such a way as to accomplish their mission. The program evaluation and resource allocation activity of a planning and control process (step 5 in the model outlined in Table 2–1) includes the information collection and decision-making activities by which resources are divided among projects.

Program life cycles

Any organization may be simultaneously involved in many long-term programs, such as changing its capital structure or modifying its corporate image, and in many short-term programs, such as improving quality control or upgrading its personnel. Any dynamic organization which is continuously initiating, carrying out, and terminating programs of varying natures and time horizons is uniquely characterized by the mix and life-cycle stages of these programs.

It is useful to distinguish between two stages in the life cycle of a program, because each stage requires different methods of resource allocation. The two program stages describe (1) ongoing programs, and (2) still unauthorized new programs or major changes in existing operations.

Efficient organizations continuously review their ongoing programs to ensure that they are still appropriate to the future. Minor changes in the level of resources devoted to existing programs are usually made during the negotiations that are part of budgeting. These activities belong to the responsibility unit planning and control process (cycle 3), which will be discussed in the section on "Responsibility Unit Planning and Control" of this chapter. New programs, or major deviations from existing operations such as discontinuing a program, divesting a division, or significantly altering operations, normally cover such lengthy time spans that they will be formulated and evaluated through an annual capital expenditure procedure.

Evaluation and choice

A discussion of how still unauthorized new programs or major change projects are evaluated can be divided into two topics: (*a*) the procedure and supporting documentation that guide evaluation, and (*b*) the criteria used for evaluation.

Procedure and documentation. Many companies document their investment analysis procedure in a formal manual. This manual is prepared by the investment analysis staff, who are responsible for the coordination, development, and administration of short- and long-range capital plans, the system for reviewing and approving project appropriations, and the reports and management follow-up. Investment analysis may, in effect, be a complete subsystem in which the planning and controlling of capital expenditures are explicitly specified.

One section of the manual, for example, may categorize the projects which are to be submitted for evaluation. Projects can be classified as related to diversification, expansion, the maintenance of existing business, cost reduction, equipment replacement, research and development, or support facilities and equipment; or as related to health, morale, and safety. Other sections of the manual may specify the steps in screening a project, the approval procedure and the expenditure approval limits of the various organizational levels.

The manual usually also describes the documentation required for the initial approval of an appropriation request. The *initial appropriation request* must usually include information about the sponsoring group or department, the classification of the project, and a summary of the expenditures that lists new cash needed, use of existing assets, and the proceeds from disposable assets. A summary of the inflows, a schedule of the timing of the project, and the appropriate signatures backing the project complete the information requirements.

The investment analysis staff is usually responsible for issuing instructions and guides (e.g., cost of capital) to help each operating group prepare its capital expenditure proposals. These proposals are then reviewed by the investment analysis staff. After this review, reconciliation, and consolidation, a capital budget is presented for the approval of an operating policy or executive committee. In the event of a capital rationing situation, the investment analysis staff may use methods such as a portfolio or linear programming allocation model to determine and assign priorities to each project before presenting it for approval.

After the initial appropriation request, two other kinds of capital expenditure documentation are usually required. Whereas a capital budget establishes broad expenditure guidelines, authorization to commit corporate funds for a specific project often requires a second request and approval. The procedure is to submit a *commitment request*, similar to the initial appropriation request, which documents all the required information. This second go-around enables management to achieve greater control over expenditures. Finally, at times a *supplemental appropriation request* may be needed to request funds not originally planned for in an approved project. Often this request is handled by granting a department a supplemental appropriation in order to complete a proposed project, but not providing it with additional funds. This means that the department must find the additional funds in the total capital assigned to it. Used in this way a supplemental appropriation merely reallocates appropriations assigned to other projects and does not consume additional resources.

Evaluation criteria. Criteria and methods of project evaluation may also be specified in the manual. Projects can be evaluated by any or all of at least seven criteria: urgency, payback, accounting rate of return, undiscounted benefit cost-ratio, internal rate of return, or net present value. In addition to these normal methods of evaluation, more analytical techniques may be required, such as using Monte Carlo simulation to capture the probabilistic nature of the project, or performing sensitivity analysis.

SPECIFICATION OF THE LONG-RANGE PLAN

Specification of the long-range plan is the final step of cycle 2 of the multicycle planning process. The long-range plan is prepared within the context of the first cycle and is the input to the third cycle, responsibility unit planning and control. It describes the future relationship of an organization to its environment in terms of the scope and character of both the new and ongoing programs undertaken, the performance expected, and the resources to be committed to them. It is detailed enough to guide subsequent planning. A sample outline of a long-range plan for a manufacturing firm is presented in Table 3–1.

The plan in Table 3–1 defines and characterizes the organization's activities in terms of segments called basic business units. A business unit is a cluster of product and/or market activities that can logically be grouped together. For each business unit the plan describes the products and markets that make it up, the competitive strategy adopted (supported by appropriate industry, market, and competitive analysis), and specific performance expectations. The plan also describes the resources that will be committed, in terms of money, facilities, and personnel; and it includes a risk-return profile and a discussion of any problems the unit may face. Many organizations feel that having their managers complete plans of this comprehensiveness forces them to think through all the critical aspects of their businesses more thoroughly than they

TABLE 3–1
Typical contents of a long-range plan

1. Definition and characterization of each basic business unit (BU).
2. Broad long-term objectives of each BU.
3. Description of products that make up a BU.
    a. Markup.
    b. Distribution policy.
    c. Pricing policy.
4. Description of competitive strategy.*
5. Expected performance by product in terms of volume, growth, market share, life-cycle characteristics.
6. Resources committed.
    a. Financial.
    b. Buildings and equipment.
    c. Personnel.
7. Five-year profit plan by product.
8. Risk-return profile.
9. Work force plan to support product growth.
10. Expected problems: social responsibility, customer attitude, etc.

* Supported by appropriate industry, market, and competitive analysis.

would if only a financial plan were involved, thereby yielding considerable process benefit.

Key variables of the long-range plan

Although a long-range plan contains all the relevant information needed for responsibility unit planning, like the statement of strategic mission it may be too detailed to be communicated and remembered effectively. Therefore, key variables may again be used to convert its qualitative and quantitative aspects into a more manageable form. The key variables must be selected and expressed in a way that minimizes confusion and maximizes understanding of the long-range plan. They must be expressed so that every activity of the firm is directed toward attaining them. Key variables can provide unity of purpose by making the objectives of behavior explicit, improve coordination through communication and understanding, and facilitate goal congruence. Relating activities to KVs minimizes the danger that activities will be misdirected toward inappropriate ends.

The following are examples of result areas that may be selected as key variables: financial performance (measured by rate of return on investment); marketing effectiveness (measured by penetration in terms of number of new outlets or share of markets); product quality, service, or leadership; financial position and stability; customer attitudes; innovative skills in advertising, product development, or uses of products; public responsibility; or capability of employees. These key variables both capture the essence of the strategic mission and long-range plan of an organization, and can also be used to evaluate progress in accomplishing them.

The KVs that describe the organization's long-range plan are logically consistent with, but are more specific than, those that describe the statement of strategic mission. And just as cycle 2 is guided by the KVs of cycle 1, the KVs which describe the plans of cycle 2 in turn guide the planning involved in cycle 3. The planning and control processes that make up cycle 3 (steps 7 and 8 of Table 2–1) are discussed next.

RESPONSIBILITY UNIT PLANNING AND CONTROL

Although a long-range plan is intended to provide the guidelines and performance expectations for subordinate decision making, it must still be translated into a form suitable for execution by a responsibility unit. A responsibility unit is a set of organizational activities for which a particular individual or group can be held accountable. At its most elementary level it is one of the basic operating units that together make up the organization. The process by which an organization's long-range plan is broken down and allocated to these units of delimited responsibility constitutes the third planning and control cycle.

FIGURE 3–3
Cycle 3: Responsibility unit planning and control

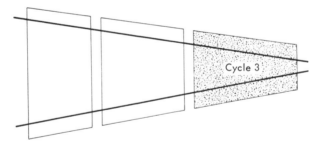

Cycle 3 (steps 7 and 8, Table 2–1) is differentiated from the previous two cycles by its shorter time horizon and its somewhat narrower objectives, which are now expressed in terms of individual responsibility. It identifies the shorter term performance targets or standards required to accomplish the long-range plans, outlines a program of activities to accomplish these expectations, describes the time span of these programs, and associates these with responsibility units. During this cycle the key variables of each responsibility unit are specified and those that are to be monitored and fed back for control are selected. In sum, cycle 3 planning integrates all short-term activities into a cohesive program of action. It is the final cycle of the multicycle process by which the broad range of activities potentially available to the organization is narrowed until specific short-term actions can be chosen.

Budgets are the most familiar means for facilitating short-range planning and control. A budget describes the activities of a responsibility unit in terms of the financial resources required to carry out these activities. Hence, a budget delineates the resources necessary to accomplish a responsibility unit's KVs. A budget is nothing more than a financially based simulation of the activities that the unit will undertake. It is therefore a planning tool, a way of testing the feasibility and desirability of alternative actions. A budget is, first, a means of expressing objectives for the responsibility unit, and secondly a basis by which performance can be evaluated. Tables 3–2 and 3–4 present a typical set of

TABLE 3–2
Operations plans

Operations budget
    1. Revenue plans
        a. Sales by district by period
        b. Sales by product by period
    2. Marketing and distribution plans
        a. Advertising and promotion expenses
        b. Wages and salaries
    3. Production plans
        a. Quantities produced by period
        b. Inventory stocks by period
        c. Material purchases
        d. Direct labor
        e. Manufacturing overhead expense
           i. Producing departments
          ii. Service departments
    4. Administrative expense budget
        a. Labor force budget and head count
        b. Overhead expenses
        c. Personnel department
    5. Special analysis
        a. Cost-volume-profit analysis
        b. By department by product
        c. By territory
Financial plans
    1. Budgeted income statement
    2. Budgeted balance sheet
        a. Depreciation provisions
    3. Cash and funds flow analysis

TABLE 3–3
Classes of key variables useful for control with examples

Qualitative only
    a. Due exercising of professional judgment
    b. Maintain ethical standards
Quantitative only
  Operational
    a. Produce X units
    b. Service Y customers
  Financial
    a. Stay within expenditure levels
    b. Achieve cost-based efficiency
    c. Achieve certain profit level
    d. Achieve specific return on invested capital
Qualitative and quantitative
    a. Level of profits
    b. Market share
    c. Reasonable innovation
    d. Effective development of management
    e. Public responsibility

TABLE 3–4

Performance reports
    1. Profit budget performance report
      a. Sales volume and mix analysis
      b. Price and economic variances
      c. Production and inventory analysis
      d. Marketing and distribution analysis
    2. Expense budget performance report
      a. Production expenses
        i. Material
       ii. Labor
      iii. Overhead
      b. Administrative expenses
    3. Financial plan analysis
      a. Balance sheet depreciation and cash flow
      b. Analysis and reconciliation

short-range responsibility unit plans and their performance reports. Some typical variables used in responsibility unit control are presented in Table 3–3.

SYSTEM EVALUATION AND ADAPTATION

Planning and control are complex, costly, time-consuming management tasks. Each cycle of an organization's planning and control process takes place in a different context under differing conditions, and it can require different methods, procedures, and degrees of organizational integration. In fact, the design of a planning and control system has all the attributes of a task requiring planning and control. Further, if a planning and control system is to be adaptable instead of rigid, that is, if it is to be continually modified to take into account new environmental conditions, there must be a mechanism to adapt it to new situations. Therefore the first step of the nine-step planning and control process model presented in Chapters 2 and 3 involves planning for the planning and control system, and the final step involves evaluation and system adaptation (Table 2–1).

The final or ninth step of the planning and control process uses information on actual performance to evaluate the system designed in step 1 and to adapt it to future requirements as required.

Just as each of the previous steps of the nine-step model can be carried out in many ways, so can the system evaluation and adaptation step. One way an organization may check if its system needs modification is by post-completion audits of capital investments. The purposes of a post-audit are simply to evaluate a project in light of initial expectations, to uncover any reasons for project failure, and to utilize this information to improve the organization's long-range planning and project evaluation. If an audit of all projects proves too expensive, some selection procedure may be invoked. For example, only major projects may be audited; e.g., those costing over $50,000. The organization must also choose a time to begin auditing the project; e.g., after a year, or after debugging and start-up have been completed. Responsibility for conducting a postaudit may be assigned either to the originator of the proposal, to an industrial engineering staff group, or to a central or financial staff member.

Another way to evaluate a planning and control system is by a detailed checklist of procedural and organizational considerations. Procedural considerations may include the following:

1. Does the system provide an appropriate amount of environmental scanning?
2. Does the system provide a clear definition and statement of strategic mission?
3. Does the system provide measures by which the firm's effectiveness in accomplishing its mission can be evaluated?
4. Does the system provide a capability or resource audit?
5. Does the system generate a sufficient number and range of alternatives?
6. Are the information flows among the various cycles in the right directions and in the right amounts?
7. Is the system sufficiently dynamic and flexible to accommodate the environment the organization is now facing?

The following questions may be asked with respect to organizational considerations:

1. Is the commitment to the system from top and middle management and from other employees sufficient to accomplish organizational mission?
2. Does the system fit the managerial style of the organization?
3. Does the system require a specific type of planning organization not now possessed?
4. Are responsibilities for planning assigned to the correct people?
5. Does the system stimulate learning?

One technologically sophisticated organization in the Cambridge, Massachusetts, area assigns the annual audit of its planning and control system to a recently employed MBA graduate. Both the company and the employee benefit from this; the latter receives a solid orientation and overview of the company, and the former is exposed to any new techniques that the student has learned in the MBA program. Another organization uses the same type of approach, but rather than assigning this task to a graduate student it hires a management consultant every four years. They really don't expect the consultant to come up with anything new; but when he or she is unable to suggest anything significant they have greater confidence that they are performing the correct functions.

Progress to the end of Part One

This book is devoted to improving performance of the first and last steps of the nine-step model that has just been surveyed: how to plan and how to evaluate planning and control systems. The approach and discussions so far have been essentially normative; that is, they are descriptions of how planning and control *ought* to be carried out. To carry out normative planning of planning and control requires a conceptual framework which can both guide the systems design process in general and also aid in specifying appropriate methods and techniques. This normative framework must provide a way to conceptualize the problem of designing a planning and control system, as well as providing a descriptive model of how an actual planning and control process is carried out. The first three chapters of this book have provided the system designer with this required normative conceptual framework as well as with a particular approach or orientation to system design.

Chapter 1 introduced an approach to system design based on the notion of specifying and implementing the system that best achieves the needed benefits that planning and control can provide. It was emphasized, for example, that there are many ways of carrying out each step in a planning and control process and that one approach to selecting the best method to carry out each step is first to specify what benefits of planning are needed (e.g., better results or process benefits). The second and third chapters describe a nine-step process model by which multicycle planning and control is conceptualized. Hence Chapters 1, 2, and 3 together provide the approach and conceptual framework required for the normative design or modification of a planning and control system. They provide the perspective and orientation which guide the system designer. The remainder of the book is devoted to providing the design methodology and the tools and techniques necessary to create a complete system.

SUMMARY

Cycle 2 of an organization's multicycle planning process produces a long-range plan consistent with the statement of strategic mission developed in cycle 1. The activities by which an organization attempts to close the planning gap expressed or implied in its statement of strategic mission are initially formulated in terms of programs and financed in terms of projects. The mix and life-cycle stages of its programs uniquely characterize every organization. New programs are one way an organization can close its planning gap. The use of direct delegation, venture teams, issue analysis, or the creation of a supportive climate, are some of the ways of stimulating the generation of new programs.

Resources are initially allocated to programs during the annual capital budgeting process. Actual commitments, however, usually require secondary justification through a commitment request. Supplementary appropriations requests and project performance evaluation reports are also part of the documentation of a project planning and control process.

An organization's long-range plan describes its future relationships with its environment in terms of the scope and character of the operations to be carried out, the performance expected, and the resources to be committed. The basic building block of the long-range plan is the program, project, or business unit. Key variables highlight the critical aspects of the long-range plan in a form that best provides directions and guidelines for subsequent planning.

Cycle 3, short-term program and responsibility unit planning, outlines the activities to be carried out by designated individuals. The budget is the most familiar tool used in this process. Financial plans, performance reports, and nonquantitative control variables all may play a role in this process.

If an organization's overall planning system is to be adaptative to new environmental conditions, explicit consideration must be paid to its planning and control. Post-completion audits of projects, question-type checklists, and detailed procedural audits are some means for testing the appropriateness of the system in use.

QUESTIONS

1. In what situations or for what types of organizations would the use of a quantified planning gap be most effective? Least effective?
2. Which of the three cycles do you think usually receives the most resources and attention? Why? Which cycle holds the greatest potential for improvement?
3. Which is the more important evaluation criterion used in choosing among projects—the rate of return on the capital invested (or net present value, and so on) or the degree to which the project fits into the strategic plans of the organization? Why?
4. To which steps in an organization's nine-step planning and control process do the methods and techniques contained in texts on managerial accounting relate?
5. What determines the linkage between cycles? Specifically, to what extent should the output of one cycle constrain subsequent planning?
6. In what situations should strategic planning be carried out independently of responsibility unit planning and control?
7. Why does the formulation of the long-range plan follow project planning and resource allocation and not precede it?

REFERENCES AND BIBLIOGRAPHY

Bower, Joseph L. *Managing the Resource Allocation Process: A Study of Corporate Planning and Investment.* Boston: Harvard Business School, 1970.

Cannon, J. T. *Business Strategy and Policy.* New York: Harcourt, Brace and World, 1968.

Cohen, K. J., and Cyert, R. M. Strategy; Formulation, implementation and monitoring. *Journal of Business,* July 1973, pp. 349–67.

Fairaizl, Alan F., and Mullick, Satinder, K. A corporate planning system. *Management Accounting* (U.S.), December 1975, pp. 13–17.

Glueck, W. F. *Business Policy: Strategy Formation and Management Actions.* New York: McGraw-Hill Book Company, 1972.

Karger, D. W. Integrated formal long-range planning, how to do it. *Long-Range Planning.* December 1973, pp. 34–38.

Lamphere, Robert J., Program Budgeting at John Hancock Life Insurance in D. Novick, ed., *Current Practices in Program Budgeting,* New York: Crang, Russell & Company, Inc., 1973.

Litschert, R. J. Some characteristics of long range planning: An industry study. *Academy of Management Journal,* September 1968, pp. 315–28.

Lorange, Peter, and Scott, Morton S.   A framework for management control systems. *Sloan Management Review*, Fall 1974, pp. 87–96.

McCaskey, Michael B.   A contingency approach to planning: Planning with goals. *Academy of Management Journal*, June 1974, pp. 281–91.

Newman, W. H.   *Constructive Control: Design and Use of Control Systems.* Englewood Cliffs, N.J.: Prentice-Hall, Inc., 1975.

Shank, John K. et al.   Balance "Creativity" and "Practicality" in Formal Planning. *Harvard Business Review*, January–February 1973, pp. 87–95.

Stokes, P. M.   *A Total Systems Approach to Management Control.* New York: American Management Associations, 1968.

Case study 3–1

Fliggleman, Feldman, Ginsberg, and Grant: Public Accountants (A)

BACKGROUND

Fliggleman, Feldman, Ginsberg, and Grant (FFGG) is a medium-sized firm of CPAs with national office in Detroit and member firms located in Chicago, New York, Boston, Philadelphia, Denver, Los Angeles, and San Francisco. The firm has a tradition of professional excellence; the number of CPA exam medal winners it has consistently attracted is far out of proportion to its size. Former members of the firm have gone on to major executive positions with the largest corporations and governmental agencies.

The client mix of FFGG covers industrial, retail, service, and financial enterprises as well as government, educational, and other nonprofit organizations. Clients range in size from small to large organizations with medium-sized businesses dominating.

The guiding philosophy of the firm is to give maximum benefits to their clients by providing individualized service. To this end FFGG strives to maintain the highest standards of professional excellence, to foster democratic involvement within the firm, and to maintain a moderate rate of growth.

EXTERNAL ENVIRONMENT

The environment in which FFGG operates is both stable and dynamic. As a professional accounting practice, it is guided by professional ethos and governed or influenced by formalized institutions such as the American Institute of Certified Public Accountants and the Securities and Exchange Commission, respectively.

The services offered by accounting firms are fairly homogeneous and standardized. Being a professional practice, overt promotional activities are forbidden. Most firms therefore rely on "quality of service" to differentiate themselves in the professional arena as well as in the marketplace. A reputation for professional excellence and word of mouth referrals are the major ways to generate additional business.

Since any given organization is likely to have the same firm audit its books each year, accounting firms usually maintain a steady clientele. Furthermore, because of the mandatory requirement for an annual audit, demand for audit services is immune to economic fluctuations.

There are also some dynamic elements in the environment which require appropriate responses. In recent years the demand for the profession's services has increased and widened in scope. Increased demand is partly a result of government requirements, and partly stimulated by the needs of growing clients. Company law has become more exacting, the complexity of tax rules has grown inordinately, and standards of accounting practice are constantly rising. Changes in these and other regulations tend to demand increasingly elaborate and sophisticated skills from the profession. Pressure has intensified by the threat—following changes in laws of negligence—of much severer claims for damages if things go wrong. Also productivity is a concern since the costs of personnel have risen rapidly recently while the fees clients are willing to pay for an audit remains relatively fixed.

One response to these changing conditions is an increasing emphasis on the quality of personnel hired by accounting firms. Firms must now offer higher salaries and provide expensive training to competent and qualified recruits. To ensure independence they are attempting to rely less on a few large clients and to distribute their work load among a variety of organizations. Some firms attempt to cope with change by diversifying into other types of services such as management consulting, which is beyond the jurisdiction of regulatory agencies and accounting institutes. Others choose to specialize in fields such as taxation and bankruptcy, as well as continuing to provide traditional auditing services.

Although accountancy is a service with few fixed costs and few economies of scale, many of these strategies require considerable financial and human resources and so larger firms hold out a much greater prospect for success. Thus medium-size and small firms attempt to compete by expanding through amalgamation and mergers. Some attempt to affiliate themselves with foreign firms or enlist foreign affiliates. In general, to the extent that accounting firms experience the strains of competition and growth, they are competitive businesses rather than professional practices.

ORGANIZATION OF THE FIRM

FFGG evolved from an association of eight independent firms, each of which developed a well-established regional practice. Some firms have more than one office. Each firm has its own internal structure. Each member firm is headed by an administrative committee annually elected by its partners. Below the partners are managers, supervisors, senior accountants, accountants, and students.

Consistent with the desires of professionals, FFGG's policy is that member firms operate largely autonomously. The national office exists to provide services to the eight member firms. It serves in maintaining uniformly high standards of practice, in staff training, research and development, and in other areas where benefits accrue to individual firms through the advantages of belonging to a large organization. The national office is headed by an annually elected management committee consisting of two partners from each of the eight member firms.

THE PLANNING AND CONTROL PROCESS

Although FFGG does not have a formalized planning and control system, it does have procedures designed to perform some of these functions. These procedures are fairly consistently applied, although ad hoc adjustments are often made to fit particular situations.

The national office primarily handles two functions—that of providing services to the member firms, and of handling decisions that affect the entire firm, most notably growth.

FFGG prefers to grow through mergers which are looked after by the national office management committee. Often, however, impetus to merge comes from a member firm. The target candidate for FFGG is a firm with aging partners and good clients since this type of firm will provide ample opportunities for FFGG men of ability to move up in the ranks, and good clients to enhance the profit position and reputation of the firm. Before a decision to merge is made, however, local reactions are thoroughly assessed. If a member firm is directly involved, it is actively consulted. Merger decisions are made at the national partnership meeting where all partners are present and must be carried by a two-thirds majority. This process of consultation and agreement is intended to assure local autonomy and to maintain democratic involvement.

The primary planning and control mechanism for FFGG is the annual budget. As the national office exists only to provide service, the budget for its services is drawn up by the management committee every spring and then submitted to the member firms for approval. Once the member firms have agreed to the total budget estimate, the members of the management committee determine each firm's assessment.

The most important planning task for each member firm is the scheduling process performed each spring. When mutually agreeable, the partners and managers within each office develop a master schedule for the next year. Estimates of each client's requirements for the coming year are based on previous years. By an iterative process all members of each office from the top down are successively assigned to clients. Continuity for each client is sought whenever possible to ensure that past knowledge and rapport are maintained. At the end of this process all members within an office know which client they will be working for, with whom they will be working, and the time during the year the work will be performed.

This scheduling process serves many purposes: first, it effectively plans and produces the plan for the following year; second, an estimate of income can be made; third, it is a short and precise procedure eliminating a lengthy and time-consuming bargaining for assignments; fourth, it indicates in advance the labor force requirements for the following year; and finally, it provides the data needed to ensure the appropriate career development of personnel through broad exposure to a wide range of clients and co-workers.

Each manager in a unit headed by a partner is responsible for setting the audit budget for each job to be performed. Prior to an audit, the manager draws up a budget, not in dollars but in work hours based on prior year requirements. This budget is then approved by the partner in charge before the audit is undertaken. During each audit, expenses and revenues are recorded and a monthly profit and loss statement is produced for each client that the partner has under audit. These monthly reports are then submitted to the firm's administrative committee where comparisons are based on last year's performance. Through this periodic reporting, partners are kept informed of their profit position and managers receive immediate feedback on how well they are fulfilling their responsibilities.

Performance evaluation is influenced by FFGG's corporate philosophy of individualized service to clients and a moderate rate of growth. Quality of service is the most important element in evaluation procedures. Hence, formal monthly and year-end evaluations by each firm's administrative committee are de-emphasized and subjective assessments are relied on.

Like most CPA firms, staff performance is constantly monitored and guidance and evaluation are provided whenever necessary. The firm's documented procedures recommend that formal evaluation programs be carried out after each assignment to provide participants with immediate feedback on their performance. However, these are often deferred indefinitely, especially during peak periods. Although participants do not actively set their own performance criteria, frequent informal evaluations ensure that they have a sufficient knowledge of the standards used to measure performance and how they are performing against these expectations.

Questions

1. Is the planning and control process used by FFGG compatible with its operating environment, the nature of its activities, and the type of people employed?
2. Does the firm carry out strategic planning, program planning and resource allocation, and/or responsibility unit planning and control?
3. What improvements would you suggest in the way planning and control are carried out in this firm?

Case study 3–2

Meat Inspection Services (A)

A series of significant events drew the government's attention to the way meat inspections were being carried out in the province. The first was a Canadian Television Network (CTV) province by province survey of inspection practices. The resulting prime time TV special alerted the public to the wide disparity in inspections carried out; e.g. between the northern and southern regions of the province. The program also reported that the hamburger being sold in many supermarkets had a significantly high bacteria count, and that meat from diseased animals was being sold in butcher shops. The program claimed that some of the meat used in processed meat products was not fit for human consumption.

Following the CTV program, several of the investigative newspapers in the province published well-researched articles on the subject. Included were accounts of salvagers supplying butchers with tainted meat. The papers reported that several butchers were repeatedly convicted for selling horse meat but, after paying nominal fines, were allowed to continue operation. These papers claimed that the provincial government was aware of these practices but had relegated the whole question of meat inspection to a low priority because of public indifference.

The stream of mail and telephone calls to members of the Provincial Legislature, which had started with the television program, now became a flood. The minister of agriculture had seen the TV program, however, and had already asked for an early report by his staff.

The Department of Agriculture (see Exhibit 1 for its organization chart) had known for some time of the disparity in meat inspection services in the province. In fact it had received a delegation from the Consumers' Association pointing out irregularities. The Department Management Committee had tentatively identified a need for some sort of action, and had given it a relatively high priority among the new initiative proposals to be included in the department's mutliyear plan.

EXHIBIT 1

Organization chart of the Provincial Government and the Department of Agriculture

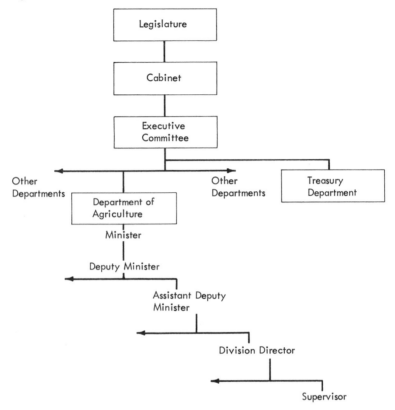

Note: A parliamentary system of government is used. Responsibility for developing and implementing policy in a parliamentary system of government is divided between elected and appointed officials as follows:

The political party electing the majority of members to the legislature holds power. The leader of that party becomes the premier; i.e., the provincial leader. His cabinet is chosen from the elected members of his party.

Responsibility for the development and approval of policy ultimately rests with the cabinet, subject to approval of the legislature. The premier is the chairman of cabinet.

The functions of government are carried out by departments consisting of appointed civil servants. The head of each department, called a minister, is an elected member of the majority party and all ministers are members of cabinet.

The Treasury Department is also headed by a cabinet minister. It has the responsibility of scrutinizing, questioning, and then approving funds for the implementation of all government programs. The Treasury Department's function is similar to that of the controller of a business organization.

PRELIMINARY INVESTIGATION

Although the director of the veterinary services division was in charge of all slaughterhouse and dead and diseased animal disposal inspection services, the deputy minister felt it was more appropriate to have the department's director of research look into these complaints, to analyse the nature of the response required, and to report back within two weeks.

The research director's report outlined the existing situation and confirmed that the province's meat inspection services were not in sound order. There were rumors of animals being improperly fed before slaughter; e.g., it was alleged that feed companies were including strychnine in the feed supplied to farmers raising chicks for them because this chemical added significant weight, and cattle were being fattened with illegal drugs. He also reported that there appeared to be too few inspectors to oversee the operations of the rendering plants which salvaged hides, oil and bone meal from dead animals. There was no licensing of traders in dead and diseased animals. He also reported the recent conviction and dismissal of one meat inspector for selling tainted meat to butchers as a sideline. And he confirmed the facts that a number of retailers had been repeatedly convicted of selling horse meat, and that the bacteria level in some hamburger being sold at retail was higher than recommended.

Based on his findings, the director of research recommended that a more in-depth study be undertaken by the department with the view to recommending some sort of action. The minister concurred with the director's recommendation. In response to a question in the legislature he stated that a study involving public hearings and the receipt of briefs would be undertaken by the Department of Agriculture.

Responsibility for this study was again given to the director of research. He was told that it was top priority and agreed to report back to the minister within two months.

THE STUDY

In discussions with his superior, the assistant deputy minister (ADM), the director of research outlined a two-phase plan for conducting the in-depth study.

Phase I—Information collection

This phase of the study would include the following aspects:

1. Advertising and then holding six public hearings.
2. Receiving and analyzing briefs from interested parties.

3. Following up sources of information within the department and other branches of government.
4. Examining the number of food inspection service systems operated both inside and outside of the province.
5. Surveying the state of inspector training.
6. Studying the administrative and records systems.
7. Studying the structure of the fresh and processed meat industry.

The director of research proposed that, at the end of Phase I, an interim presentation and report be prepared for review by the minister. This would summarize the findings to date, present possible alternatives for improvement, and outline Phase II of the study. Continuing with Phase II would then depend on the minister's evaluation of Phase I.

Phase II—Review, report preparation, and decision making

Phase II would tentatively include the following:

1. Completion of the analysis of the alternatives selected during Phase I.
2. Preparation of a policy submission to cabinet.
3. Summarization of the work, and preparation of a policy statement for the minister to make in the legislature.

PHASE I: INFORMATION COLLECTION AND ANALYSIS

The seven activities making up Phase I of the study were carried out without delay. The six public hearings were advertised and completed. Advertisements for briefs were placed and 35 were received. Following up on sources within the department, the research director pieced together a complete list of the inspections being carried out on dead animals and on the fresh and processed meat in the province. Field visits were carried out both inside and outside the province. The Treasury Department approved the hiring of consultants to conduct activities 5, 6, and 7. The consultants were hired, conducted their inquiries, and reported their findings.

During the many meetings which took place, the director and the ADM chose the four criteria they would use to select the improvement options to be presented to the minister. These were the following:

1. Amount of unfit meat reaching the public.
2. Amount of disruption to the industry.
3. Costs of providing inspection services.
4. Uniformity within the province.

They also agreed that all improvement options would have to eliminate any future complaints in the media.

RELATIONSHIP TO MINISTRY OBJECTIVES

At this point they proposed an unquantified policy aim for any new program that would be developed, namely: To provide the highest quality meat and meat products to the public at the lowest price.

The director and the ADM agreed that this objective was consistent with the department's documented overall objective: To provide the optimum agricultural system for the people of the province through the effective utilization of all available resources.

OTHER CONSIDERATIONS

In addition to ensuring that their objective coincided with the department's, they developed satisfactory answers to as many of the questions as they could anticipate such as the following: Had the analysis really concentrated on the right problem? Were there people who were actually suffering from receiving poor food? Would higher meat inspection costs push the price of meat beyond the range of most consumers? Were there procedural or administrative problems in the way inspections were being carried out that could be attended to quickly? Was this the right place for the government to make an investment in the "health" of its population?

Of all these questions the last was perhaps the toughest to deal with. There were many demands for funds to improve situations in all areas of government responsibility. Both men realized, however, that the enormous weight of public pressure for government action stirred up by the media increased the relative importance of their problem. They also recognized that there would be different rates at which any new initiatives could be implemented and that this question would need to be answered.

All these considerations were discussed in the research director's Phase I report which he presented to the Department Management Committee nine weeks after being given authorization to proceed.

KEY FINDINGS OF PHASE I

The key findings of the Phase I presentation were as follows:

Inspection both of the disposal of dead and diseased animals, and also of live animals at slaughterhouses were severely wanting. At the slaughterhouses inspectors were lax in performing their duty to inspect animals before and after slaughter. There was an insufficient number of veterinarians and lay inspectors, and the lay inspectors were insufficiently trained in animal diseases to recognize problems. Little inspection of dead and diseased animals shipped to rendering plants was carried out in the province until the mid-1960s and current efforts were erratic.

Only a few flagrant irregularities had been prosecuted; one particular example is that of meat inspectors accepting bribes from the plants in which they worked.

There were many small slaughterhouses operating in the province for only a half day to one day per week, without any inspection. These slaughterhouses were an essential part of rural life and served farmers who had two or three cows for butchering and sale to local shops. Enforcing rigid sanitary conditions on these slaughterhouses would drive them out of business.

The scare of unfit meat was driving beef prices down. Both retailers and restauranteurs reported people shifting to other products such as vegetables and fish. Foreign buyers of exported Canadian food products were also reported as being wary. Beef producers were suffering because of these events and their Provincial Association had begun lobbying members. They felt very frustrated because all this was happening to their product after it had left their control.

There was no coordinated national meat inspection policy. The federal government's Department of Agriculture was only responsible for inspecting meat products which crossed provincial boundaries, were scheduled for export, or were imported. The federal Department of Health had an overall concern with the health of the population of Canada and served as de facto inspectors of food. At the provincial level, the province was divided up into 12 regions and inspections were carried out in each under the direction of a regional veterinarian and a staff of veterinarian and lay inspectors. In addition to inspectors of the veterinary services division of the Department of Agriculture, provincial health inspectors from the Department of Health were concerned with unfit meat and were obligated by statute to report any discrepancies they observed. Provincial inspection was only required of meat slaughterhouses providing meat for sale through retailers, however. Farmers who wished to slaughter their own products and sell directly to the consumers, as they did in many markets, were not obligated to have their products inspected. Inspection at the retail level fell under the jurisdiction of municipal public health officers who inspected groceries and butcher shops as well as restaurants. There was poor communication between all levels of government with significant duplication of services in some areas and no inspections in others.

There was little evidence of cattle and chicken being fed illegal feeds although the director of research admitted this is very difficult to discover.

The provincial Department of Justice had difficulty prosecuting those found guilty of selling either horse meat or improperly killed animals because of their need for a well-documented case. Usually they were unable to secure sufficient evidence because agricultural inspectors and public health officials were not trained to keep proper notes of their visits and inspections.

There were reports that frozen beef shipped from Australia was being thawed, cut, and then refrozen before being sold.

There were widely differing attitudes and levels of interest around the province. It appeared that concern was great in the mid-size cities but in both larger cities and in the rural areas, very little was being expressed.

ALTERNATIVE STRATEGIES

After reviewing the evidence accumulated, the director suggested five actions that could be taken to improve the situation.

1. Education
   a. Inspectors. Educate both dead animal and fresh and processed meat inspectors better—have them work closer with scientists developing meat inspection evaluation techniques.
   b. Trade. Inform farmers, plant owners, workers, and dealers as to both their legal and moral obligations.
   c. General public. Inform the general public about the methods of inspection carried out, the required labels, and what to look for when buying meat.
2. Increase and improve the existing inspection system
   a. Increase both the number of lay and veterinary inspectors.
   b. Rotate inspectors among districts and plants to ensure that no collusion develops.
   c. Rely more on Humane Society agents.
   d. Rely more on provincial and municipal health officials.
   e. Require stricter controls and reporting by veterinarians treating diseased animals.
3. Improve administration
   a. Require records of all meat used to make processed meat products.
   b. Maintain detailed records of all animals and check these against tax records.
   c. Increase fines for violations.
   d. Develop an interprovincial exchange of information on diseased animals.
   e. Require tainted meat shipped to dog food manufacturers to be placed in boxes filled top and bottom with charcoal to warn anyone that it is unfit for human consumption.
4. Change inspection responsibility
   a. Contract out regional inspection services to private firms who would be licensed by the government to inspect all dead, diseased, and slaughtered animals in the province.
   b. Set up a separate governmental agency with inspection and enforcement powers.

5. Modify the structure of the industry
    a. Reduce the number of salvage and rendering plants operating in the province to ensure stricter inspection.
    b. Subsidize the reorganization and amalgamation of smaller processors into larger economic operations.
    c. Subsidize or take over the operation of plants that cannot otherwise meet sanitary conditions.
    d. Develop a government insurance program thereby reducing the need to sell diseased animals for meat.

In his presentation to the Department Management Committee, the director outlined two implementation rates—"fast" and "normal." The former meant an all-out effort to implement with money being no object, while the latter represented a well-organized but somewhat lower rate.

The director of research presented a number of charts showing the impact on the quantity of unfit meat being consumed in the province if each af these five alternatives were undertaken. He cautioned that his figures were all educated guesses at best and should be treated as such. He estimated that, at present, 1.5 percent of all meat and meat products being sold in the province was not properly inspected.

His charts showed that all options would produce dramatic reductions in the amount of uninspected meat reaching the province's population. Over time, option 5 (restructuring the industry) would produce the largest reduction in unfit meat but would also be the most expensive. Option 1 (education) would be the least expensive but would also have the minimum impact. Options 4(a) and 4(b) were essentially identical with 4(a) being somewhat lower in cost. The charts indicated that option 2 (an improved inspection system), would not produce as great a reduction as option 4 but would be the most cost effective.

The director also pointed out several additional considerations. He cautioned that there might be strong opposition and political pressure to option 5. Farmers and rural members could be expected to fight vigorously to maintain the existing patterns of rural life. He pointed out that options 2 and 4(b) would increase government staff levels, something which the government had promised not to do. He stated that although option 4(a), reprivatizing the inspection services, would result in a significant reduction in the number of people employed by the government it would require a large outlay in the early years to help private operators establish themselves.

An assistant deputy minister raised the question of how consistent each of these proposed alternatives was with the government's overall objectives for the province. The director replied that, in his opinion, it made little difference which action the department chose since all actions were consistent with overall government goals.

PRELIMINARY SCREENING AND GO AHEAD

The minister was then asked for guidance as to Phase II. He said that of the options presented, he did not feel that option 5, restructuring of the industry, would be politically acceptable. Accordingly he advised abandonment of this alternative. He was, however, sufficiently impressed by the predicted improvement of the other options to retain them for consideration. His personal preference was for option 4(a), that of handing the responsibility for inspection over to the private sector. The minister was a great believer in reducing government involvement and felt that this option represented a way to achieve that objective. He felt, however, that his cabinet colleagues should have a chance to review the other alternatives. He therefore recommended that Phase II be undertaken but with option 5 removed from further consideration.

PHASE II

The deputy minister confirmed the reassignment of the director of research to conduct Phase II.

The director now moved to complete the analysis and presentation of the alternatives selected in the Phase I review, with a view to preparing a policy submission to the Executive Committee of Cabinet. In three weeks, using the material already collected, and with the assistance of other agricultural staff, he prepared a policy paper and a formal presentation. After final review by the Department Management Committee in which the minister restated his preference for option 4(a), the paper was released ten days later.

There was some delay in discussing the policy recommendations with the Executive Committee of Cabinet, however. First, it was difficult to get on the agenda as there were a number of important issues facing cabinet at this time. When it finally made the agenda, there was not a quorum at the committee meeting. The second time it was on the agenda, the Executive Committee did not get to it. It was finally discussed on its third appearance, four weeks after being submitted.

During this discussion, many of the questions anticipated by the ADM and the director were raised and answered satisfactorily, The minister of agriculture then recommended the fastest possible implementation of option 4(a). Not only was he prepared to move it to the top of the department's list of priorities being considered in the multiyear plan, but he also felt that it should start in the current fiscal year. The Executive Committee, after giving consideration to all new issues from other departments, agreed to support this recommendation. They recommended to cabinet that this option be adopted for earliest possible implementation subject to Treasury's approval of the implementation plan. Cabinet endorsed this recommendation at their next meeting.

In somewhat greater detail, option 4(a) included the following:

1. Arranging territorial boundaries, calling for tenders and developing contractual terms for the new inspection organizations.
2. Transferring existing inspection staffs to the private sector organizations.
3. Establishing standards for the requisite knowledge of all inspectors.
4. Training and licensing all lay inspectors.
5. Ensuring the inspection and re-licensing of all agents, traders, and plants in the province.

At this point the Department of Agriculture was committed to a quantified objective: To reduce the amount of uninspected meat reaching the province's consumers from 1.5 percent to 0.6 percent of the total sold within four years of policy approval.

POLICY IMPLEMENTATION

Responsibility for policy implementation was then to be transferred to the director of veterinary services. Unfortunately, he chose this time to leave the public service and to return to private veterinary practice. Because of this, responsibility stayed with the director of research and a search was begun for a new director of veterinary services.

The director of research obtained the ADM's initial approval of a draft set of terms of reference for a working group involving himself, one of his senior analysts, a staffing specialist from the department's personnel division, and a budget accountant from the department's finance division. The director also arranged for a series of informal meetings with an analyst from the programs and estimates division of the Treasury Department.

In two meetings of this working group, they reached agreement on their terms of reference, individual responsibilities, and work schedule. The group agreed that they could only claim successful completion of their task when Treasury approved the following parts of their implementation plan:

1. A key events list with appropriate dates.
2. Budget proposals for the remainder of the fiscal year and for each of the four following years.
3. Proposals for measuring and reporting results.

They recognized that in order to obtain Treasury approval they would need to develop a number of alternatives for implementing the chosen policy option, and to present these in the format most likely to facilitate that department's understanding of them.

At this stage they recommended to the ADM that legal assistance be obtained to start drafting enabling legislation. This was approved and a legal officer was assigned to work with the group.

IMPLEMENTATION ALTERNATIVES

After approximately three weeks, the working committee was able to make a presentation to the Department Management Committee.

After confirming the policy objective, they presented two alternative schemes designed to accomplish it. The schemes were virtually identical except for the methods for training the inspectors. Scheme 1 featured centralized inspector training while scheme 2 featured decentralized training. Scheme 2 would require six more staff positions than scheme 1. Of these four could be hired on contract and released after three years once the backlog of partially trained inspectors had been cleared.

The budget estimates for 1973–74 and the next four years were virtually identical. The decentralized option would cost less in space than the centralized option. However this saving would be offset by the higher salary, transportation and communication expenses.

The working group recognized that there might be difficulties in obtaining a uniform quality of inspection training under the decentralization alternative; however they suggested that this would show up in examinations and corrective action could be taken.

For the above reasons the key events lists were identical for both schemes 1 and 2. The list showed that the new organization could be expected to have an impact on meat inspection practices in the province within 34 weeks of the date of approval.

After considerable analysis, the working group recommended adoption of decentralized training because, in most cases, the inspectors could reside at home while taking the training.

The working group recognized it had left many details to be worked out but believed it had presented sufficient information and analysis to enable the department to gain Treasury approval for an action plan. The working group also suggested that if its recommendations were acceptable to the department and to the Treasury Department, it should disband and let the new director of veterinary services carry the implementation further. Their recommendations were accepted by the Department Management Committee, subject to approval by Treasury.

PRESENTATION TO TREASURY

The director of research made the presentation to the Treasury Department outlining the objectives of the program, the commitment to establishing the key events listed, and the resources required for each alternative. Based on this presentation, Treasury recommended cabinet acceptance of the decentralized training alternative.

After the key events list was approved, a Treasury analyst suggested that the ministry make an initial progress report at some convenient point. Accordingly a date six months in the future was selected. In addition the department agreed to inform Treasury immediately if there was any deviation from the schedule of key events.

Cabinet accepted all Treasury recommendations and approval by the legislature was obtained.

PROGRAM IMPLEMENTATION

Hiring of a new director of veterinary services coincided with approval of the implementation plan by the Treasury Department. He hired four supervisors, for inspector training, contract negotiations, licensing, and administration who in turn, hired the required staff, all within the time allowed by the key events list. The new director and two of the supervisors were hired from outside the government. All others came from within the public service but from other departments.

The new director of veterinary services immediately began implementation by developing a statement of objectives for himself. After some discussion, he reached agreement with the ADM on his objectives. These covered the balance of the 1973–74 fiscal year, the start of the period of the changeover from a government run inspection services to one run by the private sector.

The director then moved to achieve the job objectives he set. He faced a number of interrelated questions in doing so, however, such as:

1.   What is the nature of the work that has to be done?
2.   How should his new organization be structured to fit this work?
3.   How should the transition between a government run service and a private run service be made?

He began to answer these questions by first subdividing the work to be done into components. A work component for him was the identifiable output of an individual or a group. The work components he identified were both controllable in terms of their costs (salaries, wages, transportation and communication, and so on) and well-defined so that responsibility could be explicity assigned.

After analyzing the future work load of his division into work components, he identified a number of quantifiable outputs for each and the staff members who could be held responsible for these. He recognized, of course, that many of these outputs required the cooperative efforts of a number of his staff and that responsibilities would overlap. Nevertheless he felt it was best to specify the results that had to be accomplished.

When the director of veterinary services drafted, discussed, and reached agreement on these outputs with the ADM, he turned to the task of establishing his subordinates' objectives.

PREPARING FOR INTERIM REPORTING

A few weeks later the new director and the Department of Agriculture's director of finance and administration met to discuss the six-month progress review which the Treasury Department had requested. One question they expected to be raised concerned the means the director of veterinary services was using to measure his performance and the performance of his division. The directors therefore agreed that a division MIS should be developed to provide the detailed information needed both for division decision making as well as for Treasury's evaluation.

Questions

1. What problem were they trying to solve?
2. How did they go about doing it?
    a. Identify and list in chronological order the activities that are described in this case, including any decisions that were made.
    b. Develop a process model (i.e., identify the cycles and the steps within cycles) describing the way the problem was solved. How many cycles can you identify?
3. What did they come up with? Evaluate the quality of their solution.
4. If you were responsible for solving this problem, what would you have done? Why?

part two

Framework and approach

Chapter outline

4

An organizational framework for situational systems design

When you have completed this chapter you will understand:

1. Some of the situational determinants of a planning and control system.
2. Some alternative organizational structures and the reasons that organizations choose different structures.
3. How differences in structure affect systems design.
4. The factors necessitating decentralization, the prerequisites for its success, and how decentralization affects systems design.
5. How the analysis of organizational structure and degree of decentralization provides an initial understanding of what a planning and control system should accomplish.

A FRAMEWORK FOR DESIGN

Any planning and control system attempts to help an organization accomplish its task and meet its expectations. The best system is the one that stimulates, assists, and guides the behavior most appropriate to the accomplishment of these expectations. System design thus involves diagnosing what the system must do and then tailoring a general model to fit these unique situational requirements.

The previous two chapters have outlined a process model and have given some examples of the tools and techniques that can make up a planning and control system. The nine-step model proposed in Chapter 2 may seem a sensible description of how an organization should plan and control its activities. However, close examination reveals that this model is far too general to be of much operational use. It is not supported by any explanation of why or where it is applicable or inapplicable. Before a particular planning system can be specified, the following questions must be answered:

1. How many cycles should the process have? And what determines the number of cycles required in a planning and control process?
2. Who should carry out each cycle, and who should have responsibility for the decisions made in each cycle? In what directions should information flow—top down, bottom up, or both ways?
3. What determines the overall timing: how often should an organization go through a complete planning process? How much time should be allotted to the performance of each cycle in the process?

The answer to these questions regarding activities, involvement and timing is simply, "It depends." The answers are contingent on the situation in which the sytem will be used. For example, the number of cycles in a planning and control process and the time required for their performance depend on the nature of the problem that an organization wants to solve, and on who is to solve it. The complexity of the problem itself may determine the number of cycles required to decompose it into manageable proportions. The number of cycles may also depend on who is to be involved in the planning. Planning may be distributed throughout various units, such as staff groups, divisions, or departments, so that each performs a cycle; or it may be handled entirely by a single organizational unit, such as one staff group. The way in which responsibility for planning is distributed depends in turn on how the organization allocates authority for decision making. Therefore, the three-cycle model presented in Table 2–1 of Chapter 2 should be regarded as a hypothetical description of a planning and control process; an actual model can be formulated only after all relevant factors have been examined.

Understanding the particular characteristics of an organization is the first step toward specifying the details of a planning and control system. This situational analysis is required to determine what is expected of each organizational responsibility unit participating in the planning and control process. Only when this information is obtained can the most appropriate planning and control system be specified. Each and every particular organizational design is chosen because it provides many benefits. But each design also carries with it many disadvantages that must be overcome. The design of the planning and control system associated with a particular organizational design must therefore ensure that the advantages of the organizational form are realized while the weaknesses are compensated.

Thus this chapter considers alternative organizational designs in order to provide some understanding of the different demands that each may place on a planning and control system.

Differentiation and decentralization

Since planning and control systems support a variety of organizational activities, and can be used to accomplish many different ends, an understanding of how an organization structures itself (differentiation) and allocates responsibility (decentralization) is necessary in order to design effective systems. First, however, it is important to point out the circular nature of the relationship between these two factors and planning and control systems.

Research has shown that organizations are generally structured in a way that helps accomplish their strategies. In other words, strategy determines structure and responsibility allocation. One purpose of a planning and control system (and the prime purpose of cycle 1 of the nine-step model discussed here, for example) is to help an organization determine what its strategy should be. And one output of the strategic planning process may be a recommendation to change the organization's structure and allocation of responsibility.

While the sense of this chronological sequence is acknowledged, it is also recognized that, like most problem solving, these decisions make up a continuous, interdependent, circular process. But if this is the case, and if it is accepted that all planning and control systems are situationally specific, where does one begin the system design activity? What is the fixed point to be used as the basis for design? What, in other words, describes the situation the system must fit if the system, in turn, may modify the situation?

Of the many dimensions that could be used to characterize organizations, the two that have been selected for the framework developed in this book are the way they are subdivided or differentiated, and the extent to which authority to make decisions is decentralized. The way an organization chooses to decompose or specialize the tasks it must accomplish in order to implement its strategy, and the degree of autonomy allowed the managers of responsibility units carrying out these tasks, significantly influence the requirements its planning and control system must satisfy. Hence these factors will be used as the "fixed" dimensions which characterize the stiuation a planning and control system must fit.

The way an organization differentiates and decentralizes itself determines what it does, how it functions, and the conditions it perceives it must satisfy in order to be successful. Differentiation into subunits (e.g., functional departments or product divisions) determines the potential scope or range of activities which each subunit can undertake. For example, if an organization is divided functionally, the relevant subsectors may be marketing, finance, and industrial relations. On the other hand, if it is subdivided by product every subunit may be involved in all of these areas of activity. But since the planning and control carried out within each subunit involve decision making, a second critical aspect is the authority to make decisions, i.e., decentralization. Decentralization determines the range of discretion allowed each subunit. For example, if all industrial relations problems are assigned to a staff group then they will not fall under the authority of a product division manager. Although they are potentially part of the manager's activity, the organization's choice to centralize them within a staff group removes them from his or her sphere of discretion. The manner in which an organization differentiates and decentralizes itself significantly influences its planning and control system requirements.

DIFFERENTIATION

An organization differentiates itself into subunits so that each faces a more homogeneous and manageable environment. Each subunit is differentiated (specialized) so that it is better able to tackle the subproblems it is assigned. Activities are grouped together in light of the material and human resources available and the nature of the information to be gathered and processed, so that the probability of effective performance will be improved.

Differentiation is necessary because organizational-environmental interaction is far too complex to be tackled holistically. Second, because the component tasks of this interaction differ significantly from each other in many ways (degree of inherent structure, amount of uncertainty, stability, and so on) organizations differentiate themselves so that the subunits that handle each of these different tasks can become specialized.

Of particular concern to the designer of a planning and control system is the nature of the activities carried out in each subunit. The nature of the organizational and environmental interaction assigned to a subunit influences its time horizon for planning, the degree of uncertainty it must contend with, its required degree of responsiveness, and the specialized skills and judgment it needs. Subunits may also differ in values, attitudes, and formality of management. These characteristics may significantly influence the type of planning and control system required by the subunit to successfully complete its task.

It is also important to understand how organizational subunits are integrated with each other and with the structure as a whole. Integration can be defined as the extent to which an organization functions as a cohesive whole. Many organizations are made up of loosely coupled, distinct segments, each with its own outlook and orientation. Coordination among subunits is necessary in order to ensure consistent goals, rational problem solving, integrated flows of information and resources, and consistent organizational behavior. But achieving effective integration and coordination depends on an understanding of how and why the organization was initially differentiated.

The degree and type of interunit integration depend on what is needed to make the set of subunits function as a whole. The choice of methods to achieve integration is thus another decision that the planning and control system designer must make. Among the alternative means that can be used are coordination by prior planning, by standardization, by information interchange, or by ad hoc committees and coordinators. Each of these choices affects planning and control in its own special way.

The more differentiated an organization is, the more different is each subunt from the other units with which it has to coordinate. There may be wide differences among the sets of key variables that characterize the actions of each unit. Therefore any differentiated organization must continually trade off the benefits of specialization against the problem of integrating its differentiated subunits into a unified whole.

The following example of some alternative structures for an oil company indicates the relationship between differentiation and integration and planning and control system requirements.

An integrated oil company must carry out the following functions: exploration (E), production from oil wells (P), transporation to refineries (Tr), manufacturing in refineries (Mf), transportation to markets (Tm), and marketing (Mr). These functions could be organized into units in any of the three ways shown in Figure 4–1. Clearly the process of

FIGURE 4–1

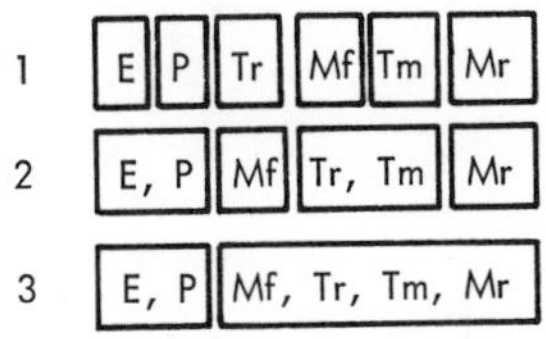

differentiation (in this case, the degree of specialization chosen) influences the scope of each unit and therefore the complexity of the planning process it will require. Structure 3 consists of only two processes while there are six in structure 1; so each of the former's two processes will be far more complex than each of the latter's six. The more specialized the organizational unit, the narrower is its scope of operations and the more limited its range of key variables. Hence, the more specialized the unit, the greater the extent to which it can develop specialized means to administer its own unique functions—but the greater the strain on communication and coordination between units. Structure 3, however, will require methods to contend with its large heterogeneous units, but possesses fewer organizational boundaries to hinder communication and coordination.

These three different structures will place different demands on a planning and control system. Let us now consider several ways in which organizations may differentiate themselves, and the different demands each will make on the design of a planning and control system.

Vertical differentiation by hierarchical level

One way an organization can differentiate itself is hierarchically; i.e., by the number of levels in its structure. Therefore it is necessary to understand the implications of hierarchical differentiation for planning and control requirements.

The most familiar and respected exposition of the effect of hierarchical differences on organizational planning and control was advanced by Anthony (1965). He conceives of a pyramidal organization differentiated into three hierarchical levels he terms strategic, administrative, and operational.

Strategic processes are those which involve the choice of objectives for an organization, the resources to be used to achieve these objectives, and the major policies which are to govern the acquisition, use, and disposition of these resources.

Administrative processes are those which involve choices among alternatives for assuring that resources are obtained and used effectively and efficiently in the accomplishment of an organization's objectives.

Operational processes are those which involve choices for assuring that specific tasks are carried out effectively and efficiently.

Anthony does not intend that these three hierarchical levels be firmly delineated within any particular organization. Rather, he merely suggests that the processes carried out at different organizational levels differ significantly from one another in many respects. Some distinctions between the processes carried out at different hierarchical levels are presented in Table 4–1.

Inspection of the continua listed in Table 4–1 reveals that in terms of both the managerial tasks to be performed and the nature of the information used, the processes carried out at different levels do differ substantially from one another. Planning at higher organizational levels is far more unstructured, uncertain, and complex, and involves far longer time horizons than at lower levels. The information used in planning at these higher levels comes more from sources outside the organization, and is more subjective, less specific and far more aggregated than the quantitative, repetitively used, detailed information of the shop floor. So, in general, the specificity and reliability of expectations, and preciseness of performance appraisal, are far greater at lower organizational echelons than at higher ones. And these differences in the nature of the tasks to be planned and controlled must be reflected in the planning and control systems designed for each level.

TABLE 4–1
Differences in managerial tasks and information used along the
strategic-operational continuum

Characteristic	Strategic	Operational
Managerial tasks		
1. Perspective	Broad—organization wide	Narrow—subunit wide
2. Time horizon	5 to 20 years	1 year or less
3. Environmental uncertainty	Very uncertain	Less uncertain
4. Complexity of process	Very complex	Much less complex
5. Degree of structure	Highly unstructured and ill-defined	Structured and defined
6. Specificity of expectations	Very general	Precisely quantified
7. Persons involved	President, vice presidents and general managers	Departmental supervisors
8. Prime skills required	Conceptual	Interpersonal
9. Output of process	Strategies and missions	Products and services
10. Appraisal of perforance	Subjective	Well defined
Nature of information used		
11. Origin	External to organization	Internal
12. Accuracy	Imprecise	Accurate
13. Specificity	Broad-brush	Detailed
14. Aggregation	Highly aggregated	Individual measures
15. Repetitiveness	Used seldomly	Used repetitively
16. Objectivity	Subjective	Precisely measured
17. Obsolescence	Less rapid	More rapid

Unstructured situations, in which the environment is constantly changing, require constant monitoring, diagnosis, independent judgment, individual decision making, and specialized problem-solving techniques. The planning and control system must guide and assist managers of unstructured tasks in coping with change and uncertainty. In more structured situations, where requirements can be specified, planning and control may present less of a problem. Instead, it may emphasize motivation and coordination of the tasks to be performed, rather than general decision making.

The degree of structure inherent in managerial tasks at different organizational levels can be depicted graphically as shown in Figure 4–2.

FIGURE 4–2

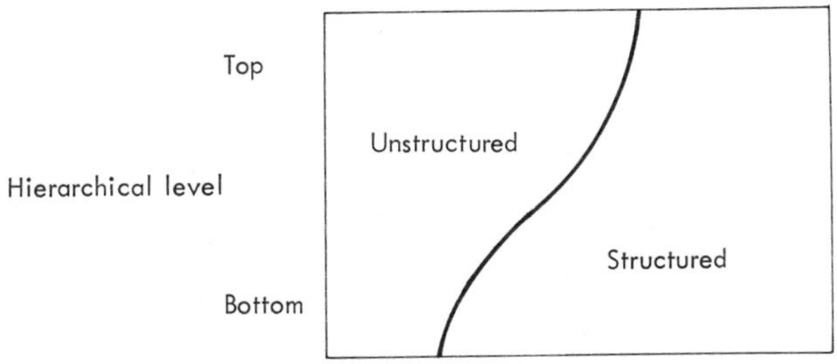

In general, the higher the hierarchical level, the greater the percentage of unstructured tasks. But unstructured tasks are some part of most managerial jobs at all levels. Degree of task structure is a significant determinant of a system's design. Differences in the planning and control of structured and unstructured tasks are therefore thoroughly covered in Chapters 6 and 7.

Horizontal differentiation

In addition to hierarchical structuring, the groups within an organization can be differentiated in several other ways, for example: (a) by the function they perform (e.g., sales or production); (b) by the resources they handle (e.g., money, people, or information); (c) by the product they handle; (d) by the territory they service; or (e) by the customers they serve. Choice of a basis for differentiation is complicated by the fact that no organizational unit is confined to one dimension alone, nor is one dimension usually dominant over all the others. The manner of differentiation, then, will be determined by the relative importance of each of these dimensions, and complex trade-offs are involved in deciding how an organization should be specialized.

These trade-offs are the reason that an understanding of organizational differentiation is mandatory for planning and control system design. Each choice of organizational structure carries with it many advantages and benefits. However, it also creates difficulties and disadvantages that must be recognized and compensated for. The objective of a planning and control system must therefore be to ensure that the benefits of a particular choice in structure are realized and its weaknesses ameliorated to the extent possible. The actual distribution of these strengths and weaknesses will vary among organizations, of course, and so adds another dimension to the clinical or diagnostic approach to situational systems design taken here.

Let us now look at two specific types of horizontal differentiation in light of the benefits and drawbacks they involve. Finally, we will briefly consider matrix organizations, which are designed to combine the advantages and minimize the drawbacks of each of these alternatives.

Differentiation by product. An organization is usually differentiated by product when its strategy dictates fast market response, or when it has problems in coordination. For example, if an organization has communication difficulties between marketing and research and development, and interactive problem solving between them is mandatory for success, then it may organize by product.

The foremost advantages of product line organization are that each unit is motivated to accomplish a single objective—its product's success—and that efficiency can therefore be measured by actual market performance. Members of a product group have a clear role and their contribution to the organization is easily recognized. There is an ease of environmental scanning and capability evaluation because these are related to a single purpose. And since managerial decision making must consider all aspects of an end product, this organizational form is ideally suited to the training of management.

On the other hand, product organizations are more expensive than functional ones because economies of specialization are sacrificed; each subunit must duplicate the functions of all the other subunits. The quality of the functional skills involved is generally lower because a professional environment is lacking. In addition, the viewpoint of the managers involved with products may be narrow and lack an overall corporate perspective. And from an accounting standpoint, product organizations are difficult to administer because of the cost allocations required.

The planning and control characteristics of a product organization may be described under four points. (1) Because there is little interaction among product groups, local planning is possible, as is localized control. (2) An organization's total system therefore will consist of a number of component systems, each related to a product. (3) Since each unit has it own functional inputs and is relatively self-sufficient, bottom-up planning is possible; top management need only coordinate and optimize the portfolio of product units that make up the total organization. (4) Further, performance evaluation is facilitated because efficiency measures can be based on market tests.

Differentiation by function. An organization differentiates itself by function, such as marketing, finance, personnel, or reseach and development, when each function's activities are performed repetitively in order that specialization and technical competence can be emphasized. Such organizations usually have a limited number of homogeneous product lines, and economies of scale are of greater importance than rapid market response and effective coordination. For example, organizations whose product life cycles are long enough to allow sequential, step-by-step planning, and which can be coordinated by top management, are in general, functionally organized.

The primary characteristic of a functional organization is specialization. Each functional group has enough members to form a critical mass and to achieve economies of scale. There is consistency within departments, as well as a comfortable climate for specialists because they are dealing with similar people with common skills and a common empathy with one another. Therefore, professional standards prevail and career paths are clearly defined. In a functional organization it is easier to hire good people and develop their skills because the demands on new employees are well defined.

One difficulty of a functional organization is that the efficiency of each function's contribution to the overall organization can only really be measured when revenue is ultimately received. The contributions of individual departments such as production or marketing can only arbitrarily be approximated. Performance evaluation is more difficult because functions perform tasks with varying time horizons. Some are concerned with immediate results, while others must keep the longer term in mind. Since each unit has only a functional perspective, environmental scanning must be coordinated, which requires more involvement by top management. Also, each unit's objective differs from that of the total organization, which may result in extremely narrow outlooks and specialized decision focuses. Since considerable communication among functions is necessary for effective planning, there is a tremendous load on the communication channels.

The requirements that a planning and control system must satisfy in a functional organization are strongly influenced by the interdependencies among the functions and the necessity for horizontal and vertical communication. Global overall planning by top management is usually required to achieve coordination. Because of this, formulating the organization's strategic mission is usually a corporate level task, which in turn implies that a top-down planning process is the only one practicable.

Matrix organizations

The matrix form of organization attempts to take advantage of the strengths of both product and functional structures. This type of organization is built around individuals who are subproduct, subfunction managers responsible simultaneously to both product line and functional managers. These two authority relationships are separate but equal. This organizational form attempts to combine the benefits of a functional form (e.g., specialized personnel, clear career paths, and so on) with the lower level decision making and cohesion that characterizes product organizations.

The most common type of organization using this form is one that was originally organized along functional lines but which now needs to process information and make decisions by product lines. Its antecedents may be one of the following:

Many functional organizations relied on task forces when crises arose in which they had to make decisions quickly. Responsibility for decisions was assigned to specialized individuals who could communicate directly with each function. An ideal task force contained the mix of authority, information, and knowledge to solve the problem at hand by cutting across functional lines. Examples of the problems handled are the design of information systems for more than one organizational unit, or the design and development of a new product from research and development to final market test. As problems that required cross-functional communication recurred, task forces became more permanent and finally evolved into permanent problem-oriented units.

A second antecedent of matrix organizations is the use of product managers in functional organizations. The position of product manager was created to solve problems similar to those for which task forces were needed. The product manager was given responsibility to coordinate the functional inputs necessary for the successful marketing of his product. Usually he had no formal authority and relied on managerial ability and interpersonal skills to accomplish the task. Unfortunately, the specialists in advertising, promotion, and finance who had to provide inputs to the program for a product often considered themselves as part of their functional group and had little identity with the product. Thus a matrix form was introduced to overcome the product manager's lack of authority, and to encourage functional specialists to identify with products.

The third antecedent of matrix organizations is the project form of organization originally used in managing construction projects. The U.S. government, in order to control costs and meet schedules, demanded that its high technology and aerospace contractors organize in relation to projects and use network-based project planning and control techniques such as PERT (program evaluation and review technique). Because these firms were functionally organized, they added a second (project) dimension in order to meet government requirements. And hence their evolution to matrix forms.

The following are examples of matrix relationships:

1. Shoe department manager in a retail store whose responsibility is limited to selling the product assigned to him.

The shoe department manager is simultaneously responsible to both the buyer of the merchandise he handles and to the store manager responsible for the overall performance of the store.

2. Subproduct, subfunction manager.

	Finance manager	Advertising manager	Distribution manager
Manager, product A	☐	☐	☐
Manager, product B	☐	☐	☐

Functional specialists may be part of a product group and simultaneously part of their functional group.

The planning and control mechanisms needed to support this most complex of organizational forms are exceedingly difficult to provide. Within a pure matrix organization there are two sets of authority relationships in effect simultaneously. Matrix organizations therefore require dual planning and control systems, and a uniform balance of power must be maintained between the two in terms of the budgets prepared, information provided, and rewards for effective performance. Although there have been claims that this organizational form can be successfully implemented (Goggin, 1974), sufficient experience has not yet been accumulated to reach a conclusion.

Line versus staff

Finally, to complete the discussion of organizational differentiation it is necessary to distinguish between line and staff functions. Much confusion exists about these terms. For our purposes, the terms line and staff will be used to distinguish the organizational relationship between two entities. Two units are assumed to be in line relationship to one another if the manager of one has formal authority over the manager of the other. On the other hand, they are in a staff relationship to each other if the relationship is not based on formal authority. A staff unit's function can be strictly advisory, such as finance, research, or public relations, or it can be based on specifically delegated functional authority such as the services performed by maintenance or accounting. The supervisor of a staff group has line authority over his or her subordinates, of course. The role of line versus staff groups in planning and control processes will be thoroughly covered in Chapter 10, "Staff Roles and Organizational Relationships," so further discussion will be deferred until then.

DECENTRALIZATION

In order to determine system requirements, a system designer should understand the nature of the environment with which each responsibility unit must contend, and the key variables of each unit. But understanding the implications of differentiation alone is not sufficient to draw conclusions about the planning and control system requirements of any organizational unit. Differentiation determines organizational structure, the scope of each unit, and its potential range of activities. However, another key element in describing the activities of any responsibility unit is the extent to which it is allocated responsibility. Thus, while differentiation determines what each responsibility unit is potentially capable of doing, it is decentralization that determines what decisions it is accountable for.

Purpose and definition

The degree of decentralization chosen by an organization depends on many factors. Perhaps the foremost of these is size. An organization decentralizes when it becomes so large that communication channels to the top become overloaded. This is especially true when organizational processes are highly complex or rapidly changing, involve a great deal of uncertainty, or are of an unstructured nature. Organizations which require fast responses to environmental changes, and/or who must stimulate interest and initiative, must rely on the skills and judgments of lower level management. Organizations which handle a wide variety of information processing and decision making, and which can make few economies of scale, tend to decentralize.

Decentralization may encompass the ability of an organizational unit to choose its objectives, its time span for accountability, the resources it employs, the expenditure levels it can commit to, the sphere of activity it embraces, or the methods it uses to accomplish objectives. Its degree of decentralization defines an organizational unit's range of discretion. The degree of decision freedom, the extent to which an organizational unit is free to rely on its own judgment, is a measure of the extent to which responsibility has been decentralized.

A common indicator of decentralization is the level at which organizational decision making takes place. This can be measured by the limit of expenditure allowed each level. Decentralization is inversely related to the amount of information an organizational unit transfers upward without first using it. Or, if it is assumed that level of compensation is related to the importance of the decisions a manager makes, then decentralization can be measured by the proportion of the total organizational salary bill allocated to a particular unit.

Benefits and weaknesses

From an administrative standpoint decentralization has many benefits. First, it frees top management from the necessity of day-to-day involvement in operations and limits the quantity and detail of information they must receive. Decentralization thus alleviates the overload on communication channels by pre-screening and aggregating information. It allows intraorganizational competition, flexibility, and adaptability by allowing units to function relatively autonomously. Within subunits, decentralization enhances motivation and job satisfaction by increasing discretion and individual responsibility; it stimulates the search for information by sharpening attention on local considerations; and it encourages innovation. Because decentralization forces managers to confront risk instead of passing it on to their superiors, it provides effective training and managerial development.

These benefits are not unaccompanied by pitfalls, of course. Objectives, incentives, and compensation schemes must be formulated to tie each individual subunit to the organization as a whole. Separable sets of key variables must be developed so that expectations can be decomposed and allocated to self-contained responsibility units. And a control system must be devised that will trace performance results to each responsibility unit. Also, of course, decentralization presupposes that the people to whom authority is delegated have both the ability and the desire to confront risk and make decisions.

Decentralization requires top management capable of trust, openness of communication, and supportive relationships. Decentralization works most effectively when top management acts as a sounding board for new ideas and not as a source of sanctions. It also requires top management to have mechanisms to resolve interunit conflicts, as well as the discipline to let the decentralized system work by maintaining a consistent hands-off attitude.

BEHAVIORAL DIFFERENCES BETWEEN RESPONSIBILITY UNITS

Clearly, the way an organization chooses to differentiate itself determines the nature of the task and the external environment for each of its responsibility units. It also determines the difficulty and best means of integrating these units into a unified whole. And the extent to which the organization is decentralized may affect the motivation, involvement, and level of decision making required by the managers of its responsibility units. But it is important to recognize that the way an organization differentiates and decentralizes itself also may cause varying behavioral characteristics among responsibility units. These behavioral differences are of great significance to planning and control system design in general, and to the achievement of organizational integration in particular.

Research studies have shown that organizational units may differ along any of the following lines:

1. Formality. Subunits may differ in the formality of their interpersonal relationships. The degree of formality may affect the way information is processed and decisions are made. The manner in which jobs are defined, the flexibility of roles, and the reliance on predefined rules and procedures as opposed to mutual interactions are all aspects of formality.

2. Interpersonal orientation. Members of a unit may be concerned solely with their task requirements, or have a genuine concern for their fellow workers, or both.

3. Risk preference. Members may be decided risk averters or may be willing to undertake new ventures.
4. Time orientation. They may be short-sighted or have a longer time horizon.
5. Goal orientation. They may be fixed solely on their own individual goals, or on their department's goals, or they may be concerned with the overall benefit of the organization as a whole.
6. Problem solving style. Different units may have different capabilities to handle problems. For example, a sales representative may stress interpersonal orientation, while an operations research analyst may rely more heavily on analytical abilities (Lawrence and Lorsch, 1967).

It is obvious that such factors affect the suitability of certain planning and control system tools and techniques. For example, the formality that exists within a unit might affect the utility or desirability of formal controls. Different levels of analytical ability mean that different methods and techniques of analysis must be used. And different goal orientations and time horizons may influence the choice of key variables to be communicated. Differences in behavioral characteristics certainly make integration among subunits more difficult. The problem of joint decision making and the need for interunit coordination and conflict resolution may be eased or aggravated by the manner of differentiation an organization chooses. Therefore, an awareness that behavioral differences may exist as a result of differentiation is also essential for effective planning and control systems design.

THE RELATIONSHIP OF DIFFERENTIATION AND DECENTRALIZATION TO PLANNING AND CONTROL SYSTEMS DESIGN

In this chapter it has been argued that an organization's total planning and control system is highly dependent on the structure of that organization and the degree of responsibility assigned to the subunits which comprise it. First, the manner in which an organization differentiates itself determines the scope and potential range of activities of each of its component units. Second, the extent of decentralization determines the actual sphere of discretion permitted to each unit. And finally, the manner of differentiation and decentralization determines the nature of interunit integration needed to bind the responsibility units into a cohesive whole, and the behavioral problems in doing so.

Chapter 1 listed the four components which make up a planning and control system:

1. A process model describing the cycles and steps within cycles to be carried out.

2. The tools and techniques with which each of the required steps could be carried out.
3. Specification of the individuals or groups to be involved in the process.
4. A schedule for when the events should take place.

To a significant extent, the determination of components 1, 3, and 4—determination of the appropriate activities, involvement, and the timing to be followed—depends on the way an organization is differentiated and decentralized.

Of course, the number of cycles carried out, the steps within each cycle, the amount of recycling before an acceptable solution is reached, the direction of communication flow and the number of iterations necessary before a cycle is concluded all depend on the complexity of the problems to be solved, the abilities and style of the managers concerned, and the general climate of the organization. And all of these factors must be thoroughly examined before system design decisions can be made. But the most significant determinants of these decisions are the delineation of responsibility units and their levels of discretion.

The following two examples illustrate the relationship of differentiation and decentralization to the process model, involvement, and timing of a planning and control system. The first is a simplified model of a divisionalized organization, and the second is a more involved but more realistic example of the same type of organization.

FIGURE 4–3

In this multiple-unit organization, each division may go through the three-cycle process described in Chapters 2 and 3. In addition, head office must plan the overall direction of the whole organization, as well as allocate resources to each division. Therefore, this multiunit organization may follow a five-cycle process involving three groups of participants.

Cycles
1. Overall strategy.
2. Resource allocation to divisions.
3. Division strategy.
4. Division resource allocation.

5. Specification of division performance targets.

Participants
1. Head office
   a. Management
2. Division
   a. Management
   b. Operations

The timing of these five cycles, the participants involved, and the points at which decisions are made can be depicted as a graph on an activity-involvement-timing chart as follows; each decision point is noted by a *D*.

FIGURE 4–4

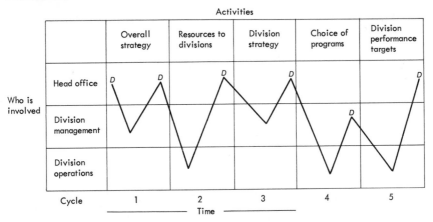

Figure 4–4 describes the following activities:

1. Head office develops the overall strategy for the organization, and communicates it to each division which may then suggest modifications to head office. Head office makes the final decision.
2. Head office then calls for resource requests. Division management confers with operations personnel and submits resource requests to head office.
3. Head office allocates its total resources to divisions and requests that they prepare statements of divisional strategy.
4. Head office approves these statements of strategy. Divisions collect detailed requests for resources from their operations personnel.
5. Divisions assign resources to operations and prepare responsibility unit short-term plans. These are consolidated and sent to head office for final approval.

This planning system is based on several assumptions with which the reader may not agree. For example, it assumes that overall corporate strategy can be developed independent of division strategies. It also assumes that division strategies should be dependent on the resources assigned to them, not vice versa. Therefore it assumes a five-cycle as opposed to a three-cycle process. However, the intent of this example is not to present a desirable or undesirable planning and control system, but merely to demonstrate the utility of an activity-involvement-timing chart in describing one, and to illustrate that different decentralization assumptions for any organizational structure will change the shape of the graph. For instance, if cycles 1 and 2 were performed completely at head office, without any communication with divisions, the chart (Figure 4–4) would show a horizontal straight line for these cycles. Alternatively, if the organization were more participative, each cycle would reach down to the operations level. In other words, differentiation and decentralization determine the shape of this graph, which illustrates the process, involvement, and timing aspects of a planning and control system.

In this second example, consider the activities, involvement, and timetable used by a product-based divisionalized organization (Fig. 4–5). The parties involved in this example are the corporate and divisional planning staff groups, corporate staff functions, and head office and divisional line managers. An annual cycle is assumed.

System Planning
    February   (① on AIT chart, Figure 4–6)
        a. Corporate planning staff (CPS) meets with company operating policy committee (OPC) and division planning staffs (DPS) to review strengths and weaknesses of last planning cycle, discuss changes to this year's process, and propose a timetable for this activity.
        b. CPS completes background studies and intelligence acquisition needed to guide development of corporate strategy.
        c. CPS prepares planning and control manual and obtains approval from OPC to distribute it to all participating corporate offices and divisions. Changes from last year discussed with divisions.
Statement of Strategic Mission
    March
        a. OPC reviews current statement of strategic mission and specifies the key strategic variables (KSVs) to be observed by all divisions. ②
        b. CPS transmits to DPS planning assumptions, environmental information, future changes possible, and risk-return criteria.
        c. Key strategic variables reviewed by divisions. ③
Program Planning and Resource Allocation
        a. Each DPS meets with its division manager (DM) to discuss

FIGURE 4–5
Product-based divisional organization

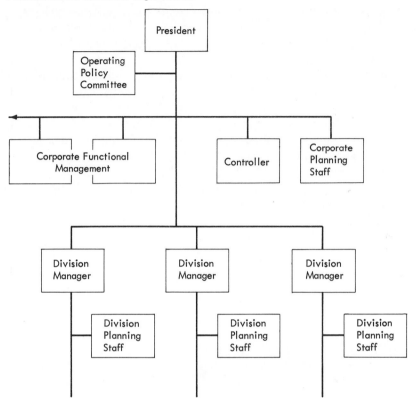

the KSVs and to plan how they will complete their plans in conformance with the procedures outlined.

b.   Corporate functional managers (CFM) meet with CPS to discuss the relationship of their plans to the rest of the organization.

c.   CPS meets with divisional planning groups when requested to solve problems or clarify requirements.

April

a.   Divisions outline their contribution to the overall strategic mission and seek tentative approval from OPC. DMs assemble the capital expenditure requests of their departmental managers.

b.   OPC approves division contributions to strategic mission. ④

c.   Divisions complete documentation of long-range plans (LRPs) and submit them to CPS. ⑤

May

a.   OPC meets to review documented plans.

b.   DM appear to present LRPs to OPC.

    c. DM undertake plans modification if required.

    d. Divisions resubmit revised LRPs.

    e. Expenditure authorization and LRPs are approved, and KPVS for program and responsibility unit planning are distributed. ⑥

Responsibility Unit Planning

  June

    a. KVs are discussed by DM with each departmental manager.

    b. Sales forecasts, overhead expenses and cost behavior analyses are prepared.

    c. Sales plan is completed.

    d. Production, inventory, materials, labor and manufacturing overhead expense budgets are completed.

  October

    a. One-year profit plan, and financial budget is submitted to corporate controller for review.

    b. DMs meet with OPC for review and approval.

    c. DMs revise profit plan.

    d. Revised profit plan reviewed by OPC and approved. ⑦

    e. Profit plans distributed to divisions.

Performance Reporting

  January

    a. Division expense budget performance report submitted to OPC.

    b. Division profit budget performance report submitted to OPC.

  March

    a. Quarterly financial budget performance report submitted.

This system is described on the Activity-Involvement-Timing (AIT) chart (Figure 4–6).

FIGURE 4–6

Activity-involvement-timing (AIT)

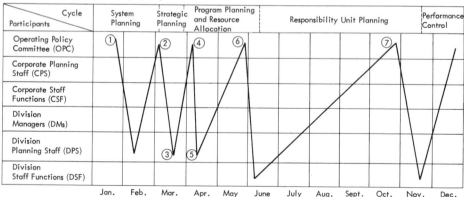

SUMMARY

This chapter has considered two distinguishing characteristics of organizations that influence planning and control systems design. Before the details of any system can be specified, these characteristics must be analyzed so that the role of each organizational unit in the planning process is clearly understood. The manner of differentiation and of decentralization are two distinguishing characteristics of all organizations.

An organization differentiates itself by developing specialized responsibility units, each capable of managing a set of specific tasks. An organization may differentiate itself vertically, assigning less structured tasks to upper level management and more structured tasks to lower level management; and it may differentiate itself horizontally into product or functional groups. Another alternative is the matrix type of organization, designed to cut across the division of product and functional groups. Whichever method of differentiation is chosen by an organization, each subunit will have its own design requirements, depending on the nature of the tasks it must perform and its relationship to the organization as a whole. While attempting to ensure maximum efficiency within each responsibility unit, the system designer must also choose appropriate methods of integrating and coordinating these units in order to assure that they best serve the purpose of the organization as a whole.

Decentralization defines the range of discretion of any organizational unit. Decentralization is needed when an organization is so large or complex that it must delegate a great deal of decision making to lower level management in order to accomplish its mission. Decentralization frees top management from the necessity of involvement in daily problems and encourages innovation and risk taking at lower levels. But it also demands special qualities of both top and lower level management, as well as control mechanisms that will both encourage independence and ensure coordination of organizational units.

An understanding of the reasons underlying an organization's manner of differentiation and decentralization is essential for the system designer to determine an appropriate process model and to specify the participants and schedule for a planning and control system.

QUESTIONS

1. What determines the number of cycles to be carried out in a planning process? Is it best to have as few cycles as possible?
2. What determines the relative amount of resources to be devoted to each cycle of a planning and control process?
3. Is it correct to say that the greater the number of levels in an organization, the greater the number of cycles that should be carried out?

4. What is top-down management? What is bottom-up management? To what extent are these consistent or conflicting? Can they be combined?

5. Is a functionally organized company more likely to be managed in a top-down fashion than one that is organized by product?

6. Can you assume that the more unstructured a task is, the more likely the authority to perform it would be decentralized?

7. What would the AIT chart for example 1 look like if the company were totally centralized? Totally decentralized?

8. Suggest and compare the key variables of a product division with those of a production, marketing, and financial division of a similar company.

9. Does a matrix organization require more planning cycles than one organized by product or by function?

REFERENCES AND BIBLIOGRAPHY

Anthony, Robert N., *Planning and Control Systems: A Framework for Analysis.* Boston: Division of Research. Harvard Business School, 1965.

Bailey, Josgan K. Organization planning: Whose responsibility? *Academy of Management Journal,* June 1964, pp. 95–108.

Bower, Joseph. Planning and control: Bottom up or top down? *Journal of General Management,* 1974, pp. 20–31.

Chandler, A. D., Jr. *Strategy and Structure.* Cambridge, Mass.: The M.I.T. Press, 1962.

Drucker, Peter F. New templates for today's organization. *Harvard Business Review, February* 1974, pp. 45–53.

Galbraith, J. R. Matrix organizational designs: How to combine functional and project forms. *Business Horizons,* February 1971, pp. 29–40.

Glueck, W. F. Organization planning and strategic planning. *Journal of Business Policy,* Autumn 1972, pp. 48–59.

Goggin, William C. How the multidimensional structure works at Dow Corning. *Harvard Business Review,* January–February 1974, pp. 54–65.

Hedley, R. Alan. Organization structure and managerial control: A case study. *Journal of General Management,* Summer 1975, pp. 55–69.

Jannig, Frederick F. Skills matrixing. *Datamation,* September 1975, pp. 71–79.

Kimberly, John R. Environmental constraints and organizational structure. A comparative analysis of rehablitation organizations. *Administrative Science Quarterly,* March 1975, pp. 1–9.

Larson, Raymond L. Decentralization in real life. *Management Accounting,* March 1974, pp. 28–32.

Lawrence, P. H., and Lorsch, J. W. *Organization and Environment: Managing Differentiation and Integration.* Boston: Division of Research, Harvard Business School, 1967.

McMahon, J. T., and Perritt, G. W. Control structure of organizations: An empirical examination. *Academy of Management Journal,* September 1971, pp. 327–40.

Morris, W. T. *Decentralization in Management Systems.* Columbus, Ohio: Ohio State University Press, 1968.

Pennings, Johannes M. The relevance of the structural-contingency model for organizational effectiveness. *Administrative Science Quarterly,* September 1975, pp. 393–410.

Reimann, Bernard C. Dimensions of structure in effective organizations: Some empirical evidence. *Academy of Management Journal,* December 1974, pp. 693–708.

Rhennan, Eric. *Organization Theory for Long-Range Planning.* New York: Wiley, 1973.

Schwerdiman, J. S. *Strategy and Long-Range Planning for the Multinational Corporation,* New York: Praeger, 1973.

Vancil, Richard F., and Lorange, Peter. Strategic planning in diversified companies. *Harvard Business Review,* January–February 1975, pp. 81–90.

Walker, A. H., and Lorsch, J. W. Organizational choice: Product versus function. In J. W. Lorsch and P. H. Lawrence, eds., *Studies in Organization Design.* Homewood, Ill.: Irwin, 1970.

Case study 4–1

Ford Motor Company

HISTORICAL BACKGROUND

Following World War II, the Ford Motor Company was in a financial crisis. Henry Ford II found himself in charge of "an enormous, shapeless, unmanageable mass."[1] The immediate reaction to the crisis was to attempt to duplicate the success of General Motors by copying GM's organizational structure.

General Motors is divided into broad groups. The automobile and truck group contains the Chevrolet, Buick, Oldsmobile, Pontiac, Cadillac, and GM truck divisions. Each car division is a relatively autonomous profit center headed by a vice president—general manager reporting to a group vice president who in turn reports to the executive vice president. Since each car line has complete responsibility for its own research, engineering and styling, each division general manager is served by almost as complete a staff as if he were operating an independent business. Each has his own engineering, manufacturing, purchasing, marketing, accounting, and personnel staff. Car divisions are free to buy components from outside suppliers if an inside supplier is not available or if the price is not suitable. The company is coordinated through the philosophy of centralized policies guiding decentralized divisional operations. This is an especially appropriate philosophy for General Motors since the com-

---

[1] "There's Another Generation of Whiz Kids at Ford," *Fortune Magazine,* January 1967.

pany came into being through the consolidation of several independent automobile manufacturers.

No such inherent product differentiation was prevalent in the Ford structure of 1945. In addition, the dominance and competence of General Motors was a significant external factor. Nonetheless, to solve its problems, Ford hired many former GM executives who tried to impose the GM pattern on it.

Attempts at copying GM even went as far as the formation of five separate car divisions. The strategy of copying General Motors, especially the decision to match each and every one of GM's car lines with a Ford offering led to the introduction of the Edsel. The Edsel was planned and designed in 1955, a year of booming sales for middle-range cars such as Buick, Oldsmobile, and Dodge. However, by the time the car appeared in 1957, market tastes had shifted considerably and the car was a disastrous failure.

The magnitude of this failure brought a slow realization that a unique organization structure and strategy was necessary for Ford. The inability to respond to market shifts and the lack of success in attempting to fill every niche in the automobile market with a separate auto line forced Ford's management, especially Henry Ford II, to concede that what was good for General Motors and America was not necessarily good for Ford. A new organization and a new strategy would have to be sought to contend with General Motors dominance and strategies.

Henry Ford recognized the need to develop an organization geared to the exploitation of opportunities. Adaptability and fast response had to become key strategic considerations. "We are like Chinese bandits. We hit them and run. We can't meet GM head on because of their sheer fire power."[2] These needs—to exploit opportunities in a market dominated by General Motors and to be more responsive to market shifts—led to Ford's functional organizational form.

FORD'S STRUCTURE

In terms of 1973 dollar sales, Ford is the third largest industrial company in the world and, with worldwide sales of 6 million cars and trucks, is the second largest automobile manufacturer.

As shown in Exhibit 1, administration of the company is divided between the chairman of the board, and the president. Ford Diversified Products, Ford International Automotive, and North American Automotive Operations report to the president, as do the operations staff. The general council, and the finance, personnel, and public relations staff report to the chairman.

As seen in Exhibit 2, the company is functionally organized. North

---

[2] Ibid.

EXHIBIT 1
Simplified Ford organizational chart

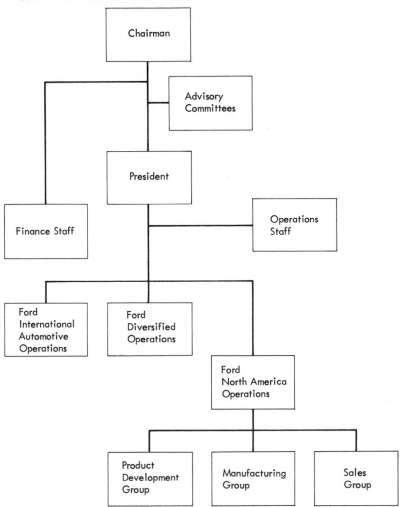

American Automotive Operations are subdivided into three groups: the product development group, the manufacturing group, and the sales group. Car planning is carried out by the product development group while sales are the responsibility of the three divisions in the sales group: Ford, Lincoln-Mercury, and Ford of Canada (i.e., the sales function itself is organized along car lines but in total, it is a separate functional division of the company). Production of the car itself is the responsibility of the manufacturing group. Manufacturing is divided into power train, body and assembly, and automotive component operations. Each

EXHIBIT 2
North American Ford operations

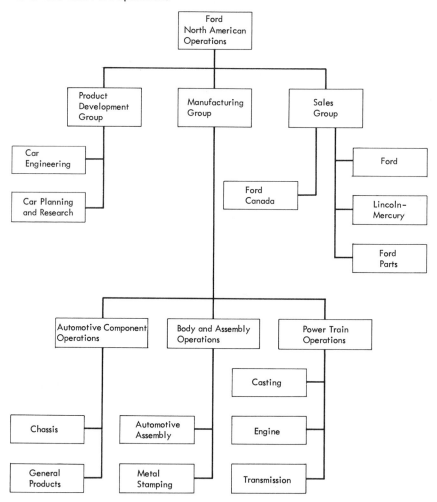

manufacturing group is responsible for its own design, engineering, and production technology.

THE PLANNING AND CONTROL PROCESS

The long-range planning process at Ford involves three steps: (1) setting objectives; (2) publishing policies, procedures, and assumptions; and (3) developing the specific strategy to achieve these objectives.[3]

---

[3] Fred G. Secrest, "The Process of Long-Range Planning at Ford Motor Company," G. Steiner (ed.), *Managerial Long-Range Planning* (New York: McGraw-Hill Book Co., 1963).

Vehicle planning is the responsibility of the operating policy committee, composed of the company's top management: the chairman, president, group vice presidents, and several staff officers. The purpose of this committee is to advise the chairman and the president on the various aspects of new product plans. Once a new product program is approved, it becomes the basis of the remainder of the planning. The product planner plays a key role in vehicle planning.

Annual planning, based on organizational units as opposed to product lines, supports the vehicle planning. Each division is held responsible for attaining a specified level of financial performance. The company therefore relies heavily on a financial planning and control system, coordinated by its finance staff. The function of the finance staff is to see that proper objectives have been set for each division, to provide uniform standards for the preparation of budgets and profit plans, and to review each budget for reasonableness. The task of actually preparing expense and profit budgets begins at the plant level, moves to the division general office level, and then to the finance staff. After staff review, each budget is presented to the chairman and president by the division general manager.

THE PRODUCT PLANNER

At present it takes approximately three years to develop a completely new model for public introduction. The need to shorten lead times so as to be more responsive to the market led Ford to create a new profession—the product planner. The duty of a product planner is to bridge the gap between division and staff groups and to balance all the factors contributing to the success or failure of a new model introduction.

Product planning for the North American market is a responsibility of the product development group. During the course of product planning, the product development office in the Car Planning and Engineering Division coordinates a number of strategic meetings among staff and divisional executives representing product planning, car engineering, styling, manufacturing, marketing, and finance. The purpose of these meetings is to discuss the merits and weaknesses, and the costs and risks of various new model alternatives. The output of these meetings is a product planning proposal that is submitted to the operating policy committee for approval.

The success of this attempt to achieve the benefits of a product differentiated organization can be seen in the conception, development, and marketing of the original Mustang. The current president of Ford, L. A. Iacocca, then serving as a product planner, convinced Henry Ford of the need for such an automobile, and was primarily responsible for moving it from the drawing board to the market in two years.

ROLE OF THE FINANCE STAFF

The finance staff plays a number of key roles in Ford's planning and control. One is in the setting of objectives. The company's principal objectives include increasing profits per share and earning a specified return on assets. Specific levels of financial performance are recommended to top management by the finance staff after a detailed study of the planning objectives used by other firms and the factors most likely to influence the company's progress. Segments of the profit per share objective are then assigned to each group such as international operations, domestic automobile sales, and so on, while a specific rate of return on assets objective is set for each of Ford's divisions and subsidiaries. The manager of each organizational unit is thus responsible for achieving a specified profit or return on asset level of performance. The finance staff determines the objectives to be achieved by each unit, subject to acceptance by its management. After a mutually agreed upon objective is arrived at, it is reported to the chairman and to the president for review and approval.

The assumptions needed to carry out long-range planning are drawn up by the various staff groups and coordinated by the finance staff. These assumptions include predictions of price levels, government fiscal policies, population trends, productivity rates, and so on. The finance staff also publishes uniform procedural rules so that all divisional planning can be developed on a common basis and presented to top management in a uniform manner.

Since the finance staff coordinates both long- and short-term planning with other functions and the operating divisions, effective integration of short- and long-term objectives is facilitated; and, reporting as it does directly to the chairman, effective control can be maintained.

THE INFLUENCE OF HENRY FORD II

An argument may be made that centralized planning and control are carried to extremes within Ford, especially by the current chairman, Henry Ford II. There are numerous examples of his personal intervention into many levels of corporate affairs. In *Fortune* Magazine, Ford was described as follows:

> He insists not only on approving styling, but he test drives every new model before it goes into production. . . . The first thing you have to understand about the company is that Henry Ford is the boss. He is the boss, he always was the boss . . . , and always will be the boss until he decides to retire. Who gets what job, down to the third echelon of management, is a question whose answer he regards very much his business.[4]

---

[4] "Henry Ford: Super Star," *Fortune* Magazine, May 1973.

Even stockholders do not pose a serious threat to Henry Ford's power. Despite the 1956 stock sale that converted Ford into a publicly held company, the Ford family retains 40 percent of the voting power. "Nothing short of a coalition that included his own admiring relatives could effectively challenge Henry Ford's power."[5]

It is clear that much of Ford's structure has been designed for centralized policy making and much of the corporate direction and control is exercised by Henry Ford himself. This centralized decision making has ensured that all functional units work in concert and, however autocratic and arbitrary, has guaranteed responsiveness. Whether corporate planning and strategy can continue to be made centrally after Henry Ford retires is a question critical to the survival of the company.

FORD'S PERFORMANCE

Perhaps the best way to describe Ford's success is to quote Henry Ford II: "We're as big today [1972] as General Motors was six years ago."[6] This closing of the gap between Ford and GM, although not an immediate objective, is certainly a measure of Ford's success.

There are many examples of Ford's ability to effectively manage its product line. The list of cars developed to fill gaps in the GM product line is impressive: Thunderbird, Falcon, Fairlane, Mustang, Maverick, Pinto, Mustang II, Granada, Monarch.

Ford is generally recognized as a leader in long-range planning and as having an excellent feel for future automobile demand. Development of the Pinto and Granada are evidence of its willingness to adapt to changing trends. In fact, for the 1974–75 model year, Ford was able to produce more compact and subcompact cars than GM, and in the 1974 model year, the only North American subcompact that was introduced was Ford's Mustang II.

In terms of market share Ford's success is again evident. While GM's U.S. market share has dropped from 44 percent to 37.5 percent, Ford has managed to at least hold its own against the onslaught of smaller imported cars.

Questions

1. With respect to planning and control, what are the disadvantages of a functional form of organization?
2. How has Ford managed to overcome these difficulties and to develop a responsive and anticipative organization?

---

[5] Ibid.
[6] Ibid.

3. If Henry Ford were not the chairman, could Ford function as it now does?
4. In the future, as Ford grows larger, will it be able to maintain this organizational form or will it have to change? If you believe it will change, in what ways? Will it become more like GM or will GM become more like Ford?

Case study 4–2

Raytheon Company

The Raytheon Company is a large, diversified, decentralized, well-managed but conservative defense contractor-conglomorate with head offices in Lexington, Massachusetts.

Large . . .

With 1971 sales of $1.3 billion, Raytheon ranked 94 among the Fortune 500. It has 45,750 employees (72nd largest employer among the Fortune 500) and approximately 29,000 shareholders.

Diversified . . .

Electronics products account for over 57 percent of Raytheon's total sales. Exploration, engineering, and construction services to the natural resource industries account for another 26 percent, while major appliance sales bring in 10 percent. Other businesses including high technology services, equipment for highway construction, and educational publishing, account for the remaining 7 percent.

Some of Raytheon's divisions are involved in the generally unrelated businesses as follows:

Missiles	Seismograph service
Sonar systems	Textbook publishing
Radar tracking systems	Computer services
Data display devices	Reservation systems
Major home appliances	Phonograph records
Industrial plant design	Learning systems
Construction management	Highway construction

Decentralized . . .

Raytheon is made up of over 20 semiautonomous profit center divisions, organized into two groups: the commercial and the government group. The divisions within each group report to a group vice president who, in turn, reports to the executive vice president. Exhibit 1 shows the company organization chart. These executives form the executive council which is the central strategy formulation and decision-making group for the company. Divisions operate relatively autonomously, however, within this policy framework. The principle management and information and control tool is the monthly divisional profit and loss statement, and top management's focus is strongly on the "bottom line."

Well-managed but conservative . . .

Raytheon's balance sheet indicates conservative financial orientation of the company. Pretax income covers interest expense more than six times and its current ratio is maintained at about 1.9. All segments of the business are profitable. Its financial ratios compare very favorably with those of other aerospace companies and with electrical appliance industry. Over the five years, 1967–71, it outperformed all multiindustry companies except 3M.

Defense contractor-conglomorate . . .

In terms of markets, 49 percent of Raytheon's 1971 sales were to the U.S. government, primarily the defense department, with the remainder to commercial markets.

PLANNING AT RAYTHEON

Planning at all levels of Raytheon is the responsibility of line management. The nature and scope of the planning activities carried out by corporate, group, and divisional line managers, suit the particular needs of each level.

The responsibilities of the vice president—corporate planning are outlined in Exhibit 2. His corporate planning group provides three general types of inputs to the divisional planning process. First, it provides a schedule outlining the dates by which the plans should be prepared and ready for submission. The general outline of this schedule, presented in Exhibit 3, is supported annually by detailed schedules. Second, it provides corporate assumptions to the divisions annually. A listing of the more general assumptions applicable to divisional planning is presented in Exhibit 4. Third, format guidelines are provided to the divisions for the preparation and presentation of their plans and also for the presentation of monthly reports. Standard formats are used so that plans may be more easily interpreted by corporate management. The divisions, however, develop their own detailed schedules and formats for their own intradivisional planning. Edited excerpts from the Raytheon's planning and performance reporting procedures are presented in Appendices A and B, respectively.

DIVISION CHARTERS

Charters are used to delineate and assign responsibilities to each division. A division's charter defines the nature of each division's business, intracompany relationships, and profit center responsibilities so as to avoid conflict or confusion caused by the overlap of missions and to ensure proper integration among divisions. Division charters identify business areas, usually taken to be specific products or markets, and these basic business units are the building blocks by which divisions plan.

PERFORMANCE GOALS

It is the practice of Raytheon's corporate management to develop a series of performance goals for internal use, and an abbreviated set of measures for public consumption. Internal short-term goals are established through the company's annual budget system, which is the responsibility of the office of the controller. Longer term performance goals consist of criteria indicating the size and operational quality of the company five years hence. These are reviewed and reconfirmed annually as part of the preparation of the five-year business plan. Objectives for outside use are established for five-year terms and are restated or reconfirmed every year. For example, the goals set in 1970 to be achieved by 1975 included figures for total sales, sales of commercial products, sales of all products and services outside of the United States and earnings per common share, expressed as annual growth rates over the period 1970 to 1975.

PLANNING CYCLE

The annual planning cycle begins in June when corporate assumptions and guidelines are issued to the divisions. However, throughout the preparation period the divisional vice presidents are kept aware of what is going on so they have an intimate knowledge of these assumptions before they are issued. Planning is carried out during the summer. In late September, the divisions review their plans internally and establish their requests for capital and for research and development funds. During October, the divisions present their plans to their group vice president. As in most formal planning processes, review and reformulation proceeds interactively until the group vice presidents are satisfied with the plans.

Once the group vice presidents are satisfied, the divisions make formal presentations to corporate management (see Appendix A). This usually takes place in early to mid-November. Following this meeting the first year of the plan is detailed and becomes the budget for the following year.

The capital and facilities plans and related appropriations requests are prepared at the same time as the five-year business plan. In the fall of each year, in accordance with schedules established by government and commercial group executives, all divisions present their requirements for new capital equipment and facilities. Detailed reviews of these plans are required by the vice president—controller, vice president—engineering, and vice president—manufacturing prior to their presentation to the group vice presidents.

PERFORMANCE CONTROL

Performance reporting (see Appendix B) is carried on monthly and is quantitatively based. A monthly meeting is held at which each division manager presents a detailed report of his activities to corporate management. In many meetings more than one division manager is present so that all division managers are aware of the progress of their peers. Divisions are compared not only to their own budgeted targets, but also to the performance of similar operations external to the company. In this way performance, relative both to their own expectations and also to competition, is kept clearly in mind.

In addition to these performance reviews, corporate management visits each division quarterly in order to become intimately familiar with what is going on, to learn of the problems that division management is having, and to discuss the means by which they intend to solve these problems. During these visits, division and corporate management have the opportunity to communicate, establish expectations, and discuss resource requirements for the future.

Questions

1. How is the president of Raytheon able to plan and control the activities of such a large and diversified company?
2. Is Raytheon's comprehensive and formally documented planning and control system compatible with the operation of a decentralized organization? Is Raytheon really decentralized?
3. What purposes must the planning and control system satisfy from the standpoint of corporate management and of division management?
   How well does Raytheon's system satisfy these two sets of requirements?

EXHIBIT 1
Company organization

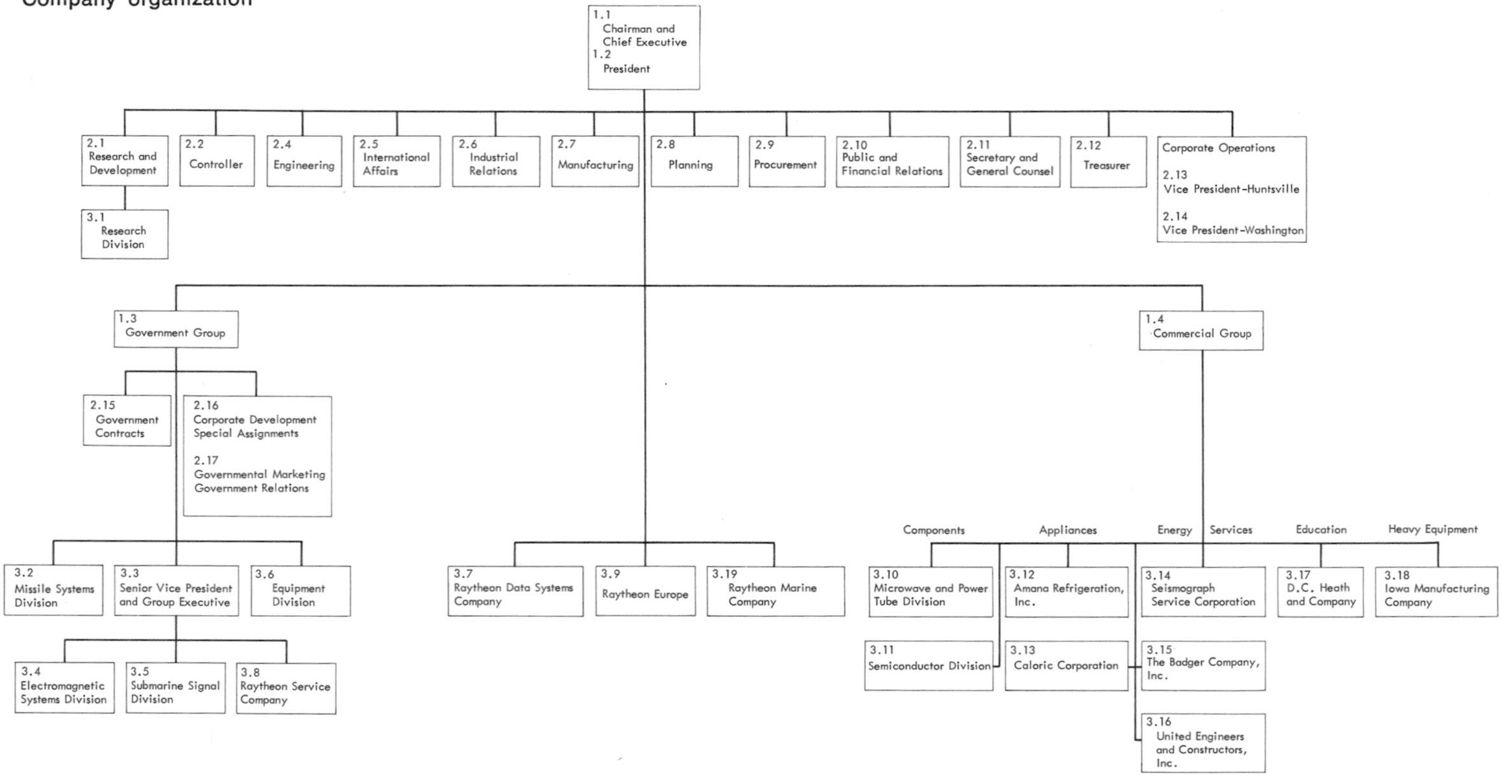

EXHIBIT 2
Responsibilities and reporting relationships

Subject: Duties and responsibilities: Vice president—planning

PURPOSE:

To provide a Company Staff office which will assist the executive office in the establishment of broad company policy relating to the longer range, the determination of company objectives and goals, and the development of implementing key strategies; provide staff guidance and coordination to the companywide planning function; and develop and provide staff support to the acquisition and divestment programs of the Company.

DUTIES AND RESPONSIBILITIES:

Business Development
1. Identify, evaluate, and recommend new growth sectors.
2. Identify and/or evaluate acquisition candidates.
3. Coordinate companywide cooperative new business projects.

Planning
4. Oversee formal long-range planning cycle; issue instructions for plan preparation.
5. Evaluate plans; evaluate operational performance basis for plans.
6. Develop guidelines for, and make evaluation of, performance by divisions and subsidiaries against plans.
7. Recommend new corporate goals and objectives.

Counsel
8. Develop and provide advice and counsel in application of mathematical methods to business problems.
9. Provide guidance and assistance in evaluation of division-/ subsidiary company-developed new business opportunities.

Data Base
10. Develop and maintain cost-effective market, business, and economic data bases.

ORGANIZATIONAL RELATIONSHIPS:

The vice president—planning reports administratively to the executive vice president and functionally to the executive office.

He works closely with the executive office, group executives, the vice president—international affairs, and the vice president and general manager of Raytheon Europe, to achieve the best possible global business planning effort at all levels. He maintains close liaison with division general managers, subsidiary company presidents, and other company staff office heads in providing continuing guidance and assistance in the planning area.

EXHIBIT 3
Schedule of key events

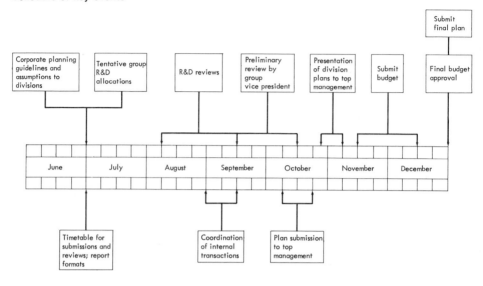

EXHIBIT 4
Company objectives

Subject: Basic objectives

The following objectives will guide Raytheon Company's planning and operating activities:

1. Conduct the progress of the business such that Raytheon Company maintains a reputation for being an aggressively managed growth company that markets quality products and services at competitive prices.
2. Achieve levels of profitability, relative to sales and to assets employed, greater than the medians of industry competitors in markets in which Raytheon Company participates.
3. Develop and maintain a balanced participation in private and public segments of the U.S. gross national product.
4. Maintain a leadership position in the electronics technologies, and remain in the forefront of those other technologies identified as important to the future of the company.
5. Maintain and broaden the company's stature as a technology-based company, exploiting areas of systems management, equipment manufacture, and component production which offer opportunities for profit and growth, commensurate with the risks involved.
6. Expand selectively upon Raytheon's present position as an international company through exchanges of technology, in order to

participate in the growing markets outside the United States.

7. Maintain and improve the company's image as a socially sensitive corporate citizen of integrity and honesty, and with the determination to deal forthrightly and fairly with stockholders, customers, suppliers, and employees.

8. Develop within the company programs to maximize the potential of all human resources.

9. Take every reasonable measure to maintain growth and continuity in businesses to which the company is committed, taking into consideration responsibilities to customers, employees, and communities throughout the world. With equal vigor, withdraw from existing markets which no longer can provide an acceptable return on investment, again including consideration of responsibilities to customers, employees, and communities throughout the world.

10. Manage the company through the use of central policy and objectives, and provide equitable systems of measurement for the guidance and control of decentralized profit centers.

APPENDIX A: GENERAL POLICIES AND PROCEDURES

SUBJECT: FIVE-YEAR BUSINESS PLAN

A. *Purpose.* This policy and procedure establishes the broad guidelines for preparation and annual review of division and subsidiary company five-year business plans. Economic and other specific guidelines and assumptions will be issued annually by the planning office.

B. *Policy.* Planning, as used herein, defines an approach to making and implementing business decisions involving the identification of and choices among alternatives. While planning is not simply the preparation of written plans, a degree of formality is required in the planning process. Formal planning imposes a beneficial discipline upon those important management thoughts and actions affecting the company's survival and future profit growth. It forces an appraisal of the present situation, the company's strengths and weaknesses and the competitive environment in which it operates. Formal planning directs attention to the problem of what the company wishes to become, not just what it is. It requires anticipation and management of change with a program of actions as opposed to reacting to actions of others. Most important, it causes purposeful identification of opportunities to make a profit from new activities or new ways of doing things.

It is Raytheon's policy to place highest priority on planning as a working tool of management. Planning will be a principal responsibility of all employees in positions of management and will be an important element in performance reviews. Principal emphasis in planning will be on the selection and profitable exploitation of opportunities. Consequently, particular attention will be given to market sensitivity in identifying alternative opportunities and to subsequent formulation of supporting objectives and strategy.

The five-year business plans of the operating divisions and subsidiary companies are to be updated as important changes occur. To provide an opportunity for executive office review, a current version of the plan covering the forthcoming budget year and four subsequent years will be submitted to the executive office in mid-October of each year. A company strategy meeting will be scheduled for late October or early November, at which time formal presentation to, and review by, company management will occur. The guidance provided at the company strategy meeting will confirm the basis for developing the next year's budget.

C. *Applicability.* This policy and procedure is applicable to all divisions, separate operations, and all majority-owned subsidiary companies of Raytheon.

D. *Responsibilities.* Division general managers and subsidiary company presidents are responsible for compliance with this policy and for the development and implementation of division or subsidiary company procedures, as appropriate.

E. *Introduction*
   1. The business plans are summarized by the use of information exhibits and by an accompanying commentary. This commentary should be held to a minimum, would by preference be in outline form, and should cover the following principal points (organized, as appropriate, by business area):
      a. The charter of the division or subsidiary company and its underlying management philosophy.
      b. Current and future circumstances of the served market.
      c. The division's or subsidiary company's percentage penetration of the served market vis-à-vis major competition.
      d. Objectives of the business area or product line grouping, given the presumptions of the above two points.
      e. Strategies to be followed to achieve the stated objectives.
      f. Significant, longer range problems to be faced in achieving the objectives, including consideration of manpower, plant and equipment, and other resources.
      g. Management development.
      h. Interrelationships with other divisions and subsidiary companies of Raytheon.

2. The information exhibits and commentaries are assembled into a plans book which forms the data base for examining and evaluating the direction and growth performance of the Raytheon Company. Except for assignment to group executives, and members of division and subsidiary company organizations in which the plans were developed, such books (the number of copies is specified each year) are distributed only to the planning office from which a controlled reassignment is made.

3. Presentations of the plans, after appropriate review and approval by the group executives, are made by invitation to the company's operating and staff management group in the fall of each year. Such presentations cover the points set forth in Sections (b)–(h) above, and provide the basis for intracompany discussion directed toward the objectives of better coordination, cooperation, and management effectiveness. Information shown at these presentations is drawn from the data base and commentaries set forth in the plans books. Separate instructions are provided by the planning office relative to the outline for plan presentations.

4. The first year of the five-year planning period (including changes that result from the fall meeting) is detailed under the direction of the controller's office for measurement purposes and, upon approval, is established by the executive office as the company's profit budget.

F. *Procedure.* It is suggested that the plans book be organized in accordance with the following generalized outline and the related commentary. Specific exhibit titles and applicability to divisions and subsidiary companies are set forth in Section G below. Discussions as to the content of exhibits and other explanatory material are set forth below along with facsimiles of the information exhibits.

1. Executive summary. This section is devoted to the general manager's or president's summary of important aspects of his division or subsidiary company. The general manager's summary and the comparison with budget and last year's plan may be presented in whatever format is appropriate to the general manager's or president's style of presentation; the remaining subsections are to be submitted on the forms as noted in Section G below.

2. The business area or product line summaries. This section contains the fundamental objectives, strategies, assumptions, and discussions of expected results for each of the business area or product line groupings identified for the purpose and as specified by the group executives.

Separate program or product line detail should be prepared and held available under the guidance of the division planning office.

3. Functional plans. This section contains the analyses, plans, and strategies for developing and improving the functional organizations of the division or subsidiary company. This review would include an assessment in some depth of personal skills on hand, expected departures and replacements, and entirely new requirements for expansion and upgrading, and would cover at least the major function of the controller, industrial relations, manufacturing, marketing, research, and engineering.

4. Facilities requirements. This section is composed of information exhibits discussing, (a) floor space, (b) the relationship between floor space and manpower, and (c) laboratory and manufacturing machinery and equipment requirements (including scientific data processing equipment).

5. Divisional statistical summaries. This section contains particular summary exhibits which have proved to be of importance in support of plans, or which are useful as reference throughout the year.

6. Information processing systems (IPS) planning data. This section contains summary information concerning IPS cost and employee count, major systems development projects, processing load, and significant equipment changes.

7. Raytheon Europe. This group is comprised of both government oriented and commercial businesses. Plans Books will be made up by selecting forms from the exhibits to this procedure, as appropriate. Each subsidiary company within Raytheon Europe will have a separate plan. Plans should be submitted in U.S. dollars, and the current conversion rate used should be indicated as a footnote.

G. *Plans book organization*

Executive Summary
General Manager's Summary.
Comparison with Budget and Last Year's Plan.
Summary of Key Measures.
Summary of Key Measures by Business Area.
√ Summary of Key Measures by Operation or Product Line.
Planning Highlights—(Extended).
√ Planning Highlights.
Planning Milestones.
Business Area or Product Line Summaries
√ Business Area Objectives and Strategies.

√ Operation or Product Line Objectives.

    Business Area Summary—Government.

    Operation or Product Line Summary.

    Project Funding Sheet—Government.

    Program Summary—Government.

Functional Plans

    (Discussion in prose form.)

√ Manpower Requirements (End of Period).

Facilities Requirements

    √ Summary of Floor Space Requirements by Major Locations.

    √ Summary of Floor Space/Manpower Relationship.

    √ Summary of Machinery and Equipment Requirements.

    Summary of Manufacturing Load by Program Served.

Divisional Statistical Summaries

    Summary of IWRs OUT

    Summary of IWRs IN

    Long-Range Balance Sheet and Funding Plan.

    GOR and Programmed Expenditures Summary—Government.

    Summary of Floor Space Investment Plans.

Information Processing Systems Planning Data

    For forms required, see Finance Manual

    Note: √ Indicates included in Appendix A.

RAYTHEON   SUMMARY OF KEY MEASURES BY OPERATION OR PRODUCT LINE   COMPANY
                                                                            PRIVATE
10 – 1603 (1 73)   Page 2 of 2

DIVISION' SUBSIDIARY COMPANY   DATE SUBMITTED

PROFIT AFTER TAX
(DOLLARS IN THOUSANDS)

OPERATIONS OR PRODUCT LINES SHOULD BE IDENTIFIED WITH SEGMENTS
OF VERTICAL BARS, USING ALTERNATING BLACK, GRAY, AND WHITE. THE
LEGEND SHOULD BE AT THE LEFT OF THE CHART. EXAMPLE.

OPER OR PL "A" ——

OPER OR PL "B" ——

OPER OR PL "C" ——

OPER OR PL "D" ——

OPER OR PL "E" ——

OPER OR PL "F" ——

PRIOR YR   CUR. YR   BDGT YR
19____   19____   19____   19____

PRIOR YR   CUR. YR   BDGT YR
19 ____   19 ____   19 ____   19 ____   19 ____   19 ____   19 ____

OPERATION OR PRODUCT LINE						
Listing of Operations or Product Lines is in the same sequence as in the chart above.						
TOTAL						
MEMO: PRIOR YEAR'S PLAN (TOTAL)						

RAYTHEON
10- '589 (1 73)

PLANNING HIGHLIGHTS
(DOLLARS IN MILLIONS & TENTHS)

COMPANY PRIVATE
Page 1 of 2

| DIVISION SUBSIDIARY COMPANY | | | | DATE SUBMITTED | | | |

	PRIOR YR 19 ___	CUR. YR(a) 19 ___	BDGT YR 19 ___	19 ___	19 ___	19 ___	19 ___
GROSS ORDERS RECEIVED							
OUTSIDE							
FROM OTHER RAYTHEON ENTITIES							
TOTAL							
MEMO: ORDERS PLACED WITH OTHER RAYTHEON ENTITIES							
NET SALES – TOTAL							
MEMO: FOREIGN SALES							
MEMO: NET SALES – OUTSIDE							
BACKLOG (END OF PERIOD)							
PROFIT BEFORE TAX							
NET INCOME							
RETURN ON SALES (NS-T) %							
PROGRAMMED EXPENDITURES							
INDEPENDENT RESEARCH							
INDEPENDENT DEVELOPMENT							
MARKETING, ETC. - OTHER (EXCL CORP)							
ADMINISTRATION (EXCL CORPORATE)							
MACHINERY AND EQUIPMENT							
APPROVALS – TO BE CAPITALIZED							
– TO BE LEASED							
EXPENDITURES – CARRYOVERS							
– CURRENT							
– TOTAL							
DEPRECIATION AND AMORTIZATION							
REAL ESTATE							
APPROVALS – TO BE CAPITALIZED							
– TO BE LEASED							
EXPENDITURES – CARRYOVERS							
– CURRENT							
– TOTAL							
DEPRECIATION AND AMORTIZATION							

> Under Machinery & Equipment and Real Estate the "Approvals" lines are separated into values to be capitalized and values to be leased. In both cases, the amounts to be shown represent purchase cost; the separation should be consistent with current policy and should have the concurrence of the Treasurer's Office.

PLANNING HIGHLIGHTS

(DOLLARS IN MILLIONS & TENTHS)

COMPANY
PRIVATE

Page 2 of 2

10-1590 (2-72)

DIVISION						DATE SUBMITTED		
	LAST YR	CUR. YR	BDGT YR					
	19 ___	19 ___	19 ___	19 ___	19 ___	19 ___	19 ___	

ASSETS (END OF PERIOD)
  CURRENT
  NON-CURRENT
  TOTAL

FUNDING: INC (DEC) IN CUSTOMER ADVANCES
        (INC) DEC IN TOTAL DEBT

MISCELLANEOUS
  BASE FOR CORP. G&A ASSESSMENT

  MANPOWER (END OF PERIOD)
    EMPLOYEES
    CONTRACT LABOR
    TOTAL

  MANPOWER TURNOVER
    ENGINEERING & SCIENTIFIC
    TOTAL

  ROYALTY AND KNOW-HOW INCOME (PRE-TAX)

KEY MEASURES (END OF PERIOD)
  RETURN ON SALES (NS-T)
  CURRENT ASSET TURNOVER
  TOTAL ASSET TURNOVER (NS-T)
  RETURN ON ASSETS

  NS-T PER PERSON

Manpower turnover (MT) definition:

$$\text{MT-Engineering \& Scientific (E\&S) (\%)} = \frac{\text{Employees hired for replacement-E\&S}}{\text{Total employees-E\&S (average for period)}} \times 100$$

$$\text{MT-Total (\%)} = \frac{\text{Employees hired for replacement-total}}{\text{Total employees (average for period)}} \times 100$$

Results are to be carried out to one decimal place.

Key measure definition:

$$\text{Return on Sales (ROS)} = \frac{\text{Net Income}}{\text{Net Sales (Total)}}$$

Current Asset Turnover (CAT), Total Asset Turnover (TAT), and Return on Assets (ROA) are based on 2-point average assets (beginning and end of year) rather than end-of-period. This applies to prior year-accounted and current year-forecast as well as to the plan years.

$$\text{CAT} = \frac{\text{Net Sales (Total)}}{\text{Current Assets (Average)}}$$

$$\text{TAT} = \frac{\text{Net Sales (Total)}}{\text{Total Assets (Average)}}$$

$$\text{ROA} = \text{ROS} \times \text{TAT}$$

BUSINESS AREA OBJECTIVES AND STRATEGIES

Business Area Definition

Objectives and Strategies

This is the section where specific and pointed
commentary is of critical importance. The
future of the Business Area, circumstances of
approach and attack on the market, details of
new and improved resources, anticipated response
of competitors, and the like, should be examined.
In the discussion of what is to be done to achieve
objectives, the Business Area Manager should be
as specific as possible in respect to his marketing
plan and the utilization of external aids (advertising,
brochures, and the like), to promote the Business
Area's position.

Major Markets and Principal Competition

OPERATION OR PRODUCT LINE

DEFINITION, OBJECTIVES, STRATEGIES, AND COMPETITIVE ANALYSIS

Product Line Definition   —   Identify the product line. Special market segmentations
                                        are of interest here but must be consistent with your
                                        definition of served market.

Objectives   —   Support your specific objectives for sales, profitability,
                                        and market share growth for the Five Year Plan period.

Market Characteristics   —   This should briefly cover at least:

                                        —   Market growth during past five years and
                                            Raytheon's growth in this market over the
                                            same period.

                                        —   Projected five year market growth and
                                            fundamental reason for growth.

                                        —   The most important changes in product
                                            in next five years.

                                        —   The most important changes in end-use
                                            buyer requirement in next five years.

                                        —   The identity of the ultimate customer. How
                                            do you reach him.

Strategy   —   Detail the principal points of the strategy you will use to
                                        meet your objectives and deal with the market character-
                                        istics for the five year period.

Competitive Analysis

    — Major Competitors

                                        Current Year Sales   Market Share

    _____

    _____

    _____

    _____

    _____

    Memo: Raytheon

    — Distribution Channels   List and, if appropriate, comment on distribution channels
                                        used by competitors and Raytheon. Specifically, comment
                                        on whether competitors have other products in same
                                        channels. Does Raytheon?

    — Competitive Evaluation   Comment on how Raytheon product compares with top
                                        competitors' product in terms of quality, price, utility,
                                        customer acceptance.

    — Competitive Strategy   What factors are most important in maintaining or improv-
                                        ing our competitive position? Describe Raytheon's competi-
                                        tive strategy.

MANPOWER REQUIREMENTS (END OF PERIOD)   COMPANY PRIVATE

10-1594 (4/71)

DIVISION _____   DATE SUBMITTED _____

LOCATIONS / OPERATIONS	LAST YR 19___	CUR. YR 19___	BDGT YR 19___	19___	19___	19___	19___
DIVISION HEADQUARTERS							
ADMINISTRATION							
ENGINEERING AND SCIENTIFIC							
MANUFACTURING							
MARKETING							
CONTROLLER							
INFORMATION PROCESSING SYSTEMS							
INDUSTRIAL RELATIONS							
TOTAL							
CONTRACT LABOR							
ADMINISTRATION							
ENGINEERING AND SCIENTIFIC							
MANUFACTURING							
TOTAL							
ADMINISTRATION							
ENGINEERING AND SCIENTIFIC							
MANUFACTURING							
MARKETING							
CONTROLLER							
INFORMATION PROCESSING SYSTEMS							
INDUSTRIAL RELATIONS							
TOTAL							
ADMINISTRATION							
ENGINEERING AND SCIENTIFIC							
MANUFACTURING							
MARKETING							
CONTROLLER							
INFORMATION PROCESSING SYSTEMS							
INDUSTRIAL RELATIONS							
TOTAL							
ADMINISTRATION							
ENGINEERING AND SCIENTIFIC							
MANUFACTURING							
MARKETING							
CONTROLLER							
INFORMATION PROCESSING SYSTEMS							
INDUSTRIAL RELATIONS							
TOTAL							

Use one data set to display Division totals.

Manpower categories are as included in the Management Report.

RAYTHEON

10-1595 (7/69)

SUMMARY OF FLOOR SPACE REQUIREMENTS BY MAJOR LOCATIONS
(SQUARE FEET IN THOUSANDS)

COMPANY
PRIVATE

Page 1 of

DIVISION ————————————— COMPILED BY ————————————— DATE SUBMITTED —————————————

	TOTAL FLOOR SPACE OCCUPIED AT END OF YEAR						
	LAST YR	CUR. YR	BDGT YR				
	19 ___	19 ___	19 ___	19 ___	19 ___	19 ___	19 ___
DIVISION TOTAL							
LEASED SPACE – LONG TERM							
– SHORT TERM							
– TOTAL							
RAYTHEON-OWNED SPACE							
GOVERNMENT-OWNED SPACE							
TOTAL SPACE OCCUPIED							

COMMENTARY:

> This exhibit shows the actual and/or intended gross floor space to be occupied at the end of each of the specified years. Accordingly, it will follow the details of planned changes in facilities and will not necessarily reflect the exact amount of space that might be efficiently utilizable at any given point. Commentary should be added as appropriate.

LEASED SPACE – LONG TERM							
– SHORT TERM							
– TOTAL							
RAYTHEON-OWNED SPACE							
GOVERNMENT-OWNED SPACE							
TOTAL SPACE OCCUPIED							

COMMENTARY:

> Leased space is considered "long term" if commitment is for five years or more.

LEASED SPACE – LONG TERM							
– SHORT TERM							
– TOTAL							
RAYTHEON-OWNED SPACE							
GOVERNMENT-OWNED SPACE							
TOTAL SPACE OCCUPIED							

COMMENTARY:

RAYTHEON

10–1596 (1/73)

SUMMARY OF FLOOR SPACE / MANPOWER RELATIONSHIP   COMPANY
                                                                          PRIVATE

DIVISION/SUBSIDIARY COMPANY	LOCATION	DATE SUBMITTED

Floor space and manpower are plotted as a graph on this form.

The lines represent total manpower and total facilities, not changes.

The scales should be so constructed so that 150 square feet corresponds to one man. This is so that the relative positions of the facilities and manpower lines can be used as a rough guide of the number of square feet per man being planned for.

Example:

MANPOWER
(IN THOUSANDS)

GROSS
FLOOR
SPACE
OCCUPIED
(IN THOUSANDS
OF
SQUARE FEET)

PRIOR YR	CUR. YR	BDGT YR				
19 ____	19 ____	19 ____	19 ____	19 ____	19 ____	19 ____

SQUARE FEET/MAN
(AVERAGE):

MANPOWER _ _ _ _ _

FLOOR SPACE _____

SUMMARY OF MACHINERY AND EQUIPMENT REQUIREMENTS

COMPANY PRIVATE

(EXCLUDING BUSINESS DATA PROCESSING EQUIPMENT)

(DOLLARS IN THOUSANDS)

Page 1 of ___

10−1597 (1 73)

| DIVISION SUBSIDIARY COMPANY | | | | | | | DATE SUBMITTED |

	ADDITIONS DURING THE CALENDAR YEAR						
	PRIOR YR 19 ___	CUR. YR 19 ___	BDGT YR 19 ___	19 ___	19 ___	19 ___	19 ___

DIVISION TOTAL
- NEW CAPABILITY
- COST REDUCTION
- REPLACEMENT & MODERNIZATION
- INCREASED CAPACITY
- POLLUTION CONTROL REQUIREMENTS
- SAFETY REQUIREMENTS
- OTHER

TOTAL
- MEMO: CONTRACT REQUIRED

- NEW CAPABILITY
- COST REDUCTION
- REPLACEMENT & MODERNIZATION
- INCREASED CAPACITY
- POLLUTION CONTROL REQUIREMENTS
- SAFETY REQUIREMENTS
- OTHER

TOTAL
- MEMO: CONTRACT REQUIRED

- NEW CAPABILITY
- COST REDUCTION
- REPLACEMENT & MODERNIZATION
- INCREASED CAPACITY
- POLLUTION CONTROL REQUIREMENTS
- SAFETY REQUIREMENTS
- OTHER

TOTAL
- MEMO: CONTRACT REQUIRED

- NEW CAPABILITY
- COST REDUCTION
- REPLACEMENT & MODERNIZATION
- INCREASED CAPACITY
- POLLUTION CONTROL REQUIREMENTS
- SAFETY REQUIREMENTS
- OTHER

TOTAL
- MEMO: CONTRACT REQUIRED

This exhibit discusses additions only. Do not net out disposals. No Business Data Processing equipment should be included in this exhibit.

The first section of this form is a division total. Subsequent sections provide a breakdown by facility.

Some machinery and equipment requirements may fit more than one of the categories listed (e.g., replacement/modernization and cost reduction). In such cases, the item should be classified under the item that provides the principal justification for the requirement.

Further information regarding pollution control requirements may be obtained from J. K. Rogers, Manager Environmental Quality, ext. 496, Lexington. Information on safety requirements, including the Occupational Health and Safety Act of 1970, may be obtained from G. E. Luedke, Director-Safety, ext. 608, Lexington.

APPENDIX B: FINANCE POLICIES AND PROCEDURES

SUBJECT: MIFA[1] FINANCIAL REPORTING SYSTEM

A. *Purpose.* The compilation of MIFA financial reports, which include budgets, management reports, financial and operating meeting review slides, and general reports, requires standard formats to assure effective presentation of key financial data and to provide uniformity for Raytheon Company consolidation. Certain reports are exhibited in this policy and procedure to show an interrelated cross section of the scope of data utilized and are arranged in subject sequence.

B. *Policy.* MIFA financial reports are compiled for company management to evaluate the financial performance of divisions, subsidiary companies, and Raytheon Company consolidated.

C. *Applicability.* This policy and procedure applies to all divisions and subsidiary companies.

D. *Responsibilities.* Division and subsidiary company controllers are responsible for effecting this policy and procedure.

E. *Procedure*

Responsibility		*Action*
Division and subsidiary company controllers	1.	Compile MIFA financial reports.
	2.	Submit reports to Manager–Budgets, Forecasts, and Financial Analysis, Lexington in accordance with required due dates.
Manager–Budgets, Forecasts, and Financial Analysis	3.	Reviews reports submitted and distributes to company management.
	4.	Prepares projector slides of certain division/subsidiary company reports and distributes copies for review and discussion at the monthly financial and operating review meetings.
	5.	Combines division/subsidiary company reports into Raytheon Company consolidated reports and distributes to company management.
		NOTE: Where a certain current data may not be available from a division/subsidiary company for the Raytheon Company consolidation, the most recent applicable data available from the division/subsidiary company is selected.

---

[1] Management information and financial analysis.

REPORT TITLE	REPORT NO.
HIGHLIGHTS	103 (Annual Budget)
DUE DATE	GENERAL REQUIREMENTS

SPECIAL REQUIREMENTS

Summarize key operating budget data for the budget year and quarters, and compare with accounted/forecast results for the previous year and quarters. Major budget changes (if any) from the Five-Year Business Plan or previous budgets are explained at the bottom of the report. (This report is used as a vehicle of appraisal for subsequent formal approval by the Executive Office.)

RELATED REPORTS	
EXHIBITED	NOT EXHIBITED

REPRESENTATIVE FORMAT

(SIMILAR FORMATS, IF ANY, ARE LISTED BY FORMAT LETTER IN POLICY AND PROCEDURE NO. 25 3003 310)

RAYTHEON 1kl   Private

HIGHLIGHTS
($ in mil except Income,
Expend & Capital in thou)

Report 103
Annual Budget
YEAR(Jan-Dec)   :19

	PRIOR QUARTERS and YEAR 19							CURRENT QUARTERS and YEAR 19					
	PLAN	ACCOUNTED/FORECAST						PLAN	BUDGET				
	*Tot Yr Jan-Dec	*Tot Yr Jan-Dec	1st Qtr Jan-Mar	2nd Qtr Apr-Jun	3rd Qtr Jul-Sep	4th Qtr Oct-Dec		Tot Yr Jan-Dec	Tot Yr Jan-Dec	1st Qtr Jan-Mar	2nd Qtr Apr-Jun	3rd Qtr Jul-Sep	4th Qtr Oct-Dec
$							GROSS ORDER RECEIPTS–Tot	$					
W							SALES ORD BKLG–Tot (end of FUTURE WKS in BKLG–T per)	W					
$							NET SALES–Total	$					
							NET INCOME						
							CURRENT ASSETS (end NON–CURRENT ASSETS of TOTAL ASSETS per)						
							TOT FINANCING (end of per) FINANCING(Incr)Decr–YTD						
X							RECEIV TURN(sales) (annual INVENTORY TURN(cost) rate)	X					
							CURRENT ASSET TURN (an- NON–CUR DETRACTOR nual TOTAL ASSET TURN rate)						
%							RETURN on SALES RETURN on ASSETS (annual RETURN on EQUITY rate)	%					
							CAPITAL REQUIREMENTS: Pri Yr Balances (at beg) Current Year Approvals						
							Expenditures Deprec & Amortiz						
E							EMPLOYEE COUNT(end of per)	E					
$							COST to MANUFACTURE	$					
							PROGRAMMED EXPEND: Independent Research						
							Independent Development						
							Marketing						
							Administration(excl Corp)						

*Includes Accounted period thru   Plan   Fcst

W-Weeks, X-Times, %-Percent, E-Employees

** End of year

RECONCILIATION of PLAN/BUDGET CHANGES

Month (MR)	Description (full year)	Sales ($ in mil)	Income ($ in thou)	Assets ** ($ in mil)

REPORT TITLE	REPORT NO.
HIGHLIGHTS	203 (Monthly Management Report)
DUE DATE	GENERAL REQUIREMENTS

SPECIAL REQUIREMENTS
Summarize key operating accounted/forecast data for the current month, next three months, and current year and compare with related budgets. Provide accounted/forecast data by quarters for the current year and compare with accounted results by quarter for the prior year.

RELATED REPORTS	
EXHIBITED	NOT EXHIBITED

REPRESENTATIVE FORMAT

(SIMILAR FORMATS, IF ANY, ARE LISTED BY FORMAT LETTER IN POLICY AND PROCEDURE NO. 25 3003 310)

RAYTHEON Bd   Private

HIGHLIGHTS

(dollars in mil except NI in thou)

Report 203

Monthly Management Report

:19

ACCOUNTED

CURRENT YEAR to DATE 19
(Jan –)

	Budget	Accounted
$		

GROSS ORDER RECEIPTS-Total
BACKLOG-Total (end of period)

NET SALES-Total
NET INCOME

CURRENT ASSETS (end of
TOTAL ASSETS period)
FINANCING(Increase)Decrease-YTD

X

CURRENT ASSET TURNOVER (annual
TOTAL ASSET TURNOVER rate)

%

RETURN on SALES
RETURN on ASSETS (annual
RETURN on EQUITY rate)

CURRENT MONTH
( )

	Budget	Forecast	Accounted
$			

X

%

FORECAST

NEXT ( ) MONTHS (–)

	Budget	Forecast
$		

NEXT YR-1ST Q (Jan-Mar)

Budget	Forecast

GROSS ORDER RECEIPTS-Total
BACKLOG-Total (end of period)

NET SALES-Total
NET INCOME

CURRENT ASSETS (end of
TOTAL ASSETS period)
FINANCING(Increase)Decrease-YTD

X

CURRENT ASSET TURNOVER (annual
TOTAL ASSET TURNOVER rate)

%

RETURN on SALES
RETURN on ASSETS (annual
RETURN on EQUITY rate)

YEAR 19
(Jan – Dec)

	Budget	Prev Fcst	New Fcst
$			

X

%

QUARTERLY TRENDS

PRIOR YEAR 19 ACCOUNTED

	1st Q (J-M)	2nd Q (A-J)	3rd Q (J-S)	4th Q (O-D)
$				

NET SALES-Total
NET INCOME

CURRENT ASSETS (end of
TOTAL ASSETS period

X

RECEIVABLE TURNOVER(sales (annual
INVENTORY TURNOVER(cost) rate)

CURRENT ASSET TURNOVER (an-
NON-CUR ASSET DETRACTOR nual
TOTAL ASSET TURNOVER rate)

%

RETURN on SALES
RETURN on ASSETS (annual rate)

(up-dated quarterly)
EMPLOYEE COUNT (end of
FUTURE WKS in BACKLOG period)

E
W

CUR YR 19 ACTD/FCST   **NEXT YR**

	1st Q (J-M)	2nd Q (A-J)	3rd Q (J-S)	4th Q (O-D)	1st Q Fcst (J-M)
$					

X

%

E
W

REPORT TITLE	REPORT NO.
BALANCE SHEET AND FUNDING	105 (Annual Budget)

DUE DATE	GENERAL REQUIREMENTS

SPECIAL REQUIREMENTS

Provide balance sheet budget data by accounts for the budget year by months, and summarize cumulative related financing requirements, comparing such with accounted/forecast results for the previous year.

RELATED REPORTS	
EXHIBITED	NOT EXHIBITED

REPRESENTATIVE FORMAT

(SIMILAR FORMATS, IF ANY, ARE LISTED BY FORMAT LETTER IN POLICY AND PROCEDURE NO. 25 3003 310)

RAYTHEON   Ae   Private

BALANCE SHEET and FUNDING

(dollars in millions)

Report 105
Annual Budget
YEAR (Jan–Dec)   :19

BALANCE SHEET (end of period)

PRI YR 19 A/F Dec	Beg 1/1	Jan	Feb	Mar	Apr	May	Jun		Jul	Aug	Sep	Oct	Nov	Dec
$								Cash & Temp Invest	$					
								US Govt-Billed (net)						
								US Govt-Unbilled (net)						
								Other Customers						
								Total Accts Receivable						
								FP Contr in Progress (net)						
								Other						
								Total Inventories						
								IWR Asset Adjustment						
								Prepaid Expenses						
								TOTAL CURRENT ASSETS						
								Long-Term Receivables						
								Investments						
								Prop, Plant & Equip-Gross						
								-(Res)						
								-Net						
								Def Charges & Oth Assets						
								TOTAL ASSETS						
								Advance Payments (net)						
								Accounts Payable						
								Accr Exp-Sal, Wages, Comm						
								Fed & Fgn Income Taxes						
								Oth Accr Expenses						
								TOTAL CURRENT LIABIL						
								Notes Payable						
								Intercompany Loans						
								Interdivision Accts						
								TOTAL FINANCING						
								EQUITY						
								TOTAL LIAB & EQUITY						

FUNDING (Year to Date)

PRI YR 19 A/F Jan-Dec	J-J	J-F	J-M	J-A	J-M	J-J		J-J	J-A	J-S	J-O	J-N	J-D
$							Net Income (Loss)	$					
							Depreciation & Amortiz (Add to Prop, Plant & Equip)						
							Prop, Plant & Eq Disp (net)						
							Other Assets (Incr) Decr						
							Cur Liab Incr (Decr)						
							FINANCING (Incr) Decr						

REPORT TITLE	REPORT NO.
BALANCE SHEET AND FUNDING	205 (Monthly Management Report)

DUE DATE	GENERAL REQUIREMENTS

SPECIAL REQUIREMENTS

Provide balance sheet account/forecast data by accounts for the current month, next three months and current year and compare with related budgets, and prior month accounted results. Summarize cumulative accounted/forecast financing requirements for the current month, next three months, and current year, comparing such with related budgets and prior month and prior year-to-date accounted results. The accounted portions of the balance sheet section of this report are derived in substance from the Accounting Trial Balance Schedule No. 51, Balance Sheet (Form No. 10-0021).

RELATED REPORTS	
EXHIBITED	NOT EXHIBITED

REPRESENTATIVE FORMAT

(SIMILAR FORMATS, IF ANY, ARE LISTED BY FORMAT LETTER IN POLICY AND PROCEDURE NO. 25 3003 310)

RAYTHEON Ag   Private

BALANCE SHEET and FUNDING

(dollars in millions)

Report 205
Monthly Management Report
; 19

CURRENT YR 19		PRIOR MONTH	CURRENT MONTH			BALANCE SHEET (end of period)	NEXT THREE MONTHS						YEAR 19		NEXT YR 19
(Beg 1/1)		( )	( )				( )		( )		( )		( )		(Beg 1/1)
Bdgt	Actd	Actd	Bdgt	Fcst	Actd		Bdgt	Fcst	Bdgt	Fcst	Bdgt	Fcst	Bdgt	Fcst	F/A
$						Cash & Temp Invest $									
						US Govt-Billed (net)									
						US Govt-Unbilled (net)									
						Other Customers									
						Total Accts Receiv									
						FP Cont in Prog (net)									
						Other									
						Total Inventories									
						IWR Asset Adj									
						Prepaid Expenses									
						TOTAL CUR ASSETS									
						Long-Term Receiv									
						Investments									
						Prop, Plant & Eq-Gr									
						– (Res)									
						– Net									
						Def Chgs & Oth Assets									
						TOTAL ASSETS									
						Adv Payments (net)									
						Accts Payable									
						Acc Sal, Wages, Comm									
						Fed & Fgn Inc Taxes									
						Oth Acc Expenses									
						TOTAL CUR LIABIL									
						Notes Payable									
						Intercompany Loans									
						Interdivision Accts									
						TOTAL FINANCING									
						EQUITY									
						TOTAL LIAB & EQTY									

PRIOR YTD 19	PRIOR MONTH	CURRENT MONTH			FUNDING (Year to Date)	NEXT THREE MONTHS						YEAR 19	
(Jan-)	(Jan-)	(Jan-)				(Jan-)		(Jan-)		(Jan-)		(Jan-)	
Actd	Actd	Bdgt	Fcst	Actd		Bdgt	Fcst	Bdgt	Fcst	Bdgt	Fcst	Bdgt	Fcst
$					Net Income (Loss) $								
					Deprec & Amortiz (Add to P, P&E)								
					P, P&E Dispos (net)								
					Oth Assets (Inc) Dec								
					Cur Liab Inc (Dec)								
					FINANCING (Inc) Dec								

DUE DATE	GENERAL REQUIREMENTS

SPECIAL REQUIREMENTS

Provide income statement budget data by accounts for the budget year and months, and compare with accounted/forecast results for the previous year.

RELATED REPORTS

EXHIBITED	NOT EXHIBITED

REPRESENTATIVE FORMAT

(SIMILAR FORMATS, IF ANY, ARE LISTED BY FORMAT LETTER IN POLICY AND PROCEDURE NO. 25 3003 310)

RAYTHEON PTe Private

(incl Machlett)

MICROWAVE & POWER TUBE

INCOME STATEMENT

(dollars in thousands)

Report 109

Annual Budget

YEAR (Jan–Dec)   :19

PRI YR 19 A/F Jan–Dec	CUR YR 19 BDGT Jan–Dec	Jan	Feb	Mar	Apr	May	Jun		Jul	Aug	Sep	Oct	Nov	Dec
			CURRENT YEAR 19	BUDGET						CURRENT YEAR 19	BUDGET			
$								Gross Sales–Total	$					
								Deductions						
								NET SALES–Total						
								Standard Product Cost						
								Fixed Overhead						
								Manufacturing Variance						
								Inventory Adjustment						
								Royalty Expense						
								Product Warranty						
								Other Cost of Sales						
								TOTAL COST of SALES						
								GROSS MARGIN						
								Independent Development						
								Operation Marketing						
								Division Marketing						
								Operation Administration						
								Division Administration						
								Independent Research						
								Corporate Administration						
								ICD Interest(Inc)Exp–Net						
								Other Interest Expense						
								(Royalty Income)						
								Oth(Income)Expense–Net						
								TOTAL OTHER COSTS						
								PROFIT before TAX						
								Federal Income Tax						
								Investment Tax Credit						
								NET INCOME						

REPORT TITLE	REPORT NO.
SALES AND PROFITS	134 (Annual Budget)
DUE DATE	GENERAL REQUIREMENTS

SPECIAL REQUIREMENTS
Provide sales and profit budget data by operation for the budget year and months, and compare with accounted/forecast results for the previous year.

RELATED REPORTS	
EXHIBITED	NOT EXHIBITED

REPRESENTATIVE FORMAT

(SIMILAR FORMATS, IF ANY, ARE LISTED BY FORMAT LETTER IN POLICY AND PROCEDURE NO. 25 3003 310)

RAYTHEON PTc   Private
(including Machlett)
MICROWAVE & P TUBE

SALES and PROFITS
- By Operation -
(Sales $ in mil & hund, Income $ in thou)

Report 134
Annual Budget
YEAR (Jan-Dec)   :19

PRIOR YEAR 19 A/F	CURRENT YEAR 19 BUDGET	CURRENT YEAR MONTHS 19 BUDGET						OPERATION Category	CURRENT YEAR MONTHS 19 BUDGET					
Jan-Dec	Jan-Dec	Jan	Feb	Mar	Apr	May	Jun		Jul	Aug	Sep	Oct	Nov	Dec
$								MICROWAVE TUBE(MTO) Net Sales	$					
%								Net Income Return on Sales	%					
$								MACHLETT LABS Net Sales	$					
%								Net Income Return on Sales	%					
$								INDUSTRIAL COMP(ICO) Net Sales	$					
%								Net Income Return on Sales	%					
$								MEDICAL ELECTRONICS Net Sales	$					
%								Net Income Return on Sales	%					
$								SPECIAL MICRO(SMDO) Net Sales	$					
%								Net Income Return on Sales	%					
$								DISTRIB PRODUCTS(DPO) Net Sales	$					
%								Net Income Return on Sales	%					
$								NEW PRODUCTS Net Sales	$					
%								Net Income Return on Sales	%					
$								TOTAL OTHER Net Sales	$					
%								Net Income Return on Sales	%					
$								TOTAL DIVISION Net Sales	$					
%								Net Income Return on Sales	%					

REPORT TITLE	REPORT NO.
FORECAST FLASH DATA	714 (Monthly General Report)
DUE DATE	GENERAL REQUIREMENTS

SPECIAL REQUIREMENTS
Provide early management report sales, profit, and related forecast data for the next three months. (This report is consolidated into Raytheon Company flash forecast and presented to the Executive Office in advance of the monthly management report.)

RELATED REPORTS

EXHIBITED	NOT EXHIBITED

REPRESENTATIVE FORMAT

(SIMILAR FORMATS, IF ANY, ARE LISTED BY FORMAT LETTER IN POLICY AND PROCEDURE NO. 25 3003 310)

RAYTHEON   Af   Private   Report 714   _____

                          ┌──────────────────────────┐
                          │   FORECAST FLASH DATA   │   Monthly General Report
                          └──────────────────────────┘
_____   (Sales and Cost/Mfr $ in mil-Profit,   _____ :19
                              Inventory & Expenditure $ in thou)

CUR YEAR to DATE 19 (Jan-) Actd		NEXT THREE MONTHS			( ) YEAR 19 (Jan-Dec) Fcst	NEXT YR 1st Q 19 (Jan-Mar) Fcst
		( ) Fcst	( ) Fcst	( ) Fcst		
	SALES and PROFITS (all Divs/Subs)					
	Net Sales-Outside					
	Net Sales-Internal Effort(Coml-Total)					
	Net Income					
	TAX RECONCILIATION (all Divs/Subs)					
	U.S. Regular-Profit before Tax -Tax -Net Income					
	U.S. Capital Gains-Profit before Tax -Tax -Net Income					
	Foreign-Profit before Tax -Tax -Net Income					
	TOTAL-Profit before Tax -Tax -Investment Tax Credit -Net Income (per above)					
	Memo -Heath Seas Adj (PAT)					
	POOL (Govt Divs/Subs-not cumulative) Cost to Mfg-Division Total -Div Tot w/o Maj Sub Cont -Subsidiary Total Independent Development Expend Bid Proposal Expenditures					
	CORP PORTION-DIV INVEN (Coml Divs) (quarterly - end of period)					
	Total					

Forecast Flash Data (except Tax data) is due the 2nd Friday of the fiscal month between 9:00 A.M.-1:00 P.M., by telephone to MIFA
The complete Forecast Flash report should be sent with the Management Report.

Chapter outline

5

System design for a responsibility unit

When you have completed this chapter you will understand:

1. The requirements that a planning and control system has to satisfy for any responsibility unit.
2. A normative approach to the design of a planning and control system.
3. Why a normative approach is superior to an incremental one, when formalization of a planning and control system is desirable and what it accomplishes.

RESPONSIBILITY UNIT SYSTEM REQUIREMENTS

A systematic approach to situational systems design requires both a framework within which to determine planning and control requirements and an approach that will satisfy these requirements. Chapter 4 has described how organizational differentiation and decentralization may influence both the number of planning and control cycles carried out and also the allocation of responsibility for their performance.

The focus in this chapter now narrows to the design requirements for a single responsibility unit. A responsibility unit or center is simply a delineated set of organizational activities and responsibilities for which a distinguishable individual or group can be held accountable. Except for the lowest organizational level, responsibility units are increasingly aggregations of subordinate units. Any responsibility unit may contribute to or be responsible for one or more cycles in the planning and control process. And so, although the focus now narrows to design for individual responsibility units, what the planning and control system must do for any particular unit still depends on the organization's manner of differentiation and decentralization. Differentiation and decentralization affect both the task-related expectations for each responsibility unit, and also behavioral differences between units; and both of these factors determine the appropriateness of a systems design.

Differentiation and decentralization influence the way an organization decomposes its planning and control process, the way it allocates responsibility to specific units, and the timing of the execution. An analysis of differentiation and decentralization therefore can provide sufficient information to at least specify an activity-involvement-timing (AIT) chart. This analysis yields a set of expectations as to the desired performance of each responsibility unit and the desired interrelationships among units. This chapter suggests a way to design a planning and control system that will assist a responsibility unit in satisfying those expectations expressed or implied by the AIT chart while matching its behavioral characteristics.

Improving performance

The purpose of the planning and control system for any focal responsibility unit is to aid the unit's managers in determining and then accomplishing what is expected of them. As discussed in Chapter 1, the system can both improve plans and decisions, and also improve managerial activities. Therefore the requirements of a system are that it stimulate, guide, and encourage the behavior appropriate to each situation, whether that behavior relates to efficiency, effectiveness, communication, a more disciplined approach to management, and so on.

Regardless of the unique requirements of a situation, there are certain universal purposes a system must satisfy. The system must link each unit's manager to the strategic mission of the organization so that he or she understands what is expected, is stimulated and aided in behaving accordingly, is reinforced appropriately, and learns from experience. More specifically, the system must (1) arouse the managers so that they are motivated to contribute to the organization's mission; (2) guide the appropriate behavior by constraining or influencing them as required; (3) help them accomplish the task requirements by either drawing attention to or helping them solve problems of planning, decision making, and controlling their sphere of responsibility; (4) provide a fair basis for evaluation; and (5) develop in them the capacity to learn and to do more. And, if the process is to be adaptative, feedback from the key variables measured must provide the input for system adaptation and evolution.

A SYSTEMATIC APPROACH TO SYSTEM DESIGN

System design is a logical process of collecting and narrowing a mass of data until system requirements are completely defined. This search should uncover all that is relevant in the situation and exclude all that is extraneous or misleading. This information is distilled and focused as the analysis moves from the overall situation to what is specifically wrong or required within it, and then finally to what can and should be done about it.

From this description of the design process it is clear that its eventual success depends in part on the initial perspective and approach. Perspective implies stepping back from a specific set of problem symptoms so as to be objective. It implies viewing the local system and its planning requirements as a problem situation within a larger context. The discussion in Chapters 1 to 4 on multicycle planning and control systems was intended to provide the required perspective. But although perspective is necessary to begin the analysis, system design also requires an operational method which will lead to a solution.

The characteristics of an orderly approach to system design are not difficult to specify. The approach must satisfy a number of criteria: (1) It must focus initially on what must be accomplished by the system if the firm is to achieve its present strategy and also adapt to future environment. (2) It must provide the system designer with a procedure to analyze the problem situation into its component parts. (3) It must allow him to probe deeper and deeper into the problem until he arrives at a degree of resolution sufficient to solve it. (4) It should continually stimulate and guide him to maintain the proper perspective so as to develop a clear understanding of the context of the situation. (5) It must be useful both to individuals and to groups by encouraging independent and interdependent judgments.

The approach must help the system designer determine what should be done, what are the best tools and techniques to do it, and then if it has been done correctly. The following nine steps are a summary of one approach.

Diagnosis
1. Understand the strategic mission of the organization within which the focal unit functions.
2. Understand the organization's expectations of the focal unit; specify the unit's measures of success (key result areas).
3. Identify the causal and intervening variables that influence success (key success factors).

Prescription
4. Select the key variables of the unit.

5. Develop a normative system to plan and control these key variables.

Prognosis

6. Define the system gap.
7. Redefine the system in light of organizational constraints and resources.

Action

8. Implement the system.

Evaluation

9. Evaluate the design and implementation decisions and adapt the system as required.

Description of the approach

1. *Understand the strategic mission of the organization within which the unit functions.* At this outermost level of examination, it is essential to understand what the organization as a whole is trying to accomplish and the strategy it is following. If the key strategic variables of the total organization are not directly identifiable, this step involves examining the firm, its environment, its organizational capabilities, stakeholder expectations, and past performance so that its KVs can be understood.

Typical questions asked in this phase of analysis are: What does the organization have to do in order to be successful? What is implied in the firm's mission other than survival—growth, diversification, product quality, development of advanced technology, worker security? Who are the customers, competitors, and suppliers of the firm? What are its resources in terms of expertise, personnel, equipment, and reputation? What characterizes the market in which it operates? What are the key success factors (differential advantages) of the firm—individual motivation, good long-term investment decisions, flexibility in product lines, marketing and selling abilities, technical expertise?

It is desirable to specify the measures of success or key result areas of the organization. What are the general yardsticks (in the form of ratios, percentages, or other quantitative or qualitative evaluations) the organization uses to evaluate its performance? How does the organization know when it is successful? These end results are the ultimate key variables the firm is attempting to influence.

2. *Understand the organization's expectations of the unit for which the system is being designed.* In this step, the rationale of the organization's differentiation and decentralization is examined in order to determine the expected contribution to the firm of the focal unit. This step defines success from the perspective of the unit itself.

At this stage it is necessary to describe how an effectively performing responsibility unit behaves. The following are typical questions to ask:

How does this unit fit into the total organization? What are the competitive advantages of the company and what does this unit have to do in order to enhance these advantages? What planning or performance does the unit contribute to the ultimate accomplishment of the organization's mission? Answering these questions involves establishing the measures of success for the unit and the measures by which it can evaluate its performance. These are the key result areas on which the unit's system focuses. Typical variables may include profit, market share, levels of customer service, or departmental growth.

3. *Identify the causal and intervening variables that influence unit performance.* Causal and intervening (or intermediate) variables are the key success factors which contribute directly or indirectly to accomplishing the unit's desired end results. For example, if sales volume is a key result area, compensation may be a causal variable and motivation an intervening one. That is, higher pay leads to higher motivation which, in turn, leads to higher sales. Key result areas and the key success factors which affect their performance can be considered to make up chains of causal, intermediate, and end-result variables; the number of variables in such a chain depends on the complexity of the activity. In this step the success measures of the unit are traced back to their causes, so as to identify the factors that must be manipulated to alter performance.

Causal variables are the independent or determining factors that, through a chain of cause and effect relationships involving intermediate variables, influence the dependent variable or accomplish the end result desired. Causal factors may have direct impact on key result areas or only work through a number of intervening steps; i.e., there may be only one cause → effect link in the chain or several. Causal factors may be controllable or uncontrollable by the unit manager. Working conditions and the perceived status of a job may both influence job satisfaction, the former may be controllable while the latter may not. And finally, it should be noted that causal and intervening variables may be of a behavioral, operational, or financial nature. The following are examples of such causal chains:

1. Higher pay → motivation → better performance.
2. Participation → job satisfaction → lower turnover.
3. Number of sales representatives → number of sales calls → greater sales.
4. Amount of quality control inspection → quality of product → more sales.
5. Dollars spent on advertising → greater profits.

In short, a causal model represents a theory of what should be taking place. It indicates to the systems designer which variables are most significant and, hence, which should be planned and controlled. And so, the validity of this model significantly influences the usefulness of the planning and control system upon which it is based.

The accuracy to which the model must be developed depends on the particular problem a responsibility unit is facing. In designing a system, it is essential to tackle the right problem. There is a need for perspective in order to isolate the correct problem and understand its relevant interactions with other parts of the organization. Therefore, the boundaries of problem definition must be extended as far as required to probe all interdependencies that are relevant. The examination must not be arbitrarily limited for the sake of a convenient model, or because some easy solution will fit an existing organizational structure.

There are limitations to this modeling process, of course. Any analysis is limited by time and costs. Furthermore, the complexity, uncertainty, and intangible factors may be difficult to reflect. But some modeling should be attempted (even if only a verbal description of how the unit operates) to avoid blunders in thinking or misplaced assumptions. Explicitly stating relationships is far superior to either pure intuition or blind application of past experience.

4. *Select the key variables of the unit.* Once the key result areas and all the basic determinants of success have been identified, they must be related to the most suitable methods of processing and gathering information. Before the system design proceeds further, however, it is necessary to identify the most important causal, intervening, and end-result variables. These are the key variables that must be planned and controlled. But which variables are of prime importance? Which are so critical to ultimate performance that they should be monitored by management for fast feedback and corrective action?

In deciding among key variables, some typical questions to ask are the following: What are the critical processes of this unit in terms of resource input, transformation, and output? What are the distinguishing characteristics of the process—personnel, finance, flexibility, responsiveness? What variables guide this process? What should be monitored in order to ensure a continuous contribution to organizational success? What is the relative importance of each of these? And how can they best be measured?

5. *Develop a normative system to plan and control these key variables.* The first four steps identify the determinants and measures of unit success, and therefore the requirements for a planning and control system. It is important that these requirements be normative and represent the design requirements of an optimal system, so that all possible alternative processes, methods and techniques, involvements, and timing can be examined. A normative system is one that would exist if there were no constraints on its implementation, such as poor management, insufficient funds, or resistance to change. The final system design may

suffer if proposals are judged prematurely and not developed into viable alternatives before evaluation. This ideal solution must then be translated into the terms used by the firm so that it can be compared with the existing system, if one exists.

6. *Define the system gap.* The existing system should now be analyzed and documented so that it is thoroughly understood. With a definition of an ideal solution, and with an understanding of the existing system, the next step is to outline the changes needed to move from the present system to the proposed one. This step defines the system gap and the likely problems in implementing the ideal system.

7. *Redefine the system in light of organizational constraints and resources.* This step is the logical continuation of the previous one. It includes analyzing the feasibility of closing the system gap in light of the constraints which determine the bounds of an acceptable solution. After this analysis, an acceptable modification of the original design can be developed.

Next the appropriate tools and techniques for implementation must be selected. The financial planning and control system and the procedures, methods, and approaches which best suit the company's organizational and planning and control requirements are some of the choices to be made. This design takes all relevant constraints and resources into consideration, such as the lack of appropriately trained personnel, the lack of capital, legal norms, and union requirements. Its purpose is to produce a feasible solution to the design problem.

8. *Implement the system.* In this second to last step, the stages leading to system changeover are specified. This transition between systems is influenced by the resources and constraints within the firm and particularly by the personalities of the individuals who have to accept the new system. An action program outlining the required steps is then designed to narrow the implementation gap.

9. *Evaluate the design and implementation decisions and adapt the system as required.* After implementation has been completed, an evaluation must be made to determine to what extent the design and implementation procedures were successful. The success of the methods used can be compared against the initial plan and so determine whether or not implementation was successful.

These steps are depicted in flow chart format in Figure 5–1.

Relationship to the multicycle model

Steps 1–4 of this systematic approach to the design of a planning and control system for a responsibility unit should be recognized as simply a restatement of the fact that planning is a multicycle process. The ap-

FIGURE 5–1
Planning and control system design

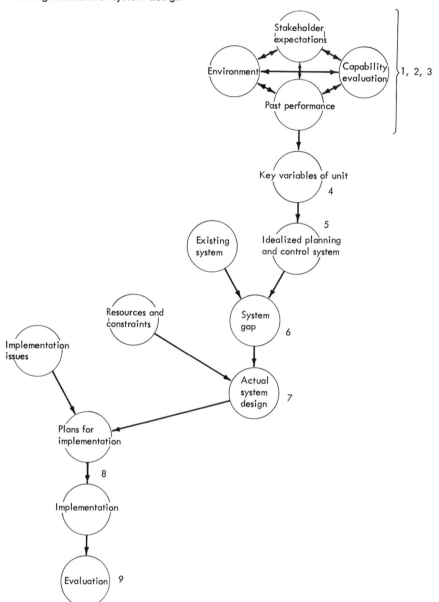

proach is a reminder that each of the cycles in a multicycle process involves establishing objectives and the strategies to achieve these objectives, and that every responsibility unit in an organization may play some part in this complex problem solving and implementation activity. In short, it is a reminder that the role a particular responsibility unit plays depends on the cycle or cycles it contributes to or has responsibility for.

The planning and controls system designer must be constantly aware that the planning in any organization can be thought of as specifying a means-ends chain, whereby attaining the objectives established for one unit is but a means of accomplishing the objectives established by higher order units. The message of Chapter 4 is that hierarchical organizations are differentiated and decentralized into responsibility units in order to clarify and execute this means-ends chain. Therefore, the logic underlying this chain must be clearly understood before the planning and control system applicable to any part of it can be designed or evaluated. It must be understood both from the standpoint of how planning is carried out in the organization as well as of how the organization is to be controlled.

The role of multicycle processes in any organization's planning has already been thoroughly discussed in this book and, hopefully, is now well understood by the reader. The cycles making up any multicycle planning activity form a nested hierarchy with each successive cycle being carried out within the guidelines and constraints established by the cycles carried out before it. This is represented by the now familiar funnel-shaped diagram on the left of Figure 5–2. Proceeding downward through a hierarchical organizational pyramid, successive cycles sequen-

FIGURE 5–2

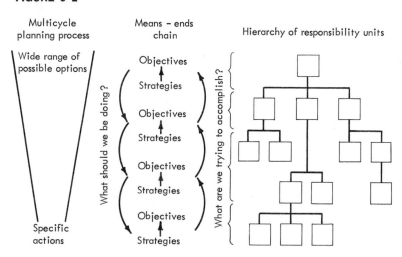

tially decompose and answer parts of the organization's key question "What should we be doing?" until specific actions can be chosen.

The conceptualization of multicycle planning as establishing a means-ends chain also facilitates the communication of expectations to each responsibility unit and the subsequent control of it. The performance expectations of each unit making up an organization are established by some multicycle planning process. Once these have been established and communicated, the management of every responsibility unit should understand what is expected of them, how they fit into the organization, and the contribution their activities make toward achieving the organization's strategic mission. Proceeding upward through this means-ends chain from the lowest to the highest levels, the manager of each responsibility unit in the organizational pyramid should understand the contribution he or she makes to the organization's strategic mission sufficiently to answer the following question: "Why am I doing what I am doing? What am I trying to accomplish and how does this contribute to the accomplishment of the organization's strategic mission?" If all responsibility unit managers in an organization can answer these questions, goal congruence and logical consistency of decision making is more likely.

Example

The staff training and development section of the personnel department is an example of a responsibility unit which exists in many organizations. This unit is established to assist in defining the managerial needs the organization will face in the future, in identifying discrepancies in managerial skills and knowledge required and available, and to provide training and assistance in developing the managers required.

Objectives. The staff training and development section can be assumed to be performing successfully when every management job in the organization is staffed by an individual with the proper training and experience, and the organization is experiencing no losses or difficulties due to inadequate managerial capability. In other words, when every manager has the exact level of skills and knowledge that the task requires, the staff training and development section is successfully accomplishing its mission. In addition, as managerial requirements change over time, this unit is responsible for identifying new requirements in advance and then taking action to develop the supply of managers required to fill positions as they come open. Thus the following two objectives apply to this responsibility unit: (1) to develop an adequate supply of managers to face current and future needs, and (2) to promote the highest quality of managerial decision making and administration.

Reason for existence. There are many alternative ways of achieving these objectives and hence the first question to be addressed in any planning process is whether or not an organization should have a staff development section. Both of the above objectives could be accomplished by other means such as improved hiring practices, improved management systems and procedures, or the better use of computer technology. These alternative strategies are illustrated in Figure 5–3. At some level of the

FIGURE 5–3
Planning for staff development

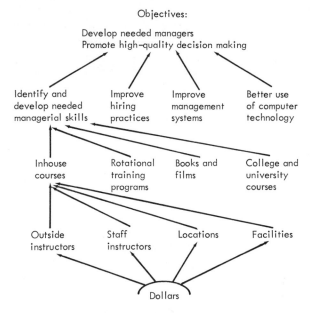

organization, the planning and control system must focus on deciding among these alternative ways of achieving the above objectives, evaluating their relative merits, and then specifying and revising resource allocation as necessary. The responsibility for doing this, however, is generally outside the scope of the staff development section itself. So it is assumed that this responsibility unit is concerned solely with identifying and developing current and future managerial knowledge and skill requirements. Thus it is assumed that the task of the staff development section is to collect the information needed to identify managerial skill requirements and then to chose the most appropriate means of developing these. Some of the choices open to it in achieving its objectives are also reflected in Figure 5–3.

Strategy. Management skills can be developed in any number of ways. The staff development section can offer its own in-house courses, attempt to operate a rotational training program, use books, films, and/or the experiences of others, or make use of college and university courses.

For each of these alternatives, a number of subsequent decisions must also be made if it is to be implemented. For example, if it chooses to operate an in-house training program, the staff development section must choose between hiring outside instructors (e.g., consultants or university faculty) and maintaining its own staff of instructors. Furthermore, it may choose to maintain its own site, to offer courses, or to make the choice of a course site the responsibility of the coordinator looking after that course (e.g., hotels or resorts). Thus, a set of instructors, coordinators, locations, and facilities make up one way of offering a course. And, of course, it is also necessary to decide how much money should be devoted to each of these staff development activities.

Key result areas. The objectives of this responsibility unit suggest the following key result areas: the quality of managerial decision making (as measured, perhaps, by organizational performance), and the availability of managers to fill positions as they become open (as measured by the losses incurred by having insufficient or deficient managers). Another key result area variable that reflects the success of this responsibility unit in carrying out its task is the rate at which the inventory of needed skills is being developed. However, the significance of these key result variables depends on the validity of the assumption that if the required skill and knowledge needs are being satisfied, the quality of decision making and administration will improve and, hence, so will organizational performance. And the assumptions underlying the activities carried out by this responsibility unit should be expressed and then probed using a causal model.

Causal model. The staff development section's approach to satisfying the need for knowledge and skills is to provide the training courses. Hence, the effectiveness of the courses offered ultimately determines the rate at which the gap between the skills and knowledge required and the skills and knowledge existing is closed. To this end this responsibility unit spends money for instructors, facilities, and the sites needed to mount courses. These variables make up a causal model of what should take place if the staff development section is spending its money and achieving its objectives.

The model depicted in Figure 5–4 graphically portrays the causal assumptions underlying the operation of the staff development section in mounting educational courses in order to improve the quality of organizational decision making and, ultimately, organizational performance. The planning and control system of the staff development section should first aid the manager in choosing the right areas to which to devote resources and then in measuring the efficiency and effectiveness at which this section is satisfying its responsibilities. The design of a planning and control system for this responsibility unit therefore involves selecting the process and activities, methods and techniques, involvement, and timing

FIGURE 5–4
Causal model of staff development
(what is *supposed* to take place)

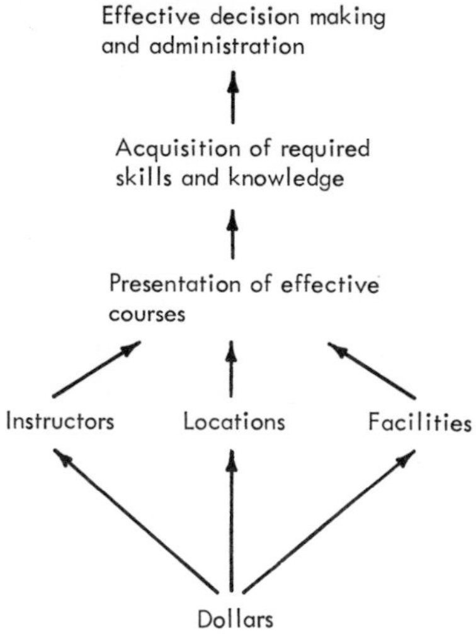

Effective decision making
and administration

Acquisition of required
skills and knowledge

Presentation of effective
courses

Instructors   Locations   Facilities

Dollars

by which plans can be initially made and then can be controlled to ensure efficiency and effectiveness.

Methods and techniques to aid planning and control. The schematic
causal model outlined in Figure 5–4 identifies many variables that could
be selected as key variables to be planned and controlled. For example,
some of the key variables suggested are the quality of decision making,
discrepancies in the managerial ability to perform each job, an inventory
of skills to be developed and the extent to which these needs exist, and
the rate at which these needs are being satisfied. The staff development
section may assume that some of these needs can be satisfied through
training. So, the characteristics of in-house courses as well as outside
courses, and the potential impact that these may have on satisfying the
required inventory of needs should be measured. If courses are offered,
the contribution of each individual instructor, each site, and the facilities
used in providing the course should be monitored so that their effectiveness can be assessed and then replaced or reconfigured as necessary.
Finally, the money spent on these activities must be measured and compared against the amount initially intended so that proper control can be
effected. Thus for purposes of planning, decision making, and control, a
number of key variables can be selected, monitored, measured, and used.

The number of tools and techniques—be they qualitative or quantitative, financial or nonfinancial, and so on—which can be used to facilitate the planning and control of this responsibility unit is extremely

large. For purposes of discussion, three aspects of the planning and control of this responsibility unit are selected and tools and techniques appropriate to each of these aspects are considered. These are the use of a questionnaire to determine needed skills and knowledge, a charge-back mechanism to assess whether or not the quality of service offered is commensurate with its cost, and an expenditures budget to assure financial control.

1. *Questionnaire survey.* In order to determine the skill and knowledge needs to be satisfied, a formal market research approach may be attempted by the staff development section. This can, of course, be done by the manager of the section or any of his or her employees by simply talking informally to managers regarding their needs, assembling these informal impressions, and from these ideas deducing a set of requirements and courses to be offered. It could be done more systematically, however, by developing a questionnaire relating to the particular problems the managers are facing, where the managers perceive their greatest deficiencies to be, and at what areas they feel it would be most beneficial to have staff development efforts directed. This questionnaire could be circulated companywide, collected and tabulated by level of job and function, and analyzed to yield suggested areas of staff development.

2. *Charge-back methods.* One question facing the designer of a planning and control system for this unit is how to go about measuring the improvement in the quality of decision making that ultimately justifies the existence of this unit. Although there are many psychometric methods that could be used to measure the key result variables identified above, qualitative improvements are perhaps best judged by those that have direct exposure to the impact of these improvements. In short, it is better to resort to a market mechanism by which individuals using the services have to sacrifice valuable resources (i.e., money) to do so, and use the results of these exchanges as a surrogate measure of whether or not improvement in quality is being achieved.

The theory underlying this approach is to have the responsibility unit price its services on some competitive basis, and then make them available on a competitive basis with outside courses. If the unit can "sell" its courses to the organization's managers and thereby at least break even on its operations (or better yet, make a profit) then it is assumed that the benefits of providing this service exceed the costs and that the improved quality of decision making is forthcoming. Hence, one component of the planning and control system for a staff development section may be to operate it on a charge-back basis thereby testing its efficiency and effectiveness.

3. *Expenditures budget.* A third planning and control technique applicable to this unit is the use of an expenditures budget to first prepare a

plan, expressed in dollars, of the activities to be undertaken by this unit during the year. On a course basis, for example, the amounts to be expended can be specified in advance and this budget can be used to control expenditures to ensure that these conform to expectation. Using a budget in this way neither measures efficiency nor effectiveness but simply explains and communicates to each individual coordinator mounting a course what is expected of him, serves as a means of securing his commitment to not expend any more than the amounts specified, and then of following up to make sure that he does just that.

Implementation constraints. Although these methods are not necessarily the best in all situations, they do represent typical choices that have to be made in designing a planning and control system for this type of responsibility unit. However, even if it is agreed that these are the best methods to use in any particular situation, it may not be possible for the supervisor of the staff development section to use these particular tools and techniques.

Assume, for example, that the personnel department (of which the staff development section is a part) is currently involved in distributing questionnaires throughout the organization to assess motivation and job satisfaction, or is involved in an organizational development effort. In this situation an additional questionnaire from the staff development section may not be permitted. What this restriction means simply is that the normative choice of a method to use cannot be implemented and another, perhaps more informal method, may have to be used even though it sacrifices some of the valuable information that could be gained if the questionnaire technique were utilized.

Similarly, other constraints may limit the use of a charge-back mechanism. The sophistication of the organization's accounting system or its general accounting policies may not allow the use of charge-backs or transfer prices. It may be a common practice in an organization that service departments operate as cost centers and do not allocate the cost of their services to those using them. In this situation the services of a staff development section are offered as a free good to be used by the employees of the organization as they deem necessary. If this constraint exists the only surrogate measurement of the effectiveness and value of the services being offered is the value of the time being devoted to these courses by the managers attending them. In order to evaluate its effectiveness, the staff development section may have to rely solely on carrying out a post-course evaluation to determine whether or not it was worth offering the course.

Although this example analysis is somewhat abbreviated and simplified, and has not specifically identified performance of the nine-step system design process model outlined above, it was carried out in accordance with this approach. The reader is therefore encouraged now to go back and review the nine-step model, and then to identify the steps carried out in the example.

The advantages of a normative approach

It is illuminating to compare the normative approach proposed here with the incremental approach frequently taken in systems design. The incremental approach begins with the givens of the design situation (e.g., organizational structure, the kind of system the president wants, the management style of current personnel, the money to be spent, and so on), and then solves the design problem within these constraints. In contrast, the normative approach advanced here begins by developing an optimal prescription of what the company should do if it were free of these constraints. Only after this has been determined does the procedure take into consideration the existing limitations and constraints, and the system designer then modifies the design accordingly.

A comparison of the ideal system needed with the actual system in use defines what has been called a system gap. The task of the designers is to narrow and, if possible, eliminate this gap, either by recommending organizational changes or by modifying their proposed system. When they then compare the actual system changes agreed upon to the gap originally defined, they have a measure of the implicit costs of making these concessions, as well as of the broader implications of the system itself.

It can reasonably be argued that it is a waste of time to ignore the constraints that must eventually be considered. However, this book will argue that the advantages of the normative approach exceed its costs. Only if the systems designer begins by specifying normative requirements can he or she know what is being sacrificed by deviating from this design. Both the normative and the incremental approach may, in the end, specify the same system, but only by taking the normative approach can the designer arrive at an imputed cost of accepting existing constraints, and hence evaluate the desirability of tackling these constraints.

Therefore it is recommended that a normative prescription be the first design in all cases, because it serves as a guide to what the system should accomplish if possible.

THE NEED FOR FORMALIZATION

Formalization of any activity involves the explicit description and documentation of its rationale and the means by which it is carried out. Formalization of planning and control, for example, implies the explicit recognition of assumptions, cause and effect relationships, methods used, and how responsibilities are assigned. It implies that there exists a disciplined way of carrying out planning. Formalization of planning and control encourages rationality and consistency in carrying out the steps of each complex problem-solving cycle. It allows for the definition and generation of information so that replanning will be facilitated. It ensures that the managers involved in planning have the opportunity to review the total process. In general, formalization leads to better learning from experience.

Formalization is especially desirable in the planning and control of complex uncertain tasks for the following reasons:

1. Most administrators are faced with large quantities of heterogeneous information which must be analyzed, filtered, and condensed. Without some framework it is almost impossible to find a semblance of order in this chaos, and reliance on intuition is the only recourse.
2. A decision maker needs to have models against which he or she can test alternative conceptions of the world, so as to reduce conceptual risk. Making explicit those environmental assumptions and cause and effect relationships underlying his or her model allows the decision maker to test their validity and evaluate alternatives more readily.
3. Any planning and control system must provide timely responses to significant changes. The system can do this only if critical assumptions and relationships are constantly monitored and deviations are reported promptly.
4. A greater transfer of knowledge within an organization is possible if the information and models used in planning and control are formalized.

Although formalization brings many benefits, any attempt to introduce it or increase its level must overcome several problems, including: (1) the reluctance of managers to explicitly state their assumptions for fear that they will be proven incorrect; (2) the general tendency of system designers to use complicated techniques that are unnecessarily complex and perhaps misunderstood by the manager who has to use them; (3) the difficulty of validating a planning model with respect both to its structure and the calibration of its parameters; and (4) the overall problem of updating and adapting models to new situations.

Formalization is needed for access to past experience and for orderly adaptation to change. There is a great deal to be learned from experience if somehow it can be captured, documented, evaluated, and preserved for later use. Unfortunately, in most organizations a great deal of planning and control is carried on as an ad hoc activity, completely divorced from ongoing administrative practices. This kind of planning and control emphasizes intuition, memory, and managerial ability instead of the development of a framework which will aid learning. New patterns and successful methods are never documented for later use. Without formalization, an organization has little opportunity to review its overall planning and control processes and to learn from experience.

SUMMARY

The purpose of a planning and control system is to aid managers in determining and accomplishing what is expected of them, and to integrate their organizational units into a unified whole, oriented to accomplishing the organization's strategic mission. Responsibility units are the basic building blocks of any organization.

The nine-step approach was presented as a guide to help the system designer specify key variables, appropriate type of financial planning and control, and other methods and techniques. The approach involved determining what should be done, how best to do it, and then if it has been done properly or needs adaptation. The normative approach recommended here first prescribes an ideal system, then modifies it to fit the constraints of the existing situation, and finally implements and evaluates the system.

The normative approach to system design ensures both that all appropriate methods and approaches are considered before they are dismissed, and that the implicit cost of accepting the constraints on the system finally adopted is recognized and evaluated.

Progressive improvement in planning and control systems can be obtained only by formalizing what is done, so that experience can be accumulated and transferred. In the absence of formalization, past experience, be it successful or unsuccessful, rests solely in the minds of individuals and leaves the organization when they do. Organizational learning, if it is to be sustained, requires formalization as a first step.

QUESTIONS

1. Suppose an organization wishes to improve its sales forecasting and must choose between using executive judgment, linear extrapolations, and statistical analyses to do so. Of what use (if any) is it to go through steps 1, 2, 3, and 4 of the system design procedure before the decision is made? What criteria should be used in deciding among these three forecasting techniques?

2. What should be the relative emphasis on key result areas and key success factors in selecting a unit's key variables? With which of the two are financial measures usually concerned?

3. In how many cycles of an organization's planning and control process will a responsibility unit normally be involved? In how many steps?

4. What role does the single-cycle planning process model described in Chapter 1 play in this system design process?

5. In modifying an existing planning and control system, is there a danger of misinterpreting problem symptoms for substantive problems? How can a system designer know when he or she has properly diagnosed the "real" problem?

6. Outline a procedure for evaluating a planning and control system. If you were called in by the president of a local organization to bid on a contract to evaluate his system, would you feel comfortable in explaining your approach to him? What questions might he ask?

7. Is there really any use in knowing the best way of carrying out a step in a planning and control process if the situation does not allow it to be done that way?

8. Are there some steps in planning that can be carried out in the same way in all situations?

9. How many ways are there to control behavior in an organization? How does one choose the ones that are best?

10. How does the approach described in Chapter 5 differ from that taken by (a) an accountant when he or she sets out to design a control system, or (b) a systems analyst when he or she sets out to design a computer-based information system?

REFERENCES AND BIBLIOGRAPHY

Dobbie, John W.   Strategic planning in large firms—Some guidelines. *Long-Range Planning*, February 1975, pp. 81–86.

Lawrence, P. R., and Lorsch, J. W.   *Organization and Environment: Managing Differentiation and Integration*. Boston: Division of Research, Harvard Business School, 1967.

Oberg, W.   Making performance appraisal relevant. *The Harvard Business Review*, January–February 1972, pp. 61–67.

Patton, A.   Why incentive plans fail. *Harvard Business Review*, May–June 1972, pp. 58–66.

Shakun, Melvin F.   Policy making under discontinuous change: The situational normativism approach. *Management Science*, October 1975, pp. 226–35.

Case study 5-1

Pfizer International in Africa

COMPANY BACKGROUND AND CHARACTERISTICS

Pfizer Corporation was founded in 1849 in Brooklyn, New York, by two young German immigrants—Charles Pfizer, a chemist and Charles Erhart, a confectioner. Initially a partnership of chemists, it was incorporated under the name Charles Pfizer and Co. in 1900, the name under which the company operated until 1970 when it was changed to Pfizer Inc. The company has been very successful. Over the decade 1963–72, sales more than doubled from $433.8 million to over $1 billion and net income increased from $40.7 million to $103.2 million.

Pfizer is grouped into five major product areas and its products are sold in over 100 countries. The distribution of sales by product is as follows.

Product line	Sales (millions of dollars)	Percent of sales
Pharmaceutical and health care products.	$ 558.8	51
Consumer products.	170.7	16
Chemicals	145.3	13
Animal and nutritional products	141.8	13
Materials science products	76.8	7
	$1,093.4	100

Source: Pfizer Inc., *Annual Report,* 1972.

Pfizer's main objective is growth and the company mission, according to one executive, is to develop and market high technology products throughout the world. "The major part of our business is specialty business," said the executive. Company strategy is to exploit its strength in product development and to remain in its areas of competence—pharmaceutical, chemical, and agricultural products.

Pfizer started geographical diversification in the early 50s and is now a full-fledged multinational corporation with over 110 production units in 37 countries in 1972.[1] Almost half of the 1972 net sales were generated in markets outside the United States. (See Exhibit 1.)

EXHIBIT 1
Pfizer Inc. sales by world markets, 1972
(millions of dollars)

Area	Sales
United States	$ 555.5
United Kingdom and Europe	261.1
Asia and Australasia	136.1
Canada and Latin America.	110.6
Africa.	30.1
Total	$1,093.4

Source: Pfizer Inc., *Annual Report.*

PFIZER INTERNATIONAL, INC.

Pfizer International is responsible for nearly all manufacturing and marketing activities outside the United States. Only three of Pfizer's Inc.'s operations—the Coty division, manufacturer and distributor of

---

[1] Pfizer, *A History of Growth* (New York: Pfizer Inc., 1972).

beauty-aid products; Howmedica, Inc., a leading manufacturer of prosthetic devices; and Quigley Company, Inc., producers of refactory specialties—handle their own international activities. International's products fall into the same categories as those of Pfizer Inc.—pharmaceuticals, agricultural, chemical, and consumer products. In 1971 and 1972, these three categories accounted for 85 to 90 percent of international sales and for substantially all of Pfizer International's pretax income.

ORGANIZATIONAL STRUCTURES

Pfizer International, with headquarters in New York City, has its own board of directors and headquarters staff. The chairman of the board and president of International reports to the chairman of the board of Pfizer, Inc., and is a member of the board of directors of Pfizer, Inc. Along with him in the office of the president are two executive vice presidents. The president oversees the European operations while one executive vice president is in charge of the Africa and Asia areas and the other the Latin-America area.

Other headquarters executives include a vice president of corporate development and law, a vice president in charge of International personnel, one vice president for each of the four product lines of International (pharmaceuticals, chemical products, consumer products, and agricultural products), a manufacturing vice president, a corporate controller, a treasurer, and two staff personnel in charge of strategic planning and projects. (See Exhibit 2 for an organization chart of Pfizer International.)

EXHIBIT 2
Pfizer International organizational chart*

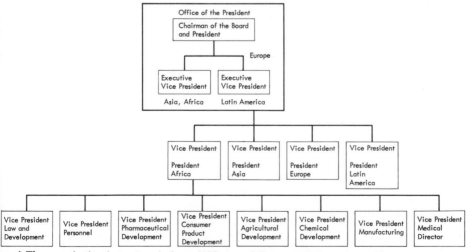

* The organizational structure is from *1972 Annual Report* and discussions with Pfizer executives. This chart was not supplied by Pfizer Inc. or Pfizer International Inc.

Four management center (or area) presidents report to the office of the president. These four executives and their staffs are resident at the management centers located in Nairobi, Kenya (Africa), Brussels (Europe), Hong Kong (Asia), and Coral Gables, Florida (Latin America).

The organization is decentralized and for every area except Africa the key operating entity is the country operation. (See Exhibit 3.) Each

EXHIBIT 3
Pfizer International organizational structure

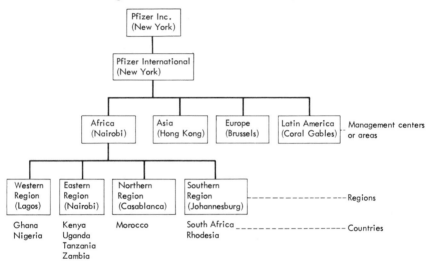

country manager has line responsibility for Pfizer's business in that country. He reports to the management center president (or regional manager in the case of Pfizer Africa). Each management center president has the responsibility of planning, developing, and carrying out Pfizer's business in his assigned area. He is responsible for "the managerial planning and integration of products imported from established plants located elsewhere; location and recommendation of potentialities of local manufacture; acquisition or establishment of plants and businesses; and direction of manufacture (where applicable) and marketing of products."[2]

Each area is a profit center, as is each region or country within it. In the larger countries, each operation within it is treated as a separate profit center.

Each country or region is run by a manager and a staff that includes a marketing manager, a controller, and, if large enough, a manufacturing manager.

_____
[2] "Pfizer International (A)," 1965 Intercollegiate Case Clearing House, Harvard University, Cambridge, Mass.

PFIZER AFRICA

The Africa area is the smallest on the basis of sales. However, Africa contains some of the fastest growing markets. Net sales for Pfizer Africa in 1973 were $36.6 million, up 20 percent from $30 million in 1972.

In 1973, Pfizer Africa with area headquarters in Nairobi had operations in eight countries with production facilities in five of them. (See Exhibit 4.)

EXHIBIT 4
Pfizer International African operations

Country	Location	Product code*
Ghana	Kumasi	E
Kenya	Nairobi	E
Nigeria	Aba	E
	Benin	E
	Ikeja	E, Y
	Kaduna	E
Rhodesia	Salisbury	A, I, J, G
South Africa	Pietermaritzburg	A, D, G, J

* See Pfizer Products and product code table.

The African area is divided into four "manageable units" called regions—West with headquarters in Lagos, East with headquarters in Nairobi, South with headquarters in Johannesburg, and North with headquarters in Casablanca. Within Pfizer's network of operations, the regional structure is unique to Africa. Each region in Africa is equivalent to a large country organization in the other areas. There is a region manager with profit and budget responsibility for each region, a controller, marketing manager, manufacturing manager, and related staff. The structure of each region is not rigid but depends upon the particular markets.

PFIZER'S OBJECTIVES AND STRATEGY IN AFRICA

Pfizer International first decided to operate through wholly owned subsidiaries (as against distributors) in Africa in the late 50s. With growth and long-term operations in mind, the immediate objectives were, according to the area manager for Africa at that time, as follows:

1. Establishing companies within the markets to satisfy local governments' plans for economic development.
2. Learning the most suitable methods of marketing and merchandising to the indigenous populations.
3. Training nationals of these countries for the eventual assumption of all managerial responsibilities.[3]

[3] L. E. Armeding, "Doing Business in Africa," *Management Looks at Africa* (New York: American Management Association, 1966), p. 56.

EXHIBIT 5
Pfizer products and product codes

A —Pharmaceuticals
B —Human vaccines
C —Animal vaccines
D —Veterinary products
E —Animal health products
E^1—Poultry breeding stock
F —Diagnostic reagents, blood serums
F^1—Antibiotic susceptibility disks and physicians' office products
F^2—Bacteriological culture media
G —Consumer health products
H —Fine chemicals
I —Antiseptics or disinfectants
J —Pesticides
K —Enzymes
L —Hops processing
M —Oxide pigments
N —Magnetic and ferrite oxides
O —Talc and other nonmetallic minerals
P —Barium and calcium metals
Q —Metal powders, high-purity metals and alloy strip
Q^1—Clad metals
R —Lime and/or limestone products
S —Toiletries
T —Cosmetics and fragrances
U —Aromatic raw materials
V —Plasticizers
W —Pyrolytic graphite, other high-temperature, high-hardness materials
X —Refractories
Y —Molded plastics
Z^1—Medical supplies and equipment
Z^2—Dental products

Source: Pfizer, *A History of Growth*, (New York: Pfizer, Inc. 1972).

Investments in the African operations were, and still are, made with full realization of the uncertainties in the environments and with long-term profitability as the criterion. One executive put it this way: "We have a very enlightened management that's prepared to take some risks." Not atypical was the wholly owned subsidiary established in Ghana in 1958 which did not yield any profit until the 1963–64 fiscal year.

Thus, in evaluating the operations in Africa, International headquarters looks beyond profits and budget reports; factors peculiar to each market are taken into consideration. This is made possible by two conditions. First, all headquarters management have had considerable field experience. Second, their frequent travels give them firsthand experience and the opportunity for informal communication.

DESCRIPTION OF THE AFRICAN MARKETS

Small market size and uncertainty are the two most distinguishing features of the African markets. Four other important variables which also differentiate these markets are information, communication, marketing facilities and the labor force. These six variables significantly influence the planning and control requirements of a multinational company in Africa.

The majority of the African countries have small markets. For example, using per capita income as a measure of size, the average African market size is only about one twentieth of the size of the European market, and about one sixth the size of the average Latin-American market. In 1972, some typical per capita incomes were as follows: Tanzania, $93; Nigeria, $133; Kenya, $163; Zambia, $153; and Chad, $66.

The main uncertainty in Africa is political. The frequent changes of leadership, usually through revolutions, have resulted in changes in strategies for economic development. For example, a country which is market oriented, and hence which encourages private investment, may after a change of leadership, adopt a socialist approach to development, and hence emphasize state ownership of property.

Economic uncertainty stems from the frequent devaluations, revaluations, price controls, and other abrupt changes in fiscal and monetary policies by the African governments. This element of uncertainty is likely to continue because its cause lies in the basic structure of the African economies. The economies of several African countries are tied to a single cash crop. For example, in Zambia it is copper, in Ghana cocoa, and in Guinea bauxite. Hence they are very susceptible to fluctuations in world commodity prices, and government fiscal and monetary policies are adjusted to these fluctuations. And, to the extent that world commodity prices will not stabilize, this element of economic uncertainty will continue.

Commercial activity is severely handicapped by a lack of information. Historical and economic data for planning is not readily available for Africa. This problem is further compounded by the long bureaucratic barriers to obtaining what is available.

Communication is also a problem. Telephone facilities within Africa are very limited. There are frequent interruptions of phone service caused by the heavy rains in some parts, and phone communications often have to go through circuitous routes. For example, a phone call from Ghana to neighboring Ivory Coast must be relayed through London and Paris. While air, road, and rail transportation facilities within and between the African countries have received serious attention recently, the existing facilities are still quite inadequate by Western standards. Also marketing communication, in general, is very poor due to the low circulation of newspapers, and the small sizes of radio and television audiences.

The final variable which distinguishes the African countries from the developed countries is the labor force. The role of wage earning employment is more recent and less prominent in Africa than it is in the developed countries. In most African countries, a substantial part of the labor force is engaged in subsistence agriculture and petty trade. There is no pool of readily available skilled laborers as in the United States and Europe.

PLANNING AND CONTROL AT PFIZER

Planning at Pfizer, Inc.

Planning at the corporate level at Pfizer Inc., involves the identification of overall corporate goals and objectives and the definition of what business(es) the company will be in. Corporate planning provides the guidelines under which planning at lower levels (such as Pfizer International) takes place.

Because research and development is central to the goals of Pfizer, Inc., all new product planning and development activities go on at the corporate level.

Planning at Pfizer International

Planning at Pfizer International occurs at two levels. The first is the strategic planning level, where long-range objectives such as choice of products, new markets, pricing, and marketing policies are articulated by Pfizer International. The second level of planning is at the operational level and consists essentially of the budget.

STRATEGIC PLANNING

Responsibility for strategic planning rests at the International headquarters. Strategic planning at Pfizer International tends to be very informal. Ideas are either generated from nuances picked up by management during their frequent visits to the field, or by ideas conceived and transmitted informally by country or area management. Ideas are evaluated, ad hoc, and either sent to the field or submitted to the corporate staff for further evaluation.

The two staff members in the New York planning group have extensive knowledge of Pfizer's product lines. They are supported by executives with firsthand market experience. Responsibility for strategic planning is based in New York, because Pfizer believes it proper to have the individuals who have the power to shape the destiny of the company determine its strategic objectives. However, managers in the field are invaluable sources of useful ideas; hence the need to diffuse strategic planning process throughout the organization.

The planning at Pfizer International is mainly concerned with new markets rather than new products. Product decisions are made within the product lines established by Pfizer Inc. Thus the strategic aspect of International's planning consists of the choosing of markets, deciding whether to manufacture in new or established plants, and setting pricing policies and performance requirements. The market, product, and operations decisions at International headquarters then become the basis for planning at the management centers.

PLANNING AT THE MANAGEMENT CENTER

Planning for each of the four areas of Pfizer International—Africa, Asia, Europe, and Latin America—is carried out at the respective management centers. These plans focus on aggregate capacity and marketing within the area. The information necessary to carry out this planning is formally provided to the management center by the budgets from the regions (in the case of Africa) and collected informally during the extensive regional traveling by management center executives. The entire operational plan for an area has a three-year horizon, of which the first year is the budget. (Pfizer used to have a five-year plan which was abandoned because the numerous uncertainties in the environment made the longer horizon unrealistic.)

Area executives are responsible for the overall operational plan, as well as for setting goals and objectives for years 2 and 3 of the plan period. Country managers are responsible for the first year of the operational plan (i.e., the budget). Guidelines for the operational plan are very loose. Countries are given wide latitude in establishing targets. The one criterion stressed by corporate management is growth. Each subsidiary is required to set a growth in profits of at least 10 percent, unless a satisfactory explanation to the contrary can be found. There is usually considerable bargaining on the budget targets, as reaching total agreement on objectives is a great concern.

The budgeting cycle is initiated from the International headquarters in New York. This usually occurs in the April preceding the budget year when instructions go out to the area managers. The cycle then proceeds through the following steps:

1. The country manager defines one-year budget targets and submits these to the regional manager.
2. The country manager negotiates targets with regional managers until agreement is reached.
3. The regional manager in turn reviews country budgets and consolidates them into a regional budget for transmittal to the area president at the management center.
4. A consolidated management budget which includes plans for year 2 and year 3 is then sent from the management center to the International headquarters in New York.

5. Finally, International staff presents a budget for all the foreign subsidiaries to the corporate staff.

BUDGET CONTENT

The budget contains a detailed account of targets articulated by the country managers to meet the strategic objectives set by corporate management. A long-range plan and statement of earnings must be filled out for each business line by area management. Details of sales, product margins, marketing expenditures, overhead, and estimated taxes for each major group must be spelled out, and, for each of these items, the growth rate and the budgeted amount must be indicated for the current and the subsequent year.

A detailed account of the estimated marketing expenses for the plan period is also required. Advertising expenses budgeted for the previous, current, and the subsequent year must be entered for each major advertising mode—trade, dealer aids, media advertising, and so on. For each of these major modes of advertising, more detail must be given. For example, for media advertising, separate entries must be made for radio, TV, newspapers, public transportation, and so forth.

CAPITAL EXPENDITURES

Capital appropriation requests from the countries must be submitted to the responsible area management for review. All capital expenditures exceeding $20,000, as well as all ventures into new countries, must be submitted to headquarters in New York for approval by the board of directors.

REPORTING AND COMMUNICATION SYSTEM

The four management centers are also the cornerstones of the reporting and control system. First, each center sends monthly P&L and operating reports to International headquarters. Second, quarterly reports containing more detailed analysis of variances are sent. And third, year-end financial and operational reports with even more detailed analysis are also forwarded.

The information transmitted from the management centers are consolidations of the reports from the various countries under their jurisdiction. Each country manager in a region submits a written report of variances and explanations to his management center every month.

Many informal and unstructured reports pour into the New York office from the field. There certainly is no shortage of reports from the field; in fact, headquarters tries to reduce the volume of data and information that flows in.

At the area level, the management center staff travel extensively to the various countries under their charge. Pfizer management believes that direct travel is a very effective mode of gathering information and acquiring knowledge on the market situation and opportunities in the subsidiaries.

PERFORMANCE EVALUATION

Pfizer relies considerably on the comparison of actual against budgeted performance. The rationale for using budget comparisons for control is Pfizer's policy of involving field managers in setting budget objectives. The company does not have rigid budgeting procedures for the subsidiaries. Instead, it recognizes that opportunities differ from country to country, and even from section to section within a particular country. During the budgeting process an operating plan believed to be optimum for that region is developed; if the manager meets this plan, performance is good.

Management recognizes that profit and loss statements are inadequate measures of performance, even where budget goals are painstakingly arrived at. Pfizer's experience in other developing countries, coupled with their commitment to contribute to the development of these countries, dictated that qualitative criteria be used in addition to financial ratios to evaluate subsidiaries in less developed countries.

Although it is difficult to formalize or characterize these qualitative criteria, Pfizer believes that they must reflect the situation at hand. Thus in Africa, for example, their criteria recognize that short-run financial returns must sometimes be traded against long-run profitability and that political and economic uncertainties beyond the control of the subsidiary manager can cause deviations from budget goals, even where these goals were reasonable a priori.

To get a better feel for how effectively the subsidiary manager is performing his duties, Pfizer's top management rely heavily on informal signals gathered during their frequent field visits. As one VP explained, "Once you are out there at the subsidiary, it is relatively easy to get a feel for how well the manager has developed his employees; to evaluate the quality of his influence on the organizational interrelationships around him; to measure the extent of the impression made on the local elite; and generally, to evaluate the executive's ability to plan, organize and control the operation he is managing."

PERSONNEL

Pfizer's policy with regard to staffing the International subsidiaries is to "hire the best man for the job, regardless of his nationality," barring certain abnormalities such as hiring a black manager for a South African subsidiary. It is conceded that there were certain advantages to be derived from employing local nationals rather than foreigners to staff the subsidiaries and that local nationals know the customs of their people better, can establish better informal connections with national officials, and are more knowledgeable about the business environment in general. However, in Pfizer's opinion, local citizenship per se is not an overwhelming predictor of managerial effectiveness.

INCENTIVE COMPENSATION

The method of incentive compensation for Pfizer's executives is the same in the United States and in the operations abroad. Performance is rewarded through a cash bonus and stock option plan. Before the beginning of the fiscal year, each manager and his supervisor agree on goals for that year. The supervisor (for example, the management center president), then evaluates the manager's performance against these goals and awards a bonus, if deserved, at the end of the year. This is done strictly at the local level; the only compensation aspects that come to International headquarters for approval are for top executives.

Questions

1. What are the key variables of the Pfizer Corporation?
2. What are the key variables of an African region and country?
3. What is your evaluation of Pfizer's way of planning and controlling their African operations?

part three
Methods and techniques of planning and control

Chapter outline

Structured and unstructured tasks
Some techniques for planning and controlling structured processes
  The use of formal models in planning
  Managed and engineered costs
  Feedback and feedforward control
    Application to fully automated processes
    Application to human processes
Motivational techniques
  The motivational role of financial objectives
  Job enrichment
  Human resource accounting
Appendix: Interpreting and responding to deviations from expectation

6

The planning and control of structured processes

When you have finished this chapter you should understand:

1. The difference between structured and unstructured processes.
2. The use of models in planning structured processes.
3. The differences between feedback and feedforward control.
4. The motivational assumptions of responsibility accounting.
5. The benefits and limitations of performance targets, human resource accounting, and the job enrichment in improving productivity.

STRUCTURED AND UNSTRUCTURED TASKS

The next four chapters discuss some of the tools and techniques used in planning and controlling responsibility units. These include methods of financial measurement as well as techniques that do not concern money. Planning and controlling responsibility units through financial budgets as cost, profit, or investment centers is a common practice. However, although the choice of financial measurements is a very important part of any planning and control system design, it is by no means the complete task. Most systems will also involve many key variables that simply do not lend themselves to financial measurement. In addition to financial measures, then, systems also require qualitative and behavioral as well as nonfinancial quantitative measures. Such considerations as organizational climate and employee satisfaction are especially relevant. As emphasized in Chapter 5, specific methods (step 8) must be selected within the perspective of overall system requirements, and it is again emphasized that the design of a comprehensive planning and control system depends both on the nature of the task involved and also on what the system must contribute to the successful accomplishment of the task.

The financial techniques to be considered in the next four chapters include responsibility accounting, budgetary control, and cost, profit, and investment-based measures of performance. Nonfinancial considerations include the motivating effects of responsibility and performance targets, job enrichment, organizational health, and management by objectives.

The essence of the contingency approach to system design taken in this book is that the choice of a technique depends on its appropriateness to the characteristics of a particular situation. Hence some criterion is needed that will describe and differentiate situations. The distinguishing characteristic chosen here is the degree of structure inherent in the tasks performed by a responsibility unit.

A comparison of responsibility units, both within and among organizations, shows that they cover a continuum of task situations. At one end of this continuum lie the completely understood, well-specified tasks which require only effort and due care for their successful execution. The disrupting effects of external influences and the need for independent judgment are minimal. In general, stable, repetitive activities or procedures which can be economically analyzed and systematized, such as clerical or assembly-line tasks, are classed as structured tasks. At the other extreme are tasks best described as judgmental, unique, novel, or simply unstructured. These require a completely different mix of problem-solving techniques and talents. The director of an advertising agency, the manager of a research and development project, or the managing partner of a law office faces tasks in which past experience may be of little relevance, and which require unique solutions.

The degree of structure inherent in a responsibility unit's task requirements has a significant influence in its planning and control system requirements. But appropriate tools and methods cannot be selected on this basis alone, because many, if not most, responsibility units perform some mixture of structured and unstructured tasks. The discussion of hierarchical differentiation in Chapter 4 noted that tasks differ in relative "structuredness" by organizational level, and showed how these differences affect the nature of the task performed and the information used. Therefore this distinction should be considered only as a convenient way of differentiating among task requirements, and not as a rigid classification criterion.

The next four chapters are intended to provide a representative sample of the many tools and techniques available to the system designer, to be used as required. The chapters do not fall neatly into the four cells of the illustrated matrix, however, since many of the concepts discussed in relation to structured tasks are also applicable to unstructured tasks, and vice versa. These techniques and ideas should therefore be considered to belong in a system designer's bag of tools, to be applied where appropriate, and not to fit into any neat scheme.

	Tools and techniques	
	Financial	Nonfinancial
Structured		
Unstructured		

Tasks (label to the left of the Structured/Unstructured rows)

This chapter focuses on the planning and control of structured processes, while Chapter 7 considers unstructured ones. Both chapters contain a mixture of material from the disciplines of accounting, statistics, and organizational behavior. To a greater or lesser extent the material may overlap with the subject matter of other courses. However, it is included here to illustrate that planning and control systems design is an integrative activity which draws on many disciplines.

SOME TECHNIQUES FOR PLANNING AND CONTROLLING STRUCTURED PROCESSES

Structured processes are those sufficiently well understood that a confident prediction can be made of their outcomes. Structured tasks are usually formalized. They involve a sequence of activities in which all choice criteria are predetermined, and they have well-established performance criteria and measures of effectiveness and efficiency. The processes to be planned and controlled may be completely automated, or they may be performed by people. Both cases are considered in this chapter.

The use of formal models in planning

Since structured processes lend themselves to analysis and formalization, formal models are useful for their planning and control. The plans that specify the conduct of a structured process may be based on three types of formal models—performance standards, relationships, or mathematical models. Performance standards are simply ratios of output to input; e.g., the output per unit time established for an assembly-line operation. Standards have been established for many defined procedures such as paying accounts payable, analyzing income tax returns, or performing preventive maintenance tasks. In fact, if economically justified, a standard can be established for most stable, repetitive activities.

Prescriptions can also be based on known relationships between two variables. Such relationships may be either linear or nonlinear. A familiar example is the use of a cost volume equation to relate spending levels to alternative levels of activity. In many organizations recurring expenses, costs of sales, and manufacturing overhead are planned and controlled in terms of historically derived relationships.

Mathematical models are a third way to prescribe behavior. These are simply multirelationship descriptions of an underlying process which can be used to plan what should take place. One familiar example of a model is a budget. A budget can be regarded as a simulation model of the firm in terms of the financial flows of its activity. Similarly, queuing models describe customer service levels at bank teller windows or at airline ticketing terminals, and can be used to plan required levels of staffing. A third example is an economic order quantity model which can be used to plan when and in what amounts inventory should optimally be replenished. These three means of prescribing behavior (standards, relationships, and models) are all formal models, which vary only in the scope and complexity of the activities they cover.

Although structured processes lend themselves to formal models more readily than do unstructured ones, it should be noted that the two types of processes are conceptually similar. Unstructured processes such as labor contract negotiations may also be planned and controlled in terms of models, but the models used are usually of the intuitive, informal variety. They are not formally articulated, and exist primarily in the head of the decision maker. Structured processes, on the other hand, because they are better understood, can be planned with formal models and can be controlled by measuring quantified deviations from expectation.

Managed and engineered costs

The distinction between unstructured and structured processes has long been recognized by accountants in their handling of managed and engineered costs. By definition, managed costs relate to tasks which are unstructured; i.e., processes for which analysis is not possible or too complex to be economical. Because a functional relationship cannot be established between the cost incurred and some measurable productive output, the estimation and control of these costs are subject to managerial discretion. Managed costs are thus a function solely of judgment. The money spent on improving employee morale or given to charity are examples of managed costs.

Engineered costs are those for which a "right" amount can be specified. These costs have to do with processes which are subject to analysis and for which a prescription can be made. A direct cost such as labor, which varies proportionally with level of activity, or an overhead cost such as the electricity to operate a machine, are typical engineered costs.

Standard costing systems are commonly employed in the administration of engineered costs for structured tasks. Task standards can be established in a number of ways. The task can be decomposed into a basic set of movements whose required performance time may be set by predetermined time standards or by methods-time-measurements (stopwatch timings). Other useful techniques are work sampling, descriptive or statistical analysis of historical data, and the application of experienced judgment.

The mechanics of a standard cost system are well documented in a host of accounting texts and will not be repeated here. In brief, plans or expectations are expressed in terms of the standards selected, and actual results are then compared against these. Control measures the deviation or variances of actual results from those expected. Usually, standard costing systems involve the computing of direct material and direct labor price, usage (efficiency) variances, and overhead spending, efficiency, and volume variances.

The distinction between engineered and managed costs, and between structured and unstructured processes, should not be related too quickly to organizational function however. Organizational units such as the controller's office or the personnel department are commonly controlled as cost centers because of the difficulty of quantifying their benefit to an organization, not because of the degree of structure of their tasks.

Feedback and feedforward control

Any process is controlled in an attempt to ensure conformance to expectations, to ensure that actions conform to plans. Remedial efforts to correct deviations from expectation may consist of modifying actions, or plans, or both. As discussed in Chapter 1, control attempts to accommodate three types of risk: the conceptual risk that plans were not correctly developed in the first place; the administrative risk that actions are not being carried out as planned; and the environmental risk that external events have changed and planned actions are no longer appropriate. The control action must match the cause of the deviation from expectation.

There are two ways of controlling a process. Feedback control attempts to ensure conformance to expectation by comparing actual performance against original expectations and then adjusting either performance or plans to diminish any deviation that exists. Feedforward control, on the other hand, monitors variables other than output or performance, variables that may change before performance itself changes. These independent variables, which influence the performance dependent variables are usually the ones originally used in devising the plan. Monitoring variables that change forward or ahead of performance allows anticipative control, as opposed to after-the-fact, or reactive, control.

A feedforward system can detect changes in these independent variables, assess their implication, modify actions, or replan if necessary, and can make these corrective adjustments before the performance variable is actually "out of control." That is, whenever a change occurs in one or more of the inputs to the planning process, corrective action starts immediately to cancel its effect before it actually affects the outcome. Feedforward control thus assures that a process continually reflects the actual conditions under which it is operating, and not the presumed conditions for which is was originally planned.

Application to fully automated processes. Fully automated processes are those which require no human intervention in the normal course of events. Although it is not a business example, perhaps the most commonly cited example of a fully automated process is a home heating system. In this system the desired temperature is set on a scale within the thermostat and a thermometer measures actual house temperature. When deviations from this level occur, the furnace of the house is turned on or off automatically, as appropriate. For the system to work, a deviation has to occur between the desired level of temperature in the house and the actual level. Whether this interval is 2°, 3°, 5°, or 10° is a function of the calibration of the system. However, it is only after the deviation has reached significant proportions that corrective action is taken to bring the temperature back up to normal; i.e., by turning on the furnace. This is an example of an automated process relying on feedback control.

A feedforward system, on the other hand, measures the outside or ambient temperature of the system before its effects have the opportunity to permeate the house. Changes in the outside temperature are fed forward into the system and corrective action is taken before actual deviations occur. For example, if the furnace requires a certain amount of time to heat up the house and the thermal barrier created by the walls resists the flow of cold into the house, these lags can be countered by a sensor outside of the house which feeds information into the system so that appropriate action can be taken before the inside temperature begins to fall.

A second example of a fully automated process is a real-time shop floor scheduling system is an automated plant. Real-time data collection terminals located throughout the plant area feed information continuously to a central computer. The computer contains a detailed model of the desired behavior of the shop, and as it receives information it recomputes the routines or algorithms necessary to predict what will take place at future intervals. In this way corrective actions, such as speeding up, slowing down, or even stopping certain components of a plant, can be taken to maintain the whole operation in balance. Real-time computer-based shop floor scheduling thus allows continuous feedforward planning, as opposed to waiting for the trouble spots to arise before corrective action is taken.

Application to human processes. A variable or flexible budget is perhaps the most familiar means of feedback and feedforward control of structured processes involving humans. The fact that the budget is adjusted to provide a realistic expectation in light of changes, such as level of activity or output, implies feedforward control. In the event of an economic downturn, or a reduction in sales volume, overhead spending levels can be adjusted accordingly so that spending remains in control. Feedforward control is commonly applied in the adjustment of staff levels or amount of discretionary expenditures, such as advertising, in economic downturns. Any subsequent deviation of spending levels from the adjusted budget figure would be reported, in which case feedback control would then be applied.

The ability to utilize feedforward control depends on the known relationships between variables which change ahead (forward) of performance, and performance itself. It cannot be used in the absence of reliable predictive relationships. The choice of a control mechanism therefore depends on the nature of the process in question. Since structured processes, by definition, are those characterized by a greater percentage of known causal relationships, feedforward or anticipative control is far more useful for them than for unstructured, uncertain tasks.

The use of feedback or feedforward control for both automated and human processes also requires that the significance of deviations from expectation be accurately assessed, so that the correct remedial action can be taken. A deviation from expectation either in performance or in some other variable may require a minor adjustment in the activities being performed, a change in plans, or even a complete revision in the way the problem is conceptualized. Or the deviation may be due to a rare transient aberration and should be ignored. Hence a key component of any control system is the means used to assess the significance of reported deviations. Some of these techniques are discussed in the Appendix to this chapter.

This section has drawn attention to the increasing number of fully automated processes to demonstrate that technical solutions to the planning and control of structured processes are not, at present, difficult to implement. There are relatively few technical constraints on the technological feasibility of such systems. The key issue is to determine the optimal trade-off between cost and technical sophistication. And in the future, as management science and industrial engineering techniques improve, and the costs of computing diminish, the ability to plan and control structured processes can be expected to improve.

Most organizations perform a host of structured tasks. At present, most are still performed by humans, not by machines. The assembly line is perhaps the example that first comes to mind; but many clerical, administrative, and secretarial tasks are just as easily specified or programmed. The planning and control of these tasks involves specifying the actions or end results required, clarifying the performance expected, motivating the worker to perform the required task so as to achieve the desired result, and then evaluating performance and taking appropriate action. All that is usually required of the worker is appropriate effort, with due care. For these tasks, modifying (optimizing) procedures or preparing better plans is not usually the main problem. Nor is it to improve control systems. Success in the performance of structured tasks by humans depends mainly on the productivity (i.e., motivation and effort) of those who have to carry out the tasks. And so the remainder of this chapter will discuss ways to motivate and maintain organizational productivity by assignment of responsibility and the establishment of financially measured performance goals, by human resource accounting, and by job enrichment.

MOTIVATIONAL TECHNIQUES

A fundamental step in the design of all planning and control systems is the assignment of responsibility. The assumed effects of responsibility significantly influence the recommendations of both behavioral scientists and accountants. Behavioral scientists suggest that trusting an individual with the responsibility for a task or goal increases his or her motivation to accomplish it. McLelland (1961) states that individuals with a high need for achievement work hardest in situations where they can take personal responsibility for goal accomplishment. Similarly, the research of Vroom (1964) and Likert (1967), reveals that job satisfaction as well as performance are related to the opportunity for self-control and to the amount of responsibility a job provides. And Argyris (1964), in his theory of integrating the individual and the organization, also emphasizes the assignment of individual responsibility.

Improving motivation is also one aim of the designers of administrative accounting systems. The assumption is that motivation is increased by the assignment of responsibility. This assumption underlies responsibility accounting in general, and financial control systems based on decentralized financial responsibility in particular. However, the assignment of responsibility to a manager is only half the task. For motivational techniques to be effective, the manager must also be assured that attempts to fulfill his or her responsibilities will be evaluated fairly. Therefore, a generally accepted constraint imposed on financial control systems is that the degree of responsibility delegated must be "fairly" assigned. That is, the measure for which managers are held responsible must also be subject to regulation or be controllable by them. With these behavioral assumptions as guidelines, accountants have designed financial planning and control systems which express expectations, record actual events, and evaluate performance in terms of financial flows.

The motivational role of financial objectives

Any financial planning and control system can be viewed not only as a means of assigning responsibility and evaluating performance, but also as a means of directly influencing motivation by the establishment of performance targets. But if the budgeted level is to serve as a target to shoot for, its relationship to differences in individual motivation should be considered. Individual differences, such as the perceived difficulty of the task or the value attached to the rewards or punishments associated with performance, must be accounted for.

Perhaps the first investigation into the relationship between individual differences in performance levels and alternate ways of setting performance targets was made by Stedry (1960). He examined the relationships between the performance levels to which an individual aspires, the budgeted levels set for him, and his ultimate performance. In Stedry's experiments, conducted in a university laboratory, 100 subjects were divided into four groups. Three groups were each given a budget of varying difficulty (low, medium, or high), and one was not given an explicit performance target at all. Each of these four groups was further divided into three subgroups. Two of these subgroups were asked to state, one before and one after receiving its budget, how much they hoped to perform; i.e., their level of aspiration. Members of the third group were not asked to state their aspirations at all. Analysis of this 4×3 matrix of responses led to the following conclusions:

When no level of aspiration was expressed, subjects who did not have a budget produced the best performance, closely followed by medium and high budgetees. Those with low budgets produced significantly poorer performance.

But when budgetees set levels of aspiration, high budgetees who set their level of aspiration after receiving their budget performed best, whereas high budgetees who set their level of aspiration before receiving their budget performed worse.

From these results Stedry (1960) concluded that the budget can be used to motivate. He states, "It seems at least reasonable to suppose that it is a proper task of budgetary control to be concerned with strategies for constant improvement in performance" (pp. 89–90). One interpretation of his findings is that communicating performance targets to subordinates before they have established their desired levels of performance tends to bring actual performance more in line with expectations. In sum, Stedry argues that one function of the budget should be to raise aspirations, thereby improving performance, rather than merely to communicate management's decisions.

Stedry's experiments were deliberately designed so that the subjects were given no knowledge of their actual performance, in order that the budget would be their primary point of reference. In normal work situations, however, task performers usually have some idea of their actual performance. Psychologists generally agree that a knowledge of actual performance either raises or lowers an individual's level of aspiration, depending on whether performance reaches or does not reach the level aspired to. It can be concluded that a higher budget, if it is attainable, will generally lead to higher performance. However, if the budget is set too high, motivation may be more than offset by failure to reach the target. In general, then, the budget level should fit the level of aspiration of the manager.

This conclusion was confirmed by a later field study by Stedry and Kay (1964), who studied groups of foremen in a large U.S. engineering plant. They found that difficult goals appeared to lead either to very good or very bad performance, in comparison with more traditional goals. In the case of very good results, it can be assumed that high levels of aspiration had been formed; in the case of very poor results, the goals may have been perceived as so difficult that the foreman withdrew from setting a level of aspiration or set one far below his normal goal.

A field study conducted by Hofstede (1967) appears to confirm the observations of Stedry and Kay. Hofstede concluded that:

> In order for a standard to function as a standard for achievement it should be tight, so tight that there is a real risk of its not being attained. This means that there should be a difference between such standards and the performance actually expected which is used in co-ordinating budgets in the accounting system. On the other hand it appears that standards which are so tight that they seem impossible destroy motivation [p. 144].

These inquiries into the motivational effects of budgeted targets have led to the recommendation to establish two company budgets—one for purposes of motivation and another for the assignment of responsibility and performance evaluation—because of the basic differences between these two processes. Dalton (1971) defines the difference between organizational control and individual control as follows. Organizational control is essentially ex post evaluation using variances, while individual or self-control "derives from individual goals and aspirations. The standards become expectations about one's own performance, and certain intermediate targets we set for ourselves. The signal for corrective action is any indication that we may not achieve our goal or meet the deadline to which we have psychologically committed ourselves" (p. 14).

It appears, then, that a budget can be used for two purposes. One is as a model to describe expected performance and also as a standard against which to measure actual events. The planning and control process uses a budget in this way by establishing standards and later analyzing the difference between actual and desired results. But the budget can also be separated from the ongoing planning and control process in order to adjust budget standards to managers who differ in levels of aspiration. If such a fit can be obtained, then the chances of better performance are significantly improved.

Although this proposal may be soundly founded in theory, few companies use a full two-budget system. One way to implement this concept, however, is to establish tight performance targets for motivation, and to budget a buffer or "slush fund" so that optimistic targets can be adjusted to realistic expectations. Establishing budgets to be motivational, while also including adjustment factors to reflect actual planned levels, is a common practice.

Job enrichment

The manner of planning and controlling structured tasks is fundamentally related to the nature of the tasks themselves. The humanization of repetitive working life by means of task restructuring, job enrichment, and more democratic processes is increasingly a subject of management literature today. There is a growing belief that something must be done to change the nature of structured tasks in our society if these tasks are to be planned and controlled effectively. Of special concern are the dull, repetitive, seemingly meaningless tasks which offer little challenge or autonomy, and which cause discontent among workers. In fact, according to the study *Work in America* (1972), the primary cause of dissatisfaction among lower level workers is the nature of their jobs. If this is the case, it is clear that assigning greater responsibility or manipulating standards of performance will do little to improve productivity. Hence there is a growing concern with discovering ways to increase the quality of performance for structured tasks.

Job enrichment, the restructuring and enriching of jobs to make them inherently more interesting, is one such attempt to increase productivity. The essential assumption of job enrichment theory is that the nature of the work performed determines to a large extent workers' satisfaction or dissatisfaction on the job. Job enrichment efforts assume that many employees seek intrinsic rewards from their work and become dissatisfied if these are not provided.

There are many conflicting opinions as to the real reasons people work, however. As one consultant has argued eloquently:

> The intrinsic nature of the work is only one factor among many that affect worker satisfaction. Moreover, the available evidence suggests that

its influence is very often subordinate to that of several other variables: pay, job security, and job rules. The inconclusive performance of job enrichment today stems largely from those programs that have neglected to consider these factors (Fein, 1974, p. 80).

From his experience and analysis, Fein concludes that the greatest progress in improving the performance of structured tasks will come in organizations where workers see that management is protecting their welfare and where productivity gains are shared with employees.

Fein's conclusions may be of critical importance to planning and control system designers. The major difficulty in administering structured tasks is simply the fact that they are structured. What must be done is well prescribed; care and effort in performance are the critical factors. What is often obscured in discussions of productivity in structured tasks is the fact that the very nature of the tasks dictates that if workers do anything to raise productivity, either the demands on them will be continuously increased, or else some workers will be penalized. Workers know that if they increase production, reduce delays, reduce crew sizes, or save time in any way, then less overtime will be available to them, some employees will be displaced, and in general the work force will be reduced. Hence the question becomes almost rhetorical: Can employees be made to voluntarily increase productivity if, in fact, greater productivity is detrimental to themselves?

There is clearly a distinction between the managerial and administrative employees who perform unstructured tasks and those who perform more structured tasks. The former have no fear of working themselves out of a job by superior performance. These employees are usually rewarded for creativity and effectiveness. However, for those performing structured tasks, increases in productivity benefit the company and please management but in general do not benefit the workers themselves. In fact, the opposite may be the case, they may suffer a loss of income either through displacement or through lack of overtime. And so any attempt to increase productivity merely by manipulating performance standards, by improving the work climate, and by enriching jobs may not achieve the desired ends. If this fundamental contradiction is to be overcome, there must be a means of allowing workers to benefit from the increased effectiveness they bring to their work.

Human resource accounting

The previous discussion has emphasized the importance of human resources as part of any planning and control activity. The amount of investment in an organization and the problem of keeping track of the impact of change amply justify a concern with organizational health. This concern has led to the development of human resource accounting systems, based on the theory of human organization advanced by Rensis Likert (1967). Likert raises the issue that managers pay attention mainly to formal measures of performance, such as costs or profits, and only consider employee-related factors such as satisfaction, group cohesion, and motivation when problems arise. Likert believes that because of their narrow focus on measured performance, managers may sometimes pressure employees in order to accomplish short-term improvements. This practice may, however, reduce the behavioral health of the organization and cause a deterioration in employee motivation and satisfaction. Since the condition of the human organization is instrumental in attaining long-run growth, this pressure is ultimately harmful to productivity (Likert and Seashore, 1958, pp. 96–108). The crux of Likert's theory is his contention that the behavioral health of an organization, as reflected by such variables as satisfaction, group cohesion, morale, or motivation, determines its overall productive capacity.

To maintain and improve productivity Likert recommends the establishment of an administrative climate in which management is sensitive to behavioral variables as well as to measured performance. Since managers tend to focus on what is measured, even though other variables may be more important, Likert suggested the establishment of a system that can measure and report behavioral variables as well as conventional performance.

Likert reasons that attention can be drawn to behavioral variables only if these are reflected in the monetary terms that management is accustomed to. Accordingly, he sought out accountants willing to broaden the scope of their endeavor to include the measurement and evaluation of the human organization. And from this collaboration of behavioral scientists and accountants the human resource accounting movement was launched.

Human resource accounting attempts to express organizational variables in monetary terms. For example, an employee may be valued at the capitalized cost of his or her training or at the total of the recruitment and training costs of a replacement. Or, direct measurements of behavioral variables such as motivation may be used in determining the amortization rates of expenditures related to increasing motivation. And it has also been suggested that if meaningful financial measures of human values cannot be derived, then measurements of the behavioral determinants of this value should be used as proxies. In sum, human resource accounting is an attempt to formally measure and report behavioral considerations that have previously been dealt with informally.

But can the measurement of behaviorable variables in fact produce useful information? Although Likert's theory has received considerable attention, there is also a substantial amount of evidence to indicate that the relationship between behavioral health and organizational performance is not as straightforward as Likert believes. In fact, the importance attached to behavioral variables may be nothing more than a vestige of the human relations era of behavioral science which stressed human-centered management, including employee satisfaction and morale. Many other relationships have been found between employee job satisfaction and performance. Several studies have concluded that the causal relationship is just the reverse; that is, work performance determines the degree of job satisfaction. Evidence accumulated over the last two decades indicates that any assumptions linking behavioral variables with performance must be qualified. Some results, such as turnover and absenteeism, may have a strong and consistent relationship with measures to promote job satisfaction; whereas others, such as actual job performance, may show no consistent relationship.

It has been shown that measuring motivation alone is not sufficient to predict performance, and that ability is one modifier of the motivation-performance relationship (Vroom, 1964). And several additional modifiers may be relevant.

> If one reflects on the kinds of conditions necessary for productive work, it becomes quite clear that motivation is only one of them. Clearly, when working conditions, the quality of leadership, the suitability of supplies and equipment, the efficiency of scheduling and coordinating procedures, or the abilities of the members of the work force are found deficient, highly motivated behavior may have either little effect on productivity or even possibly the effect of causing frustration which interferes with productivity (House and Wigdor, 1967, p. 375).

Other factors such as group cohesion, which is emphasized in Likert's theory, also may or may not be conducive to effective performance. Although it has been shown that cohesive work groups which provide their members with social satisfaction have less absenteeism than those which do not, it has also been demonstrated that group cohesion can make for either above average or below average productivity, depending upon the norms of the particular group.

In summary, then, the accumulated evidence indicates that the relationship between the behavioral condition of the human organization and performance may be direct, circular, or even reversed. Given these contradictory results, it appears that the exact effects of behavioral variables on task performance are still to be established. So the desirability of including formal behavioral measurements in a planning and control system, either in monetary or nonmonetary forms, is still questionable.

Of course, management must still pay attention to the human resources at its disposal, in order to evaluate organizational capability and for staff development and promotion. And management must also concern itself with the effects of diminished employee satisfaction, such as absenteeism and high turnover. And so at least some variables which describe the behavioral condition of an organization must be formalized and included among the key success factors in any planning and control system.

SUMMARY

Structured processes are those stable, repetitive activities or procedures which can be economically analyzed, systematized, and formalized. They include both fully automated and human activity. The distinguishing feature of a structured process is that what should take place can be known and described before the activity begins. Hence the efficient and effective performance of these tasks depends not on diagnoses, judgment, or decision-making ability but on effort and due care.

Any process can be controlled by feedback or feedforward techniques. However, the specification of an appropriate type of control depends on determining the cause of the deviations noted. A number of techniques are available to diagnose and interpret variances, extending from a subjective judgment based on the magnitude of the deviation to complex decision-theoretic value-of-information approaches, which are discussed in the Appendix.

Among the techniques suggested for increasing and maintaining employee productivity are the assignment of responsibility, the setting of performance targets in line with individual levels of aspiration, the maintenance of a healthy behavioral climate in the organization, the enrichment of tasks to make them intrinsically satisfying, and the proper allocation of economic rewards to workers. Jointly or separately these means are available to the planning and control system designer interested in improving output.

APPENDIX: INTERPRETING AND RESPONDING TO DEVIATIONS FROM EXPECTATION

Both the feedback and/or feedforward control of any task begins with the monitoring and detection of a deviation from expectation, which signals the need for action. But any deviation from expectation may be due either to random events or to permanent changes. Before it can be decided which remedial action is most appropriate, a diagnosis of the cause of the deviation is required. And hence, one of the key problems of control is interpreting the significance of the deviations which arise.

Deviations and appropriate responses

There are two types of deviation that may occur. A deviation may be caused by a *random event*, one that happened merely by chance and will rarely repeat itself. In this situation, it should be ignored and no action taken. Alternatively, the deviation may signal a need to take action; i.e., it indicates that a *permanent change* has taken place which must be countered if the process is to return to its original state.

A permanent deviation may require one of three types of responses. It may be due to an implementation error or an environmental change that requires an *adjustment in the implementation process*. For example, in a sales effort, it may signal the increased effort of a competitor and hence the need for a stronger sales effort to match it. Second, the deviation may indicate that changes in input assumptions make the original plan itself no longer appropriate. For example, in an economic downturn, expected levels of consumer expenditure may now be invalid and recalibration and replanning may be necessary. This requires returning to the planning model, inputting the new assumptions, and *deriving a new plan*. Third, a deviation may indicate that the plan itself is inappropriate, not because of its assumptions but because of the structure of the planning model itself. In this situation replanning is not appropriate because the structural relationships (i.e., the specification of the planning model) is no longer appropriate. In this situation *planning model revision* is required; and until that is done, further replanning is futile. Thus, if analyses of deviations are to be used to diagnose process malfunctions and to indicate appropriate remedial adjustments, their specification and interpretation must allow for the determination of whether adjustment, replanning, or model adaptation is required.

Ways of deciding whether to investigate variances

In deciding whether or not to investigate a variance, the following factors may be considered: (1) the probability that the variance resulted from a random, uncontrollable cause as opposed to a permanent deviation in the process which can be corrected; (2) the benefits that will result if the variance is investigated and corrected; (3) the cost of not investigating the variance and allowing it to continue; and (4) the cost of investigating.

There are several techniques, differing in their costs and required degrees of managerial sophistication, that can be used in deciding whether or not to investigate a variance. These are explained next, in order of sophistication.

Size of deviation

The simplest method, of course, is to base the investigation decision on the absolute size of a deviation. After comparing the actual to the expectation, a decision is simply made whether or not the magnitude is sufficient to warrant an investigation. A refinement to this technique is to compute the percentage deviation by comparing the difference between expected and actual, either to the actual or to the expected amounts. These two methods are perhaps the most widely used ones in assessing the significance of variances that arise in cost accounting systems.

Classical statistics

If the event in question is considered to be a random variable, its probability distribution can be used as the basis of determining whether or not a deviation was due to chance or if it indicates a permanent change in the process. Assuming, for example, that the process is governed by a normal distribution of given mean and standard deviation, it is possible to compute the probability that the deviation was due to chance by employing classical statistical hypothesis testing using normal tables.[1] Looked upon as a simple test of a hypothesis, with the expected level of performance being the hypothesized parameter and actual performance as the sample statistic, the hypothesis is either accepted or rejected based on where the actual event falls with respect to the assumed distribution. (See Figure 6-1.)

FIGURE 6-1
Normal probability distribution

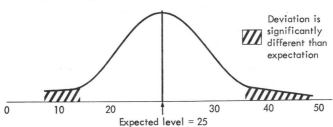

Expected level = 25

An extension of this approach, adapted from the quality control of manufactured goods, is the use of a control chart. Control limits are first established at plus or minus a specified number of standard deviations from the expected level. Over time actual events are plotted on a graph against time to determine whether or not a trend appears. Of course, until a deviation actually exceeds the prescribed limits it is not statistically significant. However, in many situations, trends become apparent

---

[1] The probability that a deviation indicates a permanent change in the process when it is in fact due to a random event is, of course, the type 1 error. The probability of accepting the process as being under control when in fact it is not, is the type 2 error.

well before deviations exceed the control limit. Hence control charts provide a form of anticipative control.

Classical statistics with cost data

A limitation in relying solely on the classical statistical approach is that the costs of investigation and the potential loss involved in not investigating are not explicitly reflected in the analysis. These costs can be estimated and included in the analysis to determine whether or not to investigate a variance as follows. Assume that an unfavorable variance if left uncorrected results in a loss L, and the cost of the investigation is C. The decision whether or not to investigate depends on the probability of two possible states which have caused the variance: (1) the variance was due to chance, or (2) the variance was due to a change in the process which can be corrected by management. If the former is true, the investigation is wasted and so is the cost of this investigation; however, if the latter is true, an investigation will presumably result in correction of the cause of the deviation. In this situation the reward will be in the form of avoiding a loss. The probability that the variance is due to chance is, of course, the area under the probability distribution curve extending from the point of deviation outward. These possibilities and costs are summarized in Table 6–1.

Let C be the cost of investigating the variance, and let L represent loss if it is not investigated. If an investigation is not carried out, the cost C will not be incurred; however, if an investigation is not carried out and the process is in need of an investigation, a loss L will be incurred. It is assumed that L is greater than C; otherwise investigation would never be warranted. Given an unfavorable variance, assume that the probability that this variance resulted from chance is p, where $p > 0$. Thus, $(1 - p)$ is the probability that the deviation was not due solely to chance.

As seen in Table 6–1, the expected cost of investigating or not investigating this variation can be calculated by multiplying each cost by

TABLE 6–1
Gross costs and benefits, probabilities, and expected costs and benefits of investigating and not investigating variances

Nature of the event	Acts		Probability
	Investigate	Do not investigate	
Random, uncontrollable	C	0	p
Controllable, correctable.	C	L	$(1 - p)$
Expected cost	C	$L(1 - p)$	1.00

its respective probability and summing over all possible events. The expected cost of investigating a variance is $C(p) + C(1 - p) = C$. The expected cost of not investigating is $(1 - p)L$. Thus, if the expected cost of investigating is less than the expected cost of not investigating, the appropriate action would be to investigate. The decision may be summarized as follows:

$$C < (1 - p)L \qquad \text{Investigate}$$
$$C > (1 - p)L \qquad \text{Do not investigate}$$

When the expected costs of these two acts are equal, a decision maker is indifferent between investigating and not investigating. Hence, by computing the probability that a variance was due to chance (using statistical tables), decision makers can then compare this probability against the probability level at which they are indifferent between investigating is not in order to determine whether they should investigate. If the probability is less than the indifference probability established by the above formulae, then the decision is to investigate; if it is greater than the indifference probability, the decision is not to investigate.

Subjective distributions

In the absence of the availability of an appropriate classical distribution such as the normal or Poisson distributions, a subjective one can be utilized. A subjective distribution is not a description of the frequency distribution of an assumed long-run trend of events but rather is a subjective expression of the experience of the individual concerned. It is simply his or her conception of the appropriate frequency distribution of possible events. The utilization of subjective probabilities is demonstrated by the following example.

Assume that a manufacturing process is producing a part with a standard cost of $10. The $10 standard consists of an ideal portion of $9 and a scrap allowance of $1; i.e., 10 percent of all parts are assumed to be scrapped. The production and cost statistics over a ten-period span are presented in Table 6–2. It is seen that over these ten years production varied from a low of 6 units to a high of 11 units and variances varied from a low of 0 to a negative variance of $50. The right-most column of the table indicates the proportion of total costs the variance reflects. Assume that the cost of investigating a variance in any one period is $20.

One method of assessing the significance of these variances is simply to average them over the ten periods and so decide whether or not the average variance exceeded the costs of investigation. In this example the average variance is $25 whereas the cost of investigation is $20, indicating that based on *average cost* an investigation is warranted.

TABLE 6–2

Period	No. of units produced	Standard cost	Actual cost	Variance	Variance (actual cost)
1.	9	90	$110	$ 20	2/11
2.	10	100	110	10	1/11
3.	11	110	110	0	0/11
4.	8	80	110	30	3/11
5.	9	90	110	20	2/11
6.	6	60	110	50	5/11
7.	11	110	110	0	0/11
8.	8	80	110	30	3/11
9.	7	70	110	40	4/11
10.	6	60	110	50	5/11
				$250	

A method employing subjective probabilities, however, would first ask an experienced executive what his probability estimate is that the scrap rate is actually .10; i.e., 10 percent, as was assumed in the standard, and the probability of its being something else. Suppose, for example, that he provided the data illustrated in Table 6–3. As seen from Table 6–3,

TABLE 6–3

Scrap rate R	Subjective probability estimate of this scrap rate p(R)	Dollar scrap loss at this defect rate L = $ (110)R	Expected loss p(R) · L
.10	0.5	$11	$ 5.50
.20	0.3	22	6.60
.25	0.2	27.50	5.50
	1.0		$17.60

the probability of a scrap rate of .10 is .5 whereas scrap rates of .20 and .25 are given probabilities of .3 and .2, respectively. Using expected loss as the criterion, it is seen that the expected loss is $17.60 per period. Hence, on an *expected value* basis, it does not pay to investigate this process since the investigation costs $20.

Subjective probabilities and additional sample information

Instead of using average or expected costs suppose it was decided to operate for one additional period, to observe the results of this period, and then to use this additional information to revise the subjective probabilities originally proposed in Table 6–3. Further assume that there was a $30 variance or 3/11 defective proportion in period 11. Let A represent this actual proportion of defective parts observed. These data are presented below in Table 6–4.

TABLE 6–4

(1) Scrap rates R	(2) Prior probability p(R)	(3) Probability (A/R) (A = 3/11)	(4) P(A,R)	(5) P(R/A)
.10. 5		.07	.035	0.23
.20. 3		.22	.066	0.43
.25. 2		.26	.052	0.34
			.153	1.00

In accordance with decision theoretic approaches, column 1 indicates the three possible scrap rates, .10, .20, and .25, while column 2 indicates the probabilities that these respective rates will occur .5, .3, and .2. If the actual variance (A) in the 11th period was $30 (3 units scrapped out of 11) then the probability of this variance occurring given the initial (prior) probabilities of the three possible scrap rates can be taken from a binomial table. For example, the probability of having 3 out of 11 (labeled event A in Table 6–4) as the proportion of the rejects in a process when the actual scrap rate; i.e., probability of rejection (R), is .10 is .07; i.e., $P(A/R) = .07$. From the binomial table it is seen that the probability of a rejection rate of 3 out of 11 when the real probability is .2 is .22. And similarly, the probability when R is actually .25 is .26. Column 4 presents data on the joint probabilities of achieving the events actually observed in period 11 when the scrap rate was as indicated. Column 5 gives the probabilities revised in light of the new information collected in period 11. This is computed from the following formula.

$$P(R/A) = \frac{R(A, R)}{P(A)}$$

where

$$P(A, R) = P(R)P(A/R)$$

This formula states that the probability that the scrap rate is actually R, given that event A took place, is the probability of both R and A taking place, divided by the marginal probability of the result A.

These a posteriori or revised probabilities in the expected value calculation (Table 6–5) show that the cost of not investigating now exceeds the cost of investigation; and hence when the additional sample information is utilized the decision is now to investigate.

Another possible refinement to this procedure involves having the al-

TABLE 6–5

R	P(R/A)	Dollar scrap loss	Expected loss
.10	0.23	$11	$ 2.53
.20	0.43	22	9.46
.25	0.34	27.50	9.52
	1.00		$21.51

ternative to choose one of several levels of investigation, each differing in cost and reliability. In the example above it was assumed that investigation would reveal what actually took place (random or not). However, it may be possible to have lower costs of investigation with 20 percent, 30 percent, and so on possibility of error and to go through two or three steps in a sequence before reaching a decision. But these are more of the matters of texts on decision theory and the interested reader is referred to the following references.

In sum then, it is seen that a deviation from expectation can be interpreted as follows: (1) on its absolute size; (2) on its relative size; (3) using classical statistics; (4) using classical statistics with cost data; (5) using subjective probability data and costs; and (6) using subjective probability data, sample information, and costs. Since structured processes are planned in terms of formal models, quantified deviation measures are usually reported. Hence the decision as to which investigative technique should be used is one of the keys to the design of control systems for structured processes.

QUESTIONS

1. Will adjusting cost standards to fit levels of aspiration improve the motivation of workers performing structured tasks? Can this be done in actual work environments?

2. Are managers who use feedforward control systems more effective than those who do not? Why?

3. What role do historical accounting data play in the development of formal models?

4. What is the role of and relationship between monetary measures and other quantitative and qualitative measures in the design of a control system?

5. If behavioral considerations are important in the design of control systems for structured tasks, what chance is there that the average plant accountant will develop an effective system?

6. To what extent do you think human resource measurements will become part of an organization's internal management accounting system? Why?

7. What are the positive and negative effects that can be expected in the future from the increasing use of computer-based information systems and management science models?

8. In what situations, if any, do you think the use of statistical techniques of control are appropriate? What are the barriers to the introduction of such techniques?

9. Could a firm operate a two-budget system (i.e., keep secret the knowledge that different expectations are being used for motivation and for financial planning)?

REFERENCES AND BIBLIOGRAPHY

Argyris, C. *Integrating the Individual and the Organization*. New York: Wiley 1964.

Balfour, C., ed. *Participation in Industry*. Totowa, N.J.: Rowman and Little-field, 1973.

Bedworth, David D. *Industrial Systems, Planning, Analysis and Control*. New York: Ronald Press 1973.

Behling, Orlando, and Shapiro, Mitchell B. Motivation theory: Source of solution or part of problem? *Business Horizons*, February 1974, pp. 59–66.

Bennet, Robert B. Motivational aspects of participation in the planning and control system. *Cost and Management*, September–October 1974, pp. 37–40.

Bierman, H.; Fouraker, J. L. E.; and Jaedicke, R. K. A use of probability and statistics in performance evaluation. *The Accounting Review*, July 1961, pp. 416–417.

Budd, J. Mark. Employee motivation through job enrichment. *Journal of Systems Management*, August 1974, pp. 34–39.

Buzby, Stephen L. Extending the applicability of probabilistic management planning and control models. *The Accounting Review*, January 1974, pp. 42–49.

Byrne, R. F., et al. *Studies in Budgeting*. New York: North-Holland Publishing Co., 1971.

Cooper, Robert. *Job Motivation and Job Design*. London: Institute of Personnel Management, 1974.

Craig, Quiester. Cost control: Whose job? *Management Accounting (U.S.)*, March 1975, pp. 22–24.

Dalton, G. W. Motivation and control in organizations. In G. W. Dalton and P. R. Lawrence (eds.), *Motivation and Control in Organizations*. Homewood, Ill.: Irwin, 1971.

Dopuch, N.; Birnberg, J.; and Demski, J. An extension of standard cost variance analysis. *The Accounting Review*, July 1967, pp. 526–536.

Edwards, James. People problems and human solutions. *Management Accounting (U.S.)*, February 1975, pp. 32–34.

Fein, Mitchell. Job enrichment: A reevaluation. *Sloan Management Review*, Winter 1974, pp. 69–88.

Fein, Mitchell. The myth of job enrichment. *The Humanist*, September–October 1973, pp. 30–32.

Gellerman, Saul W.   Doing dull work well. *Conference Board Record*, September 1974, pp. 47–52.

Hofstede, G. H.   *The Game of Budget Control*. London: Tavistock Publications, 1967.

House, R. J., and Wigdor, L. A.   Hertzberg's dual factor theory of job satisfaction and motivation, *Personnel Psychology* 1967, p. 375.

Jauch, Roger, and Skigen, Michael.   Human resource accounting. A critical evaluation. *Management Accounting*, May 1974, pp. 33–36.

Krishnan, Rama.   Democratic participation in decision making by employees in American corporations. *Academy of Management Journal*, June 1974, pp. 339–346.

Likert, R.   *The Human Organization*. New York: McGraw Hill, 1967.

Likert, R., and Seashore, S.   Making cost control work. *Harvard Business Review*, January–February 1958, pp. 96–108.

Lorange, Peter, and Scott Morton, Michael S.   A framework for management control systems. *Sloan Management Review*, Fall 1974, pp. 41–56.

McLelland, D. C.   *The Achieving Society*. New York: Van Nostrand, 1961.

Myers, M. Scott, and Flowers, Vincent S.   The feasibility and utility of human resource accounting. *California Management Review*, Summer 1974, pp. 17–23. .

Randall, P. E.   Manpower planning and control are very much the concern of the management accountant. *Management Accounting*, November 1974, pp. 294–98.

Reif, William E.; Gerrazzi, David N.; and Evans, Robert J., Jr.   Job enrichment: Who uses it and why. *Business Horizons*, February 1974, pp. 73–78.

Schleh, E. C.   Grabbing profits by the roots: A case study in "Results Management." *Management Review*, July 1972, pp. 2–13.

Shashua, Leon; Goldshmidt, Yaroov; and Shadmon, Dorikam.   Control charts for citrus packing plants. *Management Accounting (U.S.)*, March 1975, pp. 19–21.

Simpson, Howard L.   Model for participation. *Journal of Systems Management*, January 1974, pp. 30–35.

Stedry, A. C.   *Budget Control and Cost Behavior*. Englewood Cliffs, N.J.: Prentice-Hall, 1960.

Stedry, A. C., and Kay, G.   The effect of goal difficulty on performance: A field experiment. *Sloan School Working Paper*, M.I.T., No. 106–64, 1964.

Strauss, G., and Rosenstein, E.   Workers' participation: A critical view. *Industrial Relations*, 1970, pp. 197–214.

Thatcher, Ralph H.   Designing a productivity control process. *Business Horizons*, December 1975, p. 62.

The value of making each employee feel he counts. Lessons of Leadership, *Nation's Business*, October 1975, pp. 46–52.

Vroom, V. H.   *Work and Motivation*, New York: Wiley, 1964.

Whitsett, David A.   Where are your unenriched jobs? *Harvard Business Review*, January–February 1975, pp. 74–80.

Work in America. Report of a special task force to the Secretary of Health, Education and Welfare. W. E. Upjohn Institute for Employment Research. Cambridge: M.I.T. Press, 1972.

Zannetos, Z. S.   Standard costs as a first step to probability control. *Accounting Review*, April 1964, pp. 296–304.

Case study 6–1

AB Volvo

Industry has had many indications of problems developing with employees performing structured tasks. The auto industry with its monotonous assembly line has been hardest hit by boredom, high absenteeism and poor workmanship. It is estimated that 75 percent of the automobile assembly-line work is done by unskilled workers. Some auto plants now report absenteeism as high as 13 percent compared to 3 percent a few years ago. Sabotage, as experienced at the Lordstown plant of General Motors for example, is becoming a serious problem.

Recognition of the problem is, of course, a step in the direction of solving it. But there are differing opinions on how to solve it. The United Auto Workers seems to feel that more pay is the answer. Volvo, however, feels that something other than a pay increase is needed.

VOLVO'S SITUATION

Volvo was having serious difficulty in recruiting young Swedes for its assembly lines. At the main plant at Göteborg, worker turnover runs over 25 percent.[1] Because of the rate of employee turnover, Volvo has to hire and train approximately one third of its work force every year at an annual cost of $10 million to $30 million.[2]

In spite of these labor problems, AB Volvo is a rapidly growing and highly profitable company. However, although total assets and sales are growing rapidly, the cost of sales is increasing drastically, and so labor costs and expenses must be closely watched.

The Swedish attitude toward what workers need is indicated by the Swedish Prime Minister Olog Palme's comment, "The big problem is to make industrial life satisfactory for the individual. We have to bring social developments into the working places if we want to remain competitive as an industrial nation."[3] The Swedish parliament voted a bill

---

[1] "On-the-Job Commitment," *Sweden Now*, April 1974, p. 28.

[2] *Business Week*, September 9, 1972, p. 116.

[3] *Business Week*, September 9, 1972, p. 116.

permitting workers to participate in the management of all enterprises employing more than 100 persons. Union branches are entitled to two delegates on the board of directors of each individual enterprise. They will have full voting rights in all management decisions except those concerning collective bargaining. This law took effect on April 1, 1973.[4]

The following two articles describe Volvo's attempts to solve the problems of low worker job satisfaction and high turnover.

FOR VOLVO, BLUE-COLLAR JOBS NEEDN'T BE BLUE[5]

KALMAR, Sweden—Leonard Woodcock, president of the United Auto Workers of America, says "blue collar blues" are a myth—all the workers need is more money.

But he and the rest of the auto world are watching with bated breath AB Volvo's innovative attempts to humanize the assembly line.

The driving force behind the Volvo initiatives is dynamic, 39-year-old president, Pehr Gyllenhammer. At the unveiling of the new Kalmar plant in June to the European press, Gyllenhammer outlined the people parameters of its design:

"The objectives of the Kalmar works were to bring some identification with the workers to the products they were producing. . . . People in the plant should be able to communicate with each other—modern technique has isolated people on the assembly line. . . . We also wanted to establish groups because people very often function better in groups. We wanted to provide more physical freedom in the sense that people were not tied to the same spot throughout the day. We wanted to give the operators more influence on the job and their rhythm throughout the day."

A tall order for the plant designers. But they produced their answer in two months. Here are its major innovations:

1. The assembly line is broken up into 25 separate teams, each handling a complete system in the assembly process (such as the interior fittings or the safety equipment).

Within each team, the workers (numbering usually about 15) decide how to split up the work. The decisions vary from every worker performing all the operations of the system sequentially, to small groups concentrating on only two or three functions:

And if the workers can think of a better way of doing something, all they need is the approval of their "teknika," who oversees the technical aspects of the team's work.

The plant's quality control system relays to all the teams the major faults—and the examples of excellence—of the final product. So any changes in the work process produce rapid feedback—and promote competitiveness among the 25 teams.

---

[4] *International Union of Food and Allied Workers News Bulletin*, No. 3–4, 1973, p. 2.

[5] From "For Volvo, Blue-Collar Jobs Needn't Be Blue," *Financial Post*, July 27, 1974, p. 11.

2. Once a car has been fully processed by a team, it passes into a buffer zone, where it waits until the next team is ready to deal with it.

This means that each team can operate more or less independently, building up the units in the buffer zone when the workers feel like working hard and letting the stockpile run down if they want a breather.

And taking a rest in Volvo's Kalmar plant can be quite an experience. Each team is given its own rest room with a refrigerator and coffee machines. Other facilities include showers, saunas and, not to be scoffed at, an airy, bright environment with a good view of the surrounding countryside.

The feel of the plant is a shock after the assembly plants in North America, where the deafening clatter makes conversation a luxury and the machinery crammed on to the floor impresses mainly by its apparent utter confusion—and, above all, where the relentless production line dominates every person in the shop.

Volvo's Kalmar plant feels more like a public library. Even the hand tools are chosen to produce high output at low speeds.

The trick that makes all this possible is the "carrier"—an aluminum platform powered by batteries and controlled by electric impulses from a cable concealed in the floor.

It performs three functions:

It is an information store, passing to the computer its location at all times so that the computer can, in turn, keep track of it and program the instructions for each team working on that unit. Among other benefits, this means that the teams do not have to work on the units in any special order.

It transports the units around the plant from team to team automatically. It can also be controlled manually and has a special safety bumper that stops it as soon as it meets any resistance—a comforting thought when it is travelling at its top speed of 32 yards a minute.

It is also a working platform. The men or women, (there are many women workers on the Swedish assembly lines) can stand on it while it is moving. And the carrier can lift the car up or—its most impressive feature—turn the car at 90 degrees so that work on the underbody or top can be performed quite comfortably.

The overall effect is an assembly line worker's dream.

The factory cost Volvo about 10 percent more than a conventional assembly plant, but Gyllenhammer believes that increased productivity will more than make up for the higher initial capital investment.

Volvo's first deputy president, Per Ekstrom, told FP that turnover at other Swedish plants averages about 50 percent, and absenteeism on a bad day can be as much as 20 percent. That's pretty bad, even by U.S. standards.

Add to that Ekstrom's estimate that it costs the equivalent of 2.5 to four months' wages to hire and train a worker and it is obvious that any arrangement that can keep down turnover and absenteeism is going to save the company a lot of money.

In the first five months of the plant's operation, only one man in the work force of about 300 quit his job. Volvo people say it's too early to tell whether things will continue that way. But their obvious delight makes no secret of their expectations.

The second half of the year will, however, tell the real story—once the plant is brought up to capacity. By the year-end, it will provide employment for 600 people and turn out 30,000 cars a year. These figures will be doubled when the company starts a second shift.

Gyllenhammer stresses that his company means business—"Kalmar is not an experiment." He also told newsmen that the new Volvo plant in Virginia, U.S., will be modeled along the same lines as Kalmar—"though there will be some changes as a result of what we've learned at Kalmar."

The effect on the auto world in North America could be decisive. The UAW, for one, will have to decide whether blue-collar blues are really a myth.

Are people quite happy doing a boring job, if they can switch off for eight hours a day in return for a good salary that will help them enjoy their leisure time? Or do they need more "psychic income" out of their work?

The Volvo system also integrates the worker more closely with the management of the plant, because he is taking essentially managerial decisions in how he structures his work. This might require considerable adjustment from both the management and the union.

There are still some doubts, too, whether the Swedish example is suited to the American scene. The Swedes are accustomed to co-operating and do not have the fiercely independent tradition of North Americans. Groups have worked well in many cases in the U.S. and Canada—but they tend to be unpredictable and the tough, tight managers in Detroit might not like that.

But elsewhere, the Volvo idea is being extended. Umberto Agnelli, president of the Fiat Group, told FP that he was convinced that the system at Kalmar would become universal in the next 10 to 20 years. He is developing a system for Italy that would allow *individual* rather than *team* choice in the planning of the work.

Everybody else ready?

VOLVO'S VALHALLA[6]

To Henry Ford, patron saint of mass production, the new Volvo plant in Kalmar, Sweden, would seem curious indeed. It looks more like a giant repair shop than an auto factory. The working space is airy, uncluttered by stacks of spare parts. The plant is so quiet that workers can chat in normal tones, or hum along with the pop tunes playing on their cassette tape recorders. Troubleshooters on lightweight bicycles ensure a steady flow of spare parts. Sunlight plays against bright-colored walls through huge picture windows looking out on the landscape. But the most puzzling question in Ford's mind would be: What happened to the assembly line?

Busy interest. The answer is that it has been changed beyond recognition as part of an attack on an international labor problem: the growing dislike that today's young, comparatively well-educated workers have shown for tedious, repetitive factory jobs. In the U.S. and other countries, that attitude is reflected in heavy absenteeism and high turnover among factory work forces, poor-quality production and occasional strikes by workers desperate to get away from the line for a while. Volvo's system at Kalmar is attracting worldwide

---

[6] "Volvo's Valhalla," *Time*, September 16, 1974, pp. 76–79.

attention as an imaginative effort to set up a factory that will keep workers interested while busy.

Instead of a clanking, high-speed conveyor line, the Kalmar plant uses 250 "carriers"—18-ft.-long computer-guided platforms that glide silently over the concrete floor. Each carrier delivers the frame for a single Volvo 264 to each of the plant's 25 work teams. The teams consist of 15 to 25 workers who are responsible for a certain aspect of assembly; one team, for example, will install the car's electrical system and another will work on the interior finish.

The teams organize themselves as they wish and work at the speed they choose. While a worker on a conventional assembly line might spend his entire shift mounting one license-plate lamp after another, every member of a Kalmar work team may work at one time or another on all parts of the electrical system—from taillights to turn signals, head lamps, horn, fuse box and part of the electronically controlled fuel-injection system. The only requirement is that every team meet its production goal for a shift. As long as cars roll out on schedule, workers are free to take coffee breaks when they please or to refresh themselves in comfortable lounges equipped with kitchens and saunas.

The Kalmar system was worked out by Pehr Gyllenhammar, Volvo's managing director (see box). Three years ago, when he stepped in as chief executive, he had to cope with an incredibly high labor turnover rate. At Volvo's main assembly plant near Göteborg, turnover reached an annual rate of 41 percent in 1971, even though the company pays some of the highest wages in Swedish industry. The company had to spend heavily to train replacements, and the rapid turnover contributed to declines in quality that have marred Volvo's reputation for durability. Gyllenhammar was convinced that the workers simply did not like their monotonous assembly-line jobs. "As people became more educated—and Sweden spends perhaps more money per capita for education than any other country—their jobs have become less complex," he says. "That does not make sense."

Gyllenhammar assigned a task force of young executives (all under 30) to design a new plant where "machines would be the product of people and not vice versa." After two months of intensive work and study the group presented its plan. Kalmar (pop. 53,000) was chosen as a site in large part because of its high unemployment rate. Ground was broken in 1972, and 19 months later the first team-made model Volvo rolled out of the workshops.

The new plant cost $23 million, about 10 percent more than a conventional factory of the same capacity. It includes the most up-to-date devices to monitor production and promote quality control. At each team's work station, for example, a computer-connected television screen projects figures comparing the team's production goal with the number of assemblies it has actually completed. On top of the screen a yellow light flashes if the team is behind schedule; a green light comes on when it is ahead. So far, the plant is only turning out 56 cars a day, but by 1975 the company hopes to achieve annual production of 30,000 cars.

Many skeptics. A steady stream of auto executives, from Henry Ford II to Fiat Managing Director Umberto Agnelli, has visited the Kalmar plant. Some have incorporated similar ideas in their own factories. In June, for example, Fiat introduced an entirely new system of engine assembly at its plant in Termoli on the Adriatic coast; work is now performed in fixed position "islands." There are many skeptics though. Most U.S. auto executives insist that the Kalmar system would not work in American assembly plants, which serve a vastly larger market and so must turn out many more cars per day than Kalmar.

Some workers and union leaders consider the Kalmar plant less than Valhalla. "The environment is better," says Göran Nillson, 38, who worked on Volvo's conventional assembly line near Göteborg, "but you should not forget that we have the same productivity objectives as any other plant. It looks like a paradise, but we work hard." Adds Kjell Anderson, an official of the militant Swedish metal workers' union, "They haven't really changed the system and they haven't changed the hierarchy. For example, we don't think it's necessary to have a foreman when you have groups."

Gyllenhammar remains convinced that Kalmar will work. "We think the extra capital involved will be offset by increased productivity," he says. Still, Gyllenhammar is a prudent manager, and Volvo is prepared to adapt if the Kalmar experiment fails. The plant was designed in such a way that it can be reconverted into a conventional assembly line at a minimal cost.

The well-connected reformer

At first glance, a review of Pehr Gyllenhammar's meteoric career suggests that he rose to the top because he has the right relatives. In 1969, at the age of 34, the trim, handsome lawyer replaced his father as head of Skandia, Sweden's largest insurance company. Two years later he succeeded his father-in-law as managing director of Volvo, the country's biggest industrial concern. Nepotism or not, the selection has certainly paid off. Under Gyllenhammar's leadership, Volvo has not only increased its sales by 70 percent (to more than $2 billion in 1973), but has also made some far-reaching labor-relations reforms.

Gyllenhammar has skippered Volvo with the same assurance with which he pilots his 31-ft. sloop *Amanda III*. Almost immediately after taking over, he replaced a centralized management structure with four semiautonomous divisions, each of which is responsible for its own profits. He also expanded production of trucks, marine and industrial engines and other products to a point where they account for 43 percent of Volvo's sales. Pretax profits reached $90 million during the first half of this year, despite a 19 percent decline in U.S. sales of Volvo cars.

In 1971 Gyllenhammar appointed two union men as voting members of Volvo's board, a customary practice in some European nations but at that time still rare in Sweden. He also made changes at Volvo's big assembly plant near Göteborg, automating the heaviest jobs and establishing an internal placement agency to help people find more satisfying assignments. American workers will soon get a firsthand look at Gyllenhammar's style. Volvo has broken ground for a new assembly plant in Chesapeake, Va., the first automobile factory established in the U.S. by a foreign company since World War II. It is expected to begin production in late 1976.

For all the changes he has made, Gyllenhammar is no advocate of the kind of "industrial democracy" that would give workers an equal voice with management in corporate decision making. "I believe in giving workers some say in the way their job is carried out," he says, "but how can they have influence in such important executive decisions as where to put a new plant?" Although such views irritate militant Swedish unionists, Gyllenhammar's easy informality (he addresses workers with the familiar *du*, and they do likewise) and unpretentious style are the earmarks of a natural politician. Some Swedish pols have touted him as a potential leader of the liberal Folkpartiet.

Questions

1. Describe Volvo's problem in terms of the variables and the chain of causal relationships that contribute to it.
2. What alternative courses of action were potentially available to Volvo's management? What are the strengths and weaknesses of each of these approaches? Why did Volvo's management choose the one it did? Do you agree with this choice?
3. How different is this industrial task situation from managing
   a. The performance of clerical tasks in an office.
   b. A group of computer programmers.
   c. The performance of maintenance inspections on aircraft.
   d. A stenographic pool.
   e. A sales force.
4. Are such plants the wave of the future? If so, what are the implications for the design of planning and control systems?

Case study 6–2
Marvin Jenkins, General Foreman

Marvin Jenkins, general foreman of the Dibble Toy Company, had just returned from an executive development course on the behavioral aspects of budgets. The week he spent was not a vacation for him; hopefully it would help solve one of his most pressing problems—keeping the cost and output performance of the four foremen reporting to him at the level to which he aspired. Although they did not openly dispute the output levels he set for them, the foremen certainly were not committed to their attainment. In fact, their matter of fact attitude appeared to be worsening over time.

The course provided Marvin with his first exposure to the benefits of participation in budgeting and cost control. He was taught that participation implies self-control which raises self-esteem, increases involvement and commitment, and hence increases the motivation to accomplish the production levels and cost performance established. Early in the course Marvin had argued with the instructor against the practice of allowing subordinates to participate in establishing levels of performance. Marvin believed that it was a supervisor's job to lead and the subordinate's job to follow. But gradually, as he became aware of the benefits to be gained by relinquishing some control and becoming more democratic, he began to recognize that perhaps more participation could solve his problem.

July is the busiest month in the toy business—getting ready for fall shipments in time for Christmas. It is also the most difficult time to get production out, given the heat in the plant and workers' thoughts of vacation. Marvin therefore chose this month to try out his new approach.

In early June, rather than communicating the required output levels as he had traditionally done, Marvin called his four foremen together to set the levels of performance for July on a participative basis. He explained to them his belief that their knowledge of the work force and the production machinery were invaluable in establishing performance levels. He stated that he needed their help in overcoming the problems that July usually brought. He also mentioned to his foremen that sales orders for this year were about the same level as last year. He asked them to spend an evening together sometime in the next week reviewing past performance, current conditions, and the company's needs, and to suggest production levels for July. He would meet with them again in a week.

The meeting which followed did not turn out as Marvin expected, however. The four foremen appeared far more involved in the company's affairs and far more committed to their plans for July than Marvin had ever seen them. But their plan called for production at a level 20 percent below what Marvin had been instructed to produce. They argued that the additional production could be scheduled in the fall and still meet Christmas delivery dates. And they were firm in this conviction.

Question

What should Marvin do?

Case study 6–3
Nairobi Metals

The management of Nairobi Metals was not satisfied with the operation of their inventory system when they hired Sidney Charles to serve as assistant production manager in charge of inventory control. Management had many things to complain about. Materials ordered often arrived behind schedule, holding up production. The cost of many purchased parts exceeded the amounts originally estimated, and expensive emergency purchases were frequently needed. In addition, the quality of some of the goods received was questionable. Sidney's job was to put the inventory control system in working order, as quickly as possible.

Nairobi Metals was a small-scale manufacturer and distributor of home hardware products. In its plant it manufactured articles such as door knobs, hinges, fireplace equipment, and home ornamentation. Nairobi also bought similar products from other manufacturers. It then sold these to hardware stores and do-it-yourself wholesalers and retailers. The 1976 sales were about $18 million.

Nairobi had five types of inventory to be controlled. *Raw materials* consisted of die castings, bar and sheet stock, and plastic components. The other 60 percent of components' inventory was in the form of *purchased parts* or *general stores and supplies*. *Finished goods* inventory consisted of assemblies awaiting packaging. Usually, the packaged assemblies were then placed in a warehouse awaiting shipment. Once goods were transferred to the warehouse, however, they became the responsibility of the Sales Department. The final type of inventory was *materials-in-process* including all materials which had been released to various manufacturing departments and which was either on machines, in the process of being assembled, on skids or in bins. Once Inventory Control released material to the first manufacturing or assembly operation it became the responsibility of Production Control, although the policies of the Inventory Control Department had to be followed.

OBJECTIVES AND RESPONSIBILITIES

The objective given to the new assistant production manager was to provide the proper quantity of any kind of materials and/or part as specified by Product Engineering at the right place at the right time.

His responsibilities were as follows:

1. To set up and maintain inventory stocks in accordance with sales estimates.
2. To place orders for raw materials, component parts, and subassemblies required for production.
3. To maintain usage records and to purchase items for stock based on periodic reviews of these data.
4. To control all inventory: raw materials, work-in-process, supplies and finished parts.
5. To keep stock active by reviewing engineering change bulletins and using superseded items first.
6. To provide for the proper reduction or disposals of any excess or any obsolete inventories brought about by any of the following reasons: overoptimism; errors of judgment; mistakes; design obsolescence; or technical failures.

CURRENT PRACTICE

The Inventory Control Department currently issues purchase schedules for material and purchased parts to all outside vendors, either directly or through the Purchasing Department, and to manufacturing departments within the plant through the Production Control Department. It then expedites and coordinates the delivery of this material, both inside and outside, according to the required schedules.

MAJOR FUNCTIONS

The most important function in inventory control is deciding what and how many of each item to buy. At Nairobi *ordering* decisions were traditionally made in one of three ways:

a. An economic order (or manufacture) quantity was computed using data on setup charges, inventory carrying charges, requirements, obsolescence, materials handling requirements, lead time, and so on. The standard costs for each component prepared by the Cost Accounting Department were used to compute economic order quantities.
b. Check point. In this method, the level of inventory balance at which a check should be made is established and then used to determine whether or not it should be recorded.

In addition to these methods the judgment of the individuals concerned, was also followed.

Once an item is ordered, it is up to *expediting* to get it in on time. And regardless of how well planning and scheduling were carried out there always seemed to be a need for expediting. A good portion of the Inventory Control Department's resources were devoted to expediting. In fact, it was joked that at one time expediters were expediting the expediters.

The task of the expediter is to follow up on the vendor to see how he is doing and to determine whether or not shipments will arrive on time. At one time the company experimented with simply telephoning or mailing requests to vendors to indicate the date at which shipment would be made but found that this method was remarkably unreliable. Now all expediting was done by personal visits.

The third major function of the Inventory Control Department is *keeping accurate records*. The company felt it was still too small to use a computer and hence maintained a manual record system. Records were kept in a visible file, one in which each card in the file is presented so that a proportion of it is exposed, thereby enabling easy indexing.

The fourth major function of this department was *stocking*. Stocking covers all phases of inventory control that have to do with the physical handling of materials, whether raw material, work-in-process, or finished. One component of the stocking function is the operation of the Receiving Department. Another is the Stores Department where all raw material is controlled by a storekeeper. The Stores Department is responsible for the stocking and delivery of material to the proper work station when requested by Production Control. In addition to the main stock room, sub-stock rooms existed throughout the plant. The purpose of these was to hold manufactured items, subassemblies, and purchased parts at convenient locations near certain assembly lines. These sub-stock rooms were all fenced-in areas, distributed throughout the plant, looked after by stockkeepers.

The fourth task of stocking consists of accumulating subassemblies off the assembly line, and then making sure that the right quantities of these were made available to other assembly lines. If this is not properly done unbalancing of an entire line may occur.

THE CURRENT SITUATION

Management had encouraged Sidney to accept the job because they felt he could rectify the difficulties they were experiencing. They explained to him that although the previous manager of Inventory Control was rather undisciplined in his approach to the job, he had maintained a fairly accurate record-keeping system. There were extensive data available on the types of stores maintained, current stock on hand, purchase requisitions and shop order records outstanding, a detailed record of vendor follow-up procedures and vendor reliabilities, a complete file on all schedules prepared as well as on performance in meeting these, and a detailed record of all shipping schedules. Management, therefore, felt that the problem of not having adequate historical data upon which to formulate plans did not arise in this situation and that Sidney could easily utilize this data base to develop whatever controls he saw fit.

They also believed that there was no morale, motivational or attitudinal problems in the Inventory Control group. Nairobi was a very profitable, well-paying and easygoing organization, and although the ineptitude of the previous manager had caused them considerable grief and gray hair, it had not severely distorted profits. (It was enough, however, to get the previous manager fired.) Since the staff was both competent and had the correct attitude, management felt Sidney would have no trouble in quickly whipping the Inventory Control Department into shape.

Questions

1. If you were Sidney, what questions would you be asking yourself?
2. What role does a historical data base play in planning and controlling the type of operation?

Chapter outline

Some problems of unstructured processes
    Allocating resources effectively
    Increasing motivation
    Establishing appropriate feedback
Zero-base budgeting
    How zero-base budgeting works
        Developing decision packages
        Ranking packages
    Benefits of zero-base budgeting
    Implementation of the procedure
Management by objectives
    The goals of management by objectives
    How management by objectives works
    Two conceptions of MBO
        MBO for individual goal setting and appraisal
        MBO as a comprehensive approach to planning and
           control

7

The planning and control of unstructured processes

When you have completed this chapter you will understand:

1. The problems involved in planning and controlling unstructured tasks.
2. Three specific system design problems:
   a. Allocating resources effectively.
   b. Increasing motivation.
   c. Providing appropriate feedback.
3. Two proposed methods of overcoming these problems:
   a. Zero-base budgeting.
   b. Management by objectives.

SOME PROBLEMS OF UNSTRUCTURED PROCESSES

This chapter focuses on tasks whose performance relies on professional or managerial judgment. It considers the critical problems of managing managers—those individuals responsible for tasks which have no underlying model or standard of performance. As organizations plunge deeper and deeper into technological, economic, and governmental complexity, managers must contend increasingly with change, with novel and unexpected events, and with uncertainty. So the success with which an organization's planning and control system deals with unstructured tasks and managing managers is increasingly important to its overall effectiveness.

There are many substantive differences in the planning and control systems for structured and unstructured processes. For a structured process the system can answer the following questions: What was achieved? How much did it cost? How much should it have cost, based on predetermined standards or expectations? How efficient was the process? The use of models in structured situations allows control by prescription and comparison to expectations. However, in unstructured situations that involve uncertainty, novelty, ambiguity, and frequent or rapid change, or when outputs are not quantifiable or even measurable, the underlying causal relationships between inputs and outputs are far less clear. Prescribing behavior (i.e., issuing directives) and determining the effectiveness and efficiency of any behavior are difficult if not impossible tasks, and require appropriate means, both financial and nonfinancial.

As outlined in Chapter 5, any planning and control system must satisfy the following requirements:

1. It must provide objectives that allow a responsibility unit to act in its best interests and also in the best interest of the organization as a whole;
2. It must motivate the manager of each responsibility unit to achieve his or her objectives;
3. It must assist in achieving effective and efficient performance;
4. It must integrate each responsibility unit within the overall organization.

Satisfying these requirements for an unstructured situation is a difficult task.

Responsibility units that perform unstructured tasks can be planned and controlled as cost, profit, or investment centers, or with nonfinancial measures. Choice of the most appropriate form of responsibility center is one of the many decisions a system designer must make. Although the design of an effective planning and control system for unstructured processes involves a host of such problems and decisions, the present discussion will consider three fundamental issues: (1) allocating resources effectively; (2) increasing motivation; and (3) establishing appropriate feedback to provide reinforcement and control without excessive constraint. The choice among cost, profit, and investment center forms of responsibility centers will be discussed in Chapters 8 and 9.

Allocating resources effectively

An important function of any planning and control system is to determine how resources are to be allocated. Resources cannot be allocated to unstructured tasks as they are to structured ones. For an engineered task, standards can be developed per unit and, when sales volumes are forecast, resources can be allocated accordingly. For discretionary expenditures, however, neither per unit activity nor a total volume of activity can be specified. Of course, costs may be itemized to as great a degree as required (e.g., as to number of people, salaries, fringe benefits, and so on), or in relation to intended missions, such as producing financial statements or serving client needs. But because of the difficulty of measuring results, no formal model relating input to output can be devised. The specification of input-output relationships and the evaluation of efficiency rely on judgment. And so, the "correct" allocation of resources to these areas must also depend largely on judgment.

Evaluating requests for resources is a task most managers must contend with. Every student of organizations is familiar with the problem of employees who inflate their budget requests if they suspect that their requests will be cut. Several empirical studies (Argyris, 1953; Hofstede, 1967; Lowe and Shaw, 1968) indicate that submission of excessive resource requests and easily achieved performance standards is a common practice. The term "organizational slack" refers to these excessive resources.

Organizational slack is the accumulation of excess resources which have no legitimate use other than as a cushion against future difficulties. Is organizational slack a serious problem? Several research studies indicate that it is.

The concept of organizational slack was introduced by Cyert and March (1963) to explain how firms smooth environmental fluctuations by accumulating excess "fat" under favorable economic conditions, and by using up this slack when they must cut back in less favorable times. Defining organizational slack as payments made to members of an organization in excess of what is required to maintain a stable coalition, they hypothesized that during boom periods, organizations secure and disburse resources in excess of actual needs; i.e., they build up slack in various budgets. Should the environment become less favorable, however, they predicted that the accompany resource scarcity would tend to cause a reduction in excess payments, and slack would be used up.

According to another theory of slack (Williamson, 1964), individual managers attempt to achieve their own objectives while simultaneously achieving organizational objectives such as sales, profits, or return on investment. As long as organizational resources are sufficient, both personal as well as task aspirations can be satisfied. Like Cyert and March, Williamson believes that managers strive to attain their personal goals by maximizing the slack resources under their control. However, in contrast to Cyert and March, he contends that when resources become scarce slack is not used up. Instead, managers resist any reallocation of resources that could alter their preferred situation.

Schiff and Lewin (1970) also suggest that individual managers always

attempt to increase slack in order to ensure the achievement of both organizational and personal goals. They studied the budget process of
several firms and found that the slack added to many budget items cannot easily be reduced at later times because it has been spent, for example, on salary increases to managers, or on the formation or increase
of staff groups. They also found that managers tended to bargain for
lower performance criteria and to create budgetary slack by understating
revenues and overstating costs. They concluded that once established,
slack is difficult to remove.

An empirical study by Lewin and Wolf (1972) supports this contention. They examined the level of organizational slack both in economically favorable and economically unfavorable times and found that slack
tends to increase steadily over a period of time regardless of the economic climate. They found that even under less favorable conditions,
slack is not reallocated sufficiently to counter long-run declines and/or
fluctuations in profitability. They concluded that the accumulation of
organizational slack is a continuing one-way process that can only be
countered with effective administration.

These studies clearly identify one important objective of the planning
and control system for an unstructured process: the efficient allocation of
economic resources and the control of organizational slack. This chapter
discusses two means of achieving these ends—zero-base budgeting, and
management by objectives. But before turning to these, two additional
important problems must be considered.

Increasing motivation

In addition to acting as a mechanism to allocate resources, budgets
may also increase motivation. Studies have shown that performance can
be improved when expectations are made clear. On the basis of empirical
research, Locke (1968) reports that when specific goals are set, subjects
perform far better than when they are told to "do as well as you can."
It has also been found that participation in budgeting often tends to increase feelings of self-control, competence, and self-esteem. Participation
allows employees to gain a sense of commitment and so become more
motivated to achieve the objectives they have helped formulate, and it
leads to a sense of achievement from performing well. Chapter 6 has
discussed the further problem of deciding on the difficulty of the goals
to be set, where it was concluded that objectives should be difficult, but
also obtainable.

Thus, both for effective allocation of resources and for improving
motivation, the setting of difficult task objectives appears to be the best
course to follow in the administration of both structured and unstructured processes. However, from the standpoint of ensuring environ-

mental adaptation in complex situations and of effectively meeting diverse demands, it may be more desirable for management to set less demanding objectives, or to tolerate a greater degree of slack or inefficiency.

The tolerable level of slack built into any task may depend on the characteristics of the task itself. So it is argued by Argyris (1971), who notes that the intent of management information systems, which include budget and performance reports, is to help managers order and understand complexity. However, recent increases in the coverage and formalization of controls, economically produced by today's computer technology, have reduced individual flexibility. Argyris believes that an increase in control causes feelings a lack of choice, pressure, and psychological fear, which eventually lead to a decreased sense of responsibility and poorer performance. And the more uncertain the events with which the individual must cope and the more ambiguous his or her task situation, the more likely is this tendency. Therefore, one advantage of budgetary slack and less difficult budget objectives may be that they allow an employee the freedom to cope with the unexpected events of an uncertain, ambiguous environment. Hence the existence of slack may not always be demotivating or mean a wasteful use of resources. It may be the difference between a pleasant and an intolerable work environment. It appears, then, that the amount of slack that should be tolerated in a planning and control system depends on the degree of inherent uncertainty and unstructuredness of the situation, as well as on individual preferences and the ability to work under pressure.

Establishing appropriate feedback

The third issue affecting system effectiveness is the provision of appropriate feedback. Feedback on performance has two important functions: (1) it supplies an individual with the information he or she needs to continue and to improve performance; (2) it contributes toward motivation by reinforcing a sense of achievement. Since lack of information contributes to uncertainty and a sense of ambiguity, feedback provides managers of unstructured tasks with the information they need to make corrections, and so help them cope with environmental change. In addition, it is well known that feedback reinforces the incentive to achievement, partly through the greater feeling of control provided by feedback information, and partly through the feelings of competence aroused by a knowledge of what has been accomplished. It is also important for the feedback to be timed so that individuals can exercise corrective control. Prompt feedback must be provided while the memory of past performance is fresh.

However, although feedback may help to reduce ambiguity and uncertainty and also enhance motivation, feedback that comes too quickly or frequently can be dysfunctional. One danger is premature evaluation. Drawing on the job evaluation studies of Jacques (1966), Dearden (1968) has linked the notion of a manager's time span of discretion, defined as the length of time that must elapse before a superior can properly evaluate a subordinate's performance, with the performance feedback interval. He argues that if the time span of discretion is different for different jobs, then the feedback time period covered by a report should depend on the particular job and not vice versa. Dearden argues that one way of adapting a control system to different degrees of task ambiguity and uncertainty is to modify the length of the feedback interval. Contrarily, failure to adjust managers' discretionary time interval to the task they must accomplish may, if it results in premature evaluation, cause them to perceive the control system unfavorably. In fact, the intrusiveness of premature feedback may be as frustrating as excessive budgetary constraint. But in spite of these potentially dysfunctional aspects, most organizations do not vary the degree and frequency of budget performance feedback for separate tasks, even though these tasks may vary considerably in their degree of structure.

Of course, it is the improper use of the feedback information and not its timing that leads to premature evaluation and its dysfunctional consequences (such as manipulation of figures and goal displacement). But it seems to be axiomatic that whenever data become available they are used, regardless of their appropriateness for the purpose to which they are put.

These three problems—allocating resources efficiently so as to minimize slack; setting objectives that are motivating but not excessively constraining; and selecting an appropriate evaluation period—are not unrelated. Motivation, evaluation, economic slack, organizational constraint, and feedback are all closely related and interdependent. Therefore, any attempt to instruct the system designer about what to look for or what to emphasize is an impossible task. The relative importance of these factors will vary in different situations, and the only advice to be offered is—it depends. Rather than discuss solutions to each of these problems individually, the remainder of this chapter will consider two general approaches to the planning and control of unstructured tasks. This discussion, based on total approaches, is meant to capture and describe these complex interrelationships in a systematic manner.

ZERO-BASE BUDGETING

The most frequent budgeting approach to the planning, resource allocation, and control of unstructured processes can best be described as incremental. Incremental budgeting establishes expectations by adjusting the last period's allocations and expenditures in light of coming events. It is expedient, inexpensive, and frustration minimizing, and it is assumed to be a sufficiently accurate method. This is not to say that incremental budgets rely on intuition or judgment alone; ratios such as sales dollars to sales support personnel or dollars, or administrative cost to the number of transactions, may be used in the adjustment of last year's budget. However, incremental budgets rely on the last period as the frame of reference, rather than on overall analysis and synthesis. Incremental budgeting does not investigate the base amount, only the increments to it.

Zero-base budgeting is an attempt to overcome the limitations of the incremental approach. Since incremental budgeting looks at only a small fraction of the total budget, it may leave many significant questions unanswered, such as: how efficient and effective are the activities that were not evaluated? Or, should current operations be reduced or reallocated to fund new or higher priority items? The zero-base approach reviews, evaluates, and allocates all resources by asking two basic questions: where and how can money be spent most effectively; and how much should be spent?

How zero-base budgeting works

One approach to zero-base budgeting originated at Texas Instruments Ltd., and is now being promoted commercially by its developer, Peter Pyhrr (1973). This approach requires an organization to analyze all appropriation requests in detail, for current as well as new activities. It is a two-step process. The first step is to prepare "decision packages" for each activity or operation, and the second is to rank these decision packages in order of their importance.

A decision package is a document that identifies a discrete activity, function, or operation in a definitive manner so that management can evaluate and rank it against other activities and decide whether to approve or reject it (Pyhrr, 1973, p. 6). A key to the zero-base approach is the mandatory identification and evaluation of alternatives to each activity, and the development of a package for each alternative. In general, two types of alternatives are considered: (1) different ways of performing the same function or activity, such as centralizing or decentralizing an operation, employing one among others of technologies, or purchasing an activity outside versus performing it in house; and (2) different levels of effort for each activity. In this way managers can identify alternative actions at one level of expenditure and can also consider the benefits and drawbacks of additional levels of spending. Decision packages thus allow senior management to eliminate, reduce, or increase the level of spending for each activity and so reduce or shift funds.

Decision packages are usually described on a standard form which asks for information such as the following:

1. The name or title of the package.
2. The problem or service to which the package relates.
3. The actions to be taken.
4. The benefits received if it is accepted.
5. The consequences if it is not accepted.
6. Quantitative measures of performance, such as cost/effectiveness ratios.
7. The resources required to implement the package.
8. A cross-reference to other related packages; e.g., those reflecting different levels of effort or alternative ways of performing the same function.
9. Detailed costing information.
10. Any special analysis or additional explanation needed.

Once expressed in this succinct form, packages can be easily analyzed, evaluated, and ranked.

The generation and evaluation of alternatives for an activity have several advantages. For example, in times of limited resources, complete elimination of some functions may be the only possible decision if only one alternative is considered. But elimination may not be desirable or practical. Senior management may prefer to reduce the current level of effort instead of eliminating an entire function, and zero-base budgeting makes this option clear. Because the managers who develop decision packages are those who are best equipped to identify and evaluate different levels of effort, it should be their responsibility to advise senior management of these possibilities.

Developing decision packages. Three considerations that determine the organizational level at which decision packages should be developed are the availability of alternatives, the level at which meaningful decisions can be made, and the time constraints on the analysis.

Generally, decision packages are developed for discrete activities. Managers might logically begin by describing the current year's activities and operations. They can identify the current level of each activity and the methods by which it is being carried out. After they have broken their current operations down into activities, the managers can then start looking at the requirements for the coming year. It is extremely helpful, of course, if senior management issues a formal set of planning assumptions to aid each manager in determining his or her future requirements.

The preparation of decision packages usually begins with the generation of alternatives to business-as-usual activities and levels of effort. The manager may also consider new activities or programs. He or she then groups these proposed activities into one of three categories of decision packages: (1) different ways and/or different levels of effort for performing a current activity; (2) business-as-usual activities where there are no logical alternatives to the present method and level of effort; and (3) new activities and programs. Then the ranking process can begin.

Ranking packages. Management decides how much should be spent and where it should be spent by ranking all decision packages in order of decreasing benefit. It can then evaluate each cutoff level of expenditure and can study the consequences of not approving additional packages ranked below the expenditure level. Initial rankings should occur at the organizational level at which the packages are developed, so that each manager can evaluate the importance of his or her own activities. The manager at the next level up then reviews the rankings and uses them as guides to produce a single consolidated ranking for all packages presented to him or her. In this way, theoretically all packages for an entire company could be ranked. But while this single list would completely identify priorities, ranking such a large volume of packages would impose a ponderous, if not impossible, burden on top management. Terminating the ranking at the level that generated the decision packages is also unsatisfactory, because relevant trade-offs will not be identified for top management. At what level decision packages ought to be ranked depends, therefore, on a number of factors, including: (1) the number of packages to be ranked and the time and effort required to do so; (2) management's ability and willingness to rank unfamiliar activities; (3) natural groupings that provide a logical sphere of analysis, such as product or profit centres; and (4) the need for extensive review across organizational boundaries to determine trade-offs and expense levels.

Benefits of zero-base budgeting

Proponents of zero-base budgeting suggest that it will produce several benefits. It spotlights redundancy and duplication of efforts; it focuses on programs and expectations rather than on percentage increases or decreases from previous years' activities; it establishes priorities within and among responsibility units and allows comparisons to be made across organizational lines so that overall priorities can be established; and it aids performance evaluation by providing a data base which shows whether or not each activity or operation has yielded the benefits and used the costs expected.

If zero-base budgeting is used, changes in expenditure levels do not require a recycling of inputs when the budget is revised. The ranked list of decision packages already identifies those activities or programs to be added or deleted if there are changes in expenditure levels. The list of ranked decision packages can also be used during the operating year to identify activities to be reduced or expanded if expenditure levels change suddenly or if actual costs vary from expectation.

Implementation of the procedure

Should zero-base budgeting be carried out for all activities every year? Arguments against yearly repetition point out that the benefits of evaluating all activities are usually completely realized in the first year, and that little benefit will result in subsequent years because the same packages will be proposed. Programs do not change enough to warrant yearly reviews. And even if they did, the budget process is not the only way programs are reviewed. Hence it can be argued that the extra effort required to practice zero base as opposed to incremental budgeting is not worth repeating yearly.

The originator of the Texas Instruments zero-base budgeting method argues that if an organization uses an annual budget, the following two criteria should be met before annual zero-base budgeting is discontinued. First, management must be satisfied that operations are effective and efficient; second, the work environment must be reasonably stable, with no major changes in work loads, problems, needs, and so on (Pyhrr, 1973, p. 138). If these conditions are met, zero-base budgeting need be carried out only every third or fourth year.

In the interim, decision packages from earlier years can be reviewed, with changes on an exception basis and with an allowance for built-in cost increases such as wages and salaries. Decision packages can be developed for new activities, and zero-base budgeting can be applied to departments with special problems or changes. Management can then establish priorities and funding levels after reviewing the prior year's packages and rankings (with appropriate modifications) and considering the newly developed packages. This procedure allows new programs to be funded by reductions in current activities, since it is possible to evaluate new packages against last year's expenditures and rankings. Thus management is continually reviewing all its resources and allocations, and not merely considering requested increases.

In sum, the proponents of zero-base budgeting believe it is a practical way to describe expenditures, integrate planning and budgeting, identify relevant trade-offs, redirect effort and funds from lower priority to higher priority programs, and improve the overall efficiency and effectiveness of an organization.

MANAGEMENT BY OBJECTIVES

The goals of management by objectives

Because of their inherent complexity, unstructured processes cannot be planned and controlled like structured processes, by prescriptions and ex post evaluations based on predetermined standards. Even though explicitly stated expectations are needed for planning, the specific methods used in meeting the organization's objectives are not so easily controlled. For example, a manager may cut costs simply by reducing service or output. And any professional can realize greater returns merely by providing lower quality, more superficial service. Control cannot be effected in these cases by after-the-fact comparisons against known standards, but must be achieved by motivating the manager. Control requires the commitment of the person who is responsible for performing the unstructured task.

A second concern in administering unstructured processes is to ensure goal congruence. Not only must actions be efficient and effective, they must also accomplish what the organization intends. Such aberrations as hiring overqualified or excessive staff beyond organizational requirements (empire-building) must be avoided. Thus, those engaged in unstructured tasks must not only be committed, but most also be committed to objectives which are consistent with those of the organization. Management by objectives is a technique whose purpose is to secure commitment and goal congruence.

How management by objectives works

Management by objectives (MBO) is a technique designed to increase motivation, reinforce achievement, and modify behavior so that the organization's strategic mission will be achieved more efficiently. It is an interpersonal process which encourages members of an organization, by working with each other, to identify appropriate individual objectives, coordinate their efforts toward achievement of those objectives, and then evaluate their progress.

Any organization accomplishes its strategic mission by breaking it down into several cycles, identifying key variables and plans for each of these cycles, involving the managers in planning and implementation, and setting a time horizon for each activity. Since an objective is an end state or condition to be achieved by some future point in time, MBO emphasizes the future and change. It emphasizes the key result areas of performance and the way the organization intends to accomplish those results. The purposes of management by objectives are to aid managers in deriving specific objectives from general overall objectives, to ensure that these objectives are communicated to all levels of the organization, and then to structure and link these objectives to each other in an integrated chain.

As discussed in Chapter 1, the decomposition and dissemination of objectives throughout an organization can be carried out through means-ends analysis, a method of factoring general performance requirements into specific targets. Means-ends analysis starts with a general objective, discovers the means of accomplishing it, then takes this means as a more specific objective and discovers a more detailed set of means for achieving it, and so on. The assumption of MBO is that this decomposition can be carried out accurately and efficiently by interpersonal communication.

In an MBO program, each subordinate initially develops his or her own set of objectives and then, in cooperation with his or her supervisor, is coached into a final set. Both develop ideas about appropriate objectives and then reach agreement together. From this set of mutually agreed upon objectives, they develop measures of performance to be used as a basis for evaluation. During interim periods, subordinates invite coaching and advice from the supervisor. After an appropriate interval performance is evaluated by the agreed upon measures. This person-to-person planning process allows a great deal of individual control and allows organizational objectives to be related to personal objectives.

Management by objectives provides all the benefits of subordinate participation. It produces the motivational benefits of individual goal setting as well as the positive effects of feedback. In addition, individuals clearly understand what they are to accomplish because well-defined task responsibility has been established. Hence, management by objectives is both a way of planning and also a means of encouraging interpersonal communication.

A number of prerequisites are required if management by objectives is to work. Each superior must understand what he or she is supposed to do, be willing to perform the coaching function, and have the patience and self-discipline to spend time on it. And the supervisor also has to have the proper skills to carry it out. Because of the skills it requires, the implementation of MBO may necessitate an extensive educational program, with a substantial investment of both time and money. MBO must stress coaching and not evaluation, and must be firmly supported by top management. If implemented correctly, MBO can effectively draw out information, improve planning, increase involvement, and stimulate the production of bottom-up ideas. However, experience has shown that three-to-five year time spans are needed for successful implementation, and the organization must be willing to absorb the costs and frustration and to manage the conflict of continually negotiating individual objectives.

Two conceptions of MBO

To understand the different conceptions that are held about the role of MBO in organizations it is helpful to consider its origins. MBO theory stems from two diverse sources. The earliest exposition of the concept was made by Peter Drucker (1954), who held that a manager should be responsible for results rather than for his or her patterns of action. Drucker was keenly aware of the problem of how to guide subordinate activities so that they will support organizational objectives, and also of the need to coordinate among departments. He believed that the philosophy of managing by results could be applied to every manager and every business, since it pertains to the specific needs of management and also to the motivational needs of all individuals (Drucker, 1954, p. 136).

Although Drucker's theory was among the earliest, perhaps the greatest impetus to MBO was McGregor's writing on performance evaluation participation, and individual involvement (McGregor, 1957). At that time employee evaluations were based on subjective assessments by superiors. Subordinates evaluated most favorably tended to be those who possessed the traits believed to characterize successful performers, or those who could simulate these traits, rather than those who actually performed effectively. Over time, dissatisfaction with this approach arose, not because of its subjectivity or inconsistency, but because it imposed a tremendous burden on a supervisor, who had to judge the worth of a subordinate and then confront him or her with this appraisal in a personal interview. It was found that critical appraisals produced defensiveness, which, in turn, only influenced achievement in a negative way. And so, although evaluation and appraisal were intended to produce better performance, the characteristics-evaluation and appraisal interview techniques sometimes achieved just the opposite.

McGregor saw that what was needed was a shift from a situation in which a superior appraised the personal characteristics of a subordinate (which was found to make the subordinate even more self-conscious of his shortcomings and therefore even less able to correct them) to a supportive analysis or coaching situation, in which a subordinate was motivated to examine himself critically and to define constructively his strengths and potentials as well as his weaknesses. McGregor argued that objective standards of performance and not personal characteristics should be the proper criterion, and that it was better to establish objectives and appraise performance in a constructive, participative manner. This appraisal was more easily accomplished and resulted in far greater overall motivation. In this way a subordinate was allowed to break away from dependence on his superior and to control his own destiny. He could now develop and be evaluated against a well-defined index of achievement, based on his own accomplishment and independent of the attitudes and biases of others.

These two theoretical bases have led to alternative definitions of MBO and its role in the organization.

MBO for individual goal setting and appraisal. One conception of MBO is as a method of setting and reviewing individual objectives. As defined by Odiorne (1968),

> Management by objectives is a process whereby the superior and subordinate managers of an organization jointly identify its common goals, define each individual's major areas of responsibility in terms of the results expected of him, and use these measures as guides for operating the unit and assessing the contribution of each of its members (pp. 55–56).

When concrete results can be agreed upon and assigned to individuals, their progress is more visible and their motivation to accomplish these results is improved.

Wikstrom (1968) breaks down MBO into three stages:

1. Individuals and their bosses at all levels determine, agree upon, and state very precisely those specific results that are to be accomplished by some designated future date, either by the individual or the units they manage.
2. The staff go to work to achieve their objectives, presumably fired up with enthusiasm because, in the process of developing their objectives, they have become sincerely committed to them.
3. At whatever times are designated for reviewing performance, the results achieved by units and by individual managers are measured against the objectives that have been set (p. 2).

According to this formulation, MBO is a means of personal goal setting and performance appraisal. Many writers regard this as the primary function of MBO. However, a closer analysis of successful goal setting quickly reveals that it is impossible to set goals for individual managers without regard to the wider context of the organization. Therefore, MBO has also been conceptualized in far broader terms.

MBO as a comprehensive approach to planning and control. Many managers prefer to think of MBO as a top-management planning and control approach rather than merely as an aid to personnel management. The Honeywell Company, which introduced MBO in 1961, clearly saw its link with planning and control.

> There are two things that might almost be considered fundamental creeds at Honeywell: decentralized management is needed to make Honeywell work and management by objectives is needed to make decentralization work (Wikstrom, 1968, p. 21).

The comprehensive interpretation of MBO is perhaps best exemplified by the system advanced by Humble (1970).

> MBO is a dynamic system which seeks to integrate the company's needs to clarify and achieve its profit and growth goals with the manager's need to contribute and develop himself. It is a demanding and rewarding style of managing a business (p. v).

To Humble, MBO is not merely a goal-setting procedure but a style of management which begins with a formulation of corporate objectives. Formulation of individual goals is preceeded by the formulation of corporate objectives, by strategic and tactical planning, and then by the development of programs. These are then translated into organizational unit goals which generate unit improvement plans and finally job improvement plans for individual managers.

The essence of this MBO planning and control procedure is an analysis of key results; and Humble's method incorporates the notion of key variables introduced in Chapters 2 and 3. In essence, the same method used to analyze the environment of a corporation and to identify its critical success factors is also used to specify the critical components of each job within the organization. Clarifying the key result areas and success factors of each and every job to the satisfaction of the superior and the subordinate ensures not only the conscious pursuit of relevant objectives, but also a consistent management focus throughout the organization.

As an integrated planning and control process, MBO involves the following steps (Humble, 1970, p. 4):

1. Reviewing critically and restating a company's strategic and tactical plans and its key strategic variables.
2. Clarifying the key result areas of each responsibility manager and making sure that the performance standards he must achieve are in line with unit and company objectives. This process should include his contribution and ensure his commitment to the achievement of these objectives. The results are unit improvement plans which are the responsibility of each unit manager.
3. Breaking down unit improvement plans into job improvement plans that are then assigned to individual managers. These job improvement plans should make a measurable and realistic contribution to the unit's and the company's plans for better performance.
4. Providing conditions that make it possible to achieve the key results and the job improvement plans, including (a) an organizational structure which gives a manager freedom and flexibility of operation, and (b) management information that is provided in a form and with a frequency that will encourage more effective self-control and better decisions.

5. Systematically reviewing performance, both to measure progress and to identify people with potential for advancement.

The essential distinction between these two conceptions of MBO is that the approach stressing motivation and performance at the individual level presumes the prior existence of adequate organizational objectives, structure, and channels of communication. The other approach includes these antecedents within the purview of MBO, treating MBO as a comprehensive planning and control system. It should be noted that Howell (1968) has observed the evolution of MBO from the former to the latter in some companies; that is, from a method of setting individual objectives to a system for integrated planning and control. He comments that it is a slow evolution, and eventually results in a new style of management. Now, some 20 years after Drucker's first proposal, some companies are managing by results.

SUMMARY

Unstructured tasks are those which cannot be analyzed and systematized economically because they are judgmental, novel, ambiguous, or uncertain. To determine the effectiveness and efficiency with which they are carried out is a difficult, if not impossible, task. Although there are a host of problems to be solved in the design and implementation of a system to plan and control these processes, three areas are especially important: effective allocation of resources, increasing motivation, and establishment of appropriate feedback. Each of these problems involves many trade-offs, and the system designer must find the optimal point at which the system should operate. Determining what methods and levels are best in any one situation is among his or her key tasks.

Zero-base budgeting is a procedure that has been proposed to overcome the limitation imposed by the use of incremental budgeting to allocate resources. When decision packages are formulated and ranked, managers have the opportunity to express a range of alternative potential expenditures, and can then decide which programs and levels of expense are most appropriate for the funds available. Budgeting from a starting base of zero allows an organization to review all expenditures, spot redundancies and duplications, and make explicit the priorities within and among departments. This procedure can help overcome the problem of slack, which appears to be common in most organizations.

Management by objectives is a technique designed to encourage motivation, reinforce achievement, and modify behavior so that the organization's mission will be achieved more efficiently. MBO is an interpersonal process by which members of an organization, working with each other, identify appropriate individual objectives, coordinate their efforts toward achievement of these objectives, and then evaluate their progress. MBO is regarded by some as an approach to individual goal setting and appraisal which avoids the personnel problems caused by character analysis and performance appraisal interviews. Others consider it to be a comprehensive planning and control technique which begins with the specification of overall organizational objectives and key variables, and eventually translates these goals into terms of individual performance. In either case, however, the benefits of MBO include better task clarification, a greater sense of self-esteem and personal control, and greater overall commitment and motivation.

QUESTIONS

1. How serious a problem do you think each of the following is in a typical organization?
   a. Excessive constraint.
   b. Inappropriate motivation.
   c. Inefficient resource allocation.
   How would you rank the three?
2. What is the relationship of zero-base budgeting to MBO? What role does each play in the three-cycle model of planning and control described in Chapters 2 and 3? Can both techniques be used simultaneously?
3. Does the zero-base budgeting system described in this chapter assume a realistic view of how decisions are made in organizations? What are its strengths and weaknesses?
4. Is MBO the same as bottom-up planning?
5. Can MBO be used to reduce slack and improve resource allocation?
6. How can zero-base budgeting be used to increase motivation?
7. Is zero-base budgeting a method of optimizing resource allocations? Can it be applied to both capital and operating budgets?
8. Is premature evaluation a problem with MBO and zero-base budgeting?
9. If a firm has a significant entrepreneurial orientation, does incremental budgeting help assure the retention of this orientation?
10. How can a firm transfer learning involving novel tasks?

REFERENCES AND BIBLIOGRAPHY

Argyris, C. Human problems with budgets. *Harvard Business Review*, January–February 1953, pp. 97–110.

Argyris, C. Management information systems. The challenge to rationality and emotionality. *Management Science*, 1971, pp. 275–92.

Bennet, R. W. Participation in planning. *Journal of General Management*, Autumn 1971, pp. 6–11.

Carroll, Stephen J., Jr., and Tosi, Henry L., Jr. *Management by Objectives: Applications and Research*. New York: Macmillan, 1973.

Cytert, R., and March, J. *A Behavioural Theory of the Firm.* Englewood Cliffs, N.J.: Prentice-Hall, 1963.

Dearden, John. Time span in management control. *Financial Executive,* August 1968, pp. 23–30.

Drucker, P. F. *The Practice of Management.* New York: Harper & Row, 1954.

Edwards, C. Why MBO and budgetary control are related systems. *Manage-Accounting,* (U.K.) September 1974, pp. 227–31.

French, Wendell L., and Hollman, Robert W. Management by objectives: The team approach. *California Management Review,* Spring 1975, pp. 13–22.

Hofstede, G. H. *The Game of Budget Control,* Assen, Netherlands: Van Goru, 1967.

Howell, R. A. A fresh look at management by objectives. *Business Horizons,* Fall 1968, pp. 51–58.

Hrebiniak, Lawrence G. Effective job level and participation on employee attitude and perceptions of influence. *Academy of Management Journal,* December 1974, pp. 649-62.

Humble, J. W. *Improving Business Results.* New York: McGraw Hill, 1967.

Humble, J. W. *Management by Objectives in Action.* New York: McGraw-Hill, 1970.

Jacques, E. *Time-span Handbook.* Heineman, 1966.

Latham, Gary P., and Yukl, Gary A. A review of research on the application of goal setting in organizations. *Academy of Management Journal,* December 1975, pp. 824–45.

Lawler, Edward E., III. The individualized organization: Problems and promise. *California Management Review,* Winter 1974, pp. 31–39.

Lewin, A., and Wolf, C. Organizational slack: A test of the general theory. Working paper 72–20. Graduate School of Business Administration, New York University, 1972.

Locke, E. Toward a theory of task motivation and incentives. *Organizational Behavior and Human Performance,* May 1968, pp. 157–187.

Lowe, A. G., and Shaw, R. W. An analysis of managerial biasing. *Journal of Management Studies,* October 1968, pp. 304–15.

Luke, Robert A., Jr. Matching the individual and the organization. *Harvard Business Review,* May–June 1975, pp. 17–41.

McGregor, D. An uneasy look at performance appraisal. *Harvard Business Review,* 1957, pp. 89–94.

Meyer, H. H.; Kay, E.; and French, J. R. P. Split roles in performance appraisal. *Harvard Business Review,* January–February 1965, pp. 123–29.

Morrisely, George L. Without control, MBO is a waste of time. *AMACOM: Management Review,* February 1975, pp. 11–17.

Murray, Thomas J. The tough job of zero budgeting. *Dun's,* October 1974, p. 70.

Odiorne, George S. *Management by Objectives: A System of Managerial Leadership.* New York: Pitman, 1968.

Odiorne, George S.   The politics of implementing MBO. *Business Horizons,* June 1974, pp. 13–21.

Pyhrr, Peter A.   *Zero-base budgeting.* New York: John Wiley and Sons, Inc., 1973.

Raia, A. P.   *Managing by Objectives.* Glenview, Ill.: Scott, Foresman, 1974.

Schiff, M., and Lewin, A. Y.   Where traditional budgeting fails. *Financial Executive,* May 1968, pp. 51–62.

Schiff, M., and Lewin, A. Y.   The impact of people on budgets. *The Accounting Review,* April 1970, pp. 259–268.

Swieringa, Robert J.   A behavioral approach to participating budgeting. *Management Accounting (U.S.),* February 1975, pp. 35–39.

Tosi, H. L., and Carroll, S. J.   Managerial reaction to management-by-objectives. *Academy of Management Journal,* December 1968, pp. 415–26.

Wikstrom, W. S.   Managing by- and with-objectives. *Personnel Policy Study No. 212.* New York: National Industrial Conference Board, 1968.

Williamson, O. E.   *The Economics of Discretionary Behavior.* Englewood Cliffs, N.J.: Prentice-Hall, 1964.

Winning, Ethan A. MBO: What's in it for the individual? *Personnel,* March–April 1974, pp. 51–56.

Case study 7–1

Ashdale Ltd.

"Develop and implement an MBO system. That's what my big boss said, didn't he? And if that's what he wants, that's what we'll give him."

The speaker was John Freely, senior corporate budget analyst of Ashdale Ltd., and the boss he referred to was none other than Garfield Garth, the financial vice president and corporate controller. His remark was addressed to Herbert Jameson, manager of personnel relations and training for the plastics division of Ashdale. Herb was on special assignment to corporate staff to work with John on this project, under the personal direction of Garfield Garth.

Personally directing a special project was not the usual practice of Mr. Garth. After all, Ashdale is a multidivisional manufacturer of chemicals, explosives, and plastics, and Garth's reputation was developed out of his ability to prepare the corporatewide financial plans and to control costs. But although Ashdale had grown continuously since World War II to its present size of $213 million annual sales, growth had recently slowed somewhat. Corporate concern was therefore shifting from growth to increasing profitability through productivity. The operating policy committee (OPC) felt that one means of achieving this objective was through better management, and better management was what Garfield Garth was after. But at minimum cost and as soon as possible, of course.

"I've been working at corporate office for five years now and I've spoken with GG perhaps three times," said John. "He's always been aloof and remote, and has dealt mainly with my boss. That's not unusual of course. Throughout head office all communications go through formal channels. Now he's probably read a *Harvard Business Review* article linking MBO to increased productivity and is gung-ho on it. It's strange what an executive will come up with when the OPC puts the heat on. But it's up to us to come up with a scheme to make him happy. So, let's get at it."

Herb began by explaining some of the motivational theory underlying MBO. "An MBO system attempts to guide appropriate behavior by making clear what an individual's responsibility is. It builds on the principles that most individuals have a desire to satisfy higher level or self-actualization needs on the job, that they prefer to take responsibility and are achievement oriented, and that if given the opportunity, they will exercise a high degree of self-control in the performance of their tasks. A successful MBO system thus places great emphasis on communication and participation because these enable an individual to satisfy his needs for involvement and to gain a feeling of self-control. And since involvement usually leads to commitment, MBO usually leads to commitment and to higher motivation."

John looked a little puzzled at this explanation. He said: "I thought the purpose of MBO is better personnel performance evaluation through the use of more objective evaluation criteria. I never understood how it could work though because the act of appraising a man on the record of his performance against MBO objectives suffers essentially from the same shortcomings as evaluating his performance based on financial criteria. Whether expressed in MBO or in financial terms, setting fair and consistent goals for a manager is difficult. Sub-unit interdependence still remains a problem no matter how painstakingly a manager's key results analysis is carried out. And the varying time-dependent effects of decisions are clearly not avoided by an MBO system. Therefore, I always believed that MBO really adds little over what effective use of our budget system can accomplish and hence I never saw the need for it. Now you are saying that it should be regarded merely as a motivating method. I hadn't thought about it in those terms."

Herb smiled and replied: "Because MBO was initially advanced as a performance appraisal tool by personnel researchers, my comments may seem strange to you; but, in essence, I agree with you. Using MBO for performance appraisal is a mistake. Its real strength lies in its ability to motivate and in its use as a planning tool. In fact, many firms advancing MBO as an intergrated planning and control approach seldom communicate the results of a review to the manager appraised. Typically, appraisal judgments are made by the supervisor and are only reviewed by him and his own boss because these judgments are the basis for potential promotion. Further, many firms do not even regard performance against these objectives as being a basis for assessment. In reviewing job potential, many factors not linked directly with performance must be considered. And in the final analysis, job potential is really still a mystery. It is obvious that these organizations regard the strength of MBO to be its motivating effect and its ability to integrate an individual with an organization. Perhaps they even believe that if appraisal were attached to an MBO system, an impression of pressure would be created and it would lose some of its motivational benefits."

John nodded his head in agreement. "You will have no disagreement with me at that point. I thoroughly believe that the principal role of any objective should be directional. But we still have to devise an approach to establishing objectives. Based on my experience with our corporate planning system, here are my thoughts on this matter.

"To me, setting objectives is a three-step process. The first step involves identifying areas or activities that are critical to the success of the corporation. These are referred to as key result areas. Once these have been defined, the second step is to specify performance measurements for each area. For example, our production output is measured in terms of quality, quantity, and time, and resource utilization is measured by standard costing and return on investment. And the third step is to set the level of the objectives or goals which then serve as the standards against which corporate performance can be measured. That, in a nutshell, is our corporate financial planning and control approach to setting objectives."

"Your approach to setting objectives is a sound beginning," Herb said. "However, it doesn't go far enough. It is of utmost important to recognize that although objectives may provide a target to shoot for, in themselves they do not guarantee success. Plans for their achievement are also required; and it is these plans that give an organization its sense of direction and unity. Programming is the term commonly used to describe the process of laying out the steps for achieving an objective. A program indicates the steps required to achieve an objective, who is responsible for each step, and the time interval for its completion. A manager's first task in programming is to divide his actions into steps so that he can focus on each phase of his activity. He then defines the purpose of each step, states what is required to perform it, and sets forth the results expected. It is really by means of programming that a manager develops the action plans needed to achieve his objectives."

Herb continued: "As you well know, the three divisions of this company differ significantly in several respects. Marketing and sales are the strong suit of my division, plastics. We have a pronounced 'people emphasis.' My management has fought long and hard for money to invest in staff development and training and we already have a comprehensive nonfinancial evaluation system to assess performance and plan career paths. The explosives division depends on research and development for its competitive advantage and prides itself on being one of the most innovative in the industry. I have my doubts about its innovative ability, however. Regardless, it is the loosest run of the three divisions. The chemicals division is the most mature of the three and operates in a highly cyclical industry. It relies on efficient production methods to differentiate it from competition. They operate in a highly formalized manner and emphasize short-term cost control. As you're well aware, Garfield Garth comes from this division and still thinks the whole company can be run this way. Our problem is that any solution to our assignment must fit these three divisions.

"When I was notified of this assignment I sat down and wrote up what I believe to be a sound MBO system for this organization. [See appendix.] My idea is to send a guide to this system to each and every manager in the company under a covering memo by GG. Why don't you take a copy back to your office and study it. When you finish reviewing it we can meet again and discuss the matter further."

After Herb finished speaking the meeting broke up.

Question

If you were John, how would you respond?

APPENDIX

ASHDALE LIMITED

Memorandum

TO: All Managers
FROM: G. Garth

RE: Managing by Objectives

Improving productivity is a priority concern of the Operating Policy Committee. Attached is a guide to managing by objectives which could benefit each and every manager in our organization. I recommend that you begin to use it at your earliest convenience.

GUIDE TO MANAGING BY OBJECTIVES

At every level of an organization there is a natural conflict between the normal everyday problems and activities which must be handled by an individual or a work unit and the longer range thinking and planning for accomplishing change and improvement. Managing by objectives is one means of making managers stop and think and develop a strategy in writing so that the overall objectives of the organization are achieved.

Objectives are written strategies or programs for changing or improving upon the status quo. They are statements of goals and courses of action designed to keep a manager planning and thinking beyond everyday activities and problems. They may deal with any of the following: (1) highly innovative ideas which have promise of major returns and/or which add new dimensions to the business; (2) solutions to current or future problems; (3) schemes for increasing the efficiency of existing systems or procedures supporting a particular job, program, or work unit; (4) changing priorities of tasks or work units; and (5) improving the expected results for ongoing activities by appropriate revisions to work methods.

Setting objectives requires examining three questions: (1) Where are we? (2) Where do we want to go? (3) How can we get there? Thus, step 1 of formulating objectives involves analyzing what the current situation is; step 2 is the specification of the goals of the planning; and step 3 involves fleshing out the actions necessary to reach these objectives.

The following are the types of questions which may help a manager determine and specify his objectives: What am I (or what is my unit) now doing?; why am I (or we) doing it?; is there a better way of doing it?; what needs to be done that is not presently being done?; is there something I'm doing (or my unit is doing) that we could stop doing tomorrow because it no longer serves a useful purpose?; what job responsibilities do I give most attention to, and what job responsibilities do I tend to squeeze in and around the rest of my available time?; what procedures or work patterns haven't I examined in the past two years?

The steps involved in formulating effective goals and the type of questions a manager should ask himself are structured in the following three-step guide.

STEP 1

Review your responsibilities. Review your job responsibilities and the mission of the unit(s) you manage. There are four aspects to every manager's position, regardless of its level and the types of units managed. Think about what's expected from you in the following four areas of responsibility:

Organizational. Responsibility for (1) the organizational design of your unit including the number and types of jobs it in, reporting relationships, delegated authorities for decision making, spans of control, reporting and control systems, and so on; (2) effective collaboration with other organizational units whose work relates; (3) ensuring your unit works toward the goals of the larger company unit of which it is a part and in accordance with company policies, practices, etc.

Technical. Responsibility for getting the particular work of the unit you are managing—whether it be sales, research, manufacturing, engineering, or some combination (whatever your organizational unit is charged with doing)—done and done well. Accountable for directing, planning, setting standards for and controlling the actual work and work results.

Financial. Responsibility for the fiscal and monetary aspects of your unit and its contribution to profits (directly, in line unit and, indirectly, in staff units). Accountable for budgeting, approval of expenses, control of inventories, overtime and other activities that affect expenditure, conservation or use of funds.

Personnel. Responsibility for manning your organization structure with qualified personnel; hiring, firing, disciplining, communicating, motivating; recommending transfers, promotions, salary increases; maintaining morale; utilizing the time and talents of subordinates; and developing ready replacements for all key jobs in your unit.

STEP 2

Look for problems and opportunities. After you have thought about what's expected in the four areas identified under step 1, ask yourself how close you are to getting ideal results. What problems or obstacles are holding you back? What potentials could be investigated or maximized? Should you, for example:

Organizational

1. Change the basic design of your organization structure.
2. Add, abandon, or change any organizational functions or activities.
3. Examine the levels at which decisions are authorized.
4. Improve systems and reports used for management information and control purposes.
5. Establish methods to improve downward flow of information on organizational matters.
6. Work on obstacles for more effective collaboration between your unit and other units.
7. Foresee future conditions which your organization must prepare itself to handle.
8. Act upon any organizational problems which are impeding the ideal functioning of your unit.

Technical

1. Set higher standards of work output; e.g., sales quotas, manufacturing throughputs.
2. Introduce efficiencies of work flow patterns and/or systems and procedures.
3. Reduce frequencies of negative incidents; e.g., customer complaints, lost-time accidents.
4. Change priorities, redirect work and time of subordinates.
5. Identify new trends (in your field, the economy, etc.) which suggest change in the work your unit is doing or how it is being done.
6. Identify the ten most important things your unit can accomplish next year.

Financial

1. Review the major cost components of your budget and your control systems for them.
2. Make special analyses of experience under such systems to determine how well they are actually working.
3. Analyze the biggest time and cost wasters in your organization.
4. Identify your biggest difficulties in budget formulation last year.
5. Investigate what changes and innovations in systems, procedures, work standards, etc., should be pursued for increased efficiency.

Personnel

1. Plan methods for improving ready replacements for key positions including your own.
2. Establish better ways of appraising the performance and potential of individuals in your organization.
3. Establish new approaches for developing subordinates, improving morale, improving track records on promotions, transfers, turnover, etc.
4. Identify the biggest "people problems" facing your organization today and what must be done to put your organization in a better position tomorrow.

STEP 3

Establish objectives. Having identified in step 2 certain problems and opportunities, you are now ready to act upon them. Each objective has two parts: a goal to be reached and plans or strategy for reaching it. Following is a guide for going about drafting objectives:

A. State a target or goal committing you to specific results. Suppose, for example, after steps 1 and 2 you conclude your organization is not developing enough internal candidates for managerial positions. In other words, you identified a problem. Now you must translate this into a goal which will commit you to doing something to solve it, e.g.:

> Goal. Establish at least three new mechanisms for improving my organization's ability to develop more internal candidates for promotion into managerial positions.

Or suppose, after steps 1 and 2, you're not sure you have a problem but your basic organization structure hasn't changed for years and you think looking into the matter may reveal possible changes or improvements. You can commit yourself as follows:

> Goal. Study my present organization structure, and possible alternatives, and prepare a final report either justifying the status quo or recommending changes.

Always include a quantitative measurement or a definite end result like the "three mechanisms" or "final report." Without these things you're committed to produce you will have vague statements of intent with no measuring device built in to tell you at year-end whether you made the target or not.

Don't hesitate to tackle long-range or big problems which can't be resolved in one year by one goal. For example, an organization's labor force development problems are unlikely to be solved by a goal like the first above. But establishing three new development mechanisms is a good start. New or carry-over goals can be set for subsequent years. Similarly, in the second sample, one might study one's organization one year and implement necessary changes the next.

B. Next, develop your strategy for reaching the results called for by your goals. Most goals have alternative ways of reaching them and involve solving subproblems. List the specific things you're going to do to reach your goals. Add target dates.

For example, to reach the first sample goal, this might be the strategy:

1. Establish a method for identifying high performers annually.

    3/75

2. Require annual reports from their supervisors on special steps being taken to develop their capabilities further.   4/75

3. Create a new job as assistant to a key manager to which high performers can continuously be rotated for temporary assignments.

    5/75

4. Establish one task force a year on some business problem where high performers, participating with seasoned managers, will have a managerial problem-solving experience.   12/75

EXAMPLES

Examples of objectives in final form for each of the four key areas of managerial responsibility. A well-rounded set of objectives for a manager will include some for each area.

Organizational

Goal. Study my present organization structure, and possible alternatives, and prepare a final report either justifying the status quo or recommending changes

1. List the major responsibilities of each key manager (or unit) and decide whether any should be shifted, enlarged, curtailed, etc.

    2/75

2. List authorities for major types of decisions and decide whether any should be delegated to lower organizational levels.   3/75

3. Conduct a literature survey and consult with appropriate outside sources for ideas on alternative ways of structuring my organization.

    6/75

4. Prepare final written report on conclusions reached.   7/75

Technical

Goal. Institute a program at Plant X which will reduce production quality rejects by 20%

1. Request quality control specialists to identify the greatest quality problem areas and their recommended solutions.   2/75

2. Review and implement at least two recommendations this year.

    12/75

3. Draft plans for implementing other recommendations for the next year.   12/75

4. Increase quality awareness in hourly personnel by:

    a. Having plant manager and quality control specialists hold meetings with them on the economics and technical aspects of quality control.   4/75

    b. Instituting a plant program where different production units will compete on the basis of their quality records for some prize or privilege.   6/75

Financial

Goal. Have at least three cost-reduction programs in effect which by year-end will produce 10 percent savings in the subject area to which they are addressed

1. Require each unit head reporting to me to set at least one cost-reduction goal which can be implemented within his unit during the year.   1/75
2. Analyze cost-savings possibilities which will cut across all units and implement at least two of these broader cost-reduction programs.   12/75
3. Require quarterly reports from appropriate subordinates.

                                                    3, 6, 9, 12/75

Personnel

Goal. Establish at least three new mechanisms for improving my organization's ability to develop more internal candidates for promotion into managerial positions

1. Establish a method for identifying high performers annually.

                                                    3/75

2. Require annual reports from their supervisors on special steps being taken to develop their capabilities further.   4/75
3. Create a new job as assistant to a key manager to which high performers can continuously be rotated for temporary training assignments.   5/75
4. Establish one task force a year on some business problem where high performers, participating with seasoned managers, will have a managerial problem-solving experience.   12/75

Case study 7–2

Hy-Tek Computer Corporation

Jim Johnson (MBA, University of Iowa) was full of both pride and apprehension as he drove home from the sales meeting that Friday night. For the past three years since leaving business school, Jim had been a salesman for Hy-Tek, a manufacturer of fully integrated minicomputer-based business systems. Hy-Tek was a young, rapidly growing company and on joining them Jim had found an opportunity to demonstrate his ability and dedication. Now, after such a short time, he was being promoted to branch manager with a staff of two systems analysts and eight salesmen. As he drove along the highway, he recalled the immense flush of pride that welled in him as he was announced as the new manager of the north central branch. But he was also somewhat apprehensive. In three weeks he had to face his staff of eight salesmen at the annual branch planning and objective-setting meeting and he had to decide how to handle it.

Sam Bolter, the retiring north central manager and Jim's previous boss had a very simple way of setting objectives for his salesmen, a way Jim called, the "read and weep" method. Sam himself decided the objectives for each of his salesmen. And, in the three years Jim had worked for him, Sam never once chose to discuss or to disclose how he reached these objectives. The month before the annual budget period began, each man simply received a letter from Sam indicating what his expected performance for the year was to be. From Jim's own experience and from talking to his fellow salesmen he knew that the reactions to receiving objectives in this way and to the expectations themselves were always mixed. Some salesmen were happy with receiving their objectives this way, others were very unhappy, and some were indifferent. In general, Jim concluded that no overall trend could be established.

Jim had taken the opportunity of the national sales meeting to inquire about the objective-setting methods used by some of the other branch managers. Harley Tyson was known as the "Vince Lombardi" of Hy-Tek Corporation. He and his 11 salesmen were easily recognizable for all were dressed similarly; gray suit; shiny patent leather shoes, blue shirt, and muted red tie. That was the uniform of his group. Harley's branch consistently outsold every other branch to the point now where most branch managers felt that it was impossible to compete with him.

His method was simple and direct. Before a salesman could work for Harley, he had to give him a written statement committing himself to following Harley's instruction in complete detail. Harley demanded and always obtained total commitment from his salesmen. The commitment included following Harley's directions as to what to wear, how to approach a client, and how to conduct a sale. But Harley backed this demand for dedication with proven results. Furthermore, Harley gave each saleman a personal training program and set of rules to follow. These rules included for example, a promise by the salesmen not to come home before 7:00 every evening and to follow to the letter the sales pattern Harley established for him. Harley's salesmen swore by him, for they were the highest paid in the corporation.

Several salesmen had left Harley to go to work for other corporations. They had tried to introduce Harley's procedure for disciplining, training, and implementing a sales program. But, surprisingly, none had been able to succeed either in receiving the respect Harley did or achieving his results. Jim wondered whether or not he would be capable of doing so.

Walter Weger, the south central branch manager was the psychologist of the branch managers. He also had his own pet program for training, motivating, and setting objectives for his salesmen. Walter began by requiring each of his salesmen to read the book *Psychocybernetics* by Maltz. He felt that by doing so, each salesman would come to know himself better, to appreciate what he was capable of doing, and have higher self-esteem. Once he had sensitized his salesmen to their own inner capabilities, Walter followed it up with managerial and sales training so that his salesmen knew how they should act. Then finally, Walter sat down with each individual and, over a lengthy period, established individual objectives for each and every one of them. His procedure was to allow the salesmen to set their own objectives to begin with and then, after a period of negotiation and coaching by Walter, to eventually end up with a set of objectives that was satisfactory to both the salesmen and to Walter. Of course, it was no reflection on this method, but Jim knew that Walter was having trouble equaling the sales performance of the other branches.

Another branch was under the direction of Herbert Thompson. Herb had been only too happy to share with Jim his method of setting objectives for he felt that his was the only way to do it. As Herb told it, he assembles his seven salesmen for their objectives setting meeting at nine o'clock Monday morning. Precisely at nine o'clock he walks into the room and details on a flip chart his sales quotas as dictated to him by senior management. Turning to his salesmen, he tells them that they have the task of filling these quotas. He then leaves the room and allows the seven salesmen to divide up the quotas and to apportion them as they see fit. He returns at 5:00 P.M. to receive from each salesman his agreement on what portion of the quota he will achieve so that the total quota is achieved. Herb told Jim he had been using this system for five years and believes it is the most satisfactory way of setting objectives for salesmen.

Jim's problem was further complicated by the fact that his eight salesmen were a diverse lot. Ed Peters had graduated from Iowa with Jim and was a close friend of his. Four of the salesmen were slightly older and had been with Hy-Tek one or two years longer than Ed and Jim. Bill Barnes and Sig Pringle were the old-timers of the group. Each had been involved in data processing sales for over 25 years and had been with Hy-Tek since its founding nine years ago. The eighth member of the group was Paul Fogel, who had dropped out of M.I.T. after successfully completing his first year of computer science because he was bored. Paul had just completed his six-month sales training program and had been with the branch two months.

Now Jim is to enter the ranks of management and he has to adopt a style of setting objectives for his salesmen. Which should it be? The "read and weep" method, the psychological approach, the "Vince Lombardi" approach, or one of trying to achieve results and harmony through participation? Jim remembered from his university courses talk about aspiration levels and needs for achievement. He remembered somehow they were related to motivation and to the setting of objectives. He recalled vaguely that it was recommended to always set difficult objectives because individuals would then try harder. Or was it only for some individuals? Perhaps this weekend he would go down to the basement and dig through his old notes to try to find out just what was the business school approach to setting objectives for motivation. In any case, he had to decide quickly, because soon he had to face *his* salesmen.

Questions

1. What is the role of the meeting in Jim's planning and control system?
2. If you were Jim Johnson, how would you handle this meeting?

Case study 7–3

Fliggleman, Feldman, Ginsberg and Grant (B)[*]

"I don't care what old man Feldman wants us to do," said Joel Cohen. "I didn't bust my rear getting my CPA at night to now go back to being treated like an hourly worker."

The cause of this outburst was John H. R. Feldman's directive that all time spent on the job in the Detroit office be accounted for on a quarter hour basis, using daily time sheets. This request was a radical departure from the gross estimate of chargeable time senior accountants were accustomed to submitting. It was also rumored that this was only the first of a number of measures to be implemented to improve the competitive position of FFGG. Although Joel Cohen was perhaps the most vociferous of those affected, he certainly was not alone in his concern. In fact, concern of one sort or another about where the firm was headed in the future was spread throughout the hierarchy. And there was considerable speculation as to what management would do next to improve productivity.

Questions

1. Why do you think this procedure was instituted?
2. What are the strengths and weaknesses of requiring time to be recorded on a quarter hour basis?
3. If you were the managing partner of an accounting firm, would you choose to use this technique as part of your planning and control procedures?
4. How would you tackle the problem of productivity in this type of business?

---

[*] Note: This case study builds on the material presented in the A case (3–1). The A case should therefore be read before the B case is discussed.

Chapter outline

8

Profit centers

When you have completed this chapter you should understand:

1. The strengths and weaknesses of profit as a measure of performance.
2. The advantages and disadvantages of profit centers, and the conditions under which they can be implemented successfully.
3. The nature of interdependent profit centers, the function of transfer prices, and what kinds of transfer prices are most appropriate for different situations.
4. How profit centers can be effectively managed.

THE ROLE OF MONETARY MEASUREMENTS IN PLANNING AND CONTROL

Limitations of formal measurements

The selection of appropriate formal quantitative measurements is a fundamental component of most planning and control system designs. Deciding on a single criterion, multiple criteria, or a composite measure is a key concern of the system designer. It is also a difficult task because of the inherent limitations of these measurements. A single criterion measurement, such as cost or profit, may be too narrow to encompass all the objectives and activities of any complex operation. Unless a task is completely structured it will have many conflicting facets, some of which are undesirable to ultimate performance. The alternatives and trade-offs cannot be fully expressed by a single overall measurement of performance. The use of a single measurement also tends to focus interest on that factor alone, to the exclusion of other relevant key variables. And this is especially true if the other variables are not quantified. We may recall Likert's contention that the tendency of managers to focus only on monetary measurements necessitated the development of human resource accounting systems (see Chapter 6).

The use of multiple performance criteria allows qualitative or immeasurable key variables to be considered, such as social concerns, but also imposes the difficult task of selecting and weighting them appropriately. Because multiple criteria are a mixture of qualitative and quantitative measurements, it may be difficult to agree on a set of values which describes sound overall performance. The derivation of a single overall composite measurement of performance from multiple measurements requires the explicit specification of acceptable trade-offs. But because the optimal balance among objectives will change with changing conditions, the validity of the specified trade-offs, and hence of any composite measurement, depends entirely on the situation in which it is to be used. Single criterion, multiple criteria, and composite measures all have relative weaknesses, and the choice among them is situational.

All formal measurements may have further undesirable consequences when used for evaluation. Performance evaluation tends to cause the individual being evaluated to attempt to maximize short-term results, irrespective of the consequences to the organization as a whole. Any performance measurement, therefore, carries with it a number of potentially dysfunctional consequences. There may be a tendency to sacrifice long-run considerations; e.g., minimizing maintenance expense by neglecting to make repairs on capital equipment. Or, innovation may be neglected for the sake of easier tasks that can be performed efficiently.

Another undesirable behavior is the minimization of risk, so that the only tasks undertaken are those that are well understood and whose outcomes can be predicted reliably. And resentment of performance evaluation may lead people to spend time manipulating performance measurements rather than going about the business at hand. A sales manager, for example, may artificially record a sale before or after the end of an accounting period in order to change reported profit. Any evaluation of performance may cause people to feel they must make excuses or attempt to shift responsibility to others.

Dysfunctional consequences such as these arise even in the most unlikely places; for instance, in the evaluation of copywriters in an advertising agency. Many advertisers evaluate the effectiveness of their copy by the number of people who remember its content the day after they read it. Over time, copywriters have developed a number of techniques to influence day-after recall, even though many of these techniques are inappropriate for certain types and styles of advertising. Needless to say, however, when copywriters are evaluated in terms of day-after recall, their ads are usually filled with the techniques that maximize their performance evaluation.

Choosing financial performance measurements

In spite of the difficulty in specifying meaningful performance measurements, and the dangers of using them for evaluation, formal measurements play a dominant role in all planning and control systems. Monetary measurements are the most important of these. Measurements of costs are critical to financing, investment, and operating decisions. Measures expressed in accrual accounting terms may be used for internal evaluation, by means of financial statements, and for external evaluation, through annual reports. Therefore the role of money-based performance measurements, especially those relating to profits, must be considered in the design of any planning and control system.

The value of any measurement depends on the function it serves, of course. Three functions that financial measurements can serve are scorekeeping, attention getting, and problem solving. The scorekeeping function of accounting measurements is simply to tell managers how well they are doing against expectation. In their attention-getting role, accounting measurements identify deviations from expectation and draw a manager's attention to specific problem areas. This attention-getting function is the mechanism for the practice of management by exception. And having informed the managers of how well they are doing or where problems exist, a third function of these measurements is to help solve problems and overcome the barriers to better performance.

Some other ways that financial measurements can help managers perform successfully should also be considered. Accounting measurements can help a manager plan, motivate, make decisions, control, and evaluate performance. From this perspective, their relative value in a planning and control system depends on their contribution to the effective performance of these managerial functions.

Since system design is situationally determined, choice of the financial measurements to be used in any situation depends on their suitability to the objectives sought. The degree of financial decentralization is perhaps the key determinant of this choice. A responsibility unit can be planned and controlled as a cost, profit, or investment center, depending on the scope of decision making authority delegated to the unit. This range of authority is the most important factor in the choice of a monetary performance measurement. Cost, profit, and investment centers usually coincide with the allocation of authority for decisions over costs, costs and revenues, and costs, revenues, and investments, respectively. It is generally believed that the greater a manager's range of discretion, the greater are his or her perceived feelings of control, and hence the greater the motivation and involvement; yet greater, too, is the risk of inappropriate behavior. So the choice of a performance measurement and form of financial planning and control center is still a situationally determined issue, requiring the evaluation of a number of trade-offs.

The remainder of this chapter focuses on profit measures and the situational requirements for the use of profit centers. However, because the appropriate measurement of profit is a prerequisite to the use of profit as well as investment centers, most of the discussion in the chapter (especially in the sections on "Situational Requirements" and "Transfer Pricing") apply equally to both.

The distinguishing attributes of investment centers—measuring the investment base and investment-based measures of performance are considered in Chapter 9.

THE PROFIT MEASURE

Profit is a measure of financial performance which expresses the increment to wealth accumulated over some period of time. According to Hicks, it is the amount the individual can dispose of or consume and still be as well off at the end of a period as he or she was at the beginning. In this sense, profit is a measure of achievement or accomplishment, and is commonly used as a means of evaluating performance.

The traditional accounting approach measures profit in accrual terms; that is, in terms of an assumed value flow which is independent of cash or any other tangible consideration. In accrual accounting, measurement is based on acquisition (historical) costs which are traced through the accounts and matched against revenue at the time of revenue recognition (the realization point). Profit is the residual of the matching of revenue and expense (i.e., the difference between accomplishment and effort), and what is left over is considered to be the net increment from the process.

Strengths of the profit measure

In spite of criticisms, the profit measure has withstood the test of time and is still the most widely used performance measurement today. This suggests that it does have certain fundamental strengths. Profit summarizes a number of heterogeneous activities as a single homogeneous measure, money. Profit figures lend themselves to quantitative analysis, since benefits, costs, and decision criteria can all be related to the same basic measurement. Distilling complex business activities down to one common denominator facilitates communication. The profit measure allows managers to focus on a single criterion which they understand and which can be related to stakeholder expectations and evaluations. Finally, because profit is a widely used measure of performance, and because diversities in size are easily accounted for by the computation of ratios, it can be used to compare the whole range of profit-making activities.

Weaknesses of the profit measure

Accounting weaknesses. The profit measure is not without substantial drawbacks. Among the foremost of these are accounting imperfections. Profit is only an approximate surrogate for Hicks' notion of a disposable increment to wealth. It is usually based on historical costs, which are not measure of actual economic value. And because of the longevity of assets, profit is measured in a mixture of dollars of differing purchasing powers and is not in fact expressed in one homogeneous unit. Since accrual accounting involves a number of arbitrary allocations (e.g., joint or common costs, and depreciation) it is sensitive to the choice of allocation methods. Similarly, current accounting practice allows such a variety of rules that different corporations performing the same activities can report differing profits, according to their choice of accounting principles. And finally, the measurement of profit is still directed primarily toward satisfying external reporting requirements, and its use for internal purposes suffers because of this.

Multiple objectives. Even if a system were designed to correct for all of the above defects, its profit measure would still have some inherent weaknesses. The many stakeholders involved in any organization have different objectives, varying from stability to profitability, survival to risktaking, and so on. Similarly, any organization may have numerous key strategic variables, not all amenable to quantification. The organization must reflect many noneconomic considerations, such as social costs (air and noise pollution, for instance), governmental pressures, and employee morale and loyalty; these may not lend themselves to financial measurement. They impose a host of trade-offs; even, in some cases, the sacrifice of profit for the sake of other objectives. Thus it is, in fact, impossible to condense the wide diversity of organizational objectives and variables into a single homogenous dimension, and to think that this can be done is a deceptive illusion.

Time horizon. Not only is profit one dimensional, but it is usually based on only a single year's activity. Any firm's minimal objective is survival in the long run; and what's good for the short run may involve severe long-run sacrifices. A supervisor may pressure workers for short-term improvements in profitability to the extent that they leave the firm, thus destroying a key long-term asset. Or decision makers may be motivated to maximize short-run criteria at the expense of the long run. The profit figure does not reflect these long-run considerations.

No measure of opportunity loss. Profit measures what has taken place, but does not measure the effects of having rejected alternative courses of action. An essential consideration of any evaluation is not only what was done, but also what could have been done. Profit, then, is not necessarily a meaningful measure for evaluation.

Quantifiable inputs and outputs. A final limitation to the profit measure is that it requires meaningful financially based measures of inputs and outputs. Only if transactions take place at arm's length in free markets will the quantification given them be an objective representation of their actual value. Unfortunately, however, many responsibility units within an organization, such as staff groups or production or personnel functions, do not take part in such transactions. Therefore, even if the profit measure is used for these situations it can only be applied under artificial conditions.

The role of profit in planning and evaluation

Planning. Given these strengths and weaknesses of the profit measure, is profit a meaningful expression of expectation for the purposes of planning, decision making, and control? If each responsibility unit operates independently of the rest of the organization, then profit measurements do ensure goal congruence. If each organizational unit maximizes its profits, there is a benefit to the organization as a whole, since total profits are also maximized. In this situation, profit is a consistent measure of benefit to the total organization. A profit measure of expectation is also assumed to be motivational because it generates in managers the feelings of self-esteem that go along with being in business for oneself. It may also encourage a manager to search for profitable activities.

When profits are used as the means of expressing expectations, profit budgets are usually used in planning. A profit budget is simply a model of the firm in terms of financial statements that describe the organization's plans. Like all budgets, a profit budget is useful in several respects. It is a means of quantitatively expressing and reviewing expectations while simultaneously showing the interrelationship among a number of activities. It is a way of comparing expenditures to the revenues they will generate, and so implies a benefit-cost analysis. Profit budgeting can also ensure coordination because it communicates expectations and changes in expectations throughout an organization. Preparing a profit budget is a means of securing participation by low-level managers. It is also used as a basis for detecting deviations from expectation.

Given the extensive use of profit budgets in industry, it comes as no surprise that as a target for motivation, a means of ensuring goal congruence, and a technique to facilitate planning profit budgeting appears to be most appropriate. Profit thus appears to provide an extremely useful measurement for planning.

Evaluation. Profit is as widely used for measuring performance as it is for expressing expectations. Profit can be recommended as a performance measurement when the following two questions can be answered in the positive: (1) Can a fair and accepted profit expectation be established? (2) Does profit adequately describe and measure good performance?

To serve as a basis for evaluation, any performance measure must both be fully controllable by the person being evaluated, and also fit a suitable time span for the task. Profit is a composite performance measure that is a function of all the elements of a business. Not all of the components that enter into the computation of profit are controllable, and many are very uncertain. In any competitive situation many factors are beyond the control of a manager. Since all these diverse and uncontrollable factors are combined into one additive measure, the measurement is very sensitive to changes in any one of a number of areas. Therefore, it is arguable whether a fair and mutually acceptable basis for performance evaluation can be established.

The effects of any performance evaluation criterion on decision making must also be considered. Good performance requires making many decisions to cover varying time spans, and these spans overlap with each other. These decisions do not fit neatly into one specific evaluation period. Hence, any single criterion used to guide decision making must consider the whole life cycle of each program or project, and not merely its effect during one evaluation period. Because profit emphasizes the short term, it may tend to bias the selection of decision alternatives toward the short run at the expense of the long. Achieving high profits is not necessarily synonymous with maximizing the long-run welfare of the organization; and so as a basis for performance evaluation, profit appears to be of limited use. Some ways of utilizing the strengths and compensating for the weaknesses of the profit measure are discussed later in this chapter. First, however, the role of the profit center in the organization must be considered in greater detail.

PROFIT CENTERS

Situational requirements for successful implementation

When profit is used to express expectations for a responsibility unit and for evaluating its performance, that responsibility unit is known as a profit center. A profit center is a responsibility unit whose manager has responsibility for attaining a certain level of profit. Even the earliest literature on profit centers recognized that if he or she is to be evaluated on the basis of profit performance, the profit center manager must have sufficient authority to make whatever decisions are necessary to ensure an adequate profit. Joel Dean details three situational characteristics of profit centers as follows (Dean, 1955, p. 67):

1. Operational independence—each profit center manager must have the authority to make most if not all of the key operating decisions

that affect his profits, subject only to broad policy directions from the top. The areas where independence cannot exist should properly be considered to be service centers.

2. Access to sources and markets—the profit center manager must have control over all source and market decisions and be free to buy and sell in alternative markets both outside and inside the company. This freedom to trade dissolves alibis and helps establish responsibility.

3. Quantifiable costs and revenues—a profit center must be able to identify its true costs and establish a reasonable price for its product. Otherwise, measurement by profit is questionable.

The characteristics necessary for effective operation of a profit center indicate that before a responsibility unit can be considered to be a profit center, its manager must have the power to generate revenues and control sources of supply and other costs.

Identifying a responsibility unit whose revenues and costs can both be controlled by the manager is not sufficient to conclude that the unit can be planned and controlled as a profit center. At least three additional conditions must also be present.

1. Top management must be committed to decentralization. A profit center system must have the wholehearted commitment of top management. They must be willing to relinquish some of their intimate knowledge of day-to-day operations and also some of their authority to subordinates. Top management must allow the profit center manager to make the key operating decisions. Although it may be difficult to stay out of these decisions, especially in a company with only one major business, they must do so if the system is to work effectively.

2. Adequate staff and information systems. The cost of implementing a profit center system may be quite high. Most likely a new management information system will be necessary in order to provide top management with the data it needs to control decentralized operations. Further, each profit center manager will now need information to make decisions, information that was probably not available before. Accounting reports will now be the primary source of information about a unit's performance, so top management must be willing to incur the expense of providing these reports and must also know how to use them. They must also be willing to rely on their finance staff for information and for evaluation of divisions and managerial performance.

3. Capable profit center managers. A company using a profit center system must have managers capable of heading them. Often a company which has been centralized under a strong top management will not have the kind of general managers needed for this new organizational style. The implemention of profit centers requires a great deal of education to train managers up and down the line to understand and think in terms of profits. They must be made to understand that their perfor-

mance is now being measured by their contribution to company profits and that they must now make decisions based on profit contribution. Each profit center manager must be made aware of the key variables of the organization as a whole, the manager's strategic variables, and the relationship between these, so that he or she will not make decisions to maximize his or her own welfare at the expense of the organization as a whole.

The benefits of profit centers

Treating responsibility units as profit centers is one way to realize the benefits of decentralization. Recall from Chapter 4 that decentralization is an integral part of many organizational strategies. Successful decentralization brings with it the following benefits:

A way of managing large entities. In large organizations it is difficult for one manager or a small group of managers to understand every aspect of the business. Sheer size prohibits management by face-to-face contact and informal or interpersonal methods. Large organizations must therefore forego some of the benefits of integration by decomposing themselves into more manageable operating units.

Better decisions. When a large organization is divided into smaller, more manageable units it achieves many of the advantages of a small company. Because the decision makers responsible for each unit are closer to the problems in their environment, they are better able to make the relevant revenue/costs decisions. Because decision making can also be speeded up, a decentralized organization can be more responsive to environmental change. Through feedback on performance the managers see the results of their decisions and what effect their unit is having on the total company. Furthermore, because they are held responsible for all their activities, managers are far more aware of their ultimate impact and are extremely sensitive to what they are doing for the company.

Motivation. If responsibility is motivating, and monetary measures are one means of establishing responsibility, then the manager who is responsible for revenues and revenue/cost trade-offs will probably be more committed than a manager who is responsible for costs alone. Profit measures allow managers to focus on a familiar, well-understood goal, and give them the feeling of being in business for themselves.

Frees top management. By definition, decentralization frees top management. When profit centers are established, top management no longer needs to get involved in the day-to-day operations of each unit. Detail can be left to the unit manager. Top management can devote its time to more important isssues, such as strategic planning or coordinating the efforts of a number of profit centers. Because they do not have to concentrate on all elements of their business, they can practice management by exception by attending to those areas where a strong influence will be most beneficial. If one profit center begins to experience difficulty, management can then spend its time helping this center to correct its problems.

Thus it appears that management by profit centers can achieve many of the benefits of decentralization. When decentralized operating units are made into profit centers, each manager has a common goal—profit. Decentralized units can be planned and controlled according to their contribution to organizational profitability. Complete responsibility can be assigned because profit is a comprehensive measure of all activity, and each manager can then be judged on his or her ability to manage a complete operating unit as a separate and distinct business.

At the same time, central management can realize the benefits of a large organization's economies of scale by maintaining central staff functions such as economic planning, forecasting, technical analysis, accounting, and perhaps management information systems. These services can be provided to the profit centers on a charge basis to ensure that they are used efficiently.

Types of profit centers

An effective planning and control system for managers is one that motivates them to act in their best interests while simultaneously achieving what is best for the organization as a whole. Using this as the criterion for evaluation, let us examine two types of profit centers in order to determine the effectiveness of the profit measure as a basis for planning and control.

Independent (natural) profit centers. If a responsibility unit operates independently of the other units in the organization, that is, if it is effectively in its own business, then a manager who maximizes his or her own profits is also automatically maximizing the profits of the organization as a whole. The manager has discretion over sourcing of inputs and revenues to be charged. Decisions can be based on meaningful values derived from market-based, arm's-length transactions. Profit is a clear measure of efficiency and performance.

A responsibility unit which meets these criteria can be termed a natural or independent profit center. For such units, the profit measure is subject to the accounting and inherent limitations discussed above but is otherwise meaningful.

Interdependent (artificial) profit centers. Many organizational structures do not lend themselves to decomposition into natural profit centers. Because of their size, however, these organizations may still require some form of decentralization and may want to realize the benefits of a profit center system. For example, in a functionally organized automobile company (e.g., Ford, Case 4–1) the engine division or the chassis division may transfer parts to the assembly division. In an integrated oil company, the exploration and production division discovers oil and transports it to the manufacturing division which, in turn, ships it to marketing for disposal to the consumer market (Chapter 4). But to be a profit center an organizational unit must act both as a seller, with the discretion to set prices and output volumes, and as a buyer, with discretion on how much to consume at various price levels. It must also be able to choose whether to deal with a unit inside the company or with one outside.

Organizations such as the automobile and oil companies described above do not meet the criteria for profit center systems. Can units within the same organization that deal with each other regularly nevertheless be decentralized as profit centers? Many organizations do just this. Artificial or interdependent profit centers are responsibility units which are considered to be profit centers, even though they do not satisfy the usual criteria. The automobile assembly division is a good example. It can be considered to buy components from other divisions, assemble the car, and then sell it to a sales division. But clearly the assembly division manager is not free to buy and sell at will. In the absence of a free market, how are his prices to be determined?

TRANSFER PRICING

When the market conditions that give rise to natural profit centers do not obtain, problems arise in determining prices for the goods to be transferred between units. Since the prices used directly affect profit center profitability, the manner in which these prices are established critically affects the stability and effectiveness of an interdependent profit system.

A transfer price is simply the amount recorded for a transfer of goods or services between units. Although there is considerable variety in transfer price methods, only the four most popular methods will be discussed here.

1. Full-cost plus. Perhaps the simplest method of transfer pricing is to use full historical cost. The full cost of a product is the material, labor, and overhead required to produce and ship the product to the buying unit. Full costs are the most economical transfer prices to develop because they are routinely prepared for inventory evaluation. However, if goods are transferred at cost only then the selling division is only a cost center, or a profit center budgeted at zero profitability if standard costs are used as the transfer price.

Some firms have attempted to use simple cost-based transfer prices yet provide for profit by adding a normal markup to cost. Of course, this method produces an artificial profit system which is dictated by corporate policy on markups rather than by market forces. The realism of this method therefore depends on the extent to which it approximates the pricing practices in the industry as a whole.

2. *Marginal cost.* The marginal cost of a unit is the additional cost required to produce it. If the transfer pricing system is designed to ensure efficient allocation of resources then the best transfer price to use is marginal (or incremental) cost. Decision making based on incremental cost determines the benefits of the decision for the organization as a whole. At less than full capacity, marginal costs consist of the variable costs of producing and shipping goods plus any costs directly associated with the transfer. At full capacity, however, incremental costs must reflect the opportunity lost by foregoing sales to outside customers. In this situation incremental cost is equal to the market price.

3. *Market prices.* If there is an active competitive market for the goods or services transferred, the most logical pricing method to use is the market price.

4. *Negotiated prices.* In some instances profit center managers may be allowed to negotiate transfer prices with each other on whatever basis they choose. Negotiation implies, of course, that each manager has a bargaining position to begin from. This situation arises only when there are alternative sources of supply and demand. When a selling division has a choice of customers, or when a buying division has a choice of suppliers, prices can be negotiated.

Determining transfer prices

Two conditions most significantly affect the way transfer prices should be established. These are the presence of outside competition and slack resources in productive capacity.

Availability of outside competition. The presence of legitimate outside competition influences transfer pricing because it determines whether an objective value can be placed on the good or service transferred. Using market prices guarantees the optimal allocation of resources within the firm. Under competitive conditions, efficiency is assured if internal prices are no higher than external ones. Each seller is forced to meet competition and each buyer has alternative sources of supply. In fact, an internal buyer may even insist on a price below market because, in dealing intracorporately, the seller saves selling, collection, and bad debt expenses. Thus, when legitimate outside competition exists, establishing transfer prices is not difficult.

When outside sources of supply are potentially available but are not currently being used, one means of testing the efficiency of transfer prices is by securing competitive bids. However, although theoretically all internal prices should be tested by competitive bids, there are practical problems in doing so. First, it is well known that a competitor will only bid on a job if he or she has a substantial chance of getting it. Suppliers differentiate between bids requested for information only and those for which there is a possibility of securing an order. A second problem is that competitive bids may be deceptive. A supplier who wants to change the sourcing of a product from inside to outside may bid substantially lower than he otherwise would, even below his cost. He may prefer to take a short-term loss in the hope of building up dependence so that he may eventually slowly increase the price to achieve long-term profitability. Thus, when market bids are used as measures of market prices the validity of each bid must be considered individually.

In the absence of competitive market prices, economically meaningful transfer prices cannot be established. In these situations it is better for a responsibility unit to operate as a service center transferring goods at cost, rather than as a profit center. Operating decisions are best based on marginal costs, and fixed costs can be handled by central staff and allocated throughout the organization on some equitable basis. In the absence of market prices, this system is as effective a means of ensuring efficient allocation of resources as any other.

Level of productive capacity. The existence of slack in an organization's productive capacity influences transfer pricing because failing to make use of this additional capacity costs the organization as a whole. For example, assume that a buyer has the choice between an outside supplier and a division of his or her own firm. If the buying division pays an outsider anything above the marginal cost of the product to the firm, some contribution to profit and overhead will be going to the outsider. Therefore any transfer price greater than marginal costs may lead to buying decisions which are not in the best interest of the corporation as a whole, although this transfer price provides the selling division with some profit. If the marginal cost of a part to the organization is $10 and an outsider is offering to sell it at $15, accepting this offer means the sacrifice of a $5 contribution to profit and overhead. Yet if the selling division's fixed costs exceed $5, it may establish a transfer price greater than $15 so as not to incur a loss on the transaction. In this situation, the decision to source outside may be best from the standpoint of the buying division but not for the organization as a whole. Therefore, when a seller is operating at less than full capacity, transfer pricing at anything other than marginal cost may lead to decisions which do not maximize overall profits.

When outside competition exists, these two rules coincide. In a competitive situation, market prices and marginal costs are identical. In order to maximize profits each seller prices at the point where marginal cost equals marginal revenue. Therefore, at any output less than full capacity, pricing goods exchanged internally at market value both maximizes the profits of the selling division and also ensures goal congruence and consistent decision making throughout the organization.

In some instances, when a selling division is operating at full capacity and an alternative source of supply exists, prices can be set at an amount greater than marginal cost of production. In this situation, the manager of a profit center operating at full capacity may feel that he can allocate some of his productive capacity to earn a revenue greater than he is now earning; and so he may want to price to recover the opportunity loss he believes that he is incurring. If the profit center operation is truly decentralized, he should be free to price at whatever level he chooses, and the buyer should go to an outside supplier for his requirements.

The significance of transfer pricing

Since the transfer pricing problem has received a great deal of attention by economists, accountants, and management scientists over the last two decades, it may be surprising that this subject has been dispensed with as quickly as it has here. Although transfer pricing systems are of great theoretical significance and considerable practical interest, from the standpoint of organizational planning and control systems this emphasis is largely misplaced. In the absence of market-determined prices, the establishment of transfer prices either is arbitrary or else requires quantities of information far in excess of what is normally available to the manager of a profit center. Even if transfer prices are established by sophisticated analytical techniques such as linear programming, the shadow price solutions produced are still only single-period static solutions which require frequent revision to be operational. Thus in all nonmarket situations, transfer prices must either be established by negotiation or by the directives of central staff. So perhaps skill in bargaining for favorable transfer prices may be a far more important managerial asset than the ability to allocate resources efficiently. After extensively reviewing the transfer price literature from the perspectives of the theory of the firm, mathematical programming, and other analytical techniques, Abdell-Khalik and Lusk (1974) came to a similar conclusion.

TWO STYLES OF PROFIT CENTER MANAGEMENT

As noted in the discussion of key strategic variables and planning gaps in Chapter 3, expectations can be established and evaluation carried out in at least two different ways. One way is to establish specific performance expectations and to enforce firm commitment to their accomplishment. Alternatively, initially formulated expectations may serve only as guidelines; performance is later evaluated in light of the actual conditions and constraints in effect at the time of performance.

Profit as a specific performance objective

It is apparent from the preceding discussion that establishing a specific profit goal and attempting to obtain rigid commitment to this goal can have many dysfunctional consequences. Yet the benefits of ensuring that managers are sensitive to the effect of their activities on profits still makes the profit measure extremely useful. How, then, can its potentially dysfunctional consequences be averted?

One way is to adopt a management by objectives approach to commitment and evaluation and to apply this approach over short time spans of discretion. First, a level of profit is negotiated and agreed upon, and a short performance evaluation interval is set. The profit center manager also agrees to discuss all major decisions affecting profits with top management before they are finalized. These discussions ensure that no incongruent decisions are made and that no surprises occur.

Frequent communication and short evaluation periods may seem strange prescriptions for a profit center system, since they appear to negate the benefits of decentralization. However, when considered in the overall management by objectives approach, whose aims are to achieve initial commitment, periodically review performance, and coach the subordinate to achieve the objectives he or she has specified, these methods can help overcome the adverse effects of performance evaluation. This latter point is most crucial. It must be recognized that the profit center manager still makes all the decisions; his or her obligation to top management is simply to keep them fully informed and at least to use them as a sounding board before decisions are finalized. Evaluation is not merely a period-based measure of profitability; rather, it is an ongoing process that examines the quality of the decisions reached as well as their eventual results. The strength of this method is involvement and communication; if it is properly applied, it can achieve many of the motivational benefits of a management by objectives system.

Profit as a guiding objective

A second approach to profit center management is to use profit expectations merely as general objectives or guidelines. In this approach expectations are used for planning and orientation and are considered to be initial targets only. They are the best estimates that can be made at the time, and can be revised radically later on if necessary. This approach lessens the pressure on a profit center manager to maximize short-term performance. It permits him or her a greater amount of discretion. However, appropriate time spans for evaluation must still be established; too long a time interval also carries with it the risks and costs of inappropriate behavior.

If profit is used only as a general guide and performance is evaluated over a longer period of time, the following conditions must also apply. First, each profit center must be supported by an adequate information system. Detailed analyses and reconciliations of past performance to expectation must be continually provided to top management to demonstrate that the profit center manager understands what is going on. Since the profit center manager is on his or her own for a considerable time, this reporting keeps top management aware of the quality of decision making and performance. But any formal information system, regardless of how efficiently computerized it is, is still too slow to perform an early warning function for management. Continual communication between profit center managers and corporate staff is necessary. Hence the second requirement of this approach is that an appropriate climate for free and open communication be established. As in the MBO approach, the profit center manager must trust his or her superior so that communication is open and continuous.

This style of management may require the involvement of advisory staff groups, top-management committees, and perhaps a group vice president. Informal channels of communication are the real key to predicting problems in a profit center and its ability to handle them.

In this management system, evaluation takes into account the manager's explanation of his or her performance in light of existing conditions. As long as the profit center manager can justify his or her performance, and legitimate failure to perform is treated fairly, he or she need not perceive any threat or see any need to manipulate the accounts.

SUMMARY

This chapter examined the role that profit should play in establishing expectations and evaluating performance for responsibility center managers. Conceptually, profit was defined as the amount that can be disposed or consumed leaving an individual as well off at the end of a period as he or she was at the beginning. Operationally, profit is the excess of revenue over cost, measured in accrual accounting terms. The strength of the profit measure is its ability to express a host of diverse activities in one comprehensive form: its liabilities include the inability to reflect multiple objectives, to take into account the varying time horizons of programs, to measure opportunity loss, or to reflect nonquantifiable inputs and outputs.

A profit center is an operating unit whose manager has responsibility for the attainment of a given level of profit. The advantages of the profit center system are that it is a way of managing large entities through decentralization, it leads to better operating decisions because of closer proximity to the environment, it motivates managers by giving them a sense of control, and it frees top management from day-to-day operations so that they can concentrate on specific problems and long-term strategies.

There are several requirements for the successful implementation of profit centers: each center must have separate revenues and costs; it must have access to sources and markets and be free to buy and sell both inside and outside the company; and its manager must have operational independence to make the relevant decisions. In addition, top management must be committed to decentralization, the organization must have capable profit center managers, and adequate corporate and divisional staffs and information systems must be established to provide the necessary feedback to top management as well as to the manager of the decentralized unit.

Although profit is useful as a means of describing expected performance, its usefulness in performance evaluation is arguable. Profit depends on a number of factors, many of which are beyond the control of the unit manager. In addition, effective profit center decision making involves longer term considerations than can be encompassed by the single-period profit measurement. It is doubtful if a fair and accepted profit expectation can be established, or even if profit adequately describes efficient and effective performance.

Transfer prices must be established for the goods and services exchanged by interdependent organizational units operating as profit centers. Transfer prices can be based on historical costs, market prices, marginal costs, or negotiation. When outside competition exists, the independent market price for a product should be used. Although there have been a number of elegant solutions proposed for the transfer pricing problem, in the absence of competition economically meaningful transfer prices cannot be established, as arbitrary approximations only are available. In nonmarket situations it is better to operate a unit as a service center transferring goods at marginal cost than as a profit center. From the standpoint of the firm as a whole, any price paid to an outsider that exceeds the marginal cost of production for a good available from an internal source allows a contribution to fixed overhead and profit to leave the firm. Hence, to ensure the optimal allocation of economic resources within the firm, marginal costs should be used as the transfer price. When transfer prices do not equal marginal costs, one should be aware of the potential dysfunctional consequences to the corporation as a whole.

There are two styles of profit center management. One style founded on a firm commitment to a specific level of profit attainment, emphasizes close managerial involvement for short-term intervals to ensure that none of the dysfunctional consequences of firm profit expectations occurs.

An alternative style of management uses the profit measure as an initial expectation only, the best estimate for planning available at that time, and relies on ex post explanation and discussion to evaluate performance.

QUESTIONS

1. List the advantages and disadvantages of using profit as the main key result measure in a planning and control system. Do the advantages outweigh the disadvantages?
2. Does the designation of a responsibility unit as a profit center rule out the use of other key variables in its planning and control?
3. What role do profit budgets play in the three-cycle model of Chapters 2 and 3?
4. What organizational structures and/or types of responsibility unit are most likely to be planned and controlled as profit centers?
5. Does the use of a highly detailed profit budget performance reporting system negate the benefits that decentralization is supposed to bring?
6. What are the advantages and disadvantages of using full standard manufacturing cost for all intracompany transfers? If a company were currently doing this, how would you go about determining if a change in transfer pricing was desirable?
7. For what reasons would a company hold a manager responsible for profit when he or she does not control all costs and revenues? Do you think this should ever be done?
8. Does managerial style really influence the successful implementation of a profit budget system? What else is significant?

REFERENCES AND BIBLIOGRAPHY

Abdel-Khalik; Rashad, A.; and Lusk, Edward J.   Transfer pricing—a synthesis. *The Accounting Review,* January 1974, pp. 8–23.

Bernnard, Richard I.   Some problems in applying mathematical programming to opportunity costing. *Journal of Accounting Research,* Spring 1968, pp. 143–48.

Cotlar, Morton.   Performance accounting. *Management Accounting* (*U.S.*), August 1975, pp. 33–36.

Dean, Joel.   Decentralization and intra-company pricing. *Harvard Business Review,* July–August 1955, pp. 65–74.

Dearden, John.   Appraising profit center managers. *Harvard Business Review,* May–June 1968, pp. 80–87.

Dearden, John.   The case of the disputing divisions. *Harvard Business Review,* 1964, pp. 158–77.

Goetz, Billy E.   Transfer prices: An exercise in relevancy and goal congruency. *The Accounting Review,* July 1967, pp. 435–40.

Henderson, Bruce D., and Dearden, J. New systems for divisional control. *Harvard Business Review*, September–October 1966, pp. 144–61.

Mailanot, Peter. An alternative to transfer pricing. *Business Horizons*, October 1975, pp. 81–86.

Mullis, Elbert N., Jr. Variable budgeting for financial planning and control. *Management Control* (*U.S.*), February 1975, pp. 43–45.

Ridgway, V. F. Dysfunctional consequences of performance measurements. *Adminsitrative Science Quarterly*, September 1956, pp. 240–47.

Said, Kamal E. A goal-oriented budgetary process. *Management Accounting*, (*U.S.*), January 1975, pp. 31–36.

Schwab, Richard J. A contribution approach to transfer pricing. *Management Accounting* (*U.S.*), February 1975, pp. 46–48.

Solomons, David. *Divisional Performance: Measurement and Control*. Homewood, Ill., Irwin, 1968.

Watson, D. J. H., and Baumler, J. V. Transfer pricing: A behavioral context. *The Accounting Review*, July 1975, pp. 466–473.

Watson, Spencer C. A vote for R&D profit centers. *Management Accounting* (*U.S.*), April 1975, pp. 50–53.

Welsch, G. A. *Budgeting: Profit Planning and Control*, 3d ed. Englewood Cliffs, N.J.: Prentice-Hall, 1971.

Case study 8–1

European Auto

European Auto is the largest foreign luxury car dealership in Canada. It is managed and partially owned by Willy Schmidt, the retired grand prix and sports car driving champion. As the most famous racing driver ever to live in Canada, Willy had little difficulty interesting several silent partners in putting up the money for his dealership or in securing the rights to distribute such prestigious cars as Porsche, Mercedes, Ferrari, Bentley, and Lotus. European Auto's business strategy was founded on Willy's reputation as an automobile expert. It was also reputed that everyone who worked for him had to be an expert in his chosen area. Advertising stressed and customers had come to expect that European Auto stood for the highest levels of knowledge, integrity, and service.

Like most automobile dealerships, this organization was divided into four units: new car sales, used car sales, parts and service, and administration, each under the supervision of a manager who reported to Willy. (The administrative unit looked after the office paper work, payments, credit approvals, and leasing contracts.) When the dealership was started, the purpose of establishing these divisions was to allocate responsibility for structuring and supervising the work to be done. Each manager had few personnel to supervise, the physical distances between their offices were small, and so getting together for continual face-to-face meetings posed no problems. Although the four managers were not personal friends and did not socialize together off the job, relations between them were always amiable and this organizational structure proved successful.

As the dealership grew however, it became more and more apparent to Willy that this informal way of managing could no longer cope with the new demands being imposed. He himself was being drawn more and more into the public relations aspects of the business such as preparing a car for the Can-Am races and public speaking on auto safety. Another change was the movement of the parts and service operation to a new modern building one-half mile away from the showrooms. And the most shocking change was the sudden death of Wilhelm "Bill" Cushman, the used car manager, whose warm personal charm had always overcome any disagreements among the management personnel. Increased volume of operations, the need to free Willy from day-to-day management involvement, and geographical decentralization in themselves necessitated change. And the need to integrate Cash Cullhan, the new used car manager hired away from Hotspur Chev-Olds, into the organization made this an appropriate time to do it.

PROFIT CENTERS

European Auto's auditor recommended that the new car sales, used car sales, and parts and service divisions be made into profit centers, and the administrative unit into a cost center. The accountant argued that the three divisions satisfied all criteria necessary for the establishment of this form of responsibility center—each made independent revenue—cost trade-off decisions which could be measured by external market transactions. The administrative department's costs could be allocated to these three departments as equitable and reliable bases for doing so existed. Compensation was not to be tied to profits, however. Willy had the policy of always paying each employee what he believed that employee was worth to the organization, and this was independent of short-term performance.

Many large domestic auto dealerships are organized and operated in this way. New and used car selling prices are the responsibility of their respective division managers. Trade-ins on new cars are either transferred to the used car department at a negotiated (e.g., blue book) price or the new car department has the option of disposing of a car through the weekly dealer wholesale auction or to another dealer. The used car department gets its cars from new car trade-ins, used car trade-ups or trade-downs, purchases from individuals or dealers, or from the weekly dealer auction. They can also dispose of used cars through the auction. The service department prices reconditioning work to ready cars for sale by the used car department and new car predelivery inspection and tuning at an agreed upon rate.

The new profit center system was only in operation for a few weeks when it became clearly apparent to Willy that it was not working as it was supposed to. Three instances were of special concern to him.

USED CAR RECONDITIONING

First of all, Cash complained bitterly to Willy over the service department's pricing of reconditioning work. "How can I make money on used cars if I have to pay the same rates as our customers do? Work done on my cars should be the same top quality work that we always do but should be charged to me at our organization's cost. After all, we all do work for the same company."

The case in point was a 1972 Porsche 914. Cash bought it for $2,600 from an engineer who was returning to graduate school. It needed valves and rings and some body reconditioning which he estimated to cost $1,140 in total. Henry's Shell Station, run by Heinrich Finkle, quoted $1,375 to do the job; but Helmut Frisch, European Auto's service manager, wanted $1,850 for the job, take it or leave it.

Helmut's explanation was simple. "I am supposed to be in business for myself, ja? I am to maximize my profits, ja? Well I employ only the finest equipment and factory trained mechanics and these men are hard to find. My reputation for honesty, integrity, and the quality of work done is one of the strongest assets of this automobile dealership. I now have more work than I can personally supervise and have no desire to go to two shifts. Therefore, either pay my price or take your work to a cheaper Mickey Mouse garage."

"I estimate your mark up to be 60 percent on cost," Cash argued, "and that's too much for me to pay and still make a reasonable profit. If I have to spend my time farming out and supervising service work at garages all over the city, when will I have the time to sell? And what will our customers say when they find out that the work is not being done by European Auto but by somebody else?"

PREDELIVERY INSPECTION

A second problem arose between Helmut and Herman Schutz, the new car sales manager, over the cost of readying the Daimler-Benz 108 for delivery. The manufacturer's recommended procedure required three hours of a mechanic's time to perform the predelivery inspection and tuning. However Helmut felt several areas were overlooked in this procedure and that a more thorough job was required. In short, his bill was $34 more than Herman expected.

Herman protested to Willy. "I can't go elsewhere for this work and I have not requested that the thoroughness of the inspection be increased. I wasn't even asked if any of our customers complained about defects. Therefore, I don't see why I should pay for something I don't really need, I didn't request, and I can't avoid."

TRADE-INS

Thirdly, relations between Herman and Cash were also quickly disintegrating. When Cash had first came to work for European Auto Herman had taken him out for lunch several times to explain the differences in profit center relationships between the new and used car managers in a General Motors dealership and at European Auto. "Look Cash," he said, "dealing with high-volume domestic cars is different than our operations because of the availability of the wholesale market. I'm sure at Hotspur you could buy cars, and the new car manager could sell cars at will; but an $8,000 foreign sports car can't be acquired or disposed of that easily. Used car dealers won't buy them because of the specialized service requirements and so the dealer auction is of no use in disposing of cars. You and I have to be partners in trade-in deals if we are both to operate profitably."

Cash initially agreed with this proposition. Afterall, he thought, with the higher profit margins on these cars, surely deciding to accept a trade-in and negotiating a transfer price with the new car department should not be difficult. But it did not turn out that way.

One contentious point was the sharing of repair costs on defects discovered after the transfer price was negotiated. For example, a recent Jaguar XKE trade-in was in the final stages of post-reconditioning road tests when it was found that the real axle hypoid gears had to be replaced, a $380 job. The previous owner had cleverly attempted to conceal this defect by using extra viscous oil in the car's rear end, but Helmut had detected it when he checked the car out.

Herman had little sympathy for Cash's dilemma. "That's the way business is, Cash. Sometimes fewer repairs are necessary and sometimes more are necessary. On the average it will work out, so why should we bother renegotiating on one car? And if you really get stuck, you can dispose of the car without making the repair."

Cash didn't have to wait long to irritate Herman equally. Herman wanted to take a rare Ferrari Coupe in trade on a new Lamborghini. Cash said "No thanks." The market for $11,000 Ferraris was not good right now and he didn't feel he could sell it profitably given the transfer price range Herman was suggesting. And since there was already a similar Ferrari on the lot, Cash had evidence to back his contention. Herman was livid, however. This was not only the biggest deal of the year for him, but it would also place a Lamborghini in the parking lot of the ultra exclusive York Club, in view of a large number of possible buyers. He wanted to make the sale.

"If you don't want the Ferrari, I'll take it in trade and sell it myself," Herman said. "You just store it for me in your used car showroom and I will sell it".

"Sure," agreed Cash "but just be prepared to pick up your fair share of my overhead."

Question

What should Willy do?

Chapter outline

9

Investment centers

When you have completed this chapter you should understand:

1. How return on investment (ROI) and residual income (RI) are measured.
2. The advantages and disadvantages of ROI and RI.
3. The extent to which these methods are currently used to plan and control decentralized performance.
4. How these methods can be used effectively.
5. An alternative approach to planning and controlling investment performance.

RETURN ON INVESTMENT (ROI)

A company is decentralized with respect to profit responsibility when each responsibility unit manager is accountable for achieving some level of profit. The assets employed in generating this profit form the asset base of the unit. Responsibility unit managers who are responsible for their investment base as well as their profitability are known as investment center managers. The most commonly used investment-based measure of performance is return on investment (ROI), the ratio of profit to investment. Conceptually and operationally, measures of investment productivity are the most comprehensive financial measures that can be used, and investment centers are the responsibility units that operate most like autonomous businesses.

The use of ROI for financial planning and control of decentralized units, originated by the Du Pont Corporation, grew from its need to plan and evaluate the performance of the independent entities making up its diversified operations. The use of ROI solved the problem of motivating managers, ensuring consistent decision making, and controlling decentralized divisions.

As used by Du Pont, return on investment is the quotient of the accounted profit earned by a unit divided by the investment assigned to the unit. The investment is made up of both fixed assets, such as machinery and equipment, and working capital items, such as inventory, receivables, and cash. ROI allows the measurement and evaluation of each responsibility center manager according to how productively he or she uses the assets entrusted to him or her. It allows managers the latitude to make trade-off decisions between investments, revenues, and operating costs, and then to be evaluated on these decisions by one comprehensive performance figure. Planning and controlling the operations of decentralized investment centers by ROI has all the benefits of a profit center approach, and in addition can be used to measure the productivity of the assets employed.

Calculation of the investment base

Two critical procedures in the computation of ROI are specifying the investment base to be used for productivity measurements, and separating it into its controllable and noncontrollable components for evaluation. In his discussion of alternative methods of measuring an investment base, Solomons (1968) raises the following questions:

1. Should investment be interpreted to mean all assets, net assets (total assets minus liabilities), or fixed assets plus net current assets?
2. However investment is defined, how should it be measured? Should fixed assets be included at cost, net book value (i.e., deducting accumulated depreciation), or at appraised value?
3. How should assets which are either shared or controlled centrally be computed in the return on investment? That is, when a responsibility unit does not hold separate cash balances or if it does not control its own receivables, how should these be allocated?
4. When inventories are valued on a Lifo basis, is any adjustment necessary when the investment base is computed?
5. When should the investment base be measured—at the beginning or at the end of the period, or should the average over the period be used?

After an extensive analysis of the implications of each of these alternatives, Solomons concludes that for calculating returns and for evaluating performance, investment should be defined as follows:

1. Total investment is best defined as total assets. Measures of productivity should be based on the total amount of capital committed,

irrespective of how it was financed, because differences in financing strategies are irrelevant to the way assets are used, and also because financing decisions are usually made centrally rather than by the investment center manager. However, to determine controllable investment, a deduction should be made for controllable liabilities. Changing these also changes net controllable investment, which should be the basis of the ROI figure used for evaluation.

2. Fixed assets should be included at gross cost. No deduction should be made for accumulated depreciation because such arbitrary deductions, and the resulting net book values, may bear no relationship to the productivity of the assets involved. ROI based on net book value increases as accumulated depreciation increases and net book value decreases. To negate the effects of changing price levels and to establish a basis of comparison between investment centers acquiring assets at different times, index number adjustments may be used.

3. Fixed assets held under corporate control (e.g., a research laboratory or computer center) should be allocated to investment centers only if there exists a reasonable basis to do so. An alternative is to rely on a charge for services rendered, although this method involves all the difficulties of a transfer pricing scheme. The allocation of centrally controlled working capital is appropriate if a basis can be found that reflects incremental demands for such capital; for example, centrally held bank balances can be allocated on the basis of incremental cash demands while receivables can be allocated on the basis of sales. Allocated assets form part of a division's total investment, but not part of its controllable investment.

4. Investment in inventory is generally controllable and should be valued on a Fifo basis to approximate replacement cost on the balance sheet and avoid the distortions of Lifo.

5. The point in time at which the investment base should be measured depends on the length of the period considered and the time it takes for changes in assets to have an effect on profits. In calculating the rate of return for a period shorter than a quarter, the investment at the beginning of the period is a suitable base. For a longer interval, however, average investment should be used.

The five questions cited above are not an exhaustive coverage of all aspects of investment-based measurement, but they do demonstrate the types of choices to be made. A review of Solomon's recommendations and his underlying reasoning reveals how arbitrary these measurements of the investment base really are. In considering the alternatives, Solomons appears to have assessed the implications of each kind of measurement according to what appears most "correct" from the standpoint of economic productivity and performance. There is therefore a significant amount of subjectivity in his choices. One could argue that productivity measures would be better based on the appraised value of assets, not historical costs, or that index number adjustments to only a part of a company's assets produce misleading information. But debates on the "correctness" of alternative investment-based measurements could (and probably will) go on forever. As in many other accounting-related areas of contention, there are no "right" answers.

In deciding among alternative ways to compute an investment base, a system designer must consider how these measures are to be used. If their purpose is to motivate the investment center manager to behave in certain desired ways (e.g., to keep minimal levels of inventory), then they should stress the controllable components of investment. If, on the other hand, the measures are to be used as aids for decision making, they should stress economic reality. In sum, like most components of a planning and control system, how the components of an investment base should be measured depends on the characteristics of the situation and on the behavior that the measures are intended to influence.

Advantages of ROI

In addition to all the benefits of profit measures, ROI has two more advantages. The first and foremost of these is that it provides a single, comprehensive, financial measure of performance. It not only reflects the increment to wealth, such as the profit measure, but it also relates profit to the assets employed in generating it. Second, because it is expressed as a ratio, ROI is an excellent way of comparing operations of different sizes and types.

Disadvantages of ROI

When ROI was first introduced by Du Pont to control its decentralized operations, it was far superior to the methods then in use. Since then, however, numerous flaws have been uncovered in the ROI measure. Return on investment was originally intended to guide the planning and decision making of unit managers and to give top management a basis by which to control and evaluate performance. However, from both of these perspectives ROI has several defects.

First, ROI suffers from all the defects of conventional accounting measures. The numerator is profit measured in accrual accounting terms. The deficiencies of this measure were discussed in Chapter 8, where it was concluded that accounting measures of profit simply do not capture the full economic significance of all of a manager's actions and concerns. Furthermore, because ROI also requires measurement of an asset base, it suffers even more from the arbitrariness of accounting conventions. For example, many expenditures which benefit the firm for more than a single accounting period are expensed rather than capitalized, such as research and development expenditures and advertising outlays. And the historical costs at which assets are measured do not reflect their true economic value at any time subsequent to initial acquisition. Depreciation reduces book values and so increases ROI artificially. Book values are not adjusted for the changing value of the dollar, so that in times of inflation a substantial part of the reported profits may actually result from holding and using older assets while pricing products at current market levels, rather than from normal operations.

A second set of problems results from using ROI as a performance measure. As such, it should be controllable by the unit manager. However, many if not all of the assets entrusted to him are acquired through a host of past decisions outside his control. Nevertheless, these decisions are almost unavoidably reflected in any measure of performance, so that the use of ROI for evaluation may lead to distortion after all. As a measure of performance, ROI suffers not only from all the dysfunctional consequences associated with improper use of the profit measure, but it may encourage other undesirable behavior as well. Assume that the objective of an investment center manager is to maximize or at least to maintain his or her current ROI level. The manager may do so not only by improving profit performance, but also by minimizing his or her investment. For instance, minimizing assets by leasing, as opposed to buying, will have an immediate effect on ROI performance.

Pressure to achieve a specific ROI level may lead to incongruent decisions about asset replacement and disposal. In ROI performance measurement, asset replacement decisions are a function of the book value of an asset, not salvage values. Furthermore, ROI can be increased by scrapping assets which are earning less than the current ROI, thereby increasing the overall average. Scrapping unused assets increases ROI because these assets no longer are depreciated, nor do they appear in the asset base. Therefore, retaining idle assets is entirely undesirable. Also, because ROI is an overall measure of the use of assets, in some cases it can be increased by any action that reduces the asset base; and such decisions, while productive in the short run, may not be so in the long run.

Because ROI increases simply with the passage of time and depreciation (especially accelerated depreciation), it may also discourage new investments. The older the asset base of an organization, the higher is its ROI, and therefore the higher is the return required on new investments in order to maintain or improve this average. Thus there may be a tendency to keep older equipment operating as long as possible in order to show high ROI rates, even when replacement would be better in the long run.

It is important to recognize that ROI is simply the quotient of profit over investment, and may differ from an organization's cost of capital. It is also a single-year measurement, not a rate of return computed over the life cycle of an entire project. Hence while it may provide an appropriate criterion for short-term current operating decisions, it is certainly no guide for capital investments. ROI is based on current performance using existing assets, and does not reflect the cost of financing additional investments. Thus it is improper to use ROI as a decision criterion or hurdle rate against which to evaluate new investment proposals.

Investments should be made if their return exceeds the cost of making them. It is well known that different types of financing have different costs. For example, cash can be borrowed from a bank, acquired through the issuance of securities, or obtained by liquidating fixed assets. Each source of an organization's financing, be it debt or equity, carries a separate implicit or explicit cost. The weighted average of an organizations mix of financing costs is known as its cost of capital. The cost of capital for an organization is the average cost of financing its operations, and provides the decision criteria that the organization should use. If a new investment earns an amount greater than its costs, there is a net positive increment to the organization's overall worth. Therefore, if an organization's objective is to maximize the net present value of its current shareholders, then it is in the shareholders' best interest to undertake any investment whose return exceeds the organization's current cost of capital.

It is important to recognize that ROI does not measure the cost of resources to an organization; it measures only the rate currently being earned on the money already invested. And so, investment opportunities which earn less than the organization's ROI rate but more than the organization's cost of capital may be rejected because they reduce average ROI. This sort of behavior is undesirable because it foregoes potential increments to shareholder wealth. Yet once a responsibility center manager has committed himself to a specific ROI rate, it is unreasonable to expect him to propose a capital investment that will earn a lesser rate of return.

Thus it can be seen that the use of ROI as a criterion for investment decisions may lead a manager to make decisions which are incongruent with and inappropriate for overall organizational objectives. The use of ROI may not always motivate the manager to behave in a way that benefits himself while simultaneously benefiting the organization as a whole—the criterion for an effective planning and control system.

RESIDUAL INCOME (RI)

Residual income is another asset-based measure of financial performance. It is used in an attempt to overcome some of the weaknesses of

ROI and to move closer toward the net present value notion of financial decision making. The RI of an investment center is its current operating profit (revenues minus operating expenses) minus a capital charge for the assets employed in generating this profit. A capital charge is simply the cost to the firm of each particular type of asset it uses. RI is thus the net income of a responsibility unit after the cost of the capital used in its operations has been deducted.

Advantages of RI

One strength of RI is that it counters the need to maintain at least an average rate of ROI in considering new investment decisions. If an investment has a positive residual income, it will be undertaken even if its ROI is lower than the current average ROI. With an RI decision criterion, all investments will be accepted as long as they earn more than their capital costs. RI therefore encourages congruent investment decision making, so that each responsibility center is able to contribute to overall shareholder welfare by increasing the net present worth of the firm.

A second strength of RI is its use of capital charges in weighing assets. Because RI employs capital charges, each separate class of assets can be treated in a different manner, as appropriate. Assets which are more liquid and involve less risk to the firm or which are more readily available may be costed at rates substantially different from those which are hard to obtain or especially expensive. Assets which must be irretrievably committed to a project, and hence involve high risk, may be priced differently from those that can be recovered easily at full value. By pricing assets appropriately, an RI system can motivate managers to use assets in the proportions deemed most suitable from the standpoint of the organization as a whole.

Disadvantages of RI

The residual income measure shares many of the problems of ROI, however. The same problem of measuring fixed assets still exists, since the capital charges have to be applied against specific asset amounts and must be classified into controllable and noncontrollable components. Furthermore, RI is measured in absolute dollars, not as a ratio, making it more difficult to compare responsibility units of different sizes. Like ROI, RI is a comprehensive financial measurement of performance. But it cannot include nonfinancial factors, of course, so many relevant key variables may be ignored. And finally, although many of the limitations of conventional accounting can be partly ameliorated, management usually cannot or will not use accounting techniques such as annuity depreciation and replacement cost accounting that would make the use of RI more realistic.

Therefore, although residual income is a more helpful formula than ROI for making decisions about asset acquisitions, it does not overcome the dysfunctional temptation to reduce assets (so as to minimize capital charges, in this case). In short, although it is perhaps superior to ROI in some ways, it still must be applied with the greatest of care.

EFFECTIVE USE OF INVESTMENT-BASED PERFORMANCE MEASURES

The best infomation available on the use of RI and ROI comes from a survey conducted more than a decade ago. Mauriel and Anthony (1966) surveyed 3,525 U.S. companies with sales of over $20 million. Of the 2,658 companies that responded to the questionnaire, 60 percent used either ROI or RI or some combination of both in their planning and control of decentralized units. Only 3.8 percent of the total surveyed used residual income only. A follow-up study conducted by the same researchers revealed that 60 percent of their 981 respondents relied solely on ROI as a measure of responsibility center performance. The responses indicated that most companies use accounting-based measures for computing their asset base. Of the companies responding, 93 percent measured divisional performance on the basis of either gross book value (18.5 percent), net book value (73.2 percent), or a combination of these two (1.6 percent). Hence, in spite of the many deficiencies associated with the use of both ROI and RI, it appears that investment-based performance measurements are widely used in management practice today.

Investment-based performance measurements present the designer of any planning and control system with a dilemma. On the one hand it is recognized that both ROI and RI have many of the drawbacks of a single performance measurement. They do not lead to correct investment decisions because they fail to mediate effectively between the short and the long term, and to reflect both the qualitative and quantitative aspects of any business operation. Furthermore, many nonfinancial key variables and intangible considerations (e.g., services) are not reflected in a unit's investment base, and therefore cannot be accommodated by these types of measurement. But on the other hand, as the above surveys reveal, these investment-based performance measurements are in wide use today; and their acceptance by management is so widespread that it is unrealistic to assume that they will be done away with in the near future. So ways must be found to use these measures successfully. This means that if an organization relies heavily on a single performance measurement, its use ought to be accompanied both by a sharp awareness of the strengths and weaknesses of the measure, and also by an appropriate management style.

Two styles of management were discussed in Chapter 8 with respect to the use of profit measures: one based on the establishment of firm expectations combined with counselling and coaching; the other based on the establishment of expectations to be used solely as initial guidelines, with an evaluation that takes into account the circumstances of the situation as they arose. Both management styles must emphasize trust and open communication if they are to be effective. Both require the specification of appropriate key variables, the establishment of expectations in terms of these key variables, and finally, a consistent evaluation of the performance of each responsibility center manager. These requirements also hold true when investment-based performance measures are used in the planning and control system.

If an investment-based criterion is used as a firm measure of expected performance, the determinants selected for the asset base must motivate the manager to make use of his or her assets appropriately. Clearly, residual income is superior to ROI in this respect; if each individual class of assets is properly priced, the encouragement of cost minimization will automatically ensure congruent actions. As before, performance can be controlled by establishing firm expectations and then having managers report to top management at short-time intervals. The constant involvement of top management will help to avoid the dysfunctional behaviors associated with investment-based performance measures.

If investment-based performance measures are established simply as guidelines, ROI or RI measures will serve not as a basis for evaluation but as a diagnostic tool. They are monitored to detect changes over time and to suggest potential improvements. To make them more useful for this purpose, accounting practices should be modified as needed. For example, modifying depreciation schedules and capitalizing expenditures such as advertising and research and development may be appropriate for internal accounting purposes, although not for external reporting. With this approach, return on investment must be regarded simply as one of many key variables that affect performance. Again, communication between the manager of the decentralized investment center and corporate staff and management is the best way to assure an early warning of troubles to come.

AN ALTERNATIVE APPROACH TO PLANNING AND CONTROLLING INVESTMENT CENTERS

The use of RI and ROI as measures of investment center performance implies that validity of two assumptions: (1) that a single measure combining both profits and assets can describe efficient and effective behavior, and (2) that a single-period measure of performance can guide appropriate behavior. If these two assumptions are not valid, an organization must devise alternative means of planning and controlling investment centers. Specifically, it must answer the following questions:

1. What criteria should be used in making short-run operating decisions?
2. How should expenditures related to managed or discretionary short-run capacity costs (costs which cannot be associated with output) be planned and controlled?
3. How should an organization make capital investment decisions, and then evaluate the productivity of these investments?

To understand the role of investment-based performance measurements in the planning and control of any decentralized responsibility unit, it is essential to recognize that three types of decision making occur. Two of these relate to short-run decisions and performance evaluation; the third to long-run expenditures.

The first type, current operating decisions, is concerned with the net contribution of any decision to the organization's profit and overhead. The key criterion of these decisions is whether or not the benefits exceed the cost over the short run. These decisions are based solely on differential (incremental) revenues and costs; i.e., revenues as well as variable costs and other costs that will differ according to the alternative selected. All other costs, such as committed or sunk costs, are irrelevant to these decisions and their inclusion will only confuse the issue at hand. Furthermore, because of the short interval of time covered the time value of money can be ignored in these decisions. The cost-volume-profit and contribution margin decision-making procedures familiar to any student of management accounting are the applicable techniques. The effective control of operating decision making is essentially the same as the process involved in profit budgeting. The conclusions reached in Chapter 8's discussion of profit center management therefore apply here with equal force; in other words, it is possible to manage the ongoing, day-to-day process of doing business and making operating decisions using the profit measure alone.

The second set of short-run decisions relates to the capacity to carry out business in the short run. These are the costs needed to do business rather than the costs of doing business, and involve the fixed or committed costs needed to support current operations. Many components of these costs are independent of operating outputs and hence must be managed; i.e., their amounts are subject to the discretion of management rather than to an input-output relationship with volume of activity. The discussion of the allocation of resources to unstructured processes in Chapter 7 touched on many of the problems of managing discretionary expenditures. Managed cost budgets, together with allocation schemes such as zero-base budgeting and interpersonal schemes such as management by objectives, are some techniques that will ensure the effective and efficient allocation of managed resources. Hence, these resources are best planned and controlled in the manner described in Chapter 7, regardless of whether or not a single overall comprehensive performance measurement is used.

The third type of decision making and performance evaluation for investment centers relates to long-term expenditures. Capital expenditure decisions must reflect an organization's cost of capital as well as other decision criteria that reflect a time period greater than one year, such as payout period, and the relative risk in the project over its full life cycle. Capital expenditure analysis is the primary means by which an organization approves acquisition of new assets, major changes from existing operations, and also the divestment of capital assets. As described in Chapter 3, a capital expenditure analysis procedure is a comprehensive, fully documented system that must be adhered to. It is the means by which an organization ensures consistent and appropriate decision making about capital expenditures throughout its decentralized entities. In any comprehensive program of planning and control, the capital aspect of resource allocation decision making is carried out independent of financially based criteria such as ROI and RI.

Both conceptually and operationally, capital expenditure analysis should be completely divorced from short-term measurements of investment productivity. The "correctness" of any investment decision can be evaluated only over the life cycle of a project. As an approximation of this evaluation, and to the extent that its effects are not contaminated by complex interrelationships among projects, a capital expenditure audit of an ongoing project can be carried out. This audit evaluates the expenditure decision either relative to the cash flow estimates originally made for it, or relative to modifications of these estimates that reflect activities that have taken place subsequently. In either case, the evaluation of an investment cannot be carried out by ROI or RI calculations because the initial decision to invest was not made on this basis.

When the total decision making required by an organization to manage its economic resources is divided into these three broad classes, the role of measures such as ROI and RI in the planning and control of resources becomes more explicit. Each kind of decision should be kept separate and should be planned and controlled according to the specific decision process that guides it. If this is done, the arbitrary averaging, confusing interrelationships, and interperiod allocations that result from most accounting-based measurements can be avoided. Accounting measurements are useful for short-term decision making and should be used where they are relevant; but long-term capital investment decisions should be based essentially on cash flows and an organization's cost of capital, and should not be contaminated by accounting phenomena.

It should be recognized, however, that the return on investment figure derived from accounting data may be used for extracorporate evaluation. Many outsiders who rely on financial statements to assess corporate productivity examine the ratio of income to assets employed. Outsiders are, of course, forced to use financial statements because these are the only data available to them. It must therefore be recognized that, to the extent that external evaluation criteria influence internal decisions, investment-based performance measurements such as ROI may, in fact, be relevant to decisions concerning resource allocations.

SUMMARY

Investment-based performance measures, ROI and RI, are perhaps the most widely used means for planning and controlling decentralized operations. Return on investment is the ratio of operating profit to the asset base used in generating this profit, while residual income is the difference between net operating profit and the charges for the capital employed in generating this profit. Both rely heavily on conventional measures of profit, and hence suffer from all the limitations of accounting. In addition, they reflect neither the multiple objectives held by any responsibility center, nor the balance between short-term and long-term considerations, opportunity losses, or nonquantifiable inputs and outputs. They also have all the limitations of any attempt to measure fixed assets in accounting terms, such as arbitrary depreciation and an inability to reflect the changing price level of the dollar. Hence, as measures of the efficient utilization of economic resources, they are as best arbitrary approximations.

If ROI or RI must be used for performance evaluation, they can be used in either of two operating modes. One method involves the establishment of firm expectations of performance, accompanied by short-term performance reporting and a high degree of managerial involvement in decision making. Alternatively, ROI or RI can be established an initial approximations of future plans designed to guide and motivate behavior. Performance evaluation then takes into account the actual events that have taken place over the evaluation period.

Perhaps the most effective means of planning and controlling financial decision making is to differentiate between current operating decisions involving revenues and variable costs, and those which involve managed, committed, or fixed costs. Both decisions concern short periods of time but each must be handled in a different way. The third type of economic decision making concerns capital expenditure analysis. Here the criterion is the relationship of inflows to outflows, appropriately discounted by the firm's cost of capital and measured over the whole life cycle of the project. Efficient decision making maximizes the net present value of shareholder wealth. The use of measures such as ROI and RI in these three types of decision making fails to capture the significance of each individual process and hence does not do justice to any of them. A more acceptable way of controlling investment center performance is to differentiate among the various types of decisions made about the allocation of resources and to apply to each kind of decision the appropriate planning and control procedure.

QUESTIONS

1. Should ROI be used to evaluate the performance of an investment center manager? Is RI preferable for purposes of evaluation?
2. What part does an investment center manager (e.g., a divisional general manager in a product-based organization) play in the organization's overall capital budgeting system? If you were the president of this organization, what information would you want before you approved a capital investment request or a machine disposal request?
3. What role should ROI and RI measures play in the three-cycle model of Chapters 2 and 3?
4. What are the benefits and limitations of planning and controlling a responsibility unit as an investment center?
5. When should profit centers rather than investment centers be used?
6. Could zero-base budgeting, management by objectives, and human resource accounting all be applied to the management of an investment center?
7. In capital intensive industries, depreciation accounts for the majority of manufacturing expense. What role should measures of depreciation play in performance evaluation?
8. What role should the postimplementation audit of capital expenditures play in the planning and control of an investment center?

REFERENCES AND BIBLIOGRAPHY

Dearden, J. The case against ROI control. *Harvard Business Review*, May–June 1969, pp. 124–35.

Mauriel, J., and Anthony, R. N. Misevaluation of investment center performance. *Harvard Business Review*, March–April 1966, pp. 98–105.

Solomons, D. *Divisional Performance: Measurement and Control.* Homewood, Ill.: Irwin, 1968.

Case study 9–1
Simpson-Eaton Appliances Limited

THE COMPANY

Simpson-Eaton Appliance Limited is a full-line manufacturer of both gas and electric home appliances. Sales in 1975 were $173 million, with

before-tax income of $14,106,000. The company's products sell in the
upper end of the appliance price range and are of the highest quality.
Average life of a Simpson-Eaton major appliance is 10–15 years, well
above the industry average of 6 years. Overall it is one of the most
successful firms in the industry. Corporate office is in New York City
and the two manufacturing plants are located in the southeastern United
States, approximately 50 miles apart. The laundry and cooking products
plant now manufactures garbage disposals and dishwashing units in
addition to washers, dryers, ranges, and ovens. The refrigeration plant
manufactures freezers and portable home air-conditioning units in addition to refrigerators. The company's product lines are directed solely at
domestic use.

The organization chart for Simpson-Eaton is shown in Exhibit 1. There

EXHIBIT 1
Organization chart

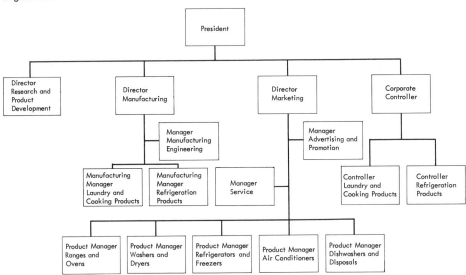

are five product line managers, one each for ranges and ovens, washers
and dryers, refrigerators and freezers, air conditioners, and dishwashers
and disposals. In addition, a manager of advertising and promotion reports to the director of marketing. The corporate controller is located in
New York City while his two plant controllers are on location at the
manufacturing facilities. The director of manufacturing and all marketing
managers reside in New York.

As a full-line appliance manufacturer S-E enjoys considerable economies of scale. It has the highest R&D level of any manufacturer in the
industry. It has also sold a sufficient number of appliances in every area of

the country either to provide factory service directly or to control the re-pair service provided customers. Being a full-line producer also helps sales because the brand loyalty developed for one appliance usually extends to others as well. (Surveys have demonstrated that brand loyalties among appliance owners is in the order of 70 percent and this is a significant factor since most manufacturers spend less than 1 percent of sales on advertising.) Simpson-Eaton also enjoys economies of scale in distribu-tion; e.g., in lower freight for full car shipments to retail outlets.

The company has a strong distribution network of retailers which is well controlled and often partly financed. Distribution is particularly strong to regional retail outlets which account for a large proportion of appliance sales nationwide. The company is especially efficient and pro-ductive; their manufacturing plants are located in areas of low-cost and highly available labor, and their component purchasing and assembly operations are extremely well planned and controlled.

TWO PROBLEMS FACING SIMPSON-EATON

In spite of its enviable position, the firm is facing two major difficulties: the first stems from the fact that the use of major appliances has reached saturation levels, implying that most sales are for replacement. For example, 92 percent of wired homes are equipped with home laundry washers, and 50–75 percent of new sales are for replacement. Almost all homes are equipped with refrigerators today and 67–70 percent of sales are for replacement. Similarly, 61–70 percent of ranges are sold as re-placements. Thus, although S-A is in a good position to capture con-sumers seeking a high-quality, long-lived major home appliance replace-ment, it is still facing a tight consumer market.

The second difficulty stems from the firm's limited share of the con-tract appliance market. Builders of new homes, condominiums, and apart-ments are extremely cost conscious and typically buy middle and lower end cost products. The contract market presently accounts for over 70 percent of built-in ranges, undercounter dishwashers, and waste disposal units sold. Contract sales accounted for one third of all appliance sales in 1975 and this percentage is increasing rapidly. It is expected that growth in contract sales will account for half the forecast growth in total appliance sales in the future.

FUTURE PLANS

In August of 1975 Harold Willis, the president of S-E, called together his directors of research and product development, manufacturing, and marketing, and his corporate controller for a meeting. At the meeting he revealed the following average increases in industry shipments over the last decade.

Percent

Refrigerators.	4.8
Freezers	3.0
Rangers	3.7
Clothes dryers	10.4
Dishwashers	14.9
Disposals	9.9
Room air conditioners	18.1

"We have been lucky to have maintained a 12 percent average annual growth in shipments over the last decade," Mr. Willis said.

However, if these figures are accurate, and I believe they are, we have reason to fear we will not be able to do so in the future unless we radically change our approach to selling appliances. To be successful in the future we must meet two challenges: first, we must continue to produce and market a high-quality, reliable home appliance. Second, we must develop and effectively market a new lower priced series of appliances that will satisfy the needs of contractors. I am confident we have the ability to carry out this strategy successfully; but we still must determine the best way of doing so. The purpose of this meeting, therefore, is to solicit your suggestions on what we should do.

THE PROPOSAL FOR INVESTMENT CENTERS

Howard Samuels, the corporate controller, was first to offer a suggestion.

For a long time I have been very concerned with the way we make capital investment decisions in this company. Our emphasis is primarily on payout period and on accounting rate of return—you know, average operating profit divided by net investment. We never consider our cost of capital, nor the complete life-cycle effects of the projects we undertake. I trace this deficiency partly to the way we plan and control our operating divisions. Our manufacturing plants are controlled as cost centers and evaluated on their ability to meet their standard cost estimates. The plant managers therefore are fixated on operating costs—labor, material, and overhead. They have absolutely no appreciation of the value of the assets they use. On the selling side, each marketing manager heads up a profit center and is evaluated on his gross profit figure (revenue less marketing costs, costs of collection, receivables lost, and so on). They therefore pay little attention to the relationship between the sales of their products and the assets required to produce these sales. According to what you have said, we now appear about to undertake a considerable number of new investments, both to maintain our current level and quality of production as well as to develop a new series of lower cost appliances. I am worried that we may not make the right investment decisions if we continue to measure performance as we now are.

The suggestion of such a possibility caught Mr. Willis' attention fully. "What do you propose we do, Howard?" he asked.

Well, I've been toying with an idea for quite a while; let me try it on you. What if we change our whole organizational outlook by combining manufacturing facilities and product lines into integrated responsibility centers? What if we make a product manager and a manufacturing manager jointly responsible for the manufacture, sale, and return on investment of each product line? Instead of two cost centers and five profit centers, I propose we have five investment centers. That is, the manager of ranges and ovens for example, and the manufacturing manager of the laundry and cooking products plant would form a team concerned with the overall return of that product line. They would be planned and controlled in terms of their rate of return on investment, and hence, would be keenly aware of the amount of investment supporting their activities. In sum, my idea is to switch this organization from its current functional planning and control structure to five investment centers as a first step toward encouraging far more effective decision making.

"Would that involve a change in organizational structure, Howard?" someone asked.

No. I think we should retain our current organizational structure and reporting relationships. All we need to do is change our managers' spheres of responsibility and also the means by which they are controlled. I think we could retain our current reporting responsibilities and achieve the effects we desire.

"Is this a matrix type organization that I read about somewhere?" asked Bill Balfour, the director of research and product development.

"Yes it is, partly," replied Howard. "And I really think it will work in our organization."

THE PROPOSED ASSET BASE

"Here is how performance will be measured," Howard continued. The managers responsible for each investment center will be charged for the assets that they use to produce and sell their products. Let's take a look at cash for instance. Currently corporate cash is handled centrally by my office and not charged to any of our managers. The actual cash balance each investment center will require is a fairly meaningless measure of the resources it really needs, of course, because the managers have quick access to corporate cash when they need it. Therefore, they do not need the safety factor that would be necesssary for an independent entity. I think the managers and I can agree upon an amount of cash that corresponds to minimum needs and each investment center will then be charged for the cash it maintains in excess of this level. If this is done, cash will be watched closely. And we need all the spare cash we can generate for our new investments.

Under our present system each product manager is not now charged with the cost of his accounts receivable. Of course, he has no real control over either credit terms or collections so it can be argued that he should not be responsible for his receivables. As a practical matter, however, there should be little complaint about a charge that depends on the sales volume of his particular sales line. By charging him for this amount, he will be aware of receivables turnover, in general, and which dealers are the causes of these problems in particular. He will be more cautious when selling to them in the future. Credit management will become especially important when we begin selling directly to contractors because many of them are very slow payers.

Coordination of inventory policy between marketing and manufacturing is especially important to our strategy. It is difficult, if not impossible, to divide responsibility for specific levels of raw materials, work-in-process, or finished goods inventory between selling and manufacturing. Clearly the forecasts of marketing and the desires of manufacturing to smooth work force scheduling and to buy materials in economical quantities both affect inventory levels. Therefore, holding both responsible for their product line's inventory and charging them appropriately should motivate both to coordinate and to optimize the levels of inventory carried.

I don't believe we should deduct current liabilities from these current assets as some companies do because neither the marketing nor the manufacturing managers have anything to say about the amount of short-term bank loans we take out, or the promptness with which bills are paid; these are corporate decisions that I make. If current liabilities were deducted, managers would be encouraged to increase current liabilities because this decreases their asset base.

A capital charge would also be applied to the book value of any fixed assets used, of course. The extraordinary wrinkle I hope to introduce, however, is the application of annuity (i.e., implicit interest) depreciation. If we were to use either straight-line or accelerated depreciation, investment costs would decline over time simply by the fact that it was being reduced by depreciation. Annuity depreciation overcomes this deficiency by deducting an amount sufficient to maintain a constant rate of return over the life of the asset. I know you fellows aren't interested in specific details, but if you are, they can be found in almost any accounting book. I'll be happy to lend you one.

Under my proposed system, capital charges would be applied against all assets. The rate would vary each year and would be specified by my office. I would communicate it to all interested parties at the beginning of the fiscal year and they would use it during that period.

Benson Brillo, the director of marketing, replied. "It sounds awfully complicated to me. Just what are you after, Howard?"

EXPECTED BENEFITS

"I know you marketers can't understand what appears to be complex financial calculations," Howard smiled.

But, by and large, this is really a simple straightforward system that will modify behavior in this organization. There is no greater incentive than an effective financial control. Here is what my system will buy us.

1. It will improve performance measurement. At present, we don't measure the performance of any of our managers in a way that matches the reasoning process by which we acquire assets. Conceptually at least, my system solves this problem by holding each manager accountable for the assets he employs in a manner which approximates the way we want capital investment decisions to be made.

2. We're about to develop a new low-priced product line. My system would result in different product prices. Our current system calculates prices on the basis of a percentage markup over manufacturing costs. Prices under the proposed system will include an allowance for a return on the assets employed in each and every product line. Furthermore, because cost will now be based on annuity depreciation, prices will tend to be more even from year to year thus avoiding the error of reducing prices when, for example, machinery is fully depreciated.

3. Under our present system of measuring performance, managers can either purchase or lease assets and we have little way of influencing what they do. However, moving to a return on investment system carries with it the tendency to lease to an excessive amount because the implicit interest in a long term noncancellable lease is less than our current ROI. The capital charge system I propose both holds each manager responsible for his assets and avoids the tendency to acquire leased assets when in fact purchasing is far more economical.

REACTION TO THE PROPOSAL

"That's quite a proposal, Howard," said Benson Brillo. "You must have been working on it for months."

> I guess you fellows don't quite understand all the intricacies of the system, so I will write it up in detailed form, work out some numerical examples, and distribute it to you. Just trust me. This is the first step toward making our managers more responsive to the investment they use and also moves us toward developing an effective capital expenditure analysis system.

They all shook their heads in disbelief.

"We will reserve judgment on your system until we see your detailed write up, Howard," said Mr. Willis. "Now, does anyone else have any suggestions?"

Questions

1. What is your evaluation of Howard Samuels' proposal?
2. What is your evaluation of the way he chose to introduce his desired changes?

part four

Organizational considerations

Chapter outline

Three staff groups that influence system design
  The planner
    Scope and objectives
    Organization of the planning department
    Career path of the planner
  The controller
    Scope and objectives
    Organization of the controller's department
    Career path of the controller
  The manager of management information systems (MIS)
    Scope and objectives
    Organization of the information processing department
    Career path of the MIS manager
Interrelationships among the three groups
Alternative organizational relationships
  Alternative roles for the planner
  Alternative roles for the controller
Other determinants of staff roles

10

Staff roles and organizational relationships

When you have finished this chapter you should understand:

1. The scope and objectives of the planning, controller's, and management information systems (MIS) departments.
2. The roles these three departments may play in planning and control system design.
3. The potential for cooperation and conflict among these three groups, and the organizational design issues that have to be resolved.
4. The personal and organizational factors that determine the roles of the planner and the controller.

THREE STAFF GROUPS THAT INFLUENCE SYSTEM DESIGN

This chapter examines the influences that three staff groups may have on planning and control system design, and how their specialized skills can be integrated and managed.

The planning and control system used by line managers is dependent on several staff specialist groups. Even if responsibility for improving the information used for decision making rests with line managers themselves, the design, implementation, and adaptation of formal information systems requires the expertise of these staff groups. Specialists combine an understanding of management with the technical knowledge of existing systems. They are abreast of recent changes in management techniques and control procedures and are aware of the available technology; they also possess the system design and implementation skills necessary to harness this information. In short, staff specialists possess the perspective and the skills for diagnosis and implementation needed to improve administrative systems. Thus their role in planning and control system design and improvement must be considered by the system designer.

The staff executives most commonly associated with planning and control systems are the corporate planner, the manager of management information systems (MIS), and the corporate controller. The staff groups that report to these three executives are concerned with long-range strategic planning, computer-based systems, and financial planning and control, respectively. Each staff executive attempts to determine management requirements and match the capabilities of his or her group to these needs. Each group devises its own strategy to accomplish its objectives. And, like all planning and control system considerations, the most appropriate strategy and the contributions that each of these staff services can make to any organization are situational. The role that these groups can or should play cannot be prescribed universally, but must be specified after an examination of the executives involved and of the situation in which they are operating.

Appropriate specification of the organizational roles and relationships of these three groups is critical to the success of the planning and control system. Since any organization has only limited resources to devote to improving its administrative effectiveness, these resources must be allocated where they contribute most. It is hoped that an understanding of the potential for conflict and cooperation among these three groups will help achieve a synergistic effect and will avoid the dysfunctional consequences of conflict.

In order to understand the role that each of these staff functions can, should, or wants to play, it is necessary to examine the followng aspects of each one: (1) the objectives and scope of the group, (2) the subfunctions that comprise it, and (3) the typical background and career path of the executives concerned.

The planner

Scope and objectives. The basic functions of the corporate planning department may include providing corporatewide policy, direction, coordination, follow-up, and assessment of any or all organizational planning activities. Among the possible activities of a corporate planning staff are:

1. Participating actively in the formulation of corporate objectives, strategies, and plans.
2. Directing the annual strategic review to ensure that corporate orientation is consistent with basic goals and objectives.
3. Providing information about customers and competitors.

4. Developing, monitoring, and revising the organzation's planning system.
5. Investigating the sociotechnological environment, and formulating assumptions and making forecasts.
6. Issuing the annual calendar of events for corporate planning.
7. Consolidating and editing plans.
8. Evaluating the plans of operating management.
9. Monitoring performance against plan.
10. Identifying opportunities for internal improvement.
11. Serving as idea sources for the chief executive officer and other members of top management.
12. Educating management about planning and planning techniques and problems.
13. Sales or market forecasting.
14. Identifying needs or opportunities for mergers, acquisitions, joint ventures, or divestments.
15. Conducting negotiations for acquisitions or divestments.
16. Serving on management committees.
17. Developing and maintaining computer-based models.

These diverse activities can be grouped broadly into three areas in which the corporate planning department can have a role.

The first possible role is as confidant, adviser, honest broker, sounding board, and catalyst. In this role the corporate planner and his or her department maintain a low profile. Their responsibilities are to ensure that planning is carried out, that the most appropriate planning methods are used, and that the planning system operates effectively. The planner collects, consolidates, coordinates, and communicates information between line managers up and down the hierarchy to ensure that effective planning takes place. His or her role is to structure the planning procedure, set up the timetable for submissions, implement new planning techniques when appropriate, and help managers to master them. In this role the planner takes no part in decision making himself; but as an independent middleman, trusted by all, bridges communication gaps between managers. He is a facilitator.

A second role is that of adviser to top management on internal affairs. In this role the planner serves as consultant on matters with which top management should be concerned. He or she may be a source for the environmental information needed by top management, but also analyzes and presents information on internal problems that may appear; e.g., by communicating regularly with investment center managers. The planner may evaluate plans as they are being formulated and take an active role in deciding what must be done. In this latter role the planner is treated like an outside expert brought in for an independent, objective view.

Although nominally a staff executive, in this role the planner functions in fact as a member of top management and will, of course, be so regarded by line managers. The planner's task is to determine the appropriate course of action and then to convey his or her ideas to management. This role is especially appropriate if the planner possesses the specialized expertise needed to answer the questions confronting the organization at this particular point in time.

A third possible role for a planner is as a consultant for mergers and divestments. The planner may function as if he or she were an independent consultant hired to advise management on matters other than ongoing activities. He or she may seek out new acquisitions and divestments, recommend the actions to be taken, and then negotiate any or all of the details.

These three roles are not completely compatible, and no one planner should attempt to fill all of them. The planner may play roles two and three simultaneously, since both require him or her to be an active decision maker who functions as part of top management, seeking the best courses for the organization to follow. Or the planner may simultaneously perform roles one and three. These are also compatible; the first is that of a passive facilitator of internal activities, and the third is that of an active, participatory adviser on external affairs. However, one planner should not attempt to perform both roles one and two, as these involve irreconcilable differences. It is difficult to conceive of a planner who on one hand can act as a sounding board and adviser privy to troubling concerns, and also as an evaluator of managerial performance.

Organization of the planning department. The organization of the planning department (better called the planning services department if no substantive planning is carried out) depends on what services are provided by the group: whether these are to teach, guide, and facilitate the organizational planning process, or to actively participate in planning, adding substance to either internal or external decision making. Planning departments responsible for corporate economics and macroeconomic forecasts will contain economists, econometricians, and perhaps computer specialists. If the planner plays a role in coordination and communication of plans, an administrative staff is necessary. And if environmental assumptions are communicated formally throughout the organization, the corporate planner may conduct the environmental surveillance and collection of this information. In some organizations, where the controller's role is restricted to accounting matters, the responsibility for budgets falls within the corporate planning department. In general, active planners who are substantive decision makers report to line executives, while those who are passive facilitators perform as staff functions. The planner may report directly to the president and hold the rank of general manager or vice president, or he or she may be subordinated to one of the line or staff vice presidents. There is no common organizational position for this department and its particular reporting relationship follows from the function it performs.

Career path of the planner. A survey carried out by the Conference Board (Brown, and O'Connor, 1974) reveals the following information about corporate planning directors: 81 percent of their sample were previously employed in another capacity by their firm; 80 percent held one or more advance degrees and 44 percent of these were MBAs; median compensation was in the $50,000–$60,000 range. The study also revealed what a recent creation the position of corporate planning director is. Of the 111 respondents, 63 indicated that they were the first incumbent and 34 percent of the remainder had but a single predecessor (p. 1). Because of the lack of data, any discussion of the career path of the corporate planner is premature. However, it appears that the majority of corporate planners go on to another function within their organization, such as supervision of a line department.

The controller

Scope and objectives. Most organizations divide the financial management functions between two executives, the controller and the treasurer. The functions of the treasurer have to do more with the acquisition and disposition of financial resources than with the planning and control of those resources. The functions of a treasurer are as follows:

1. To establish and execute programs to acquire the capital required by the business.
2. To establish and maintain an adequate market for the company's securities.
3. To maintain liaison with investment bankers, financial analysts, and shareholders.
4. To maintain adequate sources for short-term capital from banks and other institutions.
5. To maintain banking arrangements; to receive, take custody of, and disburse company money and securities and to handle the financial aspects of real estate transactions.
6. To direct the granting of credit and the collection of accounts due.
7. To invest the company's funds as required and to establish and coordinate policies for the investment of pension and trust monies.
8. To provide insurance coverage as required.

The traditional function of the controller is to manage the financial information system of the organization. The controller manages the record keeping and reporting system that supports financial accounting, cost accounting, budgeting, profit planning, capital expenditure analysis, and so forth. He or she ensures that the defined areas of financial responsibility are properly structured and that control is exercised through management by exception. The most important functions of a controller are the following:

1. To establish, coordinate, and administer systems for planning and controlling financial operations.
2. To formulate accounting policies and procedures, and systems to prepare operating data; to prepare special reports; to compare performance with plans and standards; and to report and interpret the results of operations to all levels of management.
3. To consult with management on any phase of operations as it relates to organizational objectives, and to advise on the effectiveness of organizational structure and procedures.
4. To establish and administer systematic tax policies and procedures.
5. To supervise and coordinate the preparation of reports for governmental agencies.
6. To ensure the protection of assets by appropriate internal controls and internal auditing.
7. To continuously appraise economic and social forces and governmental influences, and to interpret their effects on the business.

It is clear from the above list that the controller is usually conversant with every significant detail of the business, including the pricing of products, operation of markets, and characteristics of manufacturing. In fact, any concern of top management is a concern of the controller. Perhaps the greatest contribution a controller makes to an organization is his or her independent objective business judgment. As a member of a top-management team, not burdened with operational responsibilities, the controller can provide both the objectivity and the perspective needed to give sound business advice to operating managers caught up in day-to-day affairs. The controller is the most profit conscious of all executives in a company and his or her objective outlook can spotlight any and every aspect of the business that could profit from improvement.

Organization of the controller's department. Because controllership is a more traditional function than planning, the organization of the controller's department tends to be more uniform from company to company. Again, however, structure is a result of function. Subgroups responsible for financial accounting, cost accounting, taxation, budgets and forecasts, and internal audits are among the more common parts of a controller's staff. Units performing operations analysis, pricing analysis, capital budgeting, and project analysis are not uncommon, nor are sub-departments concerned with organization and methods or work improvement. Traditionally, the computer department has reported to the controller because he or she has usually been the heaviest user of information processing technology. In many organizations the computer department still reports to the controller. In larger organizations the controller and the treasurer are on an equal organizational level, both possibly reporting to a vice president of finance.

Career path of the controller. The controller is usually a professional accountant who has spent his or her whole career in some aspect of finance. Many controllers began as auditors with public accounting firms and later decided to join their clients' organizations. Others began as analysts or accountants and rose through the finance function to their present position. Rarely are nonfinancially trained executives appointed controllers because of the specialized knowledge that is needed of financial accounting systems and of taxation and auditing. Many organizations choose financial executives as presidents; the auto industry has a history of financially trained chief executive officers.

The manager of management information systems (MIS)

Scope and objectives. The scope of the computer-based information systems effort in an organization can be considered at two levels. The first is the level of routine data processing, the electronic processing of transactions normally involved in day-to-day operations. The design and implementation of data processing systems involves an analysis of the requirements that the system must meet and the design of an efficient way to meet these requirements, using the most appropriate computer technology. Routine data processing systems can be likened to any physical production process. They are intended to process large quantities of data to meet specified requirements at minimum cost. Routine data processing systems include the processing of payroll checks, invoices and accounts payable, accounts receivable, sales transactions, collection and recording of credit, point of sale devices, and so on. These data are required if business is to be carried out and government and accounting reporting requirements are to be met. The objective of the information system department is to perform the necessary functions at minimum cost.

In many organizations the computerization of routine data processing is now nearing completion, and attention is turning to a second phase, the development of information systems for management. This has been attempted in several ways. In some organizations, data from existing systems has been structured into a data base and made accessible to management through appropriate retrieval languages. Armed with such a system, a manager can interrogate the available data by posing queries such as "How many sales have we made in territory X?" or probe the extent to which certain types of customers have made repeated purchases. Another approach to the development of management information systems is to isolate and formalize the models used by decision makers and then to implement these models through interactive terminal-based information systems. Once a decision is structured as a model and data are incorporated, a decision maker can ask "what if" questions, such as: "If advertising is increased, will sales increase, and in what proportion?" "If we cut back on the sales force, will it have an effect on our product sales distribution?"

Third, the development of an information system may simply mean that reports are structured more to the liking of management and that feedback is provided more frequently so that managers can have the information they need when they need it, in the proper format. The overall aim of management information systems is to provide managers with the information they need to make better decisions.

In sum, it has become widely recognized that information is a resource that must be managed to improve organizational effectiveness. Over time, the role of computer-based information systems has evolved from the economical processing of transaction data to the provision of information for better management decision making. Thus managers of information processing resources must now utilize their technological expertise and knowledge of systems analysis to provide more and better information in order to improve organizational effectiveness.

Organization of the information processing department. In its simplest form, a computer system department is divided into three subunits. At the heart of the function is the computer data center where the data input, editing, machine processing, and output take place. The second subunit is the systems analysis function. For various client groups, analysts determine the requirements and feasibility of implementing a computerized system; they then prepare a set of specifications describing the requirements that the system must satisfy and an outline of the design to be programmed by the programming unit. Computer programming may be located within the same subunit as systems analysis, or it may be a separate unit. The third group provides the systems and software support. The computer systems department may also include a technical specialist responsible for internal consulting to the programming unit, and an individual who surveys available study courses and provides training for the technical specialties. There may also be a subunit whose function is to analyze new, improved equipment to determine whether additional machinery should be acquired.

Because it is closely associated with computing, the operations research or management science group of an organization may be included as a separate operating subunit within this function. The purpose of this group of analysts is to uncover situations that lend themselves to mathe-matical modeling and to implement these models on the computer either for one-shot solutions or for continuous utilization. The services provided by these analysts are potentially useful to all members of management.

Career path of the MIS manager. While there are few research data to verify any claims, it is believed that the majority of information sys-tems executives are computer professionals who have spent the majority of their careers within the computer information systems function. In general, they are knowledgeable about the technology and administra-tion of computer-related tasks such as systems design and programming. Some organizations use this position as one step in the rotational career training program of functional executives who are being prepared for senior general management positions, but this practice is still rare. If he or she is a computer professional, the manager of the information systems function can be expected to remain within this function throughout his or her career.

INTERRELATIONSHIPS AMONG THE THREE GROUPS

Each of the three staff groups discussed above, at least as part of its function, is responsible for developing and implementing information systems and analytical methods that will improve the management process. The planning services group is most concerned with ensuring that the organization anticipates change and realizes the benefits of bet-ter plans, as well as the behavioral benefits of planning as a managerial discipline. The controller develops and expresses plans in financial terms (e.g., financial forecasts, budgets, cash flows) to ensure coordination, communication, and the development of a common orientation among management, and also ensures that resources are allocated efficiently and that performance expectations are realized. The computer systems group sees to the efficient processing of routine transactional data as a service to such other organizational functions as accounting, and also uses the appropriate technology to provide better information to both line and staff decision makers.

Each staff group needs to have good relations with line management if it is to help organizational effectiveness and efficiency. Each must have the support of top management if its expertise is to be recognized and taken seriously. And each must relate to other staff groups, especially to each other, if they are to achieve their somewhat overlapping objectives. These general requirements are common to all organizations; but beyond these generalizations it is impossible to prescribe universally acceptable roles and relationships for these three groups. The specific role of each staff group will be determined by the characteristics of the situation in which it must operate and by the personalities of the participants. One important task of the planning and control system designer is therefore to understand the particular contribution that can be made by each staff group and, if possible, to specify the most appropriate organizational configuration.

The organizational position and relationships of these three staff groups should balance strengths with weaknesses, independence with interdependence, and cooperation with competition, so that each will contribute its expertise without imposing an overly narrow outlook on planning and control. Some of the decisions that have to be made are expressed in the following three groups of questions. The answers will depend on the specific problems faced by the organization, the services required from each staff group, the constraints on providing these services, and, ultimately, on the best means of satisfying the organization's requirements.

1. Should the three staff groups be independent of one another or organizationally interdependent, so that one reports to another?

The distinction between the controller's and the treasurer's function is clear. The treasurer secures funds and deals with economic events external to the corporation. The controller, on the other hand, makes the financial decisions and exercises control within organizational boundaries. The controller's mandate is to scrutinize all activities involving money and to act as deemed appropriate for his or her role. Therefore, usually the two are equal functions which both report to a senior executive, often the president or vice president of finance.

At present, the organizational relationship between the computer systems function and the users of their output varies considerably among companies. Traditionally the computer systems function reported to the controller because he was the greatest user of its services. Now the information processed by computers can be either financial or operational, pertain to the past or the future, or originate within the organization or outside it. It can involve financial decision making or labor force planning as well as the routine processing of day-to-day transactions. Therefore, the computer systems department's reporting relationships depend on the function it performs. If this is to provide better information for managers, it is often either an independent unit reporting to someone of presidential rank, or else is under the direction of its own vice president. Alternatively, the controller may retain authority over the information systems function when it is believed that this relationship does not limit its ability to serve other users as well.

The reporting relationship of the corporate planning services department is also determined by the requirements that this group must satisfy. Its position depends on whether it is to be oriented toward the problems of the external environment or to be involved in financial planning. The relationship between the controller and the planning services group is largely determined by the extent to which the latter merely supplements ongoing financial planning with its interpretation of external issues, as opposed to carrying out more extensive environmental scanning.

2. *Should each staff function be centralized in a single unit, or should it be decentralized and distributed throughout the whole organization, working within individual line groups?*

Many of the arguments for and against decentralization, as described earlier in this text, apply equally to the issue of decentralizing these staff functions. It is especially important to recognize the nature of the services provided by these groups. Each offers a largely intangible product—better information for management. But information is an integral part of each step in the management process, regardless of which process model of management is used. Hence these staff groups must provide information that is uniquely tailored to the requirements of each user.

If these staff groups are to have an impact on an organization, their advice must be fully accepted and implemented by line managers. If the staff groups are perceived as outsiders with no bona fide right or ability to assist line managers, then there will be little improvement in planning and control processes. For this reason, staff analysts are often made part of line groups and line managers are appointed leaders of project teams to change planning and control systems. The purpose of these appointments are to overcome resistance to change and to integrate line and staff functions.

The question of the extent to which staff services should be decentralized is highly complex. If cooperative involvement and quick acceptance are crucial to success, then decentralization may be required. But if economies of scale must be considered, as when the same function is being duplicated in several locations, then centralization may be more appropriate. The strengths and weaknesses of each alternative must be compared before an effective decision can be reached. Like all aspects of planning and control systems, the choice is situationally determined.

3. *Should each staff function be actively involved with the line managers they serve, or should they assume a passive role?*

Perhaps the most critical decision about the role of each staff function is to determine whether it should take an active or a passive role. Should the corporate planning services department or controller's group act as adviser, catalyst, coordinator, and teacher, or should it act as evaluator, judge, and de facto part of top management? Should it provide information and analysis to line management and then allow line managers to make decisions themselves, or should it take an active part in making specific decisions? Should the controller have authority to overrule a line manager on a decision; should both the line manager and the controller submit reports to top management for decisions; or should they be forced to reach a decision between themselves? Should management information systems analysts set out to design systems that can provide better information to management? Should they actively sell new ideas, or should they merely respond to requests by line managers? Should the staff groups be innovative or should the responsibility for innovation rest with the line managers themselves? These are perplexing questions, some of which are addressed in the next section.

ALTERNATIVE ORGANIZATIONAL RELATIONSHIPS

Alternative roles for the planner

The locus of planning is an especially contentious issue in many organizations. The unexpected events and miscalculations of recent years have caused many people to question whether organizations do, in fact, require the assistance of specialized individuals called planners in making substantive decisions to cope with the demands of the future. The alternative is to define the planner's role as a passive one, as a source of planning services only, and to keep substantive planning in the hands of the operating managers responsible for its implementation. This choice usually improves the likelihood that implementation will be smooth and consistent and lessens the problems of coordination and communication. Since participation is often an excellent means of improving motivation, one way to ensure ready acceptance of plans and objectives is to let the line managers participate in planning. The planning services adviser merely provides the procedures to carry out planning and acts as a catalyst and teacher to ensure that this is done effectively. The actual planning and decisions are the responsibility of the operating managers.

Both active and passive planning roles have strengths and weaknesses. Planning is the means by which an organization influences and adapts to its environment. Integrating planning with implementation and control and increasing the motivation of operating managers are, of course, important; but they are no more (or less) essential than ensuring that the right things are done.

External environments are becoming increasingly complex, changeable, and uncertain. As the influences of government, consumers, and domestic and foreign competition become more important, the ability to forecast, understand, and act is an organization's only assurance of survival. These abilities do not necessarily require a specialized apprenticeship in any particular industry; nor do they necessarily require a detailed knowledge of today's events. In many cases future success depends on the discovery of new opportunities; e.g., finding foreign markets or applying existing corporate resources and know-how to new fields. Success may demand immersion in volumes of published statistics, financial analyses of competitors, or the selection and use of market research techniques. The planner may have to be able to step back from the immediacy of ongoing activities in order to generate the imaginative and creative solutions that will be required for the 1980s and 1990s, and for the year 2000.

If an organization chooses to entrust the task of planning to operating management, responsibility for the company's future is in the hands of those whose skills relate to today's operations and who are committed to the status quo. Bottom-up planning by line managers brings involvement and motivation, and a greater likelihood that the plans will be effectively carried out. On the other hand, a more top-down approach, by the specialization of corporate planning in a small staff group that is detached from everyday activities, can generate the perspective and creativity needed to arrive at the answers most appropriate for a changing world. But this approach, in turn, divorces those responsible for planning from those who must ultimately execute those plans, and a way must be found to integrate the processes of planning and implementation.

The need for specialization, detachment, creativity, and innovation on the one hand, and the need for coordination, acceptance, and motivation on the other, is the trade-off to be resolved in decisions about the role of the planning department and the balance between line and staff contributions.

Alternative roles for the controller

A similar trade-off is required to specify the role of the controller. The controller may be part of either operating management or top management, or he or she may attempt to act as an independent staff function, providing information as needed and taking no active role in management. If controllers choose to be members of the line management team, they will work closely with them, offering their advice and skill for everyday analysis. In this function controllers stand to be evaluated relative to overall organizational performance and share the risks of the decisions that are reached. On the other hand, controllers may choose to define themselves not as an adviser to line management but as a member of top management, and therefore as evaluators of operating management's performance. As evaluators, the controllers familiarize themselves with every activity of the organization that requires money, ensure that resources are allocated efficiently and effectively, and report to top management on any area that could be improved. They attempt to influence the decision making of top management. In this latter role, a controller is perhaps an adversary of line management.

Role conflict is especially likely in divisionalized organizations where a divisional controller has to balance two roles. On the one hand the controller is responsible in a line relationship to the general manager of his or her division and is part of the division's management team and will be evaluated on its performance. On the other hand, since the career path of a divisional controller is usually within the finance function of the overall organization, his or her first loyalty may well be to the corporate controller, on whom his or her future career opportunities depend.

OTHER DETERMINANTS OF STAFF ROLES

The roles and reporting relationships of these staff groups depend on the characteristics and current activities of each organization. An organization's fiscal health, its traditional industry activities, and its structure may influence these roles. Mature organizations that are comfortable with their ongoing activities may have a far greater need for coordination and motivation than for innovation and disruptive change. Industries that are sophisticated, competitive, and highly technical may require a planner who is attuned to the changing market and aware of new trends. A major source of innovation in such an organization may be its research and development activities, and the integration of these activities with marketing planning may be a major factor in organizational success. The corporate planner may have to achieve this integration, especially if product managers are more involved in ongoing activities than in new product introduction. And of course, the nature of a firm's differentiation and decentralization will influence role requirements. Firms organized by product will require localized information systems oriented to product profitability, whereas planning on a functional basis requires integration and coordination among functions.

Another consideration is the management style of the chief executive officer. A chief executive officer who plays a very active role in setting the policy of the organization and who likes to make decisions himself may require a different mix of staff assistance than one who prefers to play a passive role, orchestrating and motivating his subordinates and exerting only a subtle influence on organizational direction.

Perhaps the most important determinant of the role of each staff group is the personality of the individual who heads it. The role of his group will depend to a great extent on his own analytical and interpersonal skills and ambitions. Forceful, articulate individuals, especially those with strong analytical ability and motivation, may define their role far differently than others who are shy and retiring, or not as ambitious. Some executives (risk averters, for example) will prefer the safety of a staff role in which they act only as advisers, without responsibility for actual organizational performance. Others will attempt to participate to the maximum extent possible as part of the organization's management team. And there are an infinite number of positions between these two extremes. Because these factors, like all determinants of any planning and control system, will vary from situation to situation, universal prescriptions are impossible to make.

SUMMARY

The planner, controller, and manager of computer-based information systems play significant roles in the design, implementation, and adaptation of a planning and control system. Although these three functions share common organizational objectives, their differences in scope of operations, capabilities, and career paths may lead to conflicts that can threaten successful implementation and operation of systems. Hence, the specification of appropriate roles, interrelationships, and degree of decentralization of these groups is a necessary task of the system designer.

A corporate planner may serve as an honest broker, catalyst, adviser to top management, internal consultant, or active planner. While many of these roles are internally consistent, the two roles of evaluator of plans and of participant in the preparation of plans are mutually incompatible. The responsibility of the manager of information systems includes both the economical processsing of day-to-day transaction data and also the development of better information systems for management decision making. And although the controller's functions are clearly differentiated from those of the treasurer, they may often overlap with those of the corporate planner and the information systems manager.

The potential range of activity of each staff group was described by three parameters: the extent to which its role is active or passive; whether the staff groups are independent or interdependent on each other; and whether the group is centralized or decentralized.

The role each group should play is determined by the analytical abilities, ambitions, and interpersonal skills of the executives concerned, the needs of the organization, and the operating style of the chief executive officer.

It was concluded that the role and organizational relationships of these three staff groups can only be specified situationally.

QUESTIONS

1. Who is ultimately responsible for the design and modification of an organization's planning and control system? How should this responsibility be subdivided?
2. Will the designer of a planning and control system usually also have the authority to specify staff roles and organizational relationships?
3. Can a staff group balance active participation in performance evaluation

with coaching and facilitation so that both roles are performed successfully?

4. Is a separate planning department necessary in a small organization?
5. What role would each of the three groups have in carrying out the nine-step process model described in Chapters 2 and 3?
6. What is an organization's formal information system? Who manages it?
7. What impact will future changes in information technology have on planning and control systems?
8. What role, if any, does the personnel department have in planning and control system design and/or operation?

REFERENCES AND BIBLIOGRAPHY

Adelberg, Arthur H. Management information systems and their implications. *Management Accounting (U.K.)*, October 1975, pp. 328–30.

Bacon, J. *Managing the Budget Function.* New York: National Industrial Conference Board, 1970.

Boulen, James B., and McLean, Ephraim R. An executive's guide to computer-based planning. *California Management Review,* Fall 1974, pp. 58–67.

Brown, J. K., and O'Connor, R. *Planning and the Corporate Planning Director.* New York: Conference Board, 1974.

Cleland, David I., and King, Willliam R. Organizing for long-range planning. *Business Horizons,* August 1974, pp. 25–32.

Feigenbaum, Donald S. Effective systems improve control. *Journal of Systems Management,* November 1974, pp. 7–11.

Gulley, David A., and Kane, William G. The planner's computer. *Datamation,* May 1974, pp. 64–70.

Hammond, John S., III. Do's and don'ts of computer models for planning. *Harvard Business Review,* March–April 1974, pp. 110–123.

Higgins, J. C. Corporate planning and management science. *Journal of General Management,* Spring 1972, pp. 61–65.

Hodge, Bartow. The computer in management information and control systems. *Data Management,* December 1974, pp. 26–33.

Judd, Frank. Organizing for forward motion. *Management Accounting,* April 1974, pp. 23–24.

Kriebel, C. H. The strategic dimension of computer systems planning. *Long-Range Planning,* September 1968, pp. 7–12.

Litschert, R. H. Some characteristics of organization for long-range planning. *Academy of Management Journal,* 1967, pp. 247–56.

Lorange, Peter. The planner's dual role—A survey of U.S. companies. *Long-Range Planning,* March 1973, pp. 52–58.

Meador, Charles L. Decision support systems: An application to corporate planning. *Sloan Management Review,* Winter 1974, pp. 51–68.

Mintzberg, Henry. Making management information useful. *AMACOM: Management Review,* May 1975, pp. 34–38.

Ramsden, Pamela. *Top Team Planning.* New York: Halstead, 1973.

Ransdell, William K. Managing the people who manage the computer. *Journal of Systems Management,* September 1975, pp. 18–21.

Rucker, L. Using computer models for short- and long-range planning: A case study. *The Business Quarterly,* Autumn 1969, pp. 29–37.

Simon, H. A.; Guetzkow, H.; Kozmetsky, G.; and Tyndall, G. *Centralization vs. Decentralization in Organizing the Controller's Department.* New York: Controllership Foundation, 1954.

Steiner, George A. The critical role of management in long-range planning. *Arizona Review,* April 1966, pp. 15–17.

Wilkinson, Joseph W. Specifying management's information needs. *Cost and Management,* September–October 1974, pp. 7–13.

Wilson, A. C. B. Human and organizational problems in corporate planning. *Long-Range Planning,* March 1972, pp. 67–72.

Case study 10–1

Universal Tool and Appliances

Many of the unexpected events of the 1970s caused the president of Universal Tool and Appliances to wonder whether the firm needed more long-term planning in general and a corporate planner in particular. Declines in energy availability and the conservation philosophy, accompanied by questioning of the need for certain "luxury" appliances were unsettling factors. The intense competition in the industry, the miniscule barriers to entry, the dynamic changes taking place in consumer tastes, the rate of technological innovation, the high cost of money, and the tremendous risks of new product introductions all disturbed him considerably. Perhaps, he thought, it was time to bring in someone from the outside with past experience in consumer goods and with the perspective to evaluate what UT&A was currently attempting to do and help them change course if necessary.

BACKGROUND

Universal Tool and Appliances, formed out of the merger of Denver Appliance Corporation and the Standard Manufacturing Company in 1957, is a medium-sized manufacturer of small home appliances and electrical hand tools. Total sales in 1975 from their 22 product lines (see Table 1) were about $190 million of which 34 percent were foreign and 14 percent were to resellers as private label brands. The organization chart of UT&A is presented in Table 2. In 1973 the firm moved into its

TABLE 1
Product lines

Appliances	*Tools*
Drip percolators	Electric drills
Irons	Circular saws
Toasters and toaster ovens	Reciprocating saws
Blenders	Routers
Bun warmers	Electric planes
Serving trays	Sanders
Electric toothbrushes	Bench grinders
Fans	
Clocks	
Room air conditioners	
Frying pans	
Ice crushers	
Can openers	
Shoe polishers	
Electric knives	

TABLE 2
Organizational chart

Board of Directors
President

Vice presidents and reporting personnel
   Research, design and production engineering
   Manufacturing
      Manager of fabricating
      Manager of assembly
   Marketing and sales
      Product group managers
      Manager of sales
      Manager of exports
      Manager of advertising and promotion
      Manager of market research
   Personnel and industrial relations
   Controller
      Manager of computer operations
      Director of economics and budgets
      Director of internal auditing
      Assistant controller of accounting
      Assistant controller of administrative services
   Treasurer

new modern head office and manufacturing plant located in the Midwest. Recent figures on profitability and growth are presented in Table 3.

The management of UT&A attributes its success to its market orientation (strong market research to discover needs to be satisfied) which has made it a consistent leader in product innovation and to its being able to produce tools and appliances at the cost effectiveness equal to

TABLE 3
Operating performance

Year	Gross revenues ($ million)	Operating profit margin (percent)	Net income ($ million)	Average yield on common shares (percent)
1971	$101.0	18.2%	$ 9.2	2.7%
1972	119.6	18.4	11.4	2.4
1973	146.8	18.3	13.3	2.5
1974	168.6	18.1	14.8	2.0
1975	189.7	18.3	15.8	1.8

any of its competitors. Elmo Jacobsen, the 63-year-old past founder of Denver, and now vice president of research, design and production engineering is the executive most responsible for this. A self-taught engineer, E. J. has a unique ability to take a set of functional specifications (i.e., what a product must do) and produce an aesthetically pleasing and economically manufacturable product to satisfy these needs. The XR–44 cordless electric toothbrush featuring the new oxide core self-charging battery is one of the best examples of this. This strength, combined with an efficient sales group, a reputation for reliable delivery dates, and sound after-sale service has made UT&A successful.

ORGANIZATION AND ADMINISTRATION

Although no longer a small organization, the firm has not had to change its functional organizational structure to meet the demands that growth, product proliferation, and diverse markets have placed on it. Five highly autonomous product group managers, reporting to the VP—marketing and sales, coordinate research and development, manufacturing, market research, and sales across organizational boundaries. The organization is sufficiently flexible to allow communication up, down, and across lines of authority. No executive is inaccessible to anyone who must communicate with him. Working breakfasts and lunches are the rule rather than the exception. In general any way to make doing business easier or more profitable is readily accepted.

Corporate goals are specified in terms of cost improvement expectations, profit increases and market share growth at the beginning of each profit budget period by the president, after consultation with his vice presidents. The one-year budget is then built up by product line beginning with next year's forecasted sales volume. Once sales volume by customer and product are specified, exploded bills of materials are established, production delivery and sales timing scheduled, and then these parameters are passed down to appropriate managers and supervisors. Revenue and expense budgets are approved successively until the final corporate profit budget is consolidated and presented to top management for approval. Biweekly performance reporting against this profit budget is then carried out for control.

The budgeting system, now modified and administered annually, by the director of economics and budgets, was designed and implemented by the VP and controller, Bert Whitacombe, the 38-year-old whiz kid MBA-accountant. Under his direction, budgeting was first introduced to UT&A ten years ago. Over that period the budgeting system has successfully changed the attitudes of the sales force away from maximization of sales alone, and the attitudes of manufacturing staff away from minimization of costs alone to a balanced viewpoint focused on profitability. All management is now focused on the profitability implications of any and all of their actions. The budgeting system is an exceptionally finely detailed responsibility accounting system capable of providing detailed management information for decision making. With its strong emphasis on cash flow analysis and inventory and labor control, the system is as sophisticated as any corporation is currently using. Plans to tie incentive compensation to budgeting performance are currently under consideration.

The development of computer-based management information systems, also under Bert's direction, is well in hand and should be completed within the next year when the redesign of all transaction processing systems will be completed to fit the recently installed IBM 370–145 computer. A larger computer was needed to satisfy the demands of the marketing, production, accounting and research managers in the firm. In fact, IBM is continually bringing visitors to UT&A to demonstrate the working of a successful integrated MIS. Product planning and scheduling, an integrated manufacturing and inventory system, automated requirements planning, and mathematical sales forecasting are some of the features up and running presently at UT&A.

STRATEGIC PLANNING

Strategic planning is the province of the product policy committee composed of the president, the VP of marketing and sales, the VP of research design and production, the VP and controller, and the five product group managers. The basis of this group's decisions is the strategic product life-cycle characteristics concept developed and promulgated by the McNally Consulting Group of Philadelphia. This approach combines learning curve theory, product life-cycle analysis, the notion of interaction among a portfolio of products, and the strategic implication of market share. In brief, the assumptions underlying this approach are as follows:

1. Production cost of products vary inversely with volume produced due to learning effects.

2. Because of this effect the product with the largest market share will enjoy the highest unit profit.

3. Product growth rates (rate of increase in market share) vary among products and different growth rates require different strategies regarding, for example, investment, cash management, staff requirements and necessary skills, competitive reactions, technological threats, and so on.

4. The potential market share left to be captured is an important key variable because it determines the upper limit on the potential profitability of a product.

In sum, strategic planning at UT&A means the explicit recognition that their 22 products really comprise a portfolio, each component of which may be at a different stage of its life cycle with different growth and market share potentials and hence which requires a different strategy and a different mix of resources. It is the management of this overall product portfolio that determines ultimate company success.

As part of the strategic planning process a life-cycle curve is prepared annually for each product in the UT&A portfolio (see Exhibit 1). Based

EXHIBIT 1
Strategic product life-cycle curve

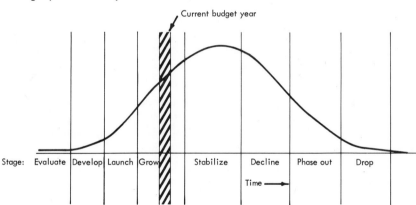

on this curve and on supplementary studies conducted as needed, the product policy committee makes the product decisions that will guide the firm's behavior in the next year.

HIRING THE CONSULTANTS

In January 1976, the president felt that some change was needed. He speculated that perhaps an outsider who could take an active part in guiding the organization by implementing his own fresh ideas would be a desirable input to the firm at this time. Accordingly, after a quick consultation with his VPs, he secured the services of McKinley and Co. to survey UT&A's needs, to advise them on the desirability of hiring a corporate planner, and the role and reporting relationships he should have within the firm.

THE CONSULTANT'S RECOMMENDATIONS

The management consultants completed their assignment and submitted their recommendations within three months. In the process of preparing their report they interviewed all the members of the upper three levels of management, reviewed current corporation plans, budgets and past performance, performed industry analysis, and reviewed all the relevant trade association documentation available. The consultants recommended the hiring of a corporate planner for UT&A. The summary of their report and the reasons they gave for this decision are presented in the Appendix.

THE DECISION

The meeting of the president and the VPs to discuss the consultants' recommendation revealed several significantly different opinions. The president was all in favor of it and suggested retaining the same consulting firm to conduct an executive search for suitable candidates. The VP—marketing and sales also thought it was a good idea to bring in someone with a fresh viewpoint. But he felt that the corporate planner should report to him since most of the planners efforts would relate to environmental change, his basic orientation. The VP—controller was against hiring someone from outside, however. He argued that the scope of the job description of his director of economics and budgets could be expanded to include formal environmental surveillance, the major deficiency in current practice that the consultant uncovered.

Elmo Jacobsen pointed out that the consultants' report made little reference to growth through diversification. He questioned the best way to check out this option and the relationship of this strategy to the planner's role. The VP—personnel questioned whether the need for a planner could perhaps be satisfied through a management committee. He felt that planning was line management's responsibility and injecting staff in this process only introduced delays, postponed the taking of hard decisions, and reduced management's commitment to implement the plans proposed. He then chuckled "Maybe we need a consultant to interpret the consultant's report."

Since the executives were unable to reach a consensus, the president decided to go ahead with the search for a suitable person in the belief that in the process of interviewing qualified candidates and in discussing the role of the corporate planner with them, each vice president would perhaps rethink his position and come around to the president's point of view.

Questions

1. What is the president's conception of the role of a corporate planner?
2. How did the other executives perceive this role?
3. Why do you think the president acted as he did? Do you agree with his actions?
4. Did the consultants earn their fee?

APPENDIX: CONSULTANTS' RECOMMENDATIONS

To the President of Universal Tool and Appliances:

The rate of change taking place in consumer attitudes, values, living habits, and economic well-being is creating very rapid change in product design and distribution techniques. As a result product managers are finding it more difficult to anticipate the events that pose major threats to future profits. Opportunities for significant new growth on a profitable basis are more difficult to find as markets change more rapidly and product life cycles become shorter.

This lack of understandability of the many variables in the market-place and technology and the inability to react to change quickly enough is generally believed to be one of the greatest threats to corporate profits and growth. It is no longer possible to rely on extrapolation of previous years' performance or on sales force estimates for future planning.

There is a growing evidence instead that sustained corporate renewal and growth is primarily achieved through the use of planned, integrated company strategies which capitalize on the opportunities found in future environmental change. In fact, it is almost a prerequisite to sustained success that management must anticipate and capitalize on change and not simply react to it. Therefore, we recommend that the new position of vice president—corporate planning, reporting directly to the president, be established to ensure that UT&A has this capability.

An organized strategic planning process provides the basis for devising ways to change the character of the corporation in terms of its products, manufacturing methods and markets. It results in the continual adjustment of corporate resources and capabilities in relation to the evolving customer needs.

The task of initiating and implementing strategic planning must lie with the president because the decisions needed are so broad in scope and crucial in nature that they affect the entire organization. However, as corporate institutions grow larger, and accumulate more and more levels between senior managers who determine strategies and consumers in the marketplace who respond, the gulf widens. As a result the task of successfully adjusting products and resources is more complex and carries greater risk of failure. Hence there is a definite need for strategic planning assistance to search out more effective ways to interrelate corporate efforts and market opportunities. And this situation is true for UT&A.

We recommend that the role of the strategic planning specialist include the performance of three basic tasks: (1) developing information about the firm and its environment; (2) evaluating alternative courses of action against stated objectives; and (3) assisting in making final strategic decisions. These three functions are detailed further below.

1. *Information leading to the creation of strategies.* One important part of strategic planning involves the comprehensive mobilization of relevant data about a company and its environment, past, present, and future. These data provide a valuable base from which to forecast environmental changes, assess the probable impact of these on the company, and plan the needed action to shape these trends. The role of a strategic planning specialist in this regard is to serve as a source for external communication to corporate management. He both provides a deliberate organized objective and consistent program of environmental surveillance encompassing sociological, demographic, political, and economic factors and also interprets the meaning of these events so as to clarify their implications for strategic action.

An important function of the corporate planner is then to use these data in the creation of new strategies for management's consideration.

2. *Evaluation and integration of strategies.* Armed with an awareness of the external environment the strategic planning specialist can identify gaps and inconsistencies in present plans and act as an early warning system for identifying plans which are off target. The results of these efforts should be strategies which are congruent with stakeholder expectations, the identification of how ongoing strategies are out of focus, and the development of long-range plans which make sense to the organization as a total entity. It should be noted however that qualitative aspects of planning and the assumptions underlying strategic actions are often much more important than quantitative factors. There may be a widespread temptation to allow numbers to dominate planning decisions and this is a tendency which must be constantly resisted.

3. *Play a supportive role to line management.* To be successful strategic planning must be an integral part of line management effort. The planning specialist can provide important assistance in this area by providing written materials to assist and guide those people within the

organization who are charged with developing corporate or divisional long-range plans and by assisting in guiding these people in the planning process through personal contact with them.

In sum, it is our opinion that the performance of these basic functions by an executive titled vice president—corporate planning reporting directly to the president would satisfy the strategic needs of Universal Tool and Appliances.

Chapter outline

Perspective and orientation
  Process models
  Assumptions
Systematic procedure for systems design/adaptation
    Express assumed relationships explicitly
    Normative systems
Selection of appropriate tools and techniques
Guidelines for successful implementation

11

Summary

The purpose of this book has been to familiarize the reader with the role, problems, and various ramifications of management planning and control systems, in order to show him or her ways to successfully design, adapt, and implement these systems. It is hoped that the text has given the reader a frame of reference and a design/adaptation procedure comfortable to him or her, and that the reader has been able to test and validate the usefulness of these procedures by analyzing the case studies presented. This final chapter will review and summarize the text material with reference to the objectives that were set out in the preface. These objectives were: (1) to provide the reader with the perspective and orientation needed to conceptualize planning and control system design and adaptation; (2) to describe a systematic diagnostic procedure that can be used to design and/or evaluate situationally determined management and control systems; and (3) to familiarize the reader with some of the tools and techniques that make up a planning and control system. To these three objectives a fourth somewhat implicit but equally important objective can now be added: (4) to convey to the system designer a guiding philosophy of implementation that will help him to effectively put to work the system design principles he has learned.

PERSPECTIVE AND ORIENTATION

The first intention of this text has been to provide the perspective and orientation needed to come to grips with the complex problem of designing or adapting a planning and control system for any given situation. To this end two general process models of planning and control were presented, along with three assumptions that underlie their application to specific situations.

Process models

Any process model of planning and control outlines the steps to be followed in performing these activities. Because the amount of planning and control carried out by any organization is vast, a multicycle model is needed to describe the way an organization plans and controls. A multicycle model details a succession of stages or cycles, starting with the most general plans in the upper echelons of the organization and concluding with specific plans at the lowest levels. Each of the cycles in a multicycle hierarchical sequence is essentially similar in process but different in its scope of inputs and outputs and in the degree of structure of the activities it includes. The seven-step single-cycle model presented in Chapter 1 is a useful way of describing what must take place in each of these cycles. The three-cycle model developed in Chapters 2 and 3 is one example of a multicycle process description.

In a multicycle process the output of one cycle becomes the input to the next. Each cycle successively narrows the range of possible behaviors until a single set of actions can be specified. The successive cycles answer questions such as: (1) What is our strategic mission and what are we trying to do in the long run? (2) How shall we develop programs and allocate our resources to these programs so as to accomplish our mission? (3) How can we best motivate, guide, and evaluate individual performance?

A multicycle hierarchical planning and control process model is simply a description of a set of linked cycles whose function is to help decompose and find solutions for the complex problem of how an organization may influence and/or adapt to its environment.

The model presented in Chapters 2 and 3 is applicable to many organizations. The first cycle of the model is strategic planning. Strategic planning involves enumerating the stakeholder expectations which influence the formulation of the organization's strategic mission. The interaction of stakeholder expectations with the organization's environmental opportunities and threats, current capabilities and resources, and past performance results in a basis for specification of the plan. The output of this cycle is a strategic plan of what the organization hopes to accomplish and the reasons it believes it can do so, as well as a set of key strategic variables that will guide subsequent planning.

The second cycle involves program planning and resource allocation. This process begins by generating and expressing ideas in terms of projects or programs. In this cycle the projects that will ultimately accomplish the strategic mission of the organization are selected and funded.

This cycle describes the specific competitive strategy to be employed; e.g., production activities, pricing, and so on.

The third cycle involves short-term program and responsibility unit planning and control: In this cycle those performance targets to be achieved by each responsibility unit manager are identified, his or her program is described in terms of specific activities, including timetables and resource constraints, and then his or her performance is reported and measured against expectations. It is in the third cycle that the unit of analysis used in planning and control changes from a program or project to a responsibility center, so that a single individual and group can be held accountable for specific performance. The manager of each responsibility unit attempts to maximize his or her unit's performance and by so doing contributes to the overall welfare of the organization.

This three-cycle process model can be applied to any organization that requires the formulation of strategy, the generation of programs and allocation of resources to these programs, and the implementation and control of these programs through responsibility units. It is not applicable to all organizations, of course, because the number of cycles suitable for any organization is situationally determined. The model was offered only to illustrate the notion of a multicycle hierarchical process which gradually resolves the complex problem of influencing and/or adapting to an uncertain environment to the point where specific action can be recommended. The number of cycles, the content, and the specific steps to be performed in each cycle are to be determined by the characteristics of each specific situation. Multicycle hierarchical process models are thus no more than a means of describing how planning and control are carried out; their main value is to provide a conceptual framework.

Assumptions

Because single- and multiple-cycle process models are only general conceptualizations of what goes on in planning and control, if they are to be used successfully in the design and/or adaptation of a planning control system, the system designer must keep in mind several assumptions. This text has emphasized three assumptions that provide a perspective on system design and are necessary to guide the application of the process models presented:

1. The objectives that guide the design or adaptation of the planning and control system must be clearly understood before design or adaptation is attempted, and preferably should be stated explicitly.

2. There is no one best planning and control system. The design specifications of any planning and control system depend on the characteristics of the situation to which it is to be applied.

3. The structure, content, implementation, and operation of any

planning and control system are interdisciplinary and integrative. They are interdisciplinary in that they require inputs from many fields of knowledge, and they are integrative in that these inputs must be combined to match the requirements of the situation at hand.

Let us examine each of these three assumptions in greater detail.

Explicit objectives. The first assumption is that the system designer must clearly understand the specific objectives that he or she hopes the planning and control system will achieve before specifying a design. This assumption grows from the situational complexity the system designer must deal with. Business is part of a complex, dynamic system, and planning and control are required to influence or adapt to this environment. The purpose of planning is to establish the situation or results that describe what a responsibility unit wants to have achieved by some future time and what it must do to reach this position. Plans express the actions and expectations that are the output of the planning process. Control is the process of ensuring conformance to these expectations. Controls are the means by which control is exercised, the tools and techniques employed to increase the probability that plans will be successful. A planning and control system can be thought of as the structure in which these activities take place. It consists of four parts: (1) a process model outlining the steps to be followed; (2) a selection of the tools and techniques needed to carry out each step of each cycle in the process; (3) a specification of the individuals and responsibility units to take part; (4) and the timetable to be followed. A planning and control system is simply the particular collection of tools, techniques, controls, procedures, responsibilities, and reporting mechanisms used by an organization to influence and/or adapt to its environment. The variety of different process models, methods, involvements, and timings that can be specified for a given situation is almost infinite. Therefore, system designers must have clearly in mind the specific results they want to achieve if they are to design the most appropriate system.

Planning can provide two types of benefits: the direct benefits of better outcomes produced by more appropriate direction, greater efficiency, and greater effectiveness; and the indirect benefits of greater communication, motivation, and participation that result from involvement in the planning process. The means of achieving one type of benefit are not necessarily the means of achieving the other. The goal of the designer may be to specify better decisions and plans, improve the management decision process through greater discipline, or achieve some weighted combination of better outcomes and the benefits that come from the planning process itself. Therefore, this text has stressed that before any system can be designed or evaluated, the specific benefits to be achieved must be explicitly stated.

Situationally determined. The second assumption is that because all planning and control systems are situationally determined, there is no one best planning system for all situations. Although planning and control in general can be applied to many aspects of management, the designer of any particular system must recognize and understand the implications of the given situation. Of course, the operation of any planning and control system influences what goes on in an organization, and the system itself can be used to change organizations. But it must be remembered that the situation that already exists significantly affects the potential influence of any planning and control system.

The following four characteristics of organizations influence any system design. The designer must assess their relative significance and possible effect on his or her planning and control system design for any given situation.

First, organizations differ widely in their objectives: they may wish to expand, grow, avoid risk, remain stable, phase themselves out, and so on. Both the nature of what they hope to accomplish and their level of achievement must be considered. Second, organizations differ in the way they are organized. The particular form of differentiation and the degree of decentralization chosen are dependent on a number of factors unique to each organization. Third, within any responsibility unit there are differences in the nature and mix of the processes being planned and controlled. Structured processes requiring only effort and due care have substantially different planning and control needs than processes that are unstructured and require imagination, judgment, and intuition for effective performance. And fourth, the system designer must recognize the whole question of management style. Some organizations have authoritarian leaders who choose to dictate and direct closely the efforts of their subordinates, while others have leaders who are democratic and prefer participative, bottom-up action. Some may be aggressive and take an anticipative, entrepreneurial stance, actively searching out new ventures, while others may prefer to be reactive, acting solely on internally generated information and waiting for deviations from expectation to stimulate additional action. These four ways in which organizations can differ do not exhaust the possibilities. Nor are these factors independent of each other. Thus the design of planning and control systems remains as much art as science, in which the judgment of the designer plays a major role.

Interdisciplinary and integrative. The third assumption is that planning and control system design is, by its very nature, interdisciplinary and integrative. Planning and control are generic processes applicable to functional areas such as production, finance, or marketing; to different organizational units such as corporations, divisions, and small responsibility units; and to a variety of resources such as money, information, or labor force. This means that the requirements of a system depend on its specific application; that is, the situation in which it is to be implemented and the purposes it is to achieve, not on any one discipline or method. System design must draw freely on all business and general academic disciplines. The expertise required to design an effective system may came from any one of three fields of knowledge:

Technical fields. Accounting, computer-based information systems, statistics, management science, and operations research, for example, all provide tools, techniques, and procedures that can be used in a planning and control system.

Behavioral science. Behavioral theories of motivation, organizational dynamics, organizational development, small group processes, and so on are all topics that cover the human aspects of system design. Ultimately it is the people, not the tools and techniques, who accomplish the goals and strategic mission of an organization. Their various motivations, capabilities, and attitudes must be understood and accommodated in a system.

The functional areas of business. The traditional business functions of marketing, finance, personnel, and production, and the related disciplines of economics, industrial relations, and so on, provide the knowledge and theory to understand the structure in which a planning and control system must operate. Knowledge of these areas is especially necessary for strategic planning: for specifying realistic objectives and making valid predictions, that make effective control possible.

These three assumptions guide the development of all process models used to conceptualize and then specify a planning and control system. Together with the general notion of a multicycle hierarchical process, they give the system designer the perspective and orientation he or she needs to begin a design and/or adaptation.

SYSTEMATIC PROCEDURE FOR SYSTEMS DESIGN/ADAPTATION

The second objective of this text was to describe a systematic, diagnostic procedure to design, implement, and evaluate situationally determined systems. Chapter 5 presented a model of a systematic approach to planning and control system design. The nine steps in this model cover diagnosis, prescription, prognosis, action, and evaluation. The model demonstrates an explicit and logical approach to the problem of system design by first determining what results are desired and then attempting to motivate and guide the behavior that best accomplishes these results. This approach not only permits the identification of a normative or ideal system but also reinforces awareness that alternative system designs are possible. The difference between the normative system and the way that planning and control are currently carried out defines a systems gap. The responsibility of the system designer is to close this gap as much as possible, given the existing constraints or barriers to implementation.

Two considerations related to the system design and evaluation procedure were especially emphasized.

Express assumed relationships explicitly. The first consideration is the importance of explicitly stating the relationships that the system design is to influence. Many planning and control system designs are applied to complex, ill-structured situations with a host of interrelated factors. The need for formalization, by relating causal, intervening variables to the key result areas that describe success, is therefore especially important in the selection of appropriate tools and techniques. Formalization helps reduce the blunders that result from abstract intuitive thinking, reveals mistakes and misplaced assumptions, and helps remove extraneous and irrelevant factors from consideration. Explicitly identifying these relationships sensitizes the system designer to look for all possible ways of influencing end results. In this way he or she can avoid premature judgments, leaping to conclusions, and mistaking symptoms for the real problems. The use of formal models, when appropriate, allows for greater consistency in decision making: Finally, the more a process can be formalized, the more likely it is that the system will be evaluated once it is in use and adapted successfully in the future.

Normative systems. The second point stressed in the systematic approach to systems design is the advantage of basing system design on a normative as opposed to an incremental approach. A normative system is the one that best meets the requirements of the situation, irrespective of the barriers to its implementation. An examination of specific problems from an abstract or conceptual point of view increases the likelihood that the most optimal solutions will be reached initially. With the normative approach the system designer is not biased by existing constraints in choosing among alternatives. A comparison of the normative design with the actual system in use defines the system gap, and the next task of the analyst is to devise methods of closing this system gap. In order to do so, he or she must outline the steps needed to change from the present situation to the proposed one. Finally, a comparison of the system as it is finally implemented with the initial proposal enables the analyst to measure the extent to which the initial plan has had to be compromised. By making this evaluation, he or she can determine the implicit cost of the existing constraints; and the ultimate implications of these constraints can be evaluated and probed if necessary.

Specification of a normative model also reflects the ethical and professional considerations of systems design. Specification of a normative system gives a measure of an ideal solution to the problem. If the designer is going to compromise (e.g., by advocating a system which satisfies local requirements but leaves the real problem unsolved) he or she will be reminded of this fact by the existence of the normative system. If all the situation allows is an incremental improvement, and if that is all the system designer can sell, then he or she should do so conscientiously and with due care. However, the system designer should not be motivated to compromise solely to satisfy the wishes of a client, or to earn an easy consulting fee.

SELECTION OF APPROPRIATE TOOLS AND TECHNIQUES

The third objective of this text was to expose the system designer to many of the tools and techniques which may be used in a planning and control system. The text distinguishes between structured and unstructured processes, as well as between different measures of financial performance and different forms of financial planning and cotrol responsibility centers.

For structured processes, a formalized, quantitative model that specifies variables and relationships can usually be employed. Because most of these relationships can be reliably specified, precise feedback and feedforward systems can be developed. Unstructured processes, however, present a greater challenge for a systems designer. He or she must simultaneously reduce the inevitable buildup of organizational slack while at the same time encouraging the motivation and adaptability of managers of decentralized units, so that they will act in the interest of the firm instead of for personal aggrandizement. Unstructured processes are much less formal and more intuitive than structured processes, and tend to be associated with larger organizations and the need for decentralization. The selection and implementation of techniques to plan and control unstructured process represent a greater challenge because of the uncertainty of their success and the trade-offs they may impose.

The advantages and disadvantages of the most widely used financial performance measurements were discussed. The discussion of tools and techniques also included human resource accounting, management by objectives, job enrichment, and financial responsibility centers such as cost, profit, and investment centers. In addition, techniques such as statistical interpretation of quantitative variances, setting goals, motivation, and reducing organizational slack by the use of zero-base budgeting were examined. This is not an exhaustive list of all tools and techniques available, of course. The broad purpose of the discussion was to bring the reader to the realization that there are many alternative ways of accomplishing any particular end. It has also been stressed that no single tool or technique can be applied universally with guaranteed success. And so it is imperative to critically evaluate the strengths and weaknesses of any method or technique in relation to the situation to which it is to be applied before a selection is made.

Many advocates of a particular tool or technique describe and emphasize at great length the problem that their technique or method can handle successfully. Too rarely, however, do they fully explain the drawbacks in its conceptualization or implementation. Inundated by the pronouncements of professors, textbooks, consultants, university courses, and personal experience, the student emerges convinced of the "correctness" of the methods proposed, eager to rush out and apply them to the nearest problem. This is the "tools in search of a problem" syndrome, and the systems designer is in great danger of being seduced by these inclinations. Too often he or she finds that the exact problem for which the method is recommended rarely arises as originally described, and that his or her attempt to implement the method runs into unexpected difficulties.

This text admits—indeed, insists upon—the uncertainty and contingent nature of most of the tools and techniques incorporated in a planning and control system (especially those aimed at motivating individuals): Not only is the difficulty of implementing a certain method emphasized, but so is the difficulty of even choosing among the various methods available. In fact, perhaps the most important message of this text is that there is no one technique—even for the most structured of processes—that does not have undesirable repercussions if implemented blindly.

It has been repeatedly stressed that this book does not (and in fact cannot) recommend specific methods for solving specific problem situations. Any technique, method, or model must be individually evaluated in light of the situation in which it is going to be used, because each problem setting involves a host of contingent factors and constraints. It is hoped that the reader has been dissuaded from narrow analysis, in an attempt to match some problem to a pet or recommended technique— the "tools in search of a problem" syndrome. It is hoped, instead, that the student has gained an understanding of, and a more thorough approach to, the problem of situational systems design. The readers will realize the benefit from this change in orientation as soon as they encounter a problem situation that does not fit their own experiences or neat textbook examples.

The approach of this text, which has avoided specific recommendations and has chosen to answer many questions with the temporizing "it depends," may appear to create some dysfunctional consequences of its own. Undoubtedly it has weakened the reader's reliance on each and every one of the techniques surveyed, be it behavioral or technical, management by objectives, or management by profit centers. But if this book has increased the reader's awareness of the conditions needed for successful selection and implementation of methods, and the dysfunctional consequences that may result from blind implementation of any method, then it has achieved its purpose. There are few simple solutions to systems design problems. Caution and critical evaluation are always called for.

The purpose of the conceptual framework, the systematic design procedure, and the discussion of tools and techniques was to accustom the system designer to look beyond obvious problem symptoms (and the most readily available tools) in order to examine the situational requirements that any tool or method must satisfy. The system designer should no longer accept a remedy without recalling from this text that no one technique is universally applicable; it must be considered with reference to organizational constraints. Before recommending any method, the designer should list its relative strengths and weaknesses, as well as the available alternatives, and then evaluate and adjudicate among them. He or she now recognizes the need to critically assess the situation on its own merits from a normative point of view and is aware that previous successful applications of any tool do not guarantee subsequent success.

It is hoped, therefore, that the uncertainty and ambiguity introduced into the discussion of tools and techniques will not be considered as a frustrating handicap; rather, it should be regarded as a useful orientation for future analysis and evaluation of tools yet to be proposed as solutions for planning and control problems. The reader has learned to select techniques that will fit the task, the expectations of accomplishment, and the specific individuals to be affected. The text has succeeded if it has given the reader a critical attitude toward some of the tools and techniques available, while demonstrating the need to select and adapt each method to the situation in which it has to be implemented.

GUIDELINES FOR SUCCESSFUL IMPLEMENTATION

The fourth objective of this text was to convey a philosophy of system implementation. A philosophy is simply a set of general principles which guide a field of knowledge. In this context it describes the outlook on organizational change in general, and on the implementation of planning and control in particular, that has been developed through the case studies. The following considerations, while not elaborated in the text, should have been demonstrated by the cases.

The first obvious factor in the success of any system change is the presence of a perceived need for the change. Just as a marketer does not set out to get a consumer to purchase a product without first arousing a need in the mind of the consumer, a system designer cannot simply go out and attempt to sell a design after it has been completed. Any proposal for change has to satisfy not only a need that is genuine, but one that is perceived to exist by the people who have to change. Unless a change is perceived to be beneficial by those who are to change, the only way to put it into effect is by coercion. But if it can be shown that change will benefit the parties directly concerned, then they will be motivated to make the change and will more readily accept a modified system.

This tenet can be conveniently summarized in the following way: a system change, no matter how good it is, does not sell itself; the perceived benefits of the change must be shown to exceed its costs and risks. Therefore, the system designer must have a concrete strategy for introducing the change. Its benefits must be perceived clearly by those who are about to change, for if there is no return to them they will be unwilling to bear the risks of change and make the necessary sacrifices.

Successful implementation of any planning and control system involves persuading, convincing, and compromising. Consequently, change is most effective when the total change desired is broken up into smaller parts which can be introduced sequentially. Following the introduction of each phase of the total change, those who have to change must receive positive feedback in the form of better performance or greater satisfaction. This positive feedback is the perceived benefit that warrants a future investment in change; it can be used for instilling confidence in the introduction of a second phase. Only in this way—by comparison with the benefits produced by change—can the risks and the costs be put in proper perspective: System implementation must always be treated as a crucial part of the system design process and should receive as much attention, if not more, than any other part.

Another lesson to be learned from these cases is the need to avoid unnecessary complexity. This tenet has two parts. The first is the idea that "the simplest methods make up the best system." This is just a restatement of the well-known principle of parsimony. Formal control mechanisms, for example, should never be used simply for the sake of sophistication when the same results could be achieved by some method of informal communication. The second part of this tenet is the need to minimize change whenever possible. The greater the change in any organizational situation, the greater the resistance to it and the greater the likelihood of dysfunctional consequences. Organizations are so complex that change inevitably has ramifications that cannot be foreseen. Unanticipated consequences can appear either locally or in subsystems far removed from the local change.

A final consideration is that any system change involves a great deal of uncertainty, especially about the success of the new methods proposed. Furthermore, many of the benefits of change may be of the intangible, managerial variety, such as improvement in the discipline of planning. Change, therefore, needs the support of a creditable source, who is willing to go out on a limb if necessary to support the change. In the real world, bottom-up change rarely occurs. Change must be initiated from the top and must be supported by senior executives. If it is not, it rarely succeeds.

Case study 11–1
United Air Lines

In 1970, United Air Lines lost nearly $40 million. The airline industry as a whole lost over $200 million. In December 1970, United's board of directors took drastic action to correct the situation. They fired the president of the company, George Keck, and replaced him with Edward Carlson. Carlson took immediate action to restore the airline to profitability. This case describes some of the activities he undertook to do so, one of which was the implementation of a profit center system.

A LOOK AT UNITED AIR LINES

In terms of revenues and assets United Air Lines is the largest airline in the free world. It carries more passengers and more revenue miles than any other airline and is the second largest transportation company in the United States (Penn-Central is the largest). Along with the rest of the industry, United achieved the highest profits in its history in 1967, $72,800,000. In 1968, United's profits fell; but in 1969, it had a good year, although not so good as 1967. Profit in 1969 was $47,600,000, high enough to place that year in the top four in the company's history.

In the mid-1960s United, like the rest of the airlines, was counting on a steady traffic increase of about 15 percent per year. Accordingly it was hiring more people, especially in administrative and management positions. It also invested heavily in new equipment, and in 1970, when it received its first 747, had financial commitments of over $980,000,000. But due to several unforeseen changes, not the least of which was the downswing in the economy, these optimistic forecasts were not to be realized.

PROBLEMS FACING UNITED

United's problems stemmed from several sources. One was the introduction of jumbo jets. TWA's introduction of 747s on transcontinental routes was very well received by the public. As a result the other airlines were forced to purchase 747s. United was somewhat late in ordering, so it lost some business to other airlines due to late delivery. Also the large investment required to introduce jumbos led the Civil Aeronautics Board

(CAB) to increase fares several times to help the airlines pay for them and this led to a reduction in total demand.

There was also difficulty in disposing of older aircraft. In the mid-1960s, any airline that was trying to sell an airplane found a ready market in smaller airlines and airlines of smaller countries. But with the introduction of the 747, United was unable to sell its smaller planes easily and was forced to carry an expensive inventory of idle aircraft.

A second problem was the industry's emphasis on market share. Frequency of service was considered a key variable in maintaining market share and this resulted in saturation of flight routes and duplication of effort. When combined with the economic downturn and use of larger planes, this meant considerable unused capacity. The airlines found themselves burdened with excess aircraft and other fixed assets whose purchases had been planned to meet the expected 15 percent growth. This excess capacity resulted in a decline of the load factor (the average percentage occupancy of a plane) from 58 percent to 50 percent. There were also high maintenance costs associated with aircraft usage. Unlike other industries, the maintenance of aircraft is subject to government regulations and cannot be neglected in unfavorable times. Unless flights are reduced, maintenance costs are constant, despite a decrease in sales.

Airline employment costs were growing rapidly in this period. Average employment costs rose at the rate of 6.8 percent per year between 1965 and 1969 and during 1970 rose by 13.3 percent to catch up with the profits of 1967–69. This was very significant since the airline industry is the highest paid in the country. United's 1970 labor productivity, as measured by enplanements per person, was at least as good or better than competitors, however.

In total, fixed costs (those not associated with boarding or flying) account for about 90 percent of United's expenses. While not growing as rapidly as variable costs, they still posed a considerable problem. Throughout the 1960s, United's fixed costs per available ton-mile (a composite measure of all services offered—passenger, freight, express, and mail) were higher than the average of the industry group in which it competes. But in 1969 and 1970, United brought its fixed costs per available ton-mile below the group's average, and all but three years of the period 1962–70, it reduced fixed costs per available ton-mile by a greater percentage than the group as a whole.

The airline industry's capital structure is one of high leverage. While this is highly favorable to shareholders in profitable periods, this is not the case in periods of economic stress. In fact, in 1970, United had interest charges of $40 million which had to be met regardless of sales. There were also leasing agreements totaling $44 million for 1970 that had to be met in the short run.

Decisions made by the CAB also influenced United unfavorably. For example, previous to 1969, United had been in competition with Pan American and Northwest Orient Airlines on the route to Hawaii. United held 60 percent of this market. However, in 1969, the Civil Aeronautics Board gave five additional airlines routes to Hawaii. This had the effect of making the route unprofitable not only for the carriers who were already on it, but also for the five new carriers to whom it was awarded. United's share of the traffic fell from 60 percent to 40 percent. In 1968, United had an operating profit of $22,400,000 on that route. By 1970, this had turned into a loss of $4,600,000.

The former president, Keck, was a strong critic of the CAB. Because of the resulting poor relations between United and the CAB, no special consideration was given United with respect to CAB legislation such as the Hawaii decision.

CHANGES IN MANAGEMENT

Keck realized the seriousness of these problems and did take action to correct them. To counter increases in wage costs, he laid off some 650 pilots, clerical workers, ground crew, and mechanics. In October of 1970, he eliminated about 156 daily flights, mostly on the unprofitable short-haul routes. But this was not enough to satisfy the board of directors.

The board felt that because the airline was so large, it had developed into a bureaucracy which could not react fast enough. Decisions were made from the top of a long, vertical chain of command. There was the continual problem of communicating timely information up and down, over vast distances, and through many levels of command; e.g., when someone in the field noticed some significant change, he simply did not know how to convey this information to the right official with the authority to act on it. They believed that as a result of the poor communications within the company there was a state of low morale which inevitably is reflected in performance, and a lack of innovation and decision making, fostered by the fact that the cost of mistakes far outweighted the benefits of success. This climate resulted in a great deal of procrastination and tendency among management to continually seek out additional information and avoid making decisions.

Conflicts about these beliefs had been developing in United's board for some time. While the company was still profitable and doing well in comparison with the rest of the industry, they lay beneath the surface. But in the first six months of 1970, United lost about $21,000,000 and the conflict began to surface. In the final quarter of 1970, losses increased and the conflict came to a head. Stock price fell from a 1967 high of $90 to a low of $20. After a series of very drastic and important meetings, United's board met in late December of 1970 and decided to replace their president.

The man they chose to replace him was Edward E. Carlson, a hotel industry executive, who had no previous experience with airlines. He was not wholly new to United, however; he had been with them about five months since United had acquired Western International Hotels. Carlson and L. P: Himmelman, president of Western International, came on the board in August following the merger of the two companies. These two men received over 220,000 shares of United's stock which gave Carlson an important voice on United's board.

Western International's growth was very rapid in the late 1960s. Between 1966 and 1970, revenues increased 82 percent to over $90,000,000 and net earnings increased by 127 percent to nearly $3,000,000. Thus Carlson had a reputation for being a strong aggressive manager and he had the influence on the board of directors; these together brought him to the presidency of United.

Carlson's appointment was announced on December 21, 1970. One of his first actions was to ask each of United's directors to prepare a list of the ten most important problems he saw and to bring the list back the Monday following Christmas. At that meeting, each director had profit at the top of his list. This was, of course, exactly what Carlson felt and he began to work to correct United's deficit.

Carlson felt that he had a very competent staff working for him. However, he believed that it had become very specialized and that United had few general managers. Thus, he focused on these two major problems: low profitability and a lack of general managers.

CARLSON'S ACTIONS

The new president continued some of the money saving programs already begun but carried them much further. He slashed United's officer corps more than 20 percent and eliminated many specialized staff positions and functions. In total he reduced payroll about 7 percent, eliminating over 5,000 employees. In an effort to reduce overcapacity and improve load factors, Carlson made numerous schedule cutbacks. The number of flights per day were reduced from 1,800 to 1,490. He canceled orders for 8 DC–10s and stretched out delivery on 15 others. Some $45 million in costs were saved as a result of this action in 1971. He also launched a sustained effort to cut costs in both operations and maintenance which resulted in a further saving of $28 million during the first year.

Carlson also devoted considerable effort to changing the internal climate within United and between United and those it had dealings with. By personal example he tried to raise morale and reorient and positively reinforce United's employee attitudes. He traveled extensively to meet with employees and held meetings and cocktail parties to hear their problems and to answer their questions. He stressed the fact that the airlines were in the business of selling the perishable product "seat miles" to people and, as such, should be oriented toward people rather than planes. No one held a minor position within the company: everyone played a key role in determining its success. Innovation and debate were encouraged while procrastination was actively discouraged. In addition to his personal efforts, a daily newsline was developed to inform all employees of key operating information. This served to foster an improved environment for communications. Everyone was given to feel responsible for assuring that information flowed both up and down the organizational structure quickly and easily. And in general, his "political campaign" in the trenches of the company met with great success.

Carlson also changed United relationship with the CAB. He assured its new chairman that United's role in the future would be one of partner rather than antagonist. He also went out of his way to meet with union leaders and discuss pertinent issues with them to ensure good future working relationships.

REORGANIZATION

Reorganization of top management occurred shortly after Keck was replaced. This served to free the president from the day-to-day responsibilities of the airline so that he could devote time to much needed long-range planning. The company was then reorganized into profit centers.

The profit center concept was to solve United's problems in several ways. First, it would make each manager in the airlines aware of his contribution to the company's profit and thus make him think more in terms of what he was doing for the company. Second, the creation of mini-airlines would necessitate the development of general managers who could handle all aspects of airline management. In order to understand his contribution to profit, each manager would have to know what each element that he was responsible for was doing. Carlson thus had three objectives in implementing the profit center concept: (1) to shorten the lines of communication within the airline; (2) to provide new nimbleness or responsiveness in the marketplace; and (3) to develop general managers who are capable of decentralized decision making.

THE OLD ORGANIZATIONAL STRUCTURE

From Exhibit 1 it can be seen that United's managers were operating primarily in a specialized, functional manner. The only managers with broad, general responsibilities were the president and the executive vice president. In terms of profit accountability, United, and the airline indus-

EXHIBIT 1
United's organization before profit centers

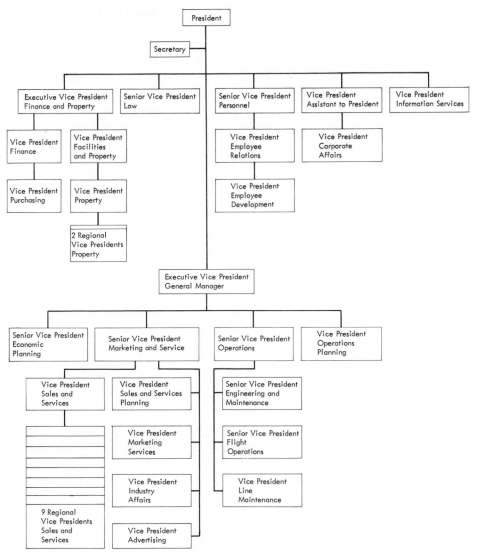

try as a whole, had chosen a system of continuing decentralization of cost control but of only pulling together profit figures at the corporate level. There were several reasons for this:

1. The difficulties involved in allocating revenues and costs on any meaningful basis to an area of responsibility, such as a station or region, are very great.

2. Airline accounting systems were developed primarily to serve cost accounting and CAB regulatory requirements with profitability only showing up in the financial statement.

3. Technical and operational problems in a rapidly growing industry placed a greater emphasis on the need to decentralize responsibility in terms of cost control, with emphasis on safety, performance, and service, rather than on the development of profitability measures. The acquisition of the primary resource, the airplane, was considered a top-management function.

Thus the lower and middle-level managers of the airline were not concerned directly with profits and were probably unaware of the effects most of their actions had on the profits of the company.

In a large airline like United, it was very easy for the local managers to feel that the company was a well from which they could draw whenever they needed anything. It was very difficult for them to see the relations of their actions to company profit. Each manager was given a budget, and was measured partially on his ability to keep within that budget; however, he was measured more on the degree of service that

EXHIBIT 2

United's organization after profit centers

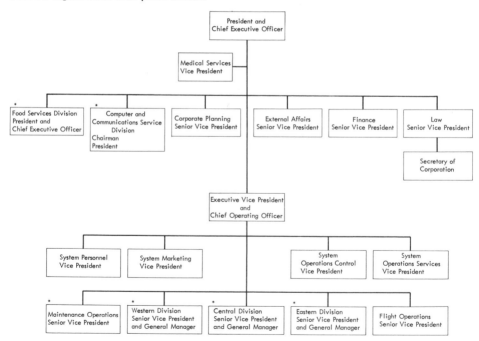

* Denotes profit centers.

he provided customers. In an industry such as air transport, which is so dependent on the relationship with customers, the service aspect of a manager's performance was often taken much more seriously than any concern about costs. Consequently, the manager was likely to devote much more time to this aspect of his job.

THE NEW ORGANIZATIONAL STRUCTURE

The new corporate organization at United is shown in Exhibit 2. The organization within the Eastern division is shown in Exhibit 3. As can be seen by comparing Exhibit 2 with Exhibit 1, there was a great change in organizational structure. United was now divided into three geographic divisions. It was decided that marketing would be decentralized but that flight operations would stay unified, although schedules would be determined by the regional VPs. The former functional organization was thus replaced by six profit centers and several corporate staff departments.

EXHIBIT 3
Eastern division organization

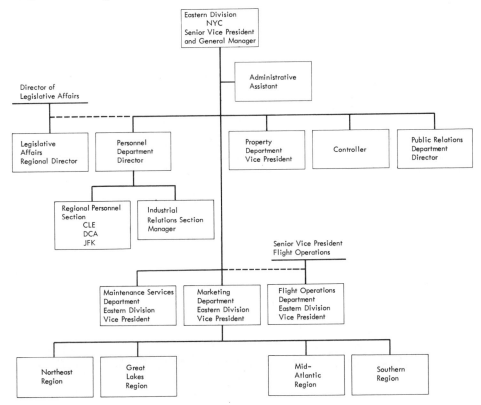

The six profit centers included three service divisions—computer and communications services division, food services division, and maintenance operations division—and the three operating divisions—Eastern, Central, and Western. The Eastern Division itself was organized similarly with functional staffs and four regions—Great Lakes, Northeast, Mid-Atlantic, and Southern—all reporting to the general manager. In January 1973, the four regions became profit centers.

Within the regions there are cost centers—the customer service centers at the airports—and revenue centers—the sales offices and reservation centers. The purpose of this approach is to emphasize the importance of controlling costs at the level where they are incurred and maximizing revenues at the point of generation. This is accomplished by providing an effective information system to monitor revenue and cost performance by regions and by each operating element of the region.

Exhibit 4 shows the organizational relationship between these elements and the division. The regional vice presidents are judged on the basis of their contribution to division profits. They are also judged on the basis of their operating ratio (expenses/revenues). The cost centers are judged by comparing unit costs to cost for the same period a year ago. They are also evaluated on a cost performance statement which is prepared in

EXHIBIT 4
Responsibility accounting within the Eastern Division

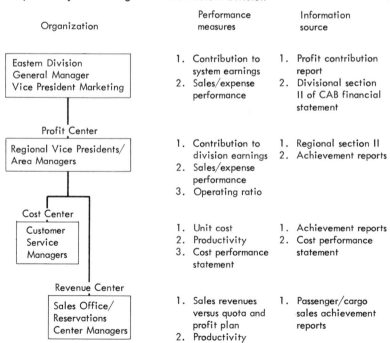

Chicago. The revenue centers are judged on the basis of sales revenue versus quota and on the basis of profit plan productivity. The two basic measures used for evaluating the airport customer service stations are the local operating ratio and the direct labor productivity ratio. The local operating ratio (expenses/revenues) gives some idea of profitability. The labor productivity ratio is:

$$\frac{\text{Equivalent passengers boarded}}{\text{Direct man hours}}$$

MANAGEMENT DEVELOPMENT

In addition to the implementation of profit centers, changes were also made to develop the general managers needed to run a profit center system. The profit center system itself was intended to develop managers, but several more direct development programs were also adopted including management by objectives and a comprehensive management identification and development process. This process was comprised of a management review in which each manager evaluated his subordinates and tried to identify those with management potential. Once a potential manager has been identified, he and his superior work together to identify his weaknesses or "development needs" and a development action plan to see that these needs are met. The Eastern Division has prepared a 37-page guideline to assist operating managers in this process. This guideline suggests in some detail how to spot management potential, how to identify development needs, what some of the most common development needs are, and how to meet some of these needs. While this development program is not strictly a part of the profit center system, it does show how serious top management felt the lack of general managers was.

THE OUTCOME

In 1973, in an era when other airlines were plagued by rising fuel and operating costs, and Pan American was on the verge of bankruptcy, United Air Lines reported a profit of $5.1 million. This reversal is, to say the least, remarkable.

Questions

1. What are United's key variables? Which ones are controllable and which are not?
2. Do United's three geographical divisions conform to the criteria usually used to distinguish when profit centers should be implemented?
3. What part did the switch to profit centers have in United's turnaround?

4. What role did Carlson play in United's turnaround?

5. How do you account for the improvement?

Case study 11–2
Meat Inspection Services (B)*

Attempting to meet the rather optimistic implementation schedule to which they were committed imposed a heavy work load on the director of veterinary services and his staff. The four supervisors (of inspector training, contract negotiations, licensing, and administration) all went to work immediately after reporting to their new jobs. Before each supervisor began work, the director instructed him on his broad mission and responsibilities, the deadlines to be met, and expected performance, but since that time had left the details of how each job was to be performed up to the individual manager. The director had enough to do himself without getting involved in his subordinates' activities. Fortunately all were experienced in somewhat similar lines of work and each had been thoroughly interviewed before he was hired, so that there was little doubt in the director's mind that they were capable of meeting their schedules and doing a good job. And their performance over the six weeks since starting work gave no reason to modify this belief. However, because of the need to meet the deadline established, there was little time for the four supervisors to become familiar with their new organization, much less to do any quiet thinking.

The director agreed with the need for good performance but was troubled by the hectic pace at which things were taking place. What troubled him was the pressure on his supervisors to act swiftly because he feared that this experience would establish a management pattern of action without adequate planning. Seat-of-the-pants action-oriented management was completely opposite to the style which the director wished to establish. He believed that planning was an important part of every manager's job.

The director's personal management philosophy was one of delegating responsibility to subordinates and of placing considerable trust in them—but only after expected results were clearly established and agreed to. Furthermore, he felt that before he could trust a subordinate to act appropriately, he had to be certain that the subordinate had thought long and hard about the goals he was committing himself to and how he would go about accomplishing them. Once he was satisfied that his managers were aware of what he expected of them and that they had planned how to accomplish these expectations, he was content first to

---

* This case study builds on the material covered in the (A) case, 3–2. That case should be reviewed before reading this one.

leave them alone to carry it out, and then to reward or punish them as required.

The director already had done a considerable amount of planning and knew exactly what he wanted each of his four subordinates to accomplish in 1974–75. Furthermore, based on his experience with them, he also had a good idea of the additional training each person required. He therefore was able to sit down and complete a statement of job objectives and goals for each of his subordinates. Examples of two of these statements are presented in the Appendix. The problem he now had to solve was how to get his subordinates committed to these goals and to planning how they would accomplish them.

One way, of course, was to go the usual MBO (management by objectives) route by first asking his subordinates to prepare a statment of objectives and plans and then to talk to each subordinate individually about these. Following this procedure, over time, he felt he could reach agreement with each subordinate as to their future plans and expected accomplishments. This "coaching" approach appeared sound in theory and although he had never used it himself personally, he was quite familiar with the underlying theory and agreed with it wholeheartedly. Unfortunately he felt he just didn't have the time to go this route.

Nor could he just give each subordinate the statement of objectives and goals he prepared because that would neither motivate them to accomplish the goals nor encourage them to plan. In fact, he was afraid that simply presenting them with the goals he alone had established could prove to be demotivating. Because his intent was to establish planning as a continual process and not a one-shot effort, he felt that this approach was inappropriate.

The director finally decided on a mixture of these two approaches. He would let each manager develop his own goals and plans, but rather than letting them proceed in an unstructured way he decided to give each a guideline to follow. He had a documented procedure that someone had once shown him in his files and felt that, with appropriate modification, it could serve the purpose satisfactorily. The guideline he developed is identical to the Guide to Managing by Objectives (see the Appendix of Case 7–1, Ashdale Ltd.).

He sent each of his four supervisors this guideline with a covering memo outlining his conception of the overall objective of each job and the specific aspects for which he expected goals to be developed (e.g., number of inspections, number of complaints received, and so on). The covering memo also indicated that the director expected supporting plans to back up each goal. The particular aspects of each job outlined in the memo to each supervisor corresponded to the goals listed in the statement the director had already prepared for him. The director hoped that later, when he met individually with each manager, they could quickly reach agreement on levels of achievement and, hence, develop a statement of objectives and goals identical to the one he had already prepared.

Questions

1. What particular *reasons* motivated the director to try to change the planning practices in his division? What should he have been trying to achieve?
2. Is the director's approach to changing his subordinates' behavior consistent with the reasons for change specified in question 1?
3. What are the strengths and what are the weaknesses in his implementation strategy? To what extent do you think the approach suited the nature of the individuals involved, the task they were performing, and the general situation? Was the use of the "Guide to Management by Objectives" more appropriate in this situation than the Ashdale one?
4. If you were the director and agreed with the needs listed in question 1, what would you have done differently? Why?

APPENDIX

OBJECTIVES AND GOALS OF THE SUPERVISOR OF ADMINISTRATION FOR FISCAL 1974–1975

Objective
  To ensure efficient, economical divisional financial and administrative support systems linked satisfactorily to government and private systems so that supervisors obtain the resources and other support required to achieve their own job objectives and goals

Goals
  1. Establish administrative policies concerning region operators such that no more than three complaints are passed to me.
  2. Ensure that valid payments to operators are cleared within three working days of invoice receipt. No more than six operator complaints requiring remedial action passed to me.
  3. Phase I MIS will be operational by November 1, 1974.
  4. MIS reports will be produced within three working days of receipt of inputs.
  5. There will be no adverse criticism in the provincial auditor's report on divisional financial or administrative matters.
  6. Financial reports will be produced within five working days of month-end.
  7. The division's relations with department office on plans and budgets will cause no complaints.

8. Administrative procedures for the division will produce no significant complaints from other directors resulting in a reprimand from the assistant deputy minister.
9. Budget will not be exceeded.
10. To attend "Managing Management Time" in February 1975.

OBJECTIVE AND GOALS FOR THE SUPERVISOR
OF TRAINING FOR FISCAL 1974–75

Objective
  To produce graduates from training courses run in an equitable, efficient manner.
Goals
1. All examination results back to trainees no later than ten working days after completion of each examination.
2. A variation in pass marks from training location to training location not greater than ±10 percent about the provincial average.
3. At least 90 percent of trainee inspectors will pass the training course.
4. Operations will not exceed the budget.
5. No more than six complaints regarding training conditions or inadequate warning of conditions and timing from course participants passed to me for investigation.
6. Input to the division's MIS will be made within two working days after month-end.
7. To complete of the "Advanced Communications" evening course given at the local university.

Case study 11–3
North Eastern Gas

In January 1977, two new members were appointed to the board of directors of North Eastern Gas. One was a young entrepreneur who had founded and developed his own metalworking firm into a multimillion dollar enterprise. The other was a financial consultant who was involved in securing long-term capital requirements for many major companies. Both were appointed just as the budgets for 1977 were being finalized. And they did not like what they found.

Their first meeting with the executives of the company led both to believe that the planning supporting preparation of the budgets had a short-term horizon which was not consistent with the long-term problems facing the natural gas industry. Furthermore, the questions they addressed to the vice presidents and the president about the future did not receive satisfactory answers. They felt therefore, that in light of the trying times ahead, North Eastern had better improve its planning practices.

The two new board members agreed, in general, with the president on the need for greater productivity from management and labor. They were terribly surprised, however, that the operating executives of the company had given little consideration to diversification as a means of maintaining the growth pattern established over the last decade. Furthermore, they learned that the company had no strategy for developing better relationships with governments. The two directors also felt that there was a need for better communication with customers, stockholders, and the general public about the significant problems facing the company so that adequate supplies of capital and product prices could be obtained. They therefore asked the president to suggest improvements in North Eastern's planning systems and requested that he make some response at their next meeting in February.

THE COMPANY

North Eastern Gas is a publicly held, regulated, gas purchase and distribution utility operating in the northeastern United States. In 1976 the company served an area populated by 4,100,000 people, and operated a gas main network of 8,254 miles. Over the last decade the company objective has been sustained growth accompanied by controlled costs. Sales in 1976 to the residential, commercial, and industrial markets were $75 million, $62 million, and $80 million, respectively, for total sales of $217 million. Net income was $26 million. This compares to total sales of $75 million and net income of $8.5 million in 1967.

Being a publicly held regulated utility serving the general public, North Eastern has the difficult task of balancing conflicting stakeholder expectations. As a capital intensive utility it has substantial financing requirements so must continually offer investors a fair rate of return. Unfortunately, the similarity of these interests with those of customers and regulatory bodies is not always appreciated.

ORGANIZATION

North Eastern is organized into eight functional departments headed by seven vice presidents and a manager. The organization chart is presented in Exhibit 1. The purchase of gas is the responsibility of the Gas Supply Department while sale is the responsibility of the Marketing and Sales Department. The physical plant and engineering necessary for the acquisition and distribution of gas is the responsibility of the Operations

EXHIBIT 1

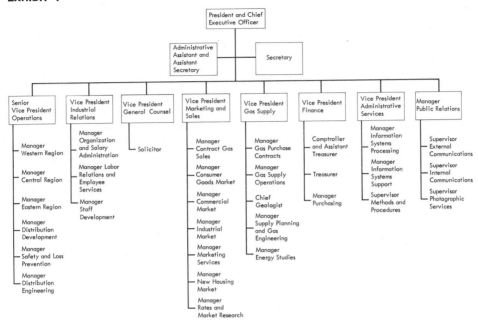

Department. Operations is divided into three regions (Western, Central, and Eastern), each headed by a region manager. The Marketing Department is subdivided by the type of customer served. The Industrial Relations, General Council, Finance, Administrative Services, and Public Relations Departments provide staff support for these activities. In total, North Eastern employs approximately 2,500.

PLANNING AND CONTROL SYSTEMS

Formal corporatewide planning at North Eastern is limited to the preparation of a capital and an operating budget. Budgets are prepared annually in November by each department of the company for the next calendar year. Information is gathered in cooperation with other departments and meetings between departments are held regularly during preparation and before budget finalization. The Finance Department, specifically the comptroller, pulls all departmental budgets together and then submits an overall budget (with individual budgets as backup) to the president for his approval. The president then holds meetings with each vice president individually and also with all vice presidents collectively before finally approving the budget. Each department head then presents his portion of the budget to the board of directors. Prior to starting on the budget, the president holds meeting with those reporting to him and out of this he develops and communicates the performance targets for the following year.

Each month of the calendar/budget year, computer reports are supplied to the president and to all department heads. Actual costs as compared to budget costs and any notable variations are questioned.

As North Eastern is a utility working on a cost-of-service basis and on a regulated rate of return, careful control must be maintained on all operating costs. Cost allocations and control are the responsibility of the individual vice presidents, with the comptroller acting as a "policeman" to ensure correct allocations. Long-range financial planning comes under the jurisdiction of the vice president of finance liaisoning with the president and other executives as required. The Finance Department is currently developing a computer model to assist decision making in this area.

CAPITAL AND OPERATING BUDGETS

As outlined in the company's policy and procedure manual, the intention of the capital budget is "to provide an organized and coordinated plan of proposed capital spending which serves as a statement of construction requirements and system expansion, an instrument of control over capital spending, a statement of cash required to finance expansion, and a source of data on which other budgets can be based." At North Eastern a capital expenditure is defined as one which improves the efficiency, output, or capacity of existing plant; extends the physical life of existing plant; or results in additional plant which has a useful life of one year.

The responsibility for the capital budgeting of each department rests with that department's vice president or manager. He approves budget requests for his area of responsibility, presents these to the president and then to the board of directors.

Items included in the capital budget are specified on appropriate capital budget request forms depending on the type of request. The rules regarding budget requests break out five types of items: Office furniture and equipment; equipment; transportation equipment; pipelines; and general. Capital budgets are prepared on a detailed basis to cover a duration of 12 months, although the company's policy and procedures manual specifies that longer term forecasting may be required on a detailed basis to justify some expenditures. Once the budget is approved, the department vice president or manager is responsible for carrying it out and is expected to conform to it. However, the policy and procedure manual explicitly notes that "a budget should not be so rigid that it restricts the efficient operation or reduces the judgment factor when a decision is required, provided that deviations from the budget plan are explainable and justifiable."

The second component of the planning and control system is the operating budget which is defined as "a management plan which states the estimated operating results expected over a certain period of time." The intent of the operating budget is to provide management and the board with "a statement of estimated revenues and expenses based on an organized and coordinated plan of activity." The operating budget serves as a guide for operating activities, a standard to measure and control actual performance throughout the year, and a tool for financial planning. Like the capital budget, the operating budget is prepared on a detailed account basis to cover a 12-month period.

Responsibility for the preparation and execution of operating budgets rests also with those reporting to the president. They are responsible for recommending the overall company plan of operation on which detailed budgets are based, specifying the funds needed to finance estimated expenditures, reviewing actual results, comparing these with budget estimates and obtaining proper explanations of significant variances, and projecting updated results throughout the budget year at least on a quarterly basis.

The responsibility for administering both the capital and operating budget systems rests with the comptroller. He establishes budget principles and rules, obtains guidelines from senior management and distributes these to all those involved in budget preparation, establishes the budget timetable, maintains the budget practice section of the policy and procedure manual, develops and controls budget forms, provides advice and assistance to managers in the preparation of their budget, receives submissions, assembles budget data and forwards these to managers as required, and then compiles the overall capital and operating budgets. The comptroller is also responsible for distributing follow-up reports on an annual, quarterly, monthly, and weekly basis as appropriate to all budget center managers and senior executives.

CURRENT SITUATION

Gas supply. Although the middle and late 1970s was a period of natural gas shortage, North Eastern has been fortunate to have an adequate supply of gas, secured under long-term contracts, to serve their existing customers. However, there is the perennial danger that changes in government policy will limit their ability to satisfy current customer requirements and restrict additional expansion. The company faces the additional uncertainty of changes in royalty and taxation regulations. At present, there appears to be insufficient natural gas to meet long-term demands unless there are new discoveries. Recognizing that existing supplies will not last forever, the company has joined several gas exploration consortia who are searching for new sources of supply.

Gas sales. The sale of natural gas for home heating purposes in the northeastern United States is significantly affected by weather conditions. The winter of 1975–76 was significantly milder than normal causing a dent in both sales and profits. Furthermore, the decline in housing starts in this period also curtailed gas sales. Gas prices doubled in 1973–76 and so North Eastern's competitive position vis-à-vis electricity and oil has eroded. Now all three sources of energy are about equivalent in price. This means that service, convenience, and public attitudes are the most significant determinants of the choice of fuel. The substantial increase in the natural gas prices over the last several years has squeezed profits, and the uncertainty of future supply still leaves the profit picture cloudy.

Operations. The operations department of North Eastern is responsible for delivering gas to customers. There is a heavy capital investment required for piping, meters, pumping and regulation stations, and related equipment. Replacing facilities has suffered from the effects of inflation and rising prices have made operating costs significantly higher than expected. Technological innovations such as the production of new large thin-walled piping for gas mains have improved the ability to distribute natural gas economically but have also provided a number of problems. On balance, the engineering aspects of this industry are stable and are well understood. Technological innovation is not expected to significantly influence this industry in the immediate future.

Research. As one of the gas utilities in the United States, North Eastern participates in many research studies coordinated by the Institute of Gas Technology (located in Chicago) and the American Gas Association. The most significant recent technological innovation affecting North Eastern has been the development of a new gas-fired water heater which has improved efficiency and recovery time.

Labor and management. Not unlike many utilities, North Eastern provides a safe, secure, and comfortable working environment for its managers. Based on its financial performance, the company has demonstrated sound managerial decision making and administrative ability. North Eastern is also progressive in that it is the first major utility in the United States to appoint a woman to a vice presidential position (vice-president—industrial relations).

The president of North Eastern is 58-year-old Stewart Dilm, an accountant and former vice-president of finance who has been in his current position for ten years. Dilm, Charles Laugherty, and Bruno Ansil, the vice presidents of finance and operations, respectively, are the last of the "old guard"—those executives who have been with the company more than 25 years. The other six executives reporting to the president are all under 40 years of age and average about 12 years of service with North Eastern.

On the labor front North Eastern has a remarkable record. It has had no major strikes over the last ten years and has had sound relationships with all its operating unions. Recently both the administrative climate and union relationships have received extra attention from the president because of his belief that the current situation facing resource-based utilities places extraordinary demands on all employees to be more productive. In both the company's annual reports as well as in speeches to service organizations he has stated that a significant investment in human capital will have to be forthcoming to prepare organizations for these new conditions.

THE PRESIDENT'S RESPONSE

In cooperation with his administrative assistant, the president developed a statement of objectives to circulate among the board of directors and also an outline of a revised corporate planning process for them to review (Exhibit 2). His statement of objectives is presented in Exhibit 3.

The planning process suggested builds on the fact that involvement brings with it the motivation to be productive. It is a multistage scheme designed to involve as many people as possible in the planning of North Eastern's operations.

At the first stage of the proposed annual planning cycle, a review of information leads to revision of the statement of objectives the president prepared this first time. The next phase involves converting these objectives into terms meaningful to each of the eight departments and reaching agreement on them. Having agreed on corporate and departmental objectives, each operating unit—whether a region, a marketing unit, or simply a budget center within a department—then formulates operational objectives. The next phase in the process involves developing programs which simultaneously accomplish these three sets of objectives. The choice of objectives and programs is followed by the development of long- and short-range plans. And following this, capital and operating budgets are prepared. These budgets then serve as the basis for performance reporting.

In his presentation to the board the president stated that this multiphase, corporatewide planning process could involve all managers who had an interest in the future of North Eastern, thereby demonstrating that each and every member of the North Eastern family could influence the future performance of the company.

EXHIBIT 2
Proposed new planning process

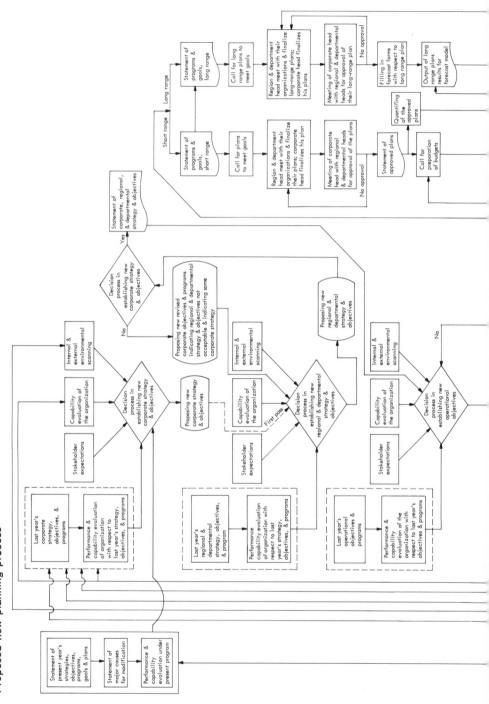

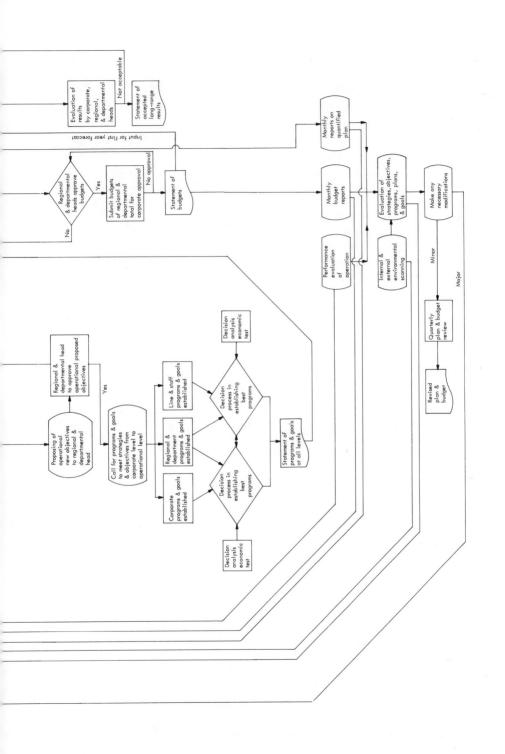

EXHIBIT 3
North Eastern Gas
Statement of objectives

The aim of North Eastern Gas is to maximize the benefits to the company's stakeholders from the most efficient and profitable use of natural gas. The company strives to do so by the following:

1. Increasing the use of installed equipment, consistent with the optimum system load factor.
2. Promoting sales of additional equipment which will result in the profitable use of gas and will render valuable customer service.
3. Promoting the sale and installation of facilities which will provide greater off-peak-hour use of plant.
4. Extending company facilities to unserved areas, if profitable.
5. Promoting conversion of competitive fuels to gas when profitable.
6. Protecting existing businesses from competitive efforts.
7. Cooperating with trade allies to maintain stable market conditions.
8. Cooperating with Chambers of Commerce, realtors, developers, bankers, and so on to bring environmentally compatible industries to the company's area of service, thereby reducing unemployment.
9. Developing a strong healthy organization capable of meeting the challenges of the future.
10. Providing employees with the opportunity to grow and develop to their fullest potential.
11. Changing the overall company philosophy and marketing policy from consumption to conservation and the best use of natural resources.
12. Providing a satisfactory rate of return to shareholders.
13. Constantly improving customer relationships by learning of any dissatisfaction with company's services and initiating corrective measures as soon as profitable.

Question

What is your opinion of the president's response?

ADDITIONAL REFERENCES AND BIBLIOGRAPHY

Anderson, Carl R., and Paine, Frank T.   Managerial perceptions and strategic behavior. *Academy of Management Journal,* December 1975, pp. 811–23.

Anthony, Robert.   Closing the loop between planning and performance. *Public Administration Review,* May–June 1971, p. 388.

Argenti, J.   *Systematic Corporate Planning.* New York: Halstead, 1974.

Baker, G. M. N.   The feasibility and utility of human resource accounting. *California Management Review,* Summer 1974, pp. 17–23.

Beatty, Richard W., and Schneier, Craig Eric.   A case for positive reinforcement. *Business Horizons,* April 1975, p. 57.

Beckhard, Richard. Strategies for large system change. *Sloan Management Review*, Winter 1975, pp. 43–56.

Bright, William L. How one company manages its human resources. *Harvard Business Review*, January–February 1976, pp. 81–93.

Brockhaus, William L. Planning for change with organization charts. *Business Horizons*, April 1974, pp. 47–51.

Cherrington, David J., and Cherrington, J. Owen. Participation, performance and appraisal. *Business Horizons*, December 1974, pp. 35–44.

Cotton, Donald B. *Companywide Planning: Concept and Process*. New York: The Macmillan Co., 1970.

Dale, B. S. Models, mergers and the planning gap. *Management Accounting*, (U.K.), April 1974, pp. 107–9.

Denning, Basil W. ed. *Corporate Planning: Selected Concepts*. New York: McGraw-Hill, 1971.

Dermer, J., and Siegel, J. P. The role of behavioral measures in accounting for human resources. *The Accounting Review*, January 1974, pp. 88–97.

Emery, J. C. *Organizational Planning and Control Systems—Theory and Technology*. New York: The Macmillan Company, 1969.

Flamholtz, Eric. *Human Resource Accounting*. Encino, Calif.: Dickenson Publishing Co., 1974.

Ford, R. N. *Motivation through Work Itself*. New York: American Management Association, 1969.

Hackman, J. Richard. Is job enrichment just a fad? *Harvard Business Review*, September–October 1975, pp. 129–38.

Hamilton, W. F., and Moses, Michael A. A computer-based corporate planning system. *Management Science*, October 1974, pp. 148–59.

Herzberg, F. *Work and the Nature of Man*. New York: World Publishing Co., 1966.

Jackson, Henry M. To forge a strategy for survival. *Public Administration Review*, Summer 1959, pp. 69–75.

Jones, H. *Preparing Company Plans*. New York: Halsted Press, 1974.

King, William R., and Cleland, David I. A new method for strategic systems planning. *Business Horizons*, August 1975, pp. 55–64.

Klein, W. H., and Murphy, D. C. *Policy: Concepts in Organizational Guidance*. Boston: Little, Brown, 1973.

Kraft, W. Philip, and Williams, Kathleen L. Job Redesign Improves Producductivity. *Personnel Journal*, July 1975, pp. 393–97.

Lorange, Peter. Divisional planning: Setting effective direction. *Sloan Management Review*, Fall 1975, pp. 77–92.

McGregor, D. An uneasy look at performance appraisal. *Harvard Business Review*, May–June, 1957, pp. 89–94.

McIntyre, Gordon. Auditing for management control. *AMA-COM: Management Review*, November 1975, pp. 49–53.

Malmlow, E. G. Corporate strategic planning in practice. *Long-Range Planning,* September 1972, pp. 29–34.

Morris, R. D. F. Budgetary control is obsolete. *Management Accounting (U.K.),* August 1968, pp. 38–41.

Myers, M. Scott, and Flowers, Vincent S. A framework for developing human assets. *California Management Review,* Summer 1974, pp. 5–16.

Nanus, B. The future oriented corporation. *Business Horizons,* February 1975, pp. 5–12.

Newman, W. H. *Constructive Control: Design and Use of Control Systems.* Englewood Cliffs, N.J.: Prentice-Hall, 1975.

Odiorne, George S. *Management by Objectives.* New York: Pitman, 1965.

Odiorne, George S. Management by objectives: Antidote to future shock. *Personnel Journal,* April 1974, pp. 258–63.

Ouchi, William G., and Maguire, Mary Ann. Organizational control: Two functions. *Administrative Science Quarterly,* December 1975, pp. 559–69.

Sayles, Leonard. Technological innovation and the planning process. *Organizational Dynamics,* Summer 1973, pp. 68–80.

Schiff, M., and Lewin, A. Y. Where traditional budgeting fails. *Financial Executive,* May 1968, p. 50.

Scott, Brian W. *Long Range Planning in American Industry.* New York: American Management Assoc., 1965.

Sheppard, H. L., and Herrick, N. Q. *Where Have all the Robots Gone?* New York: New Press, 1972.

Skousen, K. Fred, and Needles, Belverd E., Jr. *Contemporary Thought in Accounting and Organizational Control.* Encino, Calif.: Dickenson Publishing Co. Inc., 1973.

Sluxher, E. Allen, and Sims, Henry P., Jr. Commitment through MBO interviews. *Business Horizons,* April 1975, pp. 5–12.

Steiner, George A. Institutionalizing corporate social decisions. *Business Horizons,* December 1975, pp. 12–18.

Tannenbaum, Arnold S. *Control in Organizations.* New York: McGraw-Hill, 1968.

Taylor, B., and Irving A. Organized planning in major U.K. companies. *Long-Range Planning,* June 1971, pp. 22–27.

Tosi, Henry L., Jr., and Carroll, Stephen J., Jr. Management reaction to management by objectives. *Academy of Management Journal,* December 1968, pp. 415–25.

Turcotte, William E. Control systems, performance and satisfaction in two state agencies. *Administrative Science Quarterly,* March 1974, pp. 45–59.

Vancil, R. C. What kind of management control do you need? *Harvard Business Review,* March 1973, pp. 75–86.

index

Index

Case titles are given in italics.

385